DYING
TO
WIN

Why Suicide Terrorists Do It

Robert A. Pape

GIBSON SQUARE

LONDON

This edition published for the first time in 2006 in the UK by

Gibson Square Books Ltd
47 Lonsdale Square
London N1 1EW
United Kingdom

Tel: +44 (0)20 7096 1100
Fax: +44 (0)20 7993 2214

info@gibsonsquare.com
www.gibsonsquare.com

ISBN 1-903933-78-1

Contents

Contents

Future of Terrorism in the West

ON JULY 7, 2005, Al Qaeda launched its most devastating attack since 9/11—the London suicide bombings on three underground lines and one city bus, killing 52 innocent people.

Although many would have hoped that American and Western counter-terrorism efforts would have reduced the threat, the facts show otherwise. The war on terrorism is continuing to head south. On November 14 2005, four Iraqis left their country on forged passports to carry out suicide attacks against three American-related hotels in Jordan. Throughout 2005, suicide terrorism in Iraq steadily escalated to new set a new record for suicide attacks in a single year.

The reason is not a reluctance to take the offense or a failure to support democracy in Iraq. Rather, the key reason is that the West's strategy for this war is fundamentally flawed. Right now, our strategy for the war on terrorism presumes that suicide terrorism is mainly a product of an evil ideology called Islamic fundamentalism and that this ideology would produce campaigns of suicide terrorism wherever it exists and regardless of our military policies. This presumption is wrong and is leading toward foreign policies that are making our situation worse. Although multiple factors are at work, consideration of the most prominent suicide attacks in 2005 shows that the strategic logic of suicide terrorism—and especially the presence of Western combat forces in Iraq and on the Arabian Peninsula—remains the core factor driving the threat we face.

The London Bombings

Since the London bombings, many are asking how could local, middle-class, educated British Muslims kill themselves to kill others. Alas, the answer is both simple and disturbing—deep anger over Western combat forces on the Arabian Peninsula.

Since 2002, Al Qaeda has carried out 17 suicide and other terrorist bombings that killed nearly 700 people—more attacks and victims than in all the years before 9/11 combined. Although many have hoped that Western counterterrorism efforts would have weakened Al Qaeda, by the measure that counts—the ability of the group to kill us—Al Qaeda is stronger today than before 2001. The London suicide terrorist attack on July 7 and the attempted bombings on July 21 stem closely from Al Qaeda's core strategic logic, which is driven mainly by political rather than religious goals.

To make sense of Al Qaeda's campaign against the United States and its allies, *Dying to Win* compiled data on the 71 terrorists who killed themselves between 1995 and 2004 in carrying out attacks sponsored by Osama bin Laden's network. This study was able to collect the names, nationalities and detailed demographic information on 67 of these bombers, data which provides insight into the underlying causes of Al Qaeda's suicide terrorism and how the group's strategy has evolved since 2001.

Most important, the figures show that Al Qaeda is today less a product of Islamic fundamentalism than of a simple strategic goal: to compel the United States and its Western allies to withdraw combat forces from the Arabian Peninsula and other Muslim countries. Over two thirds are nationals from Sunni Muslim countries where the United States has stationed combat troops since 1990—Saudi Arabia, other states on the Arabian Peninsula, Turkey, and Afghanistan. Few or none are from many of the world's most populous Islamic fundamentalist countries. Iran—whose population is 70 million, surely steeped in Islamic fundamentalism, and three times the size of Saudi Arabia—has never produced an Al Qaeda suicide terrorist. Sudan—Islamic fundamentalist with a population almost the same size as Saudi Arabia—has also never produced one either.

Even the one third of Al Qaeda suicide attackers that are transnational in nature are powerfully motivated by anger over Western combat operations on the Arabian Peninsula. The individuals who committed the London suicide attacks are part of Al Qaeda's transnational support. Although we might like to think the London bombers' motivations were somehow exceptional, there is powerful evidence to the contrary.

First, the Al Qaeda group that claimed responsibility for the London attacks said they were to punish Great Britain for British military operations in Iraq and went on to threaten Italy and Denmark with terrorist attacks unless these states pulled their forces out of Iraq. The Al Qaeda statement was released just hours after the July 7th attack and said that "the heroic mujahideen have carried out a blessed raid in London ... in retaliation for the massacres Britain is committing in Iraq and Afghanistan."

Second, Hussein Osman, one of the four would-be July 21 bombers captured in Rome, said in his interrogation by Italian authorities: "This was not about religion. ... We watched videos of British military operations in Iraq."

Third, Mohammad Sidique Kahn, the ring-leader of the July 7th bombers, made a martyr video that Al Qaeda released several months after the attack. In it, Kahn says that the purpose of the London attacks was to punish Britain because its "democratically elected governments continuously perpetrate atrocities against my people all over the world.... Until you stop the bombing, gassing, imprisonment and torture of my people we will not stop this fight." Finally, the British home office conducted a detailed survey of the attitudes of the 1.6 million Muslims living in Britain in April 2004. This survey, located on *The Times* web site, found that, while 85 percent condemned suicide terrorism, 13 percent believed that more suicide attacks against the United States and the West were justified. The survey went further to identify the specific reason—Iraq. In other words, the principal factor driving support for suicide terrorism among British Muslims was not an evil ideology, but deep anger over British military policies on the Arabian Peninsula.

Close inspection of the pattern of Al Qaeda bombings since 9/11 helps to explain why London was selected as a target and why Al Qaeda was especially interested in attacking it in the time-frame of 2005. As *Dying to Win* shows, what is common among Al Qaeda's post-9/11 attacks is not their location but the identity of the victims killed. Since 2002, the group has killed citizens from 18 of the 20 countries that Osama bin Laden has cited as supporting the American invasions of Afghanistan and Iraq.

There is good evidence that this shift in Al Qaeda's scheme was the product of deliberate choice. In December 2003, the Norwegian intelligence service found a lengthy Qaeda planning document on a radical Islamic Web site that described a coherent strategy for compelling the United States and its allies to leave Iraq. It made clear that more spectacular attacks against the United States like those of 9/11 would be insufficient, and that it would be more effective to attack America's European allies, thus coercing them to withdraw their forces from Iraq and Afghanistan and increasing the economic and military burdens that the United States would have to bear.

In particular, the document weighed the advantages of attacking Britain, Poland and Spain, and concluded that Spain in particular, because of the high level of domestic opposition to the Iraq war, was the most vulnerable.

"It is necessary to make utmost use of the upcoming general election in Spain in March next year," the document stated. "We think that the Spanish government could not tolerate more than two, maximum three, blows, after which it will have to withdraw as a result of popular pressure. If its troops still remain in Iraq after these blows, then the victory of the Socialist Party is almost secured, and the withdrawal of the Spanish forces will be on its electoral program."

That prediction, of course, proved murderously prescient. Yet it was only one step in the plan: "Lastly, we emphasize that a withdrawal of the Spanish or Italian forces from Iraq would put huge pressure on the British presence, a pressure that Tony Blair might not be able to withstand, and hence the domino tiles would fall quickly."

The bottom line, then, is that the suicide attacks against those buses and subways in London are clearly of a piece with Al Qaeda's post-9/11 strategy. And while we don't know the full extent of the terrorist network, it is reasonable to believe that Al Qaeda has not been fundamentally weakened but has changed course and achieved significant success. The London attacks will only encourage Osama bin Laden and other Qaeda leaders in the belief that they will succeed in their ultimate aim: causing America and its allies to withdraw forces from the Muslim world.

Indeed, Americans should take little comfort in the knowledge that Al Qaeda has decided to focus over the past few years on hitting US military allies. As of 2006, this component of Al Qaeda's strategy nearly ran its course and was always viewed as a step toward adding more pressure on the United States by increasing the military and economic burden of keeping troops in Iraq and the rest of the Arabian peninsula. Further, Osama bin Laden's January 19, 2006 statement suggests that A Qaeda may also be focusing on its main target, The United States and American targets around the world. Using language similar to the 2003 document found by Norwegian intelligence, bin Laden says that although Al Qaeda has recently focused on "the capitals of the most important European countries of the aggressive coalition" in Iraq, "operations are in preparation" to carry out "similar operations in America." Given that Spain withdrew its forces from Iraq in 2004 and Britain and Italy both called for substantial withdrawals in 2006, it is unsurprising that Al Qaeda—whether in conjunction with Iraqi suicide terrorists or not—believes that the time is right to focus again on American targets.

Iraq

Most analysts are at a loss to explain why suicide terrorism is escalating in Iraq, and presume that it must be a chaotic or religious phenomenon, one without a pragmatic basis. However, suicide terrorism has a coherent strategic logic and understanding the factors actually driving terrorists to use this strategy is crucial to capping the volcano now erupting in Iraq.

A key reason why the logic of suicide terrorism in Iraq—and elsewhere—has been hard to grasp is that we have lacked robust information about the suicide attacks and the suicide attackers themselves. Recently, I have extended the database for the crucial case of Iraq, including every suicide terrorist attack in the country through the end of 2005.

Suicide terrorism in Iraq is driven not by religion, but by a clear strategic objective: to prevent the establishment of a government under the control of the United States. To do this, the terrorists are attacking targets that they hope would undermine the confidence of the Iraq population in the Iraqi government's ability to maintain order, and especially to discourage Kurds and Sunni from cooperating with the government. Although the Iraqi rebels may someday intend to foment a full-scale civil war between the Shia and Sunni communities, the facts show that this has not been the principle military objective of the resistance over the past two years.

Three patterns in the data support help to reveal the underlying logic of the suicide terrorist campaign in Iraq. The first concerns the timing of the suicide attacks. Prior to America's invasion in March 2003, Iraq had never experienced a suicide terrorist attack in its history. Since the invasion suicide terrorism has been escalating rapidly.* Iraq had 20 suicide attacks in 2003, 49 in 2004, and 125 in 2005—a new record for suicide attacks in one year. In other words, suicide terrorism has gone from nothing in all the years before the US invasion to doubling every year that nearly one hundred and fifty thousand American combat forces have been stationed there.

Second, the geographic distribution of the attacks shows a clear pattern, one that has remained remarkably constant over time. Baghdad has been the prime target, consistently hit by the great weight of all suicide attacks (45 to 60%), even as the overall number has doubled each year.** The remaining attacks have been divided fairly evenly across the three main ethnic and geographic divisions of the country outside of the capital, with the annual proportion of attacks varying from roughly 10 to 20% against targets in the Kurdish north, in Sunni triangle in the center and west, and in the Shia south. Focusing on the capital is normal for insurgency that is seeking to undermine confidence in the government.

Third, a look at the specific targets selected for attack helps to further clarify the strategic logic behind suicide terrorism in Iraq. The vast majority of attacks—over 75%—have been directed against military, government and political targets, such as government buildings, police convoys and police stations, recruiting centers, assassination of government leaders, and Western troops and contractors.*** By contrast, only a fraction—roughly 15 to 25%—have been directed at local Iraqi civilians not working for the Iraqi government or Western agencies, such as local Iraqis in mosques and crowded markets. The fraction of civilian targets rose modestly this year, but a major new trend is not yet manifest.

What fuels support for this strategic objective is the continued presence of heavy American ground forces. Although many of the targets are associated with the Iraqi government, the United States is widely viewed as the power behind the throne.

---

*   Using methods consistent with my study as a whole—double independent verification and counting tightly coordinated strikes as a team attack, see Chart 15 (Appendix I).
**   See Chart 16 (Appendix I).
***   See Chart 17 (Appendix I).

The reason is not that American forces are especially prominent; they often do keep a low profile. Rather, it is simply the basic ground truth that American military forces toppled the previous government, created the conditions to install the current regime, and remain the most potent military force in Iraq today. The presence of nearly one hundred and fifty thousand American combat troops casts doubt on the legitimacy of the Iraqi government and offers the terrorists an opportunity to mobilize resistance against a foreign occupation that is seeking to transform the local society.

The presence of American combat forces is the central basis for the recruitment appeals used by terrorist leaders in Iraq. In his famous letter to Osama bin Laden in January 2004, Abu Musab al-Zarqawi explains the main motive of the resistance is to combat an American plan to transform Iraq:

> "The Americans ... entered Iraq on the basis of a contract to create the State of Greater Israel from the Nile to the Euphrates and this Zionized American Administration thinks that in hastening the creation of Greater Israel it will hasten the arrival of the Messiah. ... America did not come here to turn around and go home ... Its immediate objectives are to be able to withdraw to its bases in complete safety, to have its hands free, and to entrust the Iraqi battlefields to the government they have installed, to which they have added an army and police forces."

Al-Zarqawi's letter goes on to single out government and military targets, as a way to undermine the American occupation:

> "Soldiers, police forces, and agents: these are the eyes, ears, and hands of the occupier who uses them to see, hear, and exert his violence. With God's help, we are determined to make them special targets in the coming period before the situation is consolidated and they have the means to proceed to arrests."

The identities of the Iraqi suicide attackers are now murky. This is not unusual in the early years of a suicide terrorist campaign. Hezbollah did not publish many of the biographies and last testaments of its suicide attackers until after the suicide operations had ended, a pattern adopted by the Tamil Tigers in Sri Lanka as well. At the moment, our best information is that the attackers are from two main sources, Sunni Iraqis and foreign fighters, principally from Saudi Arabia. The next largest groups appear to come from Syria and Kuwait. If so, this would mean that the main sources of suicide terrorists in Iraq are coming either from Iraqi itself or from the countries immediately adjacent to Iraq whose societies are most vulnerable to transformation by the presence of American combat troops—and not from the world's largest Islamic fundamentalist populations (such as Iran, Sudan, or Pakistan). This picture is fully consistent with what we now know about the strategic logic of suicide terrorism.

Jordan

The suicide attack in November 2005 in Jordan was perhaps the most worrisome of the year. On November 9, three suicide bombers launched a coordinated, team attack against three hotels in Amman that were frequented by American government officials and military contractors, killing 60 people and injuring 115 others (although no Americans). A would-be fourth suicide bomber, the wife of one of three and who had three brothers killed by American forces in Iraq , was unable to detonate her explosives and later captured by Jordanian authorities.

The next day, Zarqawi's Iraqi rebel group claimed responsibility. The statement identified the names of the three suicide terrorists, all Iraqis. This information was confirmed by the captured would-be female bomber, also an Iraqi. Zarqawi's statement also said that Jordan was attacked because it had become a "rear-base camp for the [American] Crusader army."

Much of the Western media was captivated by the female suicide bomber, a woman who showed strikingly calm nerves and disturbingly little remorse in her video-taped confession released by Jordan's security services. However, this attack was ominous for a far more important reason. For the first time, 4 Iraqi suicide attackers struck American-related targets outside of Iraq, and their forged passports could well have gained them access to any number of Western countries had they not chosen to attack in Jordan.

Although some have suggested that suicide terrorism in Iraq might well have an advantage—if they attack over there, they won't come here—the Jordan suicide attack shows that the opposite is more likely. Just as Al Qaeda carried out numerous suicide attacks against targets abroad prior to 9/11, the longer suicide terrorism continues in Iraq, the greater the risk that Iraqi suicide attackers will follow a similar trajectory against America and its allies.

The Future of Suicide Terrorism

Although terrorist leaders may harbor other goals, history shows that the presence of foreign combat forces on prized territory is the principal recruiting tool used by terrorist leaders to mobilize suicide terrorists to kill us. Suicide terrorism is mainly a demand-driven, not supply-limited phenomenon. Suicide terrorists are overwhelmingly walk-in volunteers, not long time members of terrorist groups. They do exhibit a variety of individual motivations. Some are evidently driven by social prestige, as in the case of those who make martyr videos or attack in teams of pre-existing social networks. Some are out for revenge, seeking to lash out against those whom they believe are responsible for the death of family members or close friends. Others are driven by religion. However, *Dying to* Win shows that what cuts across these various personal situations is the common motive to end the threat of a foreign occupation. Absent the goal to compel modern democracies to withdraw military forces from the territory that the terrorists view as their homeland or prize greatly, suicide terrorism hardly occurs.

These facts help to explain not only why suicide terrorist campaigns begin, but also why they end.

If suicide terrorism were mainly the product of Islamic fundamental-ism or any other evil ideology independent of circumstance, then suicide terrorism in Lebanon should not have ended when the Americans, French, and Israelis withdrew their combat forces from the country. Since Hezbollah retained its Islamic fundamentalist ideology, we should instead have witnessed suicide terrorists following the Americans to New York, the French to Paris, and the Israelis to Tel Aviv—which did not happen. Similarly, if Islamic fundamentalism is the main factor driving Palestinian suicide terrorism, we should not have seen its dramatic decline following Israel's unilateral withdrawal from Gaza and other steps in 2004 and 2005, nor, following its electoral victory in January 2006, Hamas' offer of a truce if Israel withdrew to the pre-1967 borders of the West Bank—which did happen. Although Islamic fundamentalism cannot explain the decline of suicide terrorism In Lebanon and Palestine, this pattern accords closely to the strategic logic of suicide terrorism.

So long as the war on terrorism ignores the actual strategic logic of suicide terrorism, it will likely be impossible to win and our actions may well end up helping terrorist leaders recruit many more suicide terrorists to kill us. The longer American and allied combat forces remain in Iraq and the rest of the Arabian peninsula, the greater the risk of the next 9/11 or 7/7.

May 2006

1

—

The Growing Threat

SUICIDE TERRORISM IS rising around the world, but there is great confusion as to why. Since many such attacks—including, of course, those of September 11, 2001—have been perpetrated by Muslim terrorists professing religious motives, it might seem obvious that Islamic fundamentalism is the central cause. This presumption has fueled the belief that future 9/11's can be avoided only by a wholesale transformation of Muslim societies, a core reason for broad public support in the United States for the recent conquest of Iraq.

However, the presumed connection between suicide terrorism and Islamic fundamentalism is misleading and may be encouraging domestic and foreign policies likely to worsen America's situation and to harm many Muslims needlessly.

I have compiled a database of every suicide bombing and attack around the globe from 1980 through 2003—315 attacks in all.[1] It includes every attack in which at least one terrorist killed himself or herself while attempting to kill others; it excludes attacks authorized by a national government, for example by North Korea against the South. This database is the first complete universe of suicide terrorist attacks worldwide. I have amassed and independently verified all the relevant information that could be found in English and other languages (for example, Arabic, Hebrew, Russian, and Tamil) in print and on-line. The information is drawn from suicide terrorist groups themselves, from the main organizations that collect such data in target countries, and from news media around the world. More than a "list of lists," this database probably represents the most comprehensive and reliable survey of suicide terrorist attacks that is now available.

The data show that there is little connection between suicide terrorism and Islamic fundamentalism, or any one of the world's religions. In fact, the leading instigators of suicide attacks are the Tamil Tigers in Sri Lanka, a Marxist-Leninist group whose members are from Hindu families but who are adamantly opposed to religion. This group committed 76 of the 315 incidents, more suicide attacks than Hamas.

Rather, what nearly all suicide terrorist attacks have in common is a specific secular and strategic goal: to compel modern democracies to withdraw military forces from territory that the terrorists consider to be their homeland. Religion is rarely the root cause, although it is often used as a tool by terrorist organizations in recruiting and in other efforts in service of the broader strategic objective.

Three general patterns in the data support my conclusions. First, nearly all suicide terrorist attacks occur as part of organized campaigns, not as isolated or random incidents. Of the 315 separate attacks in the period I studied, 301 could have their roots traced to large, coherent political or military campaigns.

Second, democratic states are uniquely vulnerable to suicide terrorists. The United States, France, India, Israel, Russia, Sri Lanka, and Turkey have been the targets of almost every suicide attack of the past two decades, and each country has been a democracy at the time of the incidents.

Third, suicide terrorist campaigns are directed toward a strategic objective. From Lebanon to Israel to Sri Lanka to Kashmir to Chechnya, the sponsors of every campaign have been terrorist groups trying to establish or maintain political self-determination by compelling a democratic power to withdraw from the territories they claim. Even al-Qaeda fits this pattern: although Saudi Arabia is not under American military occupation per se, a principal objective of Osama bin Laden is the expulsion of American troops from the Persian Gulf and the reduction of Washington's power and influence in the region.

Understanding suicide terrorism is essential for the promotion of American security and international peace after September 11, 2001. On that day, nineteen al-Qaeda terrorists hijacked four airlines and destroyed the

World Trade Center towers and part of the Pentagon, killing nearly 3,000 innocent people. This episode awakened Americans and the world to a new fear that previously we had barely imagined: that even at home in the United States, we were vulnerable to devastating attack by determined terrorists, willing to die to kill us.

What made the September 11 attack possible—and so unexpected and terrifying—was that willingness to die to accomplish the mission. The final instructions found in the luggage of several hijackers leave little doubt about their intentions, telling them to make

> an oath to die. . . . When the confrontation begins, strike like champions who do not want to go back to this world. . . . Check your weapons long before you leave . . . you must make your knife sharp and must not discomfort your animal during the slaughter. . . . Afterwards, we will all meet in the highest heaven. . . .[2]

The hijackers' suicide was essential to the terrible lethality of the attack, making it possible to crash airplanes into populated buildings. It also created an element of surprise, allowing the hijackers to exploit the counterterrorism measures and mind-set that had evolved to deal with ordinary terrorist threats. Perhaps most jarring, the readiness of the terrorists to die in order to kill Americans amplified our sense of vulnerability. After September 11, Americans know that we must expect that future al-Qaeda or other anti-American terrorists may be equally willing to die, and so not deterred by fear of punishment or of anything else. Such attackers would not hesitate to kill more Americans, and could succeed in carrying out equally devastating attacks—or worse—despite our best efforts to stop them.

September 11 was monstrous and shocking in scale, but it was not fundamentally unique. For more than twenty years, terrorist groups have been increasingly relying on suicide attacks to achieve major political objectives. From 1980 to 2003, terrorists across the globe waged seventeen separate campaigns of suicide terrorism, including those by Hezbollah to drive the United States, French, and Israeli forces out of Lebanon; by Palestinian terrorist groups to force Israel to abandon the West Bank and Gaza; by the Liberation Tigers of Tamil Eelam (the "Tamil Tigers") to compel the Sri Lankan government to accept an independent Tamil homeland; by al-Qaeda to pressure the United States to withdraw from the Persian Gulf region. Since August of 2003, an eighteenth campaign has begun, aimed at driving the United States out of Iraq; as of this writing, it is not yet clear how much this effort owes to indigenous forces and how much to foreigners, possibly including al-Qaeda.

More worrying, the raw number of suicide terrorist attacks is climbing. At the same time that terrorist incidents of all types have declined by nearly half, from a peak of 666 in 1987 to 348 in 2001, suicide terrorism has grown, and the trend is continuing. Suicide terrorist attacks have risen from an average of three per year in the 1980s to about ten per year in the 1990s to more than forty each year in 2001 and 2002, and nearly fifty in 2003. These include continuing campaigns by Palestinian groups against Israel and by al-Qaeda and Taliban-related forces in Saudi Arabia and Afghanistan, as well as at least twenty attacks in Iraq against U.S. troops, the United Nations, and Iraqis collaborating with the American occupation.

Although many Americans have hoped that al-Qaeda has been badly weakened by U.S. counterterrorism efforts since September 11, 2001, the data show otherwise. In 2002 and 2003, al-Qaeda conducted fifteen suicide terrorist attacks, more than in all the years before September 11 combined, killing 439 people.

Perhaps most worrying of all, suicide terrorism has become the most deadly form of terrorism. Suicide attacks amount to just 3 percent of all terrorist incidents from 1980 through 2003, but account for 48 percent of all fatalities, making the average suicide terrorist attack twelve times deadlier than other forms of terrorism—even if the immense losses of September 11 are not counted.[3] If a terrorist group does get its hands on a nuclear weapon, suicide attack is the best way to ensure the bomb will go off and the most troublesome scenario for its use.

Since September 11, 2001, the United States has responded to the growing threat of suicide terrorism by embarking on a policy to conquer Muslim countries—not simply rooting out existing havens for terrorists in Afghanistan but going further to remake Muslim societies in the Persian Gulf. To be sure, the United States must be ready to use force to protect Americans and their allies and must do so when necessary. However, the close association between foreign military occupations and the growth of suicide terrorist movements in the occupied regions should make us hesitate over any strategy centering on the transformation of Muslim societies by means of heavy military power. Although there may still be good reasons for such a strategy, we should recognize that the sustained presence of heavy American combat forces in Muslim countries is likely to *increase* the odds of the next 9/11.

To win the war on terrorism, we must have a new conception of victory. The key to lasting security lies not only in rooting out today's generation of terrorists who are actively planning to kill Americans, but also in preventing the next, potentially larger generation from rising up. America's overarching purpose must be to achieve the first goal without failing at the second. To achieve that purpose, it is essential that we understand the strategic, social, and individual logic of suicide terrorism.

Our enemies have been studying suicide terrorism for over twenty years. Now is the time to level the playing field.

2

Explaining Suicide Terrorism

MY STUDY ASSESSES the record of suicide terrorism and the state and global responses to it over the past twenty years, with a view to explaining how and why suicide terrorism has occurred and persisted, why the incidence is rising, how far the menace is likely to spread, and what can be done to contain it. Although no approach can predict the future with absolute certitude, a comprehensive analysis of the history and causes of suicide terrorism affords us the opportunity to ground our policies in a real knowledge.

My general propositions hold across a wide variety of circumstances and account for a large portion of suicide terrorism, but they have limits. My arguments are meant to account for modern suicide terrorism, especially the increasing use of suicide attack by terrorist groups from the early 1980s to the present. Modern suicide terrorist groups share a number of features. In general, they are weaker than their opponents; their political goals, if not their tactics, are broadly supported by a distinct national community; the militants have a close bond of loyalty to comrades and devotion to leaders; and they have a system of initiation and rituals signifying an individual's level of commitment to the community. Modern suicide terrorist groups may receive material assistance from states that share some of their political aspirations, but they are independent actors who rarely follow the dictates of others blindly. Perhaps most important, modern suicide terrorism is highly lethal, because the attackers' purpose is not only to die, but to use their deaths to kill the maximum number of people from the opposing community.

These commonalities make it possible to develop a general theory of modern suicide terrorism. However, the account I offer for the origins of *suicide* terrorism should not be viewed as a general explanation for terrorism as a whole. "Ordinary," nonsuicide terrorism is significantly different. It occurs under a wider variety of circumstances, for a wider variety of goals, with wider variation in the use of destructive force and in sympathy from the terrorists' national community. In addition, nonsuicide terrorism is often used by groups far smaller than those using suicide terrorism. Accordingly, we should not expect the same factors to account equally well for suicide and nonsuicide terrorism. I have set aside the broader problem of terrorism in general in order to concentrate on the specific causes of the deadlier threat, suicide terrorism.

WHAT IS SUICIDE TERRORISM?

Terrorism involves the use of violence by an organization other than a national government to intimidate or frighten a target audience.[1] In general, terrorism has two broad purposes: to gain supporters and to coerce opponents.[2] Most terrorist campaigns seek both outcomes to some extent, often aiming to change the target state's policies while simultaneously mobilizing support and recruits for the terrorists' cause. Sometimes terrorism directed at outsiders can also be a way of competing with rival groups for support within the same social movement. However, there are trade-offs between these objectives, and terrorists can strike various balances between them. These choices represent different forms of terrorism, the most important of which are "demonstrative," "destructive," and "suicide" terrorism.

"Demonstrative terrorism" is as much political theater as violence. It is directed mainly at gaining publicity, for any or all of three reasons: to recruit more activists; to gain attention to grievances from soft-liners on the other side; and to gain attention from third parties who might exert pressure on the other side. Groups that emphasize ordinary, demonstrative terrorism include the Orange Volunteers (Northern Ireland), National Liberation Army (Colombia), and Red Brigades (Italy).[3] Hostage taking, airline hijacking, and explosions announced in advance are generally intended to bring issues to the attention of the target audience. In these cases, terrorists often avoid doing serious harm, so as not to undermine sympathy for the political cause. Brian Jenkins captures the essence of demonstrative terrorism: "terrorists want a lot of people watching, not a lot of people dead."[4]

"Destructive terrorism" is more aggressive, seeking to coerce opponents with the threat of injury or death as well as to mobilize support for the cause. Destructive terrorists seek to inflict real harm on members of the target audience at the risk of losing sympathy for their cause. Exactly how groups strike the balance between harm and sympathy depends on the nature of the political goal. For instance, the Baader-Meinhof group selectively assassinated rich German industrialists, acts that alienated certain segments of German society but not others. Palestinian terrorists in the 1970s often sought to kill as many Israelis as possible, fully alienating Jewish society but still evoking sympathy from Muslim communities. Other groups that emphasize destructive terrorism include the Irish Republican Army, Revolutionary Armed Forces of Colombia (FARC), and the nineteenth-century Anarchists.[5]

"Suicide terrorism" is the most aggressive form of terrorism, pursuing coercion even at the expense of angering not only the target community but neutral audiences as well. What distinguishes a suicide terrorist is that the attacker does not expect to survive the mission and often employs a method of attack (such as a car bomb, suicide vest, or ramming an airplane into a building) that requires his or her death in order to succeed. In essence, suicide terrorists kill others at the same time that they kill themselves.[6]

The classic model of "suicide attack" that we most commonly think of today includes only situations in which the attacker kills himself or, increasingly among the Tamil Tigers and Palestinians, herself. A broader definition could include any operation that is designed in such a way that the terrorist does not expect to survive it, even if he or she is actually killed by police or other defenders. We might call such operations suicide missions instead of suicide attacks. An example would be the February 1994 Hebron Massacre: its perpetrator, Baruch Goldstein, had no plan for escape, left a note indicating he did not expect to return, and simply continued killing Palestinians until some of his victims brought him down. Such suicide missions have occurred in a number of conflicts, as in the cases of Palestinians who invade Israeli settlements on the West Bank with guns and grenades, intending to kill the inhabitants; few of these assailants escape alive.

This book counts only suicide attacks that meet the classic definition, partly because it is the common understanding of the concept, and partly because suicide missions are hard to identify reliably since we rarely know for certain that an attacker who did not kill himself or herself actually expected to die. In any event, including those suicide missions of which we can be confident would not change my basic findings.

In principle, suicide terrorism could be used for demonstrative purposes or could be limited to targeted assassinations. In practice, however, recent suicide terrorists often seek simply to kill as many people as they can. Although this maximizes the coercive leverage that can be gained from terrorism, it does so at heavier cost than other forms of terrorism. Maximizing the number of enemy killed alienates virtually everyone in the target audience, including those who might otherwise have been sympathetic to the terrorists' cause. In addition, the act of suicide creates a debate and often loss of support among moderate segments of the terrorists' community, although it may also attract support among radical elements. Thus, while coercion can be one of the aims of any form of terrorism, coercion is the paramount objective of suicide terrorism.

THE HISTORY OF SUICIDE TERRORISM

The forms of suicide terrorism that concern us most today—a driver detonating a car laden with explosives near a large, inhabited building, or a person exploding a suicide vest in a busy marketplace—were practically unknown before 1980. Instances of suicide terrorism did occur earlier, although these were mainly suicide missions rather than suicide attacks, and were much less common than they are now.

The three best known of these earlier suicide campaigns were those of the ancient Jewish Zealots, the eleventh- and twelfth-century Assassins, and the Japanese kamikazes during World War II.[7]

The world's first suicide terrorists were probably two militant Jewish revolutionary groups, the Zealots and the Sicarii.[8] Determined to liberate Judea from Roman occupation, these groups used violence to provoke a popular uprising—which historians credit with precipitating the "Jewish War" of A.D. 66—committing numerous public assassinations and other audacious acts of violence in Judea from approximately 4 B.C. to A.D. 70. They attacked their victims in broad daylight in the heart of Jerusalem and other centers using small, sicklelike daggers (*sicae* in Latin) concealed under their cloaks. Many of these must have been suicide missions, since the killers were often immediately captured and put to death—typically tortured and then crucified or burned alive.[9]

One of the earliest attacks was an attempt by ten Jewish Zealots to assassinate Herod, the ruler of Judea installed by Rome, for his role in establishing a set of institutions (such as the gymnasium and the arena, and the display of graven images of Roman emperors) that were particularly inimical to Jewish custom and law. Although the plot ultimately failed, the account of what happened when the Jews were brought before Herod presents a remarkable picture of individuals willing to die to complete their violent mission. As Josephus, the main historian of the period, says:

> They openly displayed their daggers and freely confessed that the conspiracy was justified and had taken place . . . not because of a desire for gain . . . but rather for the sake of communal customs . . . for which one is prepared to give up one's life. . . . After they had confessed their plot so openly, they were led away and, after they had endured every kind of torture, put to death.[10]

The Ismaili Assassins, a Shi'ite Muslim sect based in northwestern Iran in the eleventh and twelfth centuries, created an effective organization for the planned, systematic, and long-term use of political murder that relied on suicide missions for success. For two centuries, the Assassins' daggers terrorized and demoralized the mainly Sunni rulers of the region as well as leaders of Christian Crusader states, chalking up more than fifty dramatic murders and inspiring a new word: "assassination." Most of the Assassins' victims were political and military leaders who were so heavily guarded that even successful attackers would almost surely have to pay for that success with their lives. What made the Assassins so lethal was that their killers were willing to die to accomplish their missions and often, rather than attempting to escape, reveled in their impending death. The first successful Assassin, who killed the vizier to the Great Sultan Malikshah of Persia in 1092, exclaimed before himself being killed: "The killing of this devil is the beginning of bliss." Subsequent Assassins undertook suicide missions with similar enthusiasm.[11] These killers were routinely highly trained in the art of murder, planned clever stratagems to gain access to their victims, and also routinely expected to be caught, made no effort to escape, and considered that to survive a mission was shameful.

The Japanese kamikazes in World War II are not normally considered terrorists because they targeted solely soldiers and sailors, not civilians, and because their actions were directed and authorized by a recognized national government. History records many cases of individual soldiers who continued to fight for their country under certain-death circumstances or who, in response to a sudden threat, sacrificed themselves to save others; indeed, such sacrifice is part of our common definition of military heroism. The kamikaze program, however, was organized, planned, and persistent, not a series of individual responses to battlefield emergencies. Desperate to stop the advance of the American invasion fleet which was approaching from the Philippines, from July 1944 onward the Japanese high command organized a variety of "special attack" organizations whose pilots—commonly called kamikazes—agreed to crash their airplanes, gliders, and even manned torpedoes into U.S. naval vessels. Kamikaze raids continued for ten months, from October 25, 1944, until Japan surrendered on August 15, 1945. In total, some 3,843 pilots gave their lives. These suicide attacks did not stop the Americans, but they were four to five times more deadly than conventional strike missions and did impose high costs on the invasion forces. They damaged or sank at least 375 U.S. naval vessels, killed 12,300 American servicemen, and wounded another 36,400.[12]

Between 1945 and 1980, suicide attacks temporarily disappeared from the world scene. Although there were numerous acts of suicide by individuals in the service of political causes, there is not a single recorded instance of a suicide terrorist killing others while killing himself.

Famous self-immolations and hunger strikes did occur, but these were mainly demonstrative acts intended to evoke political sympathy and involved little risk of harming others. Mahatma Gandhi staged numerous hunger strikes against British rule in India, including in 1947; these events evoked sympathy from the British public and may have hastened Indian independence. In South Vietnam during the 1960s, Buddhist monks and nuns burned themselves to death in protest against religious persecution by the regime of the Catholic president, Ngo Dinh Diem. These horrific suicides inspired as many as 20,000 South Vietnamese to take to the streets in Saigon to demand the formation of a new government and the withdrawal of American forces. On January 19, 1969, in Czechoslovakia, a philosophy student, Jan Palach, burned himself alive in Prague's Wenceslas

Square to protest the recent Soviet invasion, a dramatic suicide that brought hundreds of thousands of people into the streets. In 1981, Bobby Sands and nine other Irish Republican Army prisoners died during a hunger strike. They failed to achieve their announced aim of compelling the British government to accord political status to IRA prisoners, but had the larger effects of strengthening Catholic perception of the British government as callous and of swelling IRA recruitment.[13]

Modern suicide terrorism—in which the attackers kill others and themselves at the same time—got its start in Lebanon the early 1980s and differs from its historical precursors in one striking way. Previously, there had rarely or never been more than one suicide terrorist campaign active at the same time. Only in recent years has suicide terrorism emerged as a tool of political coercion used by multiple actors across the globe at the same time. Suicide terrorism is increasing, both in the raw numbers of attacks and in geographical spread from one region to another.

Although not the very first modern instance, the suicide car bombing by the terrorist group called Hezbollah of the U.S. Marine barracks in Lebanon on October 23, 1983, was so spectacular—killing 241 soldiers, demolishing the building, and coinciding with a near-simultaneous second attack that killed fifty-eight French troops—that the event dominated media headlines for weeks, consumed Western national leaders for months, and encouraged terrorist groups from Hamas to the Tamil Tigers to al-Qaeda to adopt this method of attack. Hezbollah would go on to chalk up a total of thirty-six suicide attacks against American, French, and Israeli targets during the 1980s.

In the 1990s, suicide terrorism spread to several additional countries. Starting in July 1990, the Liberation Tigers of Tamil Eelam began a series of suicide attacks against Sri Lankan political leaders, military targets, and civilians, as well as using a suicide attacker to kill former prime minister Rajiv Gandhi. Suicide terrorism also spread to Israel in 1994, when the Palestinian terrorist groups Hamas and Islamic Jihad started to use suicide attacks against Israeli civilians and troops; to the Persian Gulf in 1995, when al-Qaeda initiated suicide attacks against American military targets in the region; and to Turkey in 1996, when the Kurdistan Workers Party (PKK) began suicide attacks against Turkish military and government targets.

Suicide terrorism spread further during the first years of the twenty-first century. Suicide attacks continued in Sri Lanka, Israel, and the Persian Gulf, and began to occur in new regions of the world. In 2000 and 2001, rebel groups in Chechnya launched suicide attacks against Russian targets, rebels in Kashmir conducted similar attacks against Indian targets, and al-Qaeda escalated its operations with the most spectacular suicide attack in history, the direct attack on the United States on September 11, 2001.

TABLE 1. Suicide Terrorist Campaigns, 1980–2003

Completed Campaigns

Date	Terrorists	Religion	Target Country	# Attacks
1. 1983	Hezbollah	Islam	United States, France	5
2. 1982–1985	Hezbollah	Islam	Israel	11
3. 1985–1986	Hezbollah	Islam	Israel	20
4. 1990–1994	LTTE	Hindu/secular	Sri Lanka	15
5. 1995–2000	LTTE	Hindu/secular	Sri Lanka	54
6. 1994	Hamas	Islam	Israel	2
7. 1994–1995	Hamas	Islam	Israel	9
8. 1995	BKI	Sikh	India	1
9. 1996	Hamas	Islam	Israel	4
10. 1997	Hamas	Islam	Israel	3
11. 1996	PKK	Islam/secular	Turkey	3
12. 1999	PKK	Islam/secular	Turkey	11
13. 2001	LTTE	Hindu/secular	Sri Lanka	6

Ongoing Campaigns, as of December 2003

Date	Terrorists	Religion	Target Country	# Attacks
14. 1996–	al-Qaeda	Islam	United States, Allies	21
15. 2000–	Chechens	Islam/secular	Russia	19
16. 2000–	Kashmirs	Islam	India	5
17. 2000–	several	Islam/secular	Israel	92
18. 2003–	Iraqi rebels	unknown	United States, Allies	20

Attacks Not Part of Organized Campaigns	14
Total incidents	315

Altogether, between 1980 and 2003 there were 315 suicide terrorist attacks worldwide, of which 301 were carried out as parts of eighteen organized coercive campaigns—that is, each a series of attacks that the terrorist leaders explained as aimed at gaining specific political concessions from a named target government, and which continued until the terrorist leaders deliberately abandoned the effort, either because sufficient gains were achieved or because the leaders became convinced that the effort had failed. Five suicide terrorist campaigns were still ongoing as of the beginning of 2004.

THE CONVENTIONAL WISDOM

Although terrorism has long been part of international politics, we do not have good explanations for the growing phenomenon of suicide terrorism. Traditional studies of terrorism tend to treat suicide attack as one of many tactics that terrorists use, and so do not shed much light on the recent rise of this type of attack.[14] The small number of studies that explicitly address suicide terrorism tend to focus on the irrationality of the act of suicide from the perspective of the individual attacker. As a result, they focus on individual motives for suicide—either religious indoctrination, or psychological predispositions that might drive individual suicide attackers.[15] This work is important and largely accounts for the twin explanations commonly offered in academic and journalistic accounts—that is, that suicide terrorism is a product either of indoctrination into Islamic fundamentalism or of the suicidal inclinations of individuals who would likely end their lives in any event.[16]

The first-wave explanations of suicide terrorism were developed during the 1980s and were consistent with the data from that period. However, as suicide attacks mounted from the 1990s onward, it has become increasing evident that these initial explanations are insufficient to account for which individuals become suicide terrorists and, more important, why terrorist organizations increasingly rely on this form of attack.

First, although religious motives may matter and although Islamic groups receive the most attention in Western media, modern suicide terrorism is not limited to Islamic fundamentalism. As shown in Table 1, the explicitly antireligious Tamil Tigers have committed 76 of the 315 suicide attacks, more than any other group; they are responsible for the spectacular bombing of the World Trade Center in Colombo in 1997 and the assassinations of two heads of state, Rajiv Gandhi of India and Ranasinghe Premadasa of Sri Lanka.

Even among Muslims, secular groups account for over a third of suicide attacks. The Kurdish PKK, which has used suicide bombers as part of its strategy to achieve Kurdish autonomy, is guided by the secular Marxist-

Leninist ideology of its leader, Abdullah Ocalan, rather than by Islam. Even in the conflicts most characterized by Islamic fundamentalism, groups with secular ideologies account for an important number of suicide attacks. The Popular Front for the Liberation of Palestine, a Marxist-Leninist group, and the al-Aqsa Martyrs Brigades, with allegiance to Yasser Arafat's socialist Fatah movement, together account for thirty-one of ninety-two suicide attacks against Israel, while communist and socialist groups, such as the secular Lebanese National Resistance Front, the Lebanese Communist Party, and the Syrian National Socialist Party, account for twenty-seven of thirty-six suicide attacks in Lebanon in the 1980s.

Overall, Islamic fundamentalism is associated with about half of the suicide terrorist attacks that have occurred from 1980 to 2003.[17]

Second, psychological explanations cannot explain why suicide terrorism occurs only in certain societies and at certain times. While suicide rates vary from one society to another, they do not vary enough to explain why the overwhelming majority of societies—even those experiencing political violence—exhibit no suicide terrorism but a handful of societies have experienced dozens of attacks each. This requires a political or social explanation. Similarly, while the supply of suicidal individuals may vary somewhat over time, psychological explanations cannot account for why over 95 percent of all suicide terrorist attacks occur in organized campaigns that are concentrated in time. Further, the demographic profile of suicide terrorist attackers does not fit the usual profile of suicidal individuals. Until recently, the leading experts in psychological profiles of suicide terrorists characterized them as uneducated, unemployed, socially isolated, single men in their late teens and early twenties.[18] This study, however, collects comprehensive data on the demographic characteristics of suicide terrorist attackers (see Chapter 10), which shows that they have been college educated and uneducated, married and single, men and women, isolated and socially integrated; they have ranged in age from fifteen to fifty-two.[19] In other words, suicide terrorists come from a broad array of lifestyles. Some may exhibit suicidal tendencies as these are conventionally understood, but many do not.

Recently, new explanations for suicide terrorism have begun to appear. Some have wondered whether suicide terrorism is a product of especially deep poverty or domestic political competition among various nonstate actors. The idea that suicide terrorism results from poverty is intuitively attractive. It is easier to accept that individuals with little to live for would be more willing to commit suicide than those with meaningful lives ahead of them, especially since suicide terrorism has emerged from Third World societies, all of which are poorer than Western societies.

As scholars have shown, however, poverty is a rather poor explanation for suicide terrorism.[20] A brief look at the international economic facts of life helps to explain why, especially if we control for the likely perturbing effects of the U.S. war on terrorism that led to the conquest of Afghanistan in 2001 and Iraq in 2003. As Table 2 shows, the countries plagued by suicide terrorism from 1980 to 2001 are by no means the worst off in the world; some would be considered "middle income" societies, and their people enjoy life expectancies not dramatically lower than those in the United States.

TABLE 2. 1998 Economic and Human Development Indicators for Countries and Areas Associated with Suicide Terrorism from 1980 to 2001

	GNP per capita (rank of 206)	Life Expectancy
Algeria	$1,550 (111)	71
Egypt	1,290 (121)	67
Lebanon	3,560 (80)	70
Pakistan	470 (158)	62
Saudi Arabia	6,910 (60)	72
Sri Lanka	810 (139)	73
Turkey	3,160 (85)	69
Chechnya*	2,270 (90)	66
India	450 (162)	63
West Bank	1,560 (112)	71
United States	29,240 (1)	77

Source: World Bank, *World Development Indicators* (2000)
*Data for Russia

Table 3 shows economic statistics for a dozen of the most economically hopeless states in the world, but neither these nor any of the forty-four countries that rank below India in gross national product were associated with even a single suicide terrorist attack during this period.

TABLE 3. 1998 Economic and Human Development Indicators for Poor Countries and Areas Not Associated with Suicide Terrorism from 1980 to 2001

	GNP per capita (rank of 206)	Life Expectancy
Chad	$230 (192)	48
Burundi	140 (191)	42
Ethiopia	100 (206)	43
Haiti	410 (162)	54
Mali	250 (189)	50
Mozambique	210 (195)	45
Nigeria	300 (181)	53
Niger	200 (198)	46
Rwanda	230 (192)	41
Sierra Leone	140 (202)	37
Uganda	310 (180)	42
Zambia	330 (177)	43

Source: World Bank, *World Development Indicators* (2000)

Even if we include the countries associated with suicide terrorism after the U.S. war on terrorism began, poverty remains a poor indicator of suicide terrorism. As Table 4 shows, of the five new countries that would be added to the list of those associated with suicide terrorism, only Afghanistan would be considered among the poorest forty-four countries (of 206) in the world.

TABLE 4. 1998 Economic and Human Development Indicators for Countries Associated with Suicide Terrorism Since 2001

	GNP per capita (rank of 206)	Life Expectancy
Tunisia	$2,060 (101)	72
Indonesia	640 (149)	65
Afghanistan	(not available)	46
Iraq	761–3,030 (est)	59
Morocco	1,240 (124)	67

Source: World Bank, *World Development Indicators* (2000)

The final explanation that has recently emerged is that suicide terrorism is a product of domestic competition among multiple organizations for popular support from their community. What this explanation has going for it is that it appears to correlate with some facts from the Palestinian case.[21] Starting in 1994, two separate radical groups, Hamas and Islamic Jihad, began to conduct suicide terrorist attacks that were rarely coordinated with each other and, starting in 2000, the al-Aqsa Martyrs Brigades and the Popular Front for the Liberation of Palestine launched suicide terrorist attacks as well.

However, there are good reasons to doubt that domestic political competition among rival groups is an adequate explanation either for the Palestinian case in particular or suicide terrorism in general. Even if domestic competition accounts for why multiple Palestinian groups are engaged in suicide terrorism and even if these groups are striving to outbid each other for popular support from the local community, this does not explain why suicide terrorism is so popular among the Palestinian population in the first place.[22] More important, there are many societies in which multiple violent groups compete for domestic political support without their competition leading to suicide terrorism—for instance, Somalia, Colombia, El Salvador, Nigeria, and Nicaragua—while the vast majority of cases of suicide terrorism are not associated with competition among multiple extremist organizations. The Tamil Tigers and al-Qaeda had no competitors during the periods they carried out suicide attacks, while the multiple groups that made up Hezbollah in Lebanon worked together rather than in competition with each other.

THE STRATEGIC LOGIC OF SUICIDE TERRORISM

What causes suicide terrorism? To answer this question, we must recognize that modern suicide terrorism occurs mainly in campaigns of suicide attacks carried out by organized groups for specific political goals and extending over a considerable period of time. So the core phenomenon to be explained is not an individual suicide attack, or even many such attacks considered one at a time, but the existence of protracted suicide terrorist campaigns. Although the motives of individual attackers matter, the crucial need is an explanation of the political, social, and individual conditions that jointly account for why suicide terrorist campaigns persist, why so many are occurring now, and why they occur where and when they do.

To explain suicide terrorism, it is helpful to think of a suicide terrorist campaign as the product of a three-step process, to explain each step individually, and to provide a unifying framework for the causal logic as a whole. The three principal questions are these.

First, what is the strategic logic of suicide terrorism? That is, why does suicide attack make political sense from the perspective of a terrorist organization? If terrorist organizations did not believe that suicide attack would advance their political goals, they would not do it.

Second, what is the social logic of suicide terrorism? Why does suicide attack receive mass support in some societies and not others? Without social support from the terrorists' national community, suicide terrorist campaigns could not be sustained.

Third, what is the individual logic of suicide terrorism? What makes particular people willing to give up their lives to carry out terrorist attacks? Without a ready supply of willing attackers, suicide terrorist campaigns would be much more limited in scope than they are.

Suicide terrorism depends for its existence on all three of these components—the strategic, the social, and the individual.[23] The diagram on the following page illustrates the general framework for the causal logic of suicide terrorism and supplies a brief summary of the principal mechanisms at work in each level of analysis.

The strategic logic of suicide terrorism is aimed at political coercion. The vast majority of suicide terrorist attacks are not isolated or random acts by individual fanatics, but rather occur in clusters as part of a larger campaign by an organized group to achieve a specific political goal. Moreover, the main goals of suicide terrorist groups are profoundly of this world. Suicide terrorist campaigns are primarily nationalistic, not religious, nor are they particularly Islamic. From Hezbollah in Lebanon to Hamas on the West Bank to the Liberation Tigers of Tamil Eelam in Sri Lanka, every group mounting a suicide campaign over the past two decades has had as a major objective—or as its central objective—coercing a foreign state that has military forces in what the terrorists see as their homeland to take those forces out. Further, all of the target states have been democracies, which terrorists see as more vulnerable to coercion than other types of regimes. Even al-Qaeda fits this pattern. Osama bin Laden's highest-priority objective—although he has others—is the expulsion of U.S. troops from the Persian Gulf region. Terrorists loyal to al-Qaeda routinely attack American troops, individuals from Western countries, and governments friendly to the West in Saudi Arabia and other Gulf states.

CAUSAL LOGIC OF SUICIDE TERRORISM

Strategic Level	Coercive Power	
Social Level	Mass Support	Suicide Terrorism
Individual Level	Altruistic Motive*	

*Altruistic suicides are those committed to further a goal that the individual's community supports; they are to be distinguished from egoistic suicides, which are committed to escape a life that has become intolerable. See Chapter 9.

There is a disturbing reason why suicide terrorism has been rising so rapidly: over the past two decades, suicide terrorists have learned that this strategy pays. Suicide terrorists sought to compel American and French military forces to abandon Lebanon in 1983, Israeli forces to leave Lebanon in 1985, Israeli forces to quit the Gaza Strip and the West Bank in 1994 and 1995, the Sri Lankan government to create an independent Tamil state from 1990 on, and the Turkish government to grant autonomy to the Kurds in the late 1990s. In all but the case of Turkey, the terrorists' political cause made more gains after the resort to suicide operations than it had before.

Second, suicide terrorism follows a social logic strikingly different from what many assume. Suicide terrorist groups are neither primarily criminal gangs dedicated to enriching their top leaders, nor religious cults isolated from the rest of their society. Rather, suicide terrorist organizations often command broad social support within the national communities from which they recruit, because they are seen as pursuing legitimate nationalist goals, especially liberation from foreign occupation.

Although suicide terrorism is virtually always a response to foreign occupation, only some occupations lead to this result. Suicide terrorism is most likely when the occupying power's religion differs from the religion of the occupied, for three reasons. A conflict across a religious divide increases fears that the enemy will seek to transform the occupied society; makes demonization, and therefore killing, of enemy civilians easier; and makes it easier to use one's own religion to relabel suicides that would otherwise be taboo as martyrdom instead.

Finally, what motivates individual suicide terrorists? Are suicide attackers driven by economic helplessness, social anomie, religious indoctrination, or something else? Not all suicides arise from similar causes. Emile Durkheim's famous study of suicide in nineteenth-century Europe showed that there are multiple forms of suicide. The most common is "egoistic suicide," in which personal psychological trauma leads an individual to kill himself in order to escape a painful existence. Less common is "altruistic suicide," in which high levels of social integration and respect for community values can lead normal individuals to commit suicide out of a sense of duty. Many, perhaps most, suicide terrorists fit the paradigm of altruistic suicide, at least from the point of view of those who support terrorism to further their political cause. From everyone else's point of view, suicide attacks are murders.

Few suicide attackers are social misfits, criminally insane, or professional losers. Most fit a nearly opposite profile: typically they are psychologically normal, have better than average economic prospects for their communities, and are deeply integrated into social networks and emotionally attached to their national communities. They see themselves as sacrificing their lives for the nation's good.

The bottom line, then, is that suicide terrorism is mainly a response to foreign occupation. Isolated incidents in other circumstances do occur. Religion plays a role. However, modern suicide terrorism is best understood as an extreme strategy for national liberation against democracies with troops that pose an imminent threat to control the territory the terrorists view as their homeland.

Understanding the strategic, social, and individual logics of suicide terrorism has important implications for America's war on terrorism. Our current policy debate is misguided. Neither offensive military force nor concessions alone are likely to work for long. The key problem we face is that our security depends on achieving not one goal, but two: we must defeat the current pool of terrorists seeking to launch spectacular attacks against the United States and our allies, while simultaneously undermining the conditions that will otherwise produce the next, potentially larger generation of terrorists. Accomplishing this overall purpose will require a new strategy for victory; that strategy must recognize that a trade-off exists between our two objectives, because the use of heavy offensive force to defeat today's terrorists is the most likely stimulus to the rise of more.

September 11 has changed the lives of Americans. Every day, many wonder if each airplane, building, or bus they see could be a danger to them or their families. When people themselves are weapons of war, it is hard to be confident of safety. However, the future need not be grim. Understanding the logic of suicide terrorism can help us pursue the right domestic and foreign policies to contain this deadly threat.

1 DYING TO WIN

PART I

THE STRATEGIC LOGIC OF SUICIDE TERRORISM

3

—

A Strategy for Weak Actors

MOST SUICIDE TERRORISM is undertaken as a strategic effort directed toward particular political goals; it is not simply the product of irrational individuals or an expression of fanatical hatreds. The main purpose of suicide terrorism is to use the threat of punishment to compel a target government to change policy, and most especially to cause democratic states to withdraw forces from land the terrorists perceive as their national homeland.

It is true that suicide terrorist organizations often have additional goals, such as Hamas's aim to build a religious state in Palestine or al-Qaeda's aim to do the same on the Arabian Peninsula. The existence of these ultimate goals, however, should not distract us from the fact that the proximate, operational goal of suicide operations is to gain control of territory. Neither side's views about the desirability of additional terrorist goals would matter unless the terrorists first succeed in forcing the occupying power to leave.

THE STRATEGIC VALUE OF AN ATTACKER'S WILLINGNESS TO DIE

At its core, suicide terrorism is a strategy of coercion, a means to compel a target government to change policy. The central logic of this strategy is simple: suicide terrorism attempts to inflict enough pain on the opposing society to overwhelm its interest in resisting the terrorists' demands, and so to induce the government to concede, or the population to revolt against the government. The common feature of all suicide terrorist campaigns is that they inflict punishment on the opposing society, either directly by killing civilians or indirectly by killing military personnel in circumstances that cannot lead to meaningful battlefield victory. As we shall see, suicide terrorism is rarely a onetime event, but often occurs in a series of suicide attacks. It generates coercive leverage both from the immediate panic associated with each attack and from the risk of punishment of innocents in the future.

Suicide terrorists' willingness to die magnifies the coercive effects of punishment in three ways. First, suicide attacks are generally more destructive than other terrorist attacks. An attacker who is willing to die is much more likely to accomplish the mission and to cause maximum damage to the target. Suicide attackers can conceal weapons on their own bodies and make last-minute adjustments more easily than ordinary terrorists. They are also better able to infiltrate heavily guarded targets, because they do not need escape plans or rescue teams. Suicide attackers are also able to use certain especially destructive methods such as "suicide vests" and ramming vehicles into targets. The 315 suicide terrorist attacks from 1980 to 2003 killed an average of 12 people each, not counting the unusually large number of fatalities on September 11 and also not counting the attackers themselves. During the same period, there were about 4,155 total terrorist incidents worldwide, which killed 3,207 people (also excluding September 11), or less than one person per incident. Overall, from 1980 to 2003, suicide attacks amount to 3 percent of all terrorist attacks, but account for 48 percent of total deaths due to terrorism, once again excluding September 11.[1]

Second, suicide attacks are an especially convincing way to signal the likelihood of more pain to come, because suicide itself is a costly signal, one that suggests that the attackers could not have been deterred by a threat of costly retaliation. Organizations that sponsor suicide attacks can also deliberately orchestrate the circumstances around the death of a suicide attacker to further increase expectations of future attacks. This can be called the "art of martyrdom."[2] The more suicide terrorists justify their actions on the basis of religious or ideological motives that match the beliefs of a broader national community, the more the status of terrorist martyrs is elevated, and the more plausible it becomes that others will follow in their footsteps. Suicide terrorist organizations commonly cultivate "sacrificial myths" that include elaborate sets of symbols and rituals to mark an individual attacker's death as a contribution to the nation. Suicide attackers' families also often receive material rewards both from the terrorist organizations and from other supporters. As a result, the art of martyrdom elicits popular support from the terrorists' community, reducing the moral backlash that suicide attacks might otherwise produce, and so establishes the foundation for credible signaling of more attacks to come.

Third, suicide terrorist organizations are better positioned than other terrorist groups to heighten expectations of escalating future costs by deliberately violating norms in the use of violence. They can do this by crossing thresholds of damage, by breaching taboos concerning legitimate targets, and by broadening recruitment to confound expectations about limits on the number of possible terrorists. The element of suicide itself helps increase the credibility of future attacks, because it suggests that attackers cannot be deterred. Although the capture and conviction of Timothy McVeigh gave reason for some confidence that others with similar political views might be deterred, the deaths of the September 11 hijackers did not, because Americans would have to expect that future al-Qaeda attackers would be equally willing to die.

LOGIC OF COERCION BY WEAK ACTORS

Suicide terrorism does not occur under the same circumstances as military coercion used by states, and these structural differences help to explain the logic of the strategy. In virtually all instances of international military coercion, the coercer is the stronger state and the target is the weaker state; otherwise, the coercer would likely be deterred or simply unable to execute the threats. Under these circumstances, coercers have a choice between two main coercive strategies: punishment and denial. Punishment seeks to coerce by raising the costs or risks to the target society to a level that overwhelms the value of the interests in dispute. Denial seeks to coerce by demonstrating to the target state that it simply cannot win the dispute regardless of its level of effort, and that therefore fighting to a finish is pointless—for example, because the coercer has the ability to conquer the disputed territory. Hence, although coercers may initially rely on punishment, they often have the resources to create a formidable threat to deny the opponent victory in battle and, if necessary, to achieve a brute-force military victory if the target government refuses to change its behavior. The Allied bombing of Germany in World War II, American bombing of North Vietnam in 1972, and Coalition attacks against Iraq in 1991 all fit this pattern.[3]

Suicide terrorism (and terrorism in general) occurs under the reverse structural conditions. In suicide terrorism, the coercer is the weaker actor and the target is the stronger. Although some elements of the situation remain the same, flipping the stronger and weaker sides in a coercive dispute has a dramatic change on the relative feasibility of punishment and denial. In these circumstances, denial is impossible, because military conquest is ruled out by relative weakness.

This accounts for why suicide terrorism often appears as a weapon of last resort. When rebels are strong enough to achieve their territorial aims through conventional or guerrilla means alone, there is little reason for them to accept the disapproval and costs that follow from resorting to suicide terrorism. Thus, it is not surprising that although some groups using suicide terrorism have received important external support, and some have been strong enough to wage guerrilla military campaigns as well as terrorism, none have been strong enough to have any serious prospect of achieving their political goals by conquest. The suicide terrorist group with the most significant military capacity has been the LTTE, but it has not had a real chance of controlling the whole of the homeland that it claims, including the Eastern and Northern Provinces of Sri Lanka.

So the only coercive strategy available to suicide terrorists is punishment. Although the element of "suicide" is novel and the pain inflicted on civilians is often spectacular and gruesome, the heart of suicide terrorism's strategy is the same as the coercive logic used by states when they employ air power or economic sanctions to punish an adversary: to cause mounting civilian costs to overwhelm the target state's interest in the issue in dispute and so to cause it to concede the terrorists' political demands. What creates the coercive leverage is not so much actual damage as the expectation of future damage. Targets may be economic or political, military or civilian, but in all cases the main task is less to destroy the specific targets than to convince the opposing society that it is vulnerable to more attacks in the future. These features also make suicide terrorism convenient for retaliation, a tit-for-tat interaction that generally occurs between terrorists and the defending government.[4]

The rhetoric of major suicide terrorist groups reflects the logic of coercive punishment.

Hezbollah's "Open Letter" of February 1985, the principal statement defining the purpose of the movement, said that its "great and necessary objectives" were "to put an end to foreign occupation and to adopt a regime freely wanted by the people of Lebanon" and "to expel the Americans, the French and their allies definitely from Lebanon, putting an end to any colonialist entity on our land."[5] In late 1985, Ayatollah Sayyid Muhammad Husayn Fadlallah, a spiritual leader of Hezbollah, stressed the coercive value of suicide attack: "We believe that suicide operations should only be carried out if they can bring about a political or military change in proportion to the passions that incite a person to make of his body an explosive bomb."[6]

Hamas's first communiqué, of December 14, 1987, proclaimed the general purpose of resistance as follows: "The intifada of our vigilant people in the Occupied Territories comes as a resounding rejection of the occupation and its pressures, land confiscation and the planting of settlements, and the policy of subjugation by the Zionists. . . . Let the reckless settlers beware. Our people know the way of sacrifice and martyrdom and are generous in this regard. . . . Let them understand that violence breeds nothing but violence and death bestows but death." Similarly, the Hamas Charter of 1988 states, "If an enemy invades Muslim territories, then Jihad and fighting the enemy becomes an individual duty on every Muslim."[7]

Abdel Karim, a leader of the *al-Aqsa Martyrs Brigades,* a militant group linked to Yasser Arafat's Fatah movement, said the goal of his group was "to increase losses in Israel to a point at which the Israeli public would demand a withdrawal from the West Bank and Gaza Strip."[8]

Each year, the leader of the *Liberation Tigers of Tamil Eelam,* Velupillai Prabhakaran, gives a speech to mark the anniversary of the "Heroes' Day"—July 5, 1987, the day of the first suicide attack by the LTTE. Although these speeches vary according to the events of the year, each year the core message stresses the relationship between achieving the goal of liberation from Sinhalese occupation and the willingness of the LTTE cadres to sacrifice themselves for this goal. In 1997, Prabhakaran said, "Our martyrs were extraordinary human beings. They chose the noble cause of liberating our people. Having lived and struggled for such a cause they finally sacrificed their precious lives for that higher ideal. . . . Let us continue to struggle to expel the enemy forces who have occupied our sacred land."[9]

In December 2003, *Chechnya's* rebel commander, Abu al-Walid al-Ghamidi, said, "As you have seen and noticed, most of the suicide attacks were carried out by women. . . . These women, particularly the wives of the mujahedin who were martyred, are being threatened in their homes, their honour and everything are being threatened. They do not accept being humiliated and living under occupation."[10]

Al-Qaeda's infamous fatwa against the United States, signed by Osama bin Laden and others, reads: "The ruling to kill the Americans and their allies—civilians and military—is an individual duty for every Muslim who can do it in any country in which it is possible to do it, in order to liberate the al-Aqsa Mosque and the holy mosque [Mecca] from their grip, and in order for their armies to move out of all the lands of Islam, defeated and unable to threaten any Muslim."[11]

There is also strong evidence that the leaders of terrorist groups view the offensive use of suicide attack as a means to compensate for the relative military weakness of their groups compared with their opponents.

In 1985, Daud Daud, a leader of *Hezbollah* in southern Lebanon, said: "We are prepared to sacrifice our lives—literally blow ourselves up in opposition to their tanks. . . . Since we cannot fight the enemy with weapons, we have to sacrifice our lives. And this is what is happening right now in South Lebanon."

Sayeed Siyam, a *Hamas* leader in Gaza, said, "We in Hamas consider suicide bombing attacks inside the 1948 borders"—inside Israel—"to be the card that Palestinians can play to resist the occupation. . . . We do not own Apache helicopters ourselves, so we use our own methods. Given the methods used by the Israelis, we consider the door to hell is open. Their assassination policy and the bombardment—all this theater of war inside Palestinian villages and homes—we respond to that by seeking to make Israelis feel the same, insecure inside their homes."[12]

In 1995, the secretary general of *Islamic Jihad*, Fathi al-Shaqaqi, said, "Martyrdom actions will escalate in the face of all pressures. . . . [they] are a realistic option in confronting the unequal balance of power. If we are unable to effect a balance of power now, we can achieve a balance of horror."[13]

In 1997, the *Tamil Tigers'* political spokesman, S. Thamilchelvan, gave an interview in which he explained that the group devised the use of suicide bombing as a means to compensate for the Tamils' numerical disadvantage—their population is about one-fourth that of the majority Sinhalese—and to more effectively attack the Sinhalese military and political leadership. The goal, Thamilchelvan said, was "to ensure maximum damage done with minimum loss of life."[14] The Tigers' leader, Prabhakaran, has also singled out the group's suicide commandos. In a major speech in 1998, he said, "In terms of manpower, firepower and resources, the enemy was strong and the balance of military power was in his favor. Yet we had an extraordinary weapon which was not in the arsenal of the enemy. The courage and commitment of our fighters was our most powerful weapon in the battle."[15] Similarly, he said, "The Black Tigers [suicide squad] are the self-protective armor of our race. They are the men of flame who can destroy the enemy's armed strength."[16]

EARLIER CASES ALSO HAD COERCIVE GOALS

The best known suicide operations before 1980 also had coercive aims. The Zealots, the Assassins, and the kamikazes all sought to coerce their political opponents, either to remove foreign military forces from their homeland or to prevent imminent military invasions.

The Zealots and Sicarii

Information about the first-century Jewish Zealots and Sicarii is scant. Although we know that they numbered in the "hundreds" and committed "numerous daily murders," we lack important knowledge about the groups' organizational structure and attack doctrines, and do not have a solid basis for estimating the total number of people who would have considered themselves members of these groups.

However, we do have a reasonably clear understanding of the Zealots' and Sicarii's strategic logic. According to scholars of the period, the Zealots and Sicarii adopted a strategy of violent attacks designed to provoke a massive uprising among the Jewish population against the Roman occupation. As David C. Rapoport summarizes it, "Consecutive atrocities continually narrowed prospects for a political, more mutually agreeable, solution, serving to destroy the credibility of moderates on both sides while steadily expanding the conflict."[17]

After decades of attacks, which provoked steadily escalating Roman retaliatory responses, the Zealots and Sicarii succeeded in generating two large-scale popular uprisings. These uprisings triggered the Jewish War of A.D. 66, a bloody four-year struggle that ultimately led to the destruction of the Temple in Jerusalem, extermination of the large Jewish centers in Egypt and Cyprus, and the traumatic exodus of the Jews from Judea.[18]

For the Zealots and Sicarii, the Jewish War ended at Masada. Rather than submit to Roman rule and, after years of war, probable murder, rape, and slavery, some 960 members of these groups chose to commit what remains the most famous group suicide in history. Their motives, however, were at least as much personal as political. The leader of the Sicarii, Eleazar, is said to have given the following speech just as the Romans were preparing for the final assault on the fortress:

> This grace has been given to us by God, namely to be able to die nobly and freely. . . . Only our shared death is able to protect our wives and children from violation and slavery. . . . We, who have been brought up at home in this way, should set an example to others in our readiness to die. . . . This— suicide—is commanded by our laws. Our wives and children ask for it. God himself has sent us the necessity for it.[19]

The Assassins

Like the Zealots, the Ismaili Assassins have several features in common with modern suicide terrorist groups: they were weak relative to their opponents; they were the militant arm of a broader, geographically distinct community with widely shared beliefs and practices; they had a close bond of loyalty to comrades and devotion to leaders; and they had a system of initiation and rituals signifying an individual's level of commitment to the community.

The Assassins also exploited their reputation as suicide killers for coercive purposes. Although the overarching political program of the Assassins was to overthrow the existing Sunni order and to establish the dominance of their own rulers, whom they believed to be more true to Islam, the Assassins frequently used the threat of suicide attack to compel Sunni rulers to abandon military campaigns against their strongholds and even to strike long-lasting peaceful settlements.

Territorial control was a key element of the Assassins' program. Living in the remote Elburz mountains of northern Iran, an area with many castles and a sympathetic Ismaili population, the Assassins succeeded, as the historian Bernard Lewis writes, "in creating what was virtually a territorial state."[20] Numerous sultans in Persia and Iraq sought to uproot the Ismaili menace by military force only to find themselves meeting the Assassins' daggers or accepting a negotiated settlement. In 1118, a new sultan awoke to find an ornate dagger stuck in the ground beside his bed and found a message from the Assassins' leader: "Did I not wish the Sultan well, that dagger which was struck into the hard ground would have been planted in his soft breast." The sultan did not attack the Assassins for the remainder of his ten-year rule.[21] This pattern of threatened or actual assassinations followed by mutual nonaggression pacts continued until the Mongols invaded Iran and exterminated virtually the entire Ismaili population in the Elburz mountains in 1258.

The Kamikazes

The Japanese kamikazes during World War II were regular military forces and therefore are not normally considered terrorists, although they also used suicide attack for coercive purposes. Specifically, the kamikazes' aim was not to defeat the American invasion forces, but to impose such high costs on the attacking fleet that the United States would settle for a negotiated outcome to the war. The name "kamikaze" derives from the "Divine Wind" that was said to have turned back a Mongol invasion fleet in the thirteenth century. The purpose of the "special attack" squadrons was similar, as Hichiro Naemura, a former instructor of kamikaze pilots, explained:

> I did not believe we could win the war against the overwhelmingly powerful enemy, no matter how well we fought. . . . Our special kamikaze tactics could delay the enemy's advance towards our homeland and inflict severe damage upon him. By delaying his encroachment we hoped that the enemy would agree to negotiate a truce.[22]

For Japanese leaders, suicide attack was a last resort. The first major plan for "body-crashing" attacks was Rear Admiral Kameto Kuroshima's "Invincible War Preparation" plan, which was rejected in July 1943 by a conference of high-ranking officers who believed that they could defeat the Allied forces in regular combat. However, with the fall of Saipan in July 1944 and the growing fear that Japan's defense perimeter would collapse island by island, the Japanese high command reconsidered the earlier decision. Military leaders met on July 7, 1944, and ordered new designs for planes intended specifically for suicide missions. In mid-September, a proposal for new forms of attack stated: "The primary concern was to inflict maximum destruction on the enemy; it mattered little whether the pilots had to be sacrificed or not."[23] The leading advocate of these new forms of attack, Vice Admiral Takijiro Onishi, took command of Japan's land-based air forces in the Philippines on October 17, and, within days, formed the first kamikaze squadrons, which just days later attacked

American carriers and other vessels during the great naval battle of Leyte Gulf. As Onishi explained to his senior staff officers, the only chance Japanese surface forces had to counter the invasion was to "neutralize" the U.S. carriers for at least a week, and this could only be done one way: "suicide attack units composed of Zero fighters armed with 250kg bombs, with each plane to crash-dive into an enemy carrier."[24]

Kamikaze pilots were also motivated by the belief that their sacrifice would enable Japan to avoid occupation by the United States. These individuals, who were generally graduates of special training programs for pilots or universities, often kept extensive diaries, many of which have been published. Special attack pilots volunteered for their missions. Although social pressure may have contributed to why individuals willingly stepped forward, the common explanation they give for why such missions were important was that suicide attack was the only way to stave off American occupation. Shortly before his death, one pilot wrote in his diary: "We must fight to the end so that the Japanese can create a new era by the Japanese ourselves. We cannot succumb to the 'red hair and blue eyes.' "[25]

Similarly, Wada Minoru wrote, shortly before volunteering to be a special attack pilot:

> Perhaps there is no other way to make a break-through [for Japan in the war] except by the human torpedo. The use of planes is so ineffective in causing damage to enemy vessels in relation to casualties. With radar, it is now impossible to approach aircraft carriers without being detected. . . . If human torpedoes must appear in Japan, there is no other group of people but us who would become pilots.[26]

These contemporaneous accounts agree with testimony given by senior Japanese leaders to the United States Strategic Bombing Survey after the war. When asked to account for the motivation of individual kamikaze pilots, Lieutenant General Torashiro Kawabe said:

> We believed that our spiritual convictions and moral strength could balance your material and scientific advantages. We did not consider our attacks to be "suicide." The pilot did not start out on his mission with the intention of committing suicide [i.e., of immolating himself in a spirit of despair]. He looked upon himself as a human bomb which would destroy a certain part

of the enemy fleet . . . [and] died happy in the conviction that his death was a step towards the final victory.[27]

In the end, the kamikazes did not succeed in compelling the United States to accept a negotiated surrender by Japan. They were, however, the most effective coercive tool available to Japan at the time. Aptly, the U.S. Strategic Bombing Survey summarizes the kamikazes as "macabre, effective, and supremely practical under the circumstances."[28]

4

Targeting Democracies

NO PREVIOUS ANALYSIS of suicide terrorism has been able to draw on a complete survey of suicide terrorist attacks worldwide. This drawback, together with the fact that many such attacks, including all those against Americans, have been committed by Muslims have led many in the United States to assume that Islamic fundamentalism must be the main underlying cause.[1] This, in turn, has fueled a belief that anti-American terrorism can be stopped only by wholesale transformation of Muslim societies, a belief that helped create public support of the invasion of Iraq. Comprehensive study of the phenomenon of suicide terrorism, however, shows that the presumed connection to Islamic fundamentalism is misleading.

My study surveys all 315 suicide terrorist attacks around the globe from 1980 to 2003.[2] The data show that there is not the close connection between suicide terrorism and Islamic fundamentalism that many people think. Rather, what all suicide terrorist campaigns have in common is a specific secular and strategic goal: to compel democracies to withdraw military forces from the terrorists' national homeland. Religion is rarely the root cause, although it is often used as a tool by terrorist organizations in recruiting and in other efforts in service of the broader strategic objective.

THREE PATTERNS IN SUICIDE TERRORISM

Three general patterns in the data support the conclusion that suicide terrorism is mainly a strategic phenomenon. These three properties are consistent with the above strategic logic but not with irrational behavior or religious fanaticism:

1. Timing. Nearly all suicide attacks occur in organized, coherent campaigns, not as isolated or randomly timed incidents.
2. Nationalist goals. Suicide terrorist campaigns are directed at gaining control of what the terrorists see as their national homeland, and specifically at ejecting foreign forces from that territory.
3. Target selection. All suicide terrorist campaigns in the last two decades have been aimed at democracies, which make more suitable targets from the terrorists' point of view. Nationalist movements that face non-democratic opponents have not resorted to suicide attack as a means of coercion.

Timing

Of the 315 separate suicide terrorist attacks between 1980 and 2003, 301, or 95 percent, were parts of organized, coherent campaigns, while only 14 were isolated or random events. Nine separate disputes have led to suicide terrorist campaigns: the presence of American and French forces in Lebanon; Israeli occupation of the West Bank and Gaza; the status of the Tamil regions of Sri Lanka; the status of the Kurdish region of Turkey; the Russian occupation of Chechnya; the Indian occupation of Kashmir; the Indian control of Punjab; and the presence of American forces in Iraq and in the Arabian Peninsula. Overall, however, there have been eighteen distinct campaigns, because in certain disputes the terrorists elected to suspend operations one or more times, either in response to concessions or for other reasons. Thirteen of the campaigns have ended and five were ongoing as of the end of 2003. The attacks making up each campaign were organized by the same terrorist group (or, sometimes, a set of cooperating groups, as in the ongoing "second intifada" in Israel/Palestine), clustered in time, publicly justified in terms of a specified political goal, and directed against targets related to that goal.

A suicide terrorist *campaign* can be distinguished from a string of isolated attacks. A campaign consists of an intended series of attacks that terrorist leaders explain and justify as aimed at gaining political concessions from a target government. A campaign also continues until the terrorist leaders deliberately abandon it, either because sufficient gains have been made or because the leaders believe that the effort has failed. The Babbar Khalsa International (BKI) attack on the Indian chief minister of Punjab in August 1995 meets the minimum criteria for an organized campaign, even though there was only one successful operation that clearly meets the classic definition of suicide attack. The BKI sought over a period of years to coerce India to permit Sikh independence in Punjab, publicly tied the August 1995 attack to this goal, and carried out at least one other possible (though ambiguous) suicide attack and at least one that meets the broader definition of a suicide mission. The BKI also attempted other, unsuccessful, suicide operations.[3]

TABLE 5. Suicide Terrorist Campaigns: Goals and Results

Completed Campaigns

Date	Terrorist Group	Terrorists' Goal	# Attacks/ Killed	Target Behavior
1. Apr–Dec 1983	Hezbollah	U.S./France out of Lebanon	5/393	Complete withdrawal
2. Nov 1983–Apr 1985	Hezbollah	Israel out of Lebanon	11/197	Partial withdrawal
3. June 1985–June 1986	Hezbollah	Israel out of Leb. security zone	20/156	No change
4. July 1990–Nov 1994	LTTE	Sri Lanka accept Tamil state	15/206	Negotiations
5. Apr 1995–Oct 2000	LTTE	Sri Lanka accept Tamil state	54/662	No change
6. Apr 1994	Hamas	Israel out of Palestine	2/15	Partial withdrawal from Gaza
7. Oct 1994–Aug 1995	Hamas	Israel out of Palestine	9/73	Partial withdrawal from W.B.
8. Aug 1995	BKI (Sikh)	Punjab independence	1/16	No change
9. Feb–Mar 1996	Hamas	Retaliation for Israeli assassination	4/58	No change
10. Mar–Sept 1997	Hamas	Israel out of Palestine	3/24	Hamas leader released
11. June–Oct 1996	PKK	Turkey accept Kurd autonomy	3/16	No change
12. Mar–Aug 1999	PKK	Turkey release jailed leader	11/6	No change
13. 2001	LTTE	Sri Lanka accept Tamil state	6/33	Granted autonomy

Ongoing Campaigns, as of December 2003

Date	Terrorist Group	Terrorists' Goal	# Attacks/ Killed	Target Behavior
14. 1996–	al-Qaeda	U.S. out of Saudi Arabia	21/3661	TBD
15. 2000–	Chechen rebels	Russia out of Chechnya	19/332	TBD
16. 2000–	Kashmir rebels	India out of Kashmir	5/61	TBD
17. 2000–	several	Israel out of Palestine.	92/459	TBD
18. 2003	Iraqi rebels	U.S. out of Iraq	20/262	TBD

Total incidents: 315
in campaigns: 301
isolated: 14

The most important indicator of strategic orientation is the timing of the suspension of campaigns. Suspension is most often based on a strategic decision by leaders of the terrorist organizations that further attacks would be counterproductive to their coercive purposes—for instance, in response to full or partial concessions by the target state to the terrorists' political goals. Such suspensions are often accompanied by public explanations that justify the decision to opt for a "cease-fire." Further, the terrorist organizations' discipline is usually fairly good; although there are exceptions, such announced cease-fires usually do stick for a period of months at least, normally until the terrorist leaders take a new strategic decision to resume in pursuit of goals not achieved in the earlier campaign. This pattern indicates that both terrorist leaders and their recruits are sensitive to the coercive value of the attacks.

As an example of a suicide campaign, consider Hamas's suicide attacks in 1995 to compel Israel to withdraw from towns in the West Bank. Hamas leaders deliberately held off attacking during the spring and early summer in order to give PLO negotiations with Israel an opportunity to finalize a withdrawal. However, in early July, when Hamas leaders came to believe that Israel was backsliding and delaying withdrawal, Hamas launched a series of suicide attacks. Israel accelerated the pace of its withdrawal, after which Hamas ended the campaign. Mahmud al-Zahar, a Hamas leader in Gaza, announced following the cessation of suicide attacks in October 1995:

> We must calculate the benefit and cost of continued armed operations. If we can fulfill our goals without violence, we will do so. Violence is a means, not a goal. Hamas's decision to adopt self-restraint does not contradict our aims, which include the establishment of an Islamic state instead of Israel. . . . We will never recognize Israel, but it is possible that a truce could prevail between us for days, months, or years.[4]

If suicide terrorism were mainly irrational or even disorganized, we would expect a much different pattern: political goals would not be articulated (for example, we would see references in news reports to "rogue" attacks), or the stated goals would vary considerably even within the same conflict. We would also expect the timing to be either random, or perhaps event-driven in response to particularly provocative or infuriating actions by the other side, but little if at all related to the progress of negotiations over issues in dispute that the terrorists want to influence.

Nationalist Goals

Suicide terrorism is a high-cost strategy, which makes strategic sense for a group only when crucial interests are at stake, and even then as a last resort. The reason is that suicide terrorism maximizes coercive leverage at the expense of support among the terrorists' own community and so can be sustained over time only when there already exists a high degree of commitment among the potential pool of recruits. The most important goal that a community can have is the independence of its homeland (population, property, and way of life) from foreign influence or control. As a result, a strategy of suicide terrorism is most likely to be used to achieve nationalist goals.

In fact, every suicide campaign from 1980 to 2003 has had as a major objective—or as its central objective—coercing a foreign government that has military forces in what they see as their homeland to take those forces out. Table 6 summarizes the disputes that have engendered suicide terrorist campaigns. Since 1980, there has not been a suicide terrorist campaign directed mainly against domestic opponents or against foreign opponents who did not have military forces in the terrorists' homeland. Although attacks against civilians are often the most salient to Western observers, actually every suicide terrorist campaign in the past two decades has included attacks directly against the foreign military forces in the relevant country, and most have been waged by guerrilla organizations that also use more conventional methods of attack against those forces.

Even al-Qaeda fits this pattern. Although Saudi Arabia is not under American military occupation, at least from the perspective of the United States, and although the terrorists have political objectives against the Saudi regime and others, one major objective of al-Qaeda is the expulsion of U.S. troops from the country. There have been attacks by terrorists loyal to Osama bin Laden against American troops in Saudi Arabia. To be sure, there is a major debate among Islamists over the morality of suicide attacks, but within Saudi Arabia there is little debate over al-Qaeda's objection to American forces in the region, and over 95 percent of Saudi society reportedly agrees with Bin Laden on this matter.[5]

Still, even if suicide terrorism follows a strategic logic, could some suicide terrorist campaigns be irrational in the sense that they are being waged for unrealistic goals?

In fact, some suicide terrorist groups have not been realistic in expecting the full concessions demanded of the target, but this is normal in disputes involving overlapping nationalist claims, and even for coercive

Table 6. Motivation and Targets of Suicide Terrorist Campaigns, 1980–2003

Region/Dispute	Homeland Status	Terrorist Goal	Target a Democracy?
Lebanon, 1983–86	U.S./F/IDF military presence	U.S./F/IDF withdrawal	Yes
West Bank/Gaza, 1994–	IDF military presence	IDF withdrawal	Yes
Tamils in Sri Lanka,			
1990–2001	SL military presence	SL withdrawal	Yes (1950)*
Punjab, 1995	Indian control	Punjab independence	Yes
Kurds in Turkey, 1990s	Turkey military presence	Turkey withdrawal	Yes (1983)*
Chechnya, 2000–	Russia military presence	Russian withdrawal	Yes (1993)*
Kashmir, 2000–	Indian military presence	Indian withdrawal	Yes
Arabian Peninsula,			
1996–	U.S. military presence	U.S. withdrawal	Yes
Iraq, 2003–	U.S. military presence	U.S. withdrawal	Yes

*Date established as a democracy (if not always a democracy).

Sources: Adam Przeworski, Michael E. Alvarez, Jose Antonio Cheibub, and Fernando Limongi, *Democracy and Development: Political Institutions and Well-Being in the World, 1950–1990* (Cambridge, UK: Cambridge University Press, 2000) identifies four simple rules for determining regime type. They are: (1) the chief executive must be elected; (2) the legislature must be elected; (3) there must be more than one party; and (4) there must be at least one peaceful transfer of power. By these criteria, all the targets of suicide terrorism were and are democracies. Przeworski, Alvarez, Cheibub, and Limongi code only from 1950 to 1990 but have been updated to 1999 by Carles Boix and Sebastian Rosato, "A Complete Dataset of Regimes, 1850–1999" (manuscript, University of Chicago, 2001). Freedom House also rates countries as "Free," "Partly Free," and "Not Free," using criteria for degrees of political rights and civil liberties. According to Freedom House's measures, Sri Lanka, Turkey, and Russia were all "Partly Free" when they were the targets of suicide terrorism, which puts them approximately in the middle of all countries, a score that is actually biased against this study since terrorism itself lowers a country's civil liberties rating (www.freedomhouse.org).

attempts in general. However, the ambitions of terrorist leaders are realistic in two other senses. First, suicide terrorists' political aims, if not their methods, are often more mainstream than observers realize; they generally reflect quite common, straightforward nationalist self-determination claims of their community. Second, these groups often have significant support for their policy goals with respect to the target state, goals that are typically much like those of other nationalists within their community. Differences between the terrorists and more "moderate" leaders usually concern the usefulness of a certain level of violence, and—sometimes—

the legitimacy of attacks against targets other than foreign troops in the country (such as attacks in other countries, or against third parties and civilians). Thus, it is not that terrorists pursue radical goals and then seek others' support. Rather, terrorists are simply the members of their societies who are the most optimistic about the usefulness of violence for achieving goals that many, and often most, support.

The behavior of Hamas illustrates the point. Hamas terrorism has provoked Israeli retaliation that has been costly for Palestinians, while pursuing the—apparently unrealistic—goal of abolishing the state of Israel. Although prospects of establishing an Arab state in all of "historic Palestine" may be poor, most Palestinians agree that it would be desirable if possible. Hamas's terrorist violence was in fact carefully calculated and controlled. In April 1994, as its first suicide campaign was beginning, Hamas leaders explained that "martyrdom operations" would be used to achieve intermediate objectives, such as Israeli withdrawal from the West Bank and Gaza, while the final objective of creating an Islamic state from the Jordan River to the Mediterranean may require other forms of armed resistance.[6]

Democracies as the Targets

Suicide terrorism is more likely to be employed against states with democratic political systems than against authoritarian governments, for three reasons. First, democracies are often thought to be especially vulnerable to coercive punishment. Domestic critics and international rivals, as well as terrorists, often view democracies as "soft," usually on the grounds that their publics have low thresholds of cost tolerance and high ability to affect state policy. Even if there is little evidence that democracies are easier to coerce than other regime types, this image of democracy matters.[7] Since terrorists can inflict only moderate damage by comparison with even small inter-state wars, terrorism can be expected to coerce only if the target state is viewed as especially vulnerable to punishment. Second, suicide terrorism is a tool of the weak, which means that, regardless of how much punishment the terrorists inflict, the target state almost always has the capacity to retaliate with far more extreme punishment or even by exterminating the terrorists' community. Accordingly, suicide terrorists must not only have high interests at stake, they must also be confident that their opponent will be at least somewhat restrained. Democracies are widely perceived as less likely to harm civilians, and no democratic regime has committed genocide in the twentieth century, although recent scholarship casts strong doubt on the presumption that democracies are generally more restrained than authoritarian states.[8] Finally, suicide attacks may also be harder to organize or publicize in authoritarian police states, although these possibilities are weakened by the fact that weak authoritarian states are also not targets.

In fact, the target state of every modern suicide campaign has been a democracy. The United States, France, Israel, India, Sri Lanka, Turkey, and Russia were all democracies when they were attacked by suicide terrorist campaigns, even though the last three became democracies more recently than the others. To be sure, these states vary in the degree to which they share "liberal" norms that respect minority rights; Freedom House, a respected non-profit organization that monitors democracy in countries around the world, rates Sri Lanka, Turkey, and Russia as "Partly Free" (3.5–4.5 on a 7-point scale) rather than "Free" during the relevant years, partly because of their handling of minority rights and partly because terrorism and civil violence themselves lower the freedom rating of these states. Still, all these states elect their chief executives and legislatures in multiparty elections and have seen at least one peaceful transfer of power, making them solidly democratic by standard criteria.[9]

The Kurds, who straddle Turkey and Iraq, illustrate the point that suicide terrorist campaigns are more likely to be targeted against democracies than authoritarian regimes. Although Iraq has been far more brutal toward its Kurdish population than has Turkey, violent Kurdish groups have used suicide attacks exclusively against democratic Turkey and not against the authoritarian regime in Iraq. There are plenty of national groups living under authoritarian regimes with grievances that could possibly inspire suicide terrorism, but none have.

Thus, the fact that rebels have resorted to this strategy only when they face the more suitable type of target counts against arguments that suicide terrorism is a non-strategic response, motivated mainly by fanaticism or irrational hatreds.

OCCUPATION AND SUICIDE TERRORISM

The Core Logic

At bottom, suicide terrorism is a strategy for national liberation from foreign military occupation by a democratic state. In general, foreign occupation involves the exertion of political and military control over territory by an outside group.[10] Most foreign occupations involve stationing well-armed troops on or near the occupied territory. So do military alliances. In fact, foreign occupiers have often claimed they were merely supporting a local government and so should be treated as an ally, not an "occupier."

To avoid confusion, this study defines a foreign occupation as one in which a foreign power has the ability to control the local government independent of the wishes of the local community. The key is not the number of troops actually stationed on the occupied territory, so long as enough are available, if necessary, to suppress any effort at independence. Rather, the critical requirement is that the occupying power's political control must depend on coercive assets—whether troops, police, or other security forces—that are controlled from outside the region. If control can be maintained using only police who are responsible to indigenous authorities, then the territory cannot be said to be under foreign occupation.

In addition, many or most members of the occupied community should recognize that the foreign power exerts control over the local government, even if their estimates of the magnitude of control are vague. Accordingly, the ultimate test is the political decisiveness of foreign-controlled coercive power: if political control of the local government would change—or if most of the local community believes that it would change—if the foreign military power left, then the territory is under foreign occupation. By this standard, the United States' liberation and occupation of Italy, Germany, and Japan in World War II qualifies as occupation, but American military deployments to Great Britain and France during the conflict count as military alliances.

The association between foreign occupation and suicide terrorism does not mean that religion plays no role; it does suggest that the widely shared view that suicide terrorism emanates from Islamic fundamentalism—or religious hatred in general—is wrongheaded. Since national and religious identities often overlap, distinguishing the main motive for particular suicide terrorist campaigns may seem excessively difficult. However, these two motives will not always lead terrorists to attack the same enemies. Attacking certain enemies would make sense for nationalist objectives, but not religious ones, while attacking others would make sense for religious but not nationalist reasons.

Hamas and al-Qaeda are crucial cases. Both groups espouse Islamic fundamentalist ideologies. Both charge Christians and Jews with crimes against Muslims. And both seek to overturn what they view as foreign military occupations—Hamas, to end Israeli occupation of Palestinian land; al-Qaeda, to drive out what it sees as the American occupation of the Arabian Peninsula since 1990 as well as of Afghanistan since 2001 and Iraq since 2003.

Comparison of target selection for Hamas and al-Qaeda shows that combating foreign military occupation is more central than religious motives for both groups. If religious hostility were paramount, one would expect both Hamas and al-Qaeda to attack both Christians and Jews. Similarly, if revenge for perceived injuries were a central motive, one would expect both groups to attack both the United States and Israel. However, each group in fact concentrates its efforts against the opponent that actually has troops stationed on what it sees as its homeland territory. Hamas concentrates almost all of its effort against Israel and has not attacked the United States or American citizens outside of Israel and Palestine. Al-Qaeda's main effort has been against the United States and against American allies that have deployed troops in Afghanistan and Iraq; al-Qaeda has never attacked Israel and has rarely attacked Jewish targets elsewhere. Although Hamas complains that the United States supports Israel's occupation of Palestine, and al-Qaeda says that Israel and Jews control American foreign policy, neither group actually expends significant effort to attack opponents who do not have troops occupying their homeland.

Hamas

In the June 1967 war, Israel captured the West Bank, the Gaza Strip, and East Jerusalem. East Jerusalem was immediately annexed to Israel, while the West Bank and Gaza have remained under Israeli occupation since then. As of 2001, there were about 2.7 million Palestinians living in the Occupied Territories. Although the overwhelming majority of Palestinians in the Occupied Territories detest Israel's occupation, and although strikes, protests, and other forms of nonviolent resistance began as early as 1972, for many years most of the Palestinian population preferred to accept the benefits of the economic modernization that occurred under Israeli rule rather than support violent rebellion.[11] Beginning in 1987, however, Palestinian resistance to Israeli occupation grew progressively from violent (but unarmed) rebellion in the first intifada from 1987 to 1992, to protracted guerrilla war and suicide terrorism in the 1990s, to large-scale suicide terrorism since the start of the second intifada in September 2000.

We do not know exactly why the Palestinian rebellion against Israeli occupation began when it did. Few observers at the time expected an uprising in 1987, especially since, by this time, Palestinians had been under

Israeli rule for twenty years. That the rebellion has continued and esca-lated for a decade and a half, while not wholly unexpected, has disap-pointed those who expected the Oslo peace negotiations to reduce Palestinian resistance.

However, we do know that Islamic fundamentalism did not play a role in the initiation of the rebellion. The first intifada was largely a sponta-neous uprising of independent grassroots activists and was quickly sup-ported by the main Palestinian nationalist organization, Fatah, a secular movement. The most important Islamist organization that has played a role in Palestinian politics and in suicide terrorism, Hamas, did not yet exist in 1987.

One factor that probably did contribute significantly to the rise and per-sistence of the Palestinian rebellion was the increasing encroachment of Jewish settlers on Palestinian land. As Chart 1 shows, during the first thir-teen years of the occupation (1967 to 1980), only about 12,000 Jewish set-tlers resided in the Occupied Territories. From 1980 to 1995, this number increased more than tenfold, to 146,000, and by a further 50 percent from 1995 to 2002, to 226,000.[12] The growth of Jewish settlements not only con-sumed more land and water, but also required progressive expansion of the Israeli military presence in the West Bank and Gaza, including more and more checkpoints that made it difficult for Palestinians to travel or even carry out ordinary business. The second intifada appears to be a response to the failure of the Oslo peace process to lead to full Israeli withdrawal from the Occupied Territories, and especially the failure of the Camp David negotiations in August 2000. The growing number of Jewish settlers likely contributed to this sense of failure.

Palestinian suicide terrorist attacks began in April 1994 and continued at a rate of about three a year until the start of the second intifada, when the number rose to over twenty a year. Although two Islamist organiza-tions, Hamas and Palestinian Islamic Jihad, have conducted the majority of Palestinian suicide attacks (79 out of 110 attacks between 1994 and 2003), there is strong evidence that Islamic fundamentalism has not been the driving force behind Palestinian suicide terrorism.[13] The most impor-tant evidence is the trajectory of Palestinian public support for suicide op-erations, because this is necessary to their persistence over time. However, as Table 7 shows, public opinion polls show that suicide operations have consistently commanded much more support than Hamas or even all Is-lamist groups combined. Support for suicide terrorism was roughly flat during the 1990s, and rose sharply with the start of the second intifada.

CHART 1. JEWISH SETTLERS IN WEST BANK AND GAZA

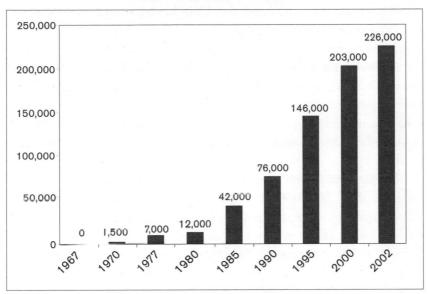

Sources: Israeli Central Bureau of Statistics, Israel Yearbook and Almanac, Jewish Telegraphic Agency (JTA), *Jerusalem Post* (August 8, 2001; February 3, 2003).

Support for Hamas and other Islamist groups also remained steady during the 1990s and rose at the start of the second intifada, although not as dramatically as support for suicide terrorism. The rise in support for Hamas and Islamic Jihad cannot be the main cause of the rise in support of suicide terrorism, because the latter is a much broader phenomenon. Indeed, support for the Islamist groups is more likely an effect of the rising popularity of suicide terrorism than a cause of it.

Table 7. Palestinian Support for Suicide Attacks and Islamic Groups, 1995–2003

Support for:	1995	1997	2001	2002	2003
Suicide operations	29%	29%	73%	68%	61%
Hamas	15%	12%	20%	20%	23%
All Islamic groups	19%	18%	28%	27%	30%

Source: Jerusalem Media and Communication Centre polls, 1995 to 2003. The table records the average of polls taken each year (1–3 per year).

The most likely explanation for the growth of popular support for suicide terrorism is not rising fundamentalism, then, but simply the intensified rebellion itself or increased Israeli use of force against the rebellion. Indeed, one poll conducted in April 2002 found that 65 percent of the Palestinians who supported suicide operations cited as a main reason Israeli military incursions.[14] Moreover, once the second intifada began and suicide terrorism became more popular, non-Islamist groups, such as the Marxist-oriented Popular Front for the Liberation of Palestine and the al-Aqsa Martyrs Brigades, also began using suicide operations, which also suggests that the phenomenon is not tightly driven by Islamic fundamentalism.

In addition, as Table 8 shows, throughout the 1990s Hamas commanded far less support than Fatah, the main secular Palestinian nationalist organization, attaining rough parity only when Fatah support declined during the second intifada. Hence, a possible additional cause of the rise in support for Hamas may be frustration with Fatah's failure to compel Israel to withdraw. While support for Islamist views may have risen somewhat over the past twenty years, there is no evidence that Hamas or any other Islamist group has made domestic political gains through the use of suicide operations. In fact, support for both groups has followed a similar trajectory, with both at constant low levels through the 1990s and both rising to higher but still constant levels after the second intifada began in fall 2000.

Table 8. Palestinian Support for Suicide Attacks and Islamic Groups, 1993–2003

Support for:	1993	1994	1995	1996	1997	1998	1999	2000	2001	2002	2003
Fatah	58%	41%	44%	37%	38%	34%	33%	34%	31%	29%	26%
Hamas	18%	13%	15%	9%	12%	14%	12%	16%	20%	20%	23%
Islamic Jihad	na	4%	3%	1%	2%	2%	2%	3%	5%	5%	6%

Source: Jerusalem Media and Communication Centre Polls, 1993–2003. Average of polls taken each year (1–3 per year).

From 1994 to 2003, there have been more than 100 Palestinian suicide terrorist attacks. All of these attacks have been directed against Israeli targets in Israel or the Occupied Territories. Although Palestinian terrorist groups have used ordinary, non-suicide tactics to attack a small number of Israeli targets outside the region, there have been no attempts to kill Americans, Europeans, or Christians, and no general campaign to attack Jews living outside of Palestine. The pattern of the suicide attacks over the past decade suggests that the Palestinian terrorists are concentrating their fire against the state that is actually occupying the territory they view as their homeland.

Al-Qaeda

Al-Qaeda is an Islamic fundamentalist terrorist organization whose central purpose is to end the American occupation of the Arabian Peninsula. Like Hamas, al-Qaeda derives its core ideology from the tradition of the Muslim Brotherhood, which stresses the obligation on Muslims to resist Western imperialism and to work toward the establishment of an Islamic regime. Unlike Hamas, however, al-Qaeda draws its membership from the transnational community of Muslim believers, not from a single country. Also unlike Hamas, while al-Qaeda focuses principally on a particular territory (the Arabian Peninsula), the group also emphasizes grievances of Muslims in multiple countries and seeks to establish Islamic regimes in all of them.[15]

The close relationship between Islamic fundamentalism and the membership of al-Qaeda has given many Americans the impression that religion is the main force driving al-Qaeda's suicide operations. On November 8, 2001, President George W. Bush addressed the nation, saying: "We are the target of enemies who boast they want to kill—kill all Americans, kill all Jews, and kill all Christians. . . . This new enemy seeks to destroy our freedom and impose its views. . . . We wage a war to save civilization itself."[16]

However, to ascribe al-Qaeda's suicide campaign to religion alone would not be accurate. The targets that al-Qaeda has attacked, and the strategic logic articulated by Osama bin Laden to explain how suicide operations are expected to help achieve al-Qaeda's goals, both suggest that al-Qaeda's principal motive is to end foreign military occupation of the Arabian Peninsula and other Muslim regions. The United States and its allies who have been under al-Qaeda's fire do export democratic, liberal, capitalist, and (arguably) Christian values to the Muslim world. The critical question is a counterfactual one: would these religious or ideological provocations suffice if the United States and European allies did not also station troops in the Middle East?

The evidence suggests that answer is no. The taproot of al-Qaeda's animosity to its enemies is what they do, not who they are.

First, consider the identity of al-Qaeda's suicide attackers. From 1995 to

2003, seventy-one al-Qaeda suicide attackers completed their missions and actually killed themselves. The Chicago Project on Suicide Terrorism collected information from a variety of languages on these attackers, ascertaining the names of fifty-six and the nationalities of sixty-seven. The majority were from Saudi Arabia and other Persian Gulf states. Although there is clearly some transnational support, the movement would probably pose little threat to the United States and might even collapse without this core support from Persian Gulf states.

Further, if religious, social, or economic grievances were primary, then al-Qaeda should have been interested in combating three enemies—the United States, Europe, and Israel—with more or less equal weight and with little regard for the target states' military policies. However, al-Qaeda's timing and choice of targets shows that religious and ideological factors are not the forces driving the strategic logic of this suicide terrorist campaign.

The United States has been exporting cultural values that are anathema to Islamic fundamentalism for several decades, but bin Laden and the al-Qaeda organization did not turn toward attacking the United States until after 1990, when the United States sent troops to Saudi Arabia, Qatar, and Bahrain.

CHART 2. NATIONALITY OF AL-QAEDA SUICIDE ATTACKERS

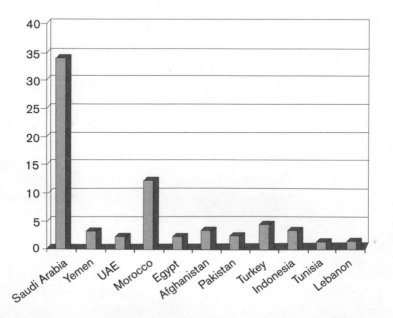

Source: Chicago Project on Suicide Terrorism, 2004.

CHART 3. U.S. MILITARY FORCES ON THE ARABIAN PENINSULA, 1980 TO 2001

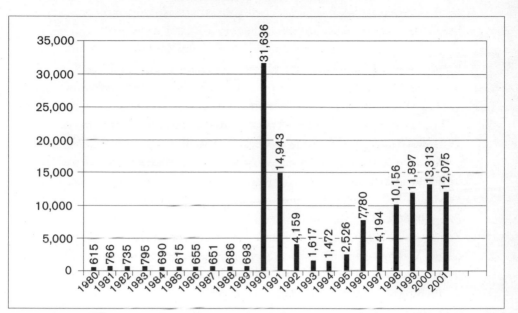

Legend for Chart 3

Year*	U.S. Troops in Persian Gulf	Year*	U.S. Troops in Persian Gulf
1980	615	1991	14,943
1981	766	1992	4,159
1982	735	1993	1,617
1983	795	1994	1,472
1984	690	1995	2,526
1985	615	1996	7,780
1986	655	1997	4,194
1987	651	1998	10,156
1988	686	1999	11,897
1989	693	2000	13,313
1990	31,636	2001	12,075

*September 30 of each year

Source: Directorate for Information Operations and Reports, "Active Duty Military Personnel by Country" (Washington, D.C.: Department of Defense, 1980–2001).

Not only the timing of the campaign against the United States but also bin Laden's public statements reflect a focus on U.S. occupation of Arabia. In 1996, bin Laden issued a lengthy statement explaining the motives behind his campaign against the United States:

> The people of Islam have suffered from aggression, iniquity and injustice imposed on them by the Zionist-Crusader alliance and their collaborators. . . . The latest and the greatest of these aggressions, incurred by the Muslims since the death of the Prophet . . . is the occupation of the land of the two Holy Places [the cities of Mecca and Medina] — the foundation of the house of Islam. . . . The explosion at Riyadh and Al-Khobar [he is referring to the June 25, 1996, attack on the Khobar Towers apartment complex, which killed nineteen] is a warning of this volcanic eruption emerging as a result of the severe oppression, suffering, excessive iniquity, humiliation and poverty. . . . [I]t is essential to hit the main enemy who divided the Ummah [the Muslim community] into small and little countries and pushed it, for the last few decades, into a state of confusion. . . . Clearly after Belief (Imaan) there is no more important duty than pushing the American enemy out of the holy land [Arabia].[17]

In his famous 1998 fatwa, "Jihad Against Jews and Crusaders," bin Laden asserted:

> The Arabian Peninsula has never . . . been stormed by any forces like the crusader armies spreading in it like locusts, eating its riches and wiping out its plantations. . . . For over seven years the United States has been occupying the lands of Islam in the holiest of places, the Arabian Peninsula, plundering its riches, dictating to its rulers, humiliating its people, terrorizing its neighbors, and turning its bases in the Peninsula into a spearhead through which to fight the neighboring Muslim peoples. . . . We issue the following fatwa to all Muslims: The ruling to kill the Americans and their allies — civilians and military — is an individual duty for every Muslim who can do it in any country in which it is possible to do it, in order to liberate the al-Aqsa Mosque and the holy mosque [Mecca] from their grip, and in order for their armies to move out of all the lands of Islam, defeated and unable to threaten any Muslim.[18]

To be sure, bin Laden may have his own personal reasons for pursuing this campaign against the United States. One may speculate that he is ultimately motivated by revenge for how the United States abandoned Muslim fighters in Afghanistan after the victory against the Soviet Union in 1988, or that he is driven by a peculiar brand of Yemeni religious nationalism related to the Wahhabi strand of Islam. However, even if bin Laden has such private motives, they do not form the basis of his public appeals to gain support within his own community. When bin Laden appeals for support, he focuses on American military policies that have led to the occupation of Muslim countries. Bin Laden surely hates the United States, but it is his public opposition to American military policies that ultimately matters.

Although Europeans do not pose as great a cultural threat to Muslim society as does the United States, European societies have also been a source of economic, social, and religious pressure on traditional Muslim values for decades. Until recently, however, al-Qaeda has not selected European countries or citizens for attack, nor did bin Laden's public statements mention any grievances against them. This changed following the arrival of European troops in Afghanistan in 2001 and in Iraq in 2003. From 2002 to 2003, Europeans became al-Qaeda's most frequent target: ten of fifteen suicide attacks during this period were directed mainly at European or Australian citizens, although these people were in Muslim countries. In every one of the ten cases, the victims came from countries that had troops in Afghanistan or Iraq.

Al-Qaeda's declared strategy suggests that the motive for attacking Europeans is to undermine foreign occupation of the Arabian Peninsula and other Muslim countries. In September 2003, an al-Qaeda planning document published on a radical Islamic Web page described a coherent strategy for how to compel the United States and its allies to leave Iraq. The forty-two-page document assumed that new spectacular attacks directly against the United States would be insufficient to compel America's withdrawal, and so it would be more effective to attack America's European allies, who could be coerced to withdraw their forces, thus increasing the economic and other burdens that the United States would have to shoulder in order to continue the occupations of Afghanistan, Iraq, and the Arabian peninsula.

The document went on to evaluate the prospects of using spectacular terrorist attacks to coerce Spain, Great Britain, and Poland, concluding that Spain—because of strong domestic opposition to the Iraq war—was the most vulnerable and recommending strikes against Spain just before the March 2003 national elections. Below are important passages from the analysis of terrorist attacks on Spain:

Table 9: Al-Qaeda vs. United States and Allies Since 9/11

Date	Weapon	Target	Killed	Victims' Identity
1. Apr 11, 2002	car bomb	Synagogue, Djerba, Tunisia	21	14 Germans, 1 French
2. May 8, 2002	car bomb	Sheraton Hotel, Karachi	14	11 French
3. June 16, 2002	car bomb	US consulate, Karachi	12	12 local residents working for U.S.
4. Oct 6, 2002	boat bomb	French oil tanker, Yemen	1	1 French
5. Oct 12, 2002	car bomb	Nightclub, Bali, Indonesia	202	103 Australians; most Western
6. Nov 28, 2002	car bomb	Hotel Mombasa, Kenya	13	3 Israelis
7. May 12, 2003	3 car bombers	Riyadh, Saudi Arabia	34	8 U.S.; most Western
8. May 16, 2003	car bombs	Casablanca, Morocco	31	French, Spanish, Italians
9. June 7, 2002	car bomb	German military bus, Kabul	4	4 Germans
10. Aug 5, 2003	car bomb	Hotel Jakarta, Indonesia	15	Western tourists
11. Nov 8, 2003	car bomb	Riyadh, Saudi Arabia	17	Arabs working w/ U.S.
12. Nov 15, 2003	2 car bombs	2 synagogues, Istanbul, Turkey	25	9 Jews
13. Nov 20, 2003	2 truck bombs	British embassy, Istanbul, Turkey	31	British and Turks working for U.K.
14. Dec 25, 2003	2 truck bombs	President Musharraf, Rawalpindi, Pak	14	Leader allied to U.S.
15. Dec 28, 2003	car bomb	Airport, Kabul	5	International troops
15 attacks			439	18 of 20 countries Osama bin Laden cites as supporting U.S. troops in Iraq/Afghanistan

In order to force the Spanish government to withdraw from Iraq the resistance should deal painful blows to its forces. This should be accompanied by an information campaign clarifying the truth of the matter inside Iraq. It is necessary to make utmost use of the upcoming general election in Spain in March next year.

We think that the Spanish government could not tolerate more than two, maximum three blows, after which it will have to withdraw as a result of popular pressure. If its troops still remain in Iraq after these blows, then the victory of the Socialist Party is almost secured, and the withdrawal of the Spanish forces will be on its electoral program.

Lastly, we emphasize that a withdrawal of the Spanish or Italian forces from Iraq would put huge pressure on the British presence (in Iraq), a pressure that Tony Blair might not be able to withstand, and hence the domino tiles would fall quickly. Yet, the basic problem of making the first tile fall still remains.[19]

These strikes did occur and Spain did withdraw its forces from Iraq, just as the document predicted.

Shortly after Spain's decision to withdraw from Iraq, bin Laden issued a statement in which he offered to cease attacks on European countries that withdrew their forces from Iraq and Afghanistan:

I announce a truce with the European countries that do not attack Muslim countries. . . . [T]he door to a truce is open for three months. . . . The truce will begin when the last soldier leaves our countries [Iraq and Afghanistan]. . . . They say that we kill for the sake of killing, but reality shows that they lie. . . . [T]he Russians were only killed after attacking Afghanistan in the 1980s and Chechnya, Europeans after invading Iraq and Afghanistan[,] and the Americans in New York after supporting the Jews in Palestine and their invasion of the Arabian Peninsula. Stop spilling our blood so we can stop spilling your blood [April 15, 2004].[20]

European countries officially rejected the offer.

Israel, like the United States and Europe, is a source of Western religious, cultural, social, and economic pressure on the Muslim world, and in addition occupies land populated by Muslims and holds Islam's third most important holy city, Jerusalem. Many Muslims, including bin Laden, believe that Israel controls American foreign policy and suspect it of aiming at the conquest of additional Muslim territory.

The 1996 and 1998 statements in which bin Laden justified attacks on the United States also accuse Israel: "Division of the land of the two Holy Places, and annexing of the northerly part of it by Israel . . . is an essential demand of the Zionist-Crusader alliance. The existence of such a large country with its huge resources under the leadership of the forthcoming Islamic State, by Allah's Grace, represent a serious danger to the very existence of the Zionist state in Palestine" (1996). "If the Americans' aims behind these wars are religious and economic, the aim is also to serve the Jews' petty state and divert attention from its occupation of Jerusalem and murder of Muslims there. The best proof of this is their eagerness to destroy Iraq, the strongest neighboring Arab state, and their endeavor to fragment all the states of the region such as Iraq, Saudi Arabia, Egypt, and Sudan into paper statelets and through their disunion and weakness to guarantee Israel's survival and the continuation of the brutal crusade occupation of the Peninsula" (1998).

Unlike the United States and Europe, however, Israel has never had troops on the Arabian peninsula, or in Iraq or Afghanistan, and despite al-Qaeda's rhetoric, it has never attacked Israel and has mounted only one attack directed primarily against Jews (in Istanbul in November 2002).[21]

SEVERITY OF OCCUPATION AND SUICIDE TERRORISM

Suicide terrorism is primarily an extreme national liberation strategy used against foreign occupiers with a democratic political system. This immediately raises a core question: is suicide terrorism simply a product of the severity of the occupier's policies?

Foreign occupation can have its own logic of violence. Even when an occupying power is restrained in the use of force, the common spiral of local resistance leading to retaliation leading to more local resistance can dramatically escalate the level of harm to the civilian community. As a result, there could be a threshold of violence above which the local community becomes so desperate that it resorts to suicide terrorism because many believe they will die anyway or because they are seeking revenge for those who have died.

If severity of occupation were the main cause of suicide terrorism, then we would expect to find a consistent relationship between the magnitude of violence and the use of suicide terrorism in the nine occupations in which suicide terrorism occurred. Testing this proposition is fairly straightforward. Although precise estimates of civilian casualties are often diffi-

TABLE 10. Severity of Occupation and Suicide Terrorism

Region/Dispute	Occupied Population	Deaths from Military Presence		Suicide Terrorists	
		Total	Per 1,000	Total	Per 1,000 Deaths
Lebanon, 1982–86	1 million	19,000	19	41	2
West Bank/Gaza, 1994–	3.4 million	3,339	1	121	121
Tamils in Sri Lanka, 1990–	3.1 million	45,000	15	143	10
Sihks in Punjab, 1995	20 million	18,000	1	1	1
Kurds in Turkey, 1990s	9 million	35,000	4	14	4
Chechnya, 2000–	1.1 million	50,000	50	33	<1
Kashmir, 2000–	10 million	38,000	4	5	1
Arabian Peninsula, 1995	50 million	nil	nil	71	>71
Iraq, 2003–	25 million	12,000	2	20	10

Sources: *South Lebanon, 1948–1986: Facts and Figures* (Beirut: Dar Bilal, 1987); B'Tselem, "Intifada Fatalities, 2000–2003" (Jerusalem: Israeli Information Center for Human Rights in the Occupied Territories, 2005); "Sri Lanka: Country Profile/Quick Facts" (International Committee of the Red Cross, 2001) counts 60,000 deaths for the conflict, of which I estimate three quarters are Tamil; Harish K. Puri, et al., *Terrorism in Punjab* (New Delhi: Har-Anand Publications, 1999); David McDowall, *A Modern History of the Kurds* (New York: I. B. Tauris, 2000); "Death Toll in Chechen Wars, 1994–2003," *Novaia Gazeta* (September 10–16, 2003); K. Allan Kronstat, "India–U.S. Relations" (Washington, D.C.: Congressional Research Service, July 15, 2003); Les Roberts, et al., "Mortality Before and After the 2003 Invasion of Iraq," *Lancet*, no. 364 (October 29, 2004), pp. 1857–64, estimates 50,000 overall excess Iraqi deaths from April 2003 to December 2003, of which about 24 percent are attributed to violence; and Chicago Project on Suicide Terrorism, 2004.

cult, there are reasonably good rough estimates for the number of total deaths suffered by each occupied community, and we can compare levels across cases by controlling for population size. We can then compare the level of deaths in the occupied community to the number of suicide terrorists and see if there is a consistent relationship between the two. This method will not show the importance of small differences in occupation policies, but it will allow us to test the strongest form of the question whether harsh occupation policies routinely lead to suicide terrorism, while relatively benign occupation policies do not.

The striking finding from Table 10 is that there is no strong relationship between the level of harm suffered by the occupied community and the level of suicide terrorism. Although the number of disputes is too small to conduct tests for statistical significance, the level of harm and the number of suicide terrorists both vary dramatically and in opposite directions across the cases. The two least harmful cases—the United States in the Arabian Peninsula, and Israel in the West Bank and Gaza—account for nearly 43 percent of all suicide terrorists due to occupation (192/448), while the two most harmful—Russia in Chechnya and Israel in Lebanon—account for about 17 percent (74/448).

This does not mean that harsh occupation policies cannot drive up the level of suicide terrorism once it occurs. However, it does mean that we must look further than the severity of the occupier's policies if we are to improve our understanding of the causes of suicide terrorism.

5

Learning Terrorism Pays

THE MAIN REASON that suicide terrorism is growing is that terrorists have learned that it works. Even more troubling, the encouraging lessons that terrorists have learned from the experience of suicide terrorist campaigns since 1980 are not, for the most part, products of wild-eyed interpretations or wishful thinking. They are, rather, quite reasonable assessments of the relationship between terrorists' coercive efforts and the political gains that the terrorists have achieved in many of these cases.

To understand how terrorist groups have assessed the effectiveness of suicide terrorism requires three tasks: (1) explanation of appropriate standards for evaluating the effectiveness of coercion from the standpoint of coercers; (2) analysis of the eleven suicide terrorist campaigns that have ended as of 2001 to determine how frequently target states made concessions that were, or at least could have been interpreted as, due to suicide attack; and (3) close analysis of terrorists' learning from particular campaigns. Because some analysts see suicide terrorism as fundamentally irrational, it is important to assess whether the lessons that the terrorists drew were reasonable conclusions from the record.[1]

TERRORISTS' ASSESSMENTS OF SUICIDE TERRORISM

Terrorists, like other people, learn from experience. Since the main purpose of suicide terrorism is coercion, the lessons likely to have the greatest impact on terrorists' future behavior are those they have drawn from past campaigns about the coercive effectiveness of suicide attack.

Most analyses of coercion focus on the decision making of target states, largely to determine their vulnerability to various coercive pressures.[2] The analysis here, however, seeks to determine why terrorist coercers are increasingly attracted to a specific coercive strategy. For this purpose, we must develop a new set of standards, because assessing the value of coercive pressure for the coercer is not the same problem as assessing its impact on the target.

From the perspective of a target state, the key question is whether the value of the concession being demanded is greater than the costs imposed by the coercive pressure, regardless of what form—risk to human life, economic hardship, or something else—that pressure takes. However, from the perspective of the coercer, the key question is whether a particular coercive strategy promises to be more effective than alternative methods of influence, and so warrants continued (or increased) effort. This is especially true for terrorists who are highly committed to a particular goal and so are willing to exhaust virtually any means rather than abandoning it. In this search for an effective strategy, coercers' assessments are likely to be largely a function of estimates of the success of past efforts; for suicide terrorists, this means assessments of whether past suicide campaigns produced significant concessions.

A glance at the behavior of suicide terrorists reveals that such trade-offs between alternative methods are important in their calculations. Nearly all of the organizations that have resorted to suicide terrorism began their coercive efforts with more conventional guerrilla operations, non-suicide terrorism, or both. Hezbollah, Hamas, Islamic Jihad, the PKK, the LTTE, and al-Qaeda all used demonstrative and destructive means of violence long before resorting to suicide attack. Indeed, in looking at the trajectory of terrorist groups over time, one can see a distinct element of experimentation in the techniques and strategies used by these groups and clear movement toward the most effective means. Al-Qaeda actually prides itself on a commitment to tactical learning over time: the infamous "terrorist manual" frequently stresses the importance of writing "lessons learned" memoranda that can be shared with other members to improve the effectiveness of future attacks.

The most important analytical difficulty in assessing outcomes of coercive efforts is that successes are more ambiguous than failures. Whenever a suicide terrorist campaign, or any coercive effort, ends without obtaining significant concessions, presumably the coercers must judge the effort a failure. When, however, the target state does make policy changes in the direction of the terrorists' political goals, it may not always be reasonable to attribute this outcome to the coercive pressure of suicide terrorism. The target government's decision could have been mainly or partly a response to the punishment inflicted by the suicide attacks, but it also could be a response to another type of pressure (such as an ongoing guerrilla campaign), or to pressure from a different actor (such as one of the target state's allies or another country), or the target's policy decision may not even have been intended as a concession at all, but could have been taken for other reasons that only coincidentally moved in a direction desired by the terrorists. For example, when Israel released Sheikh Ahmed Yassin, the spiritual leader of Hamas, from prison in October 1997 it was not clear whether this was a response to coercive pressure from recent Hamas suicide attacks or to diplomatic pressure from the United States and Jordan following a bungled Israeli attempt to assassinate a Hamas leader in Jordan. How a terrorist organization makes judgments between such alternative explanations determines what lessons are learned about the future usefulness of suicide attack.

Standard principles from social psychology suggest how terrorists are likely to resolve these ambiguities. Under normal conditions, most people tend to interpret ambiguous information in ways that are consistent with their own prior beliefs and that justify their past actions.[3] Suicide terrorists, of course, are likely to have at least some initial confidence in the efficacy of suicide attack or else they would not resort to it, and the fact of having carried out such attacks gives them an interest in justifying that choice. Thus, whenever targets of suicide terrorism make a real or apparent concession and it is plausible to interpret that behavior as due to the coercive pressure of the suicide campaign, we would expect terrorists to favor that interpretation even if other interpretations are also plausible.

This does not mean that we should simply expect terrorists to interpret virtually all outcomes, regardless of evidence, as encouraging further terrorism; that would not constitute learning and would make sense only if the terrorists were deeply irrational. To control for this possibility, it is cru-cial to consider the assessments of the same events by other well-informed observers. If we find instances in which suicide terrorist leaders claim credit for coercing concessions by opponents, but few other observers share this judgment, then it would be appropriate to dismiss these interpre-tations as irrational. If, on the other hand, we find that their interpretations are shared by a significant portion of other observers, across a range of cir-cumstances and interests—from target state leaders, to others in the terror-ists' community, to neutral analysts—then we should assume that their assessments are as rational as anyone else's and should take the lessons they draw seriously. In making these judgments, the testimony of target state leaders is often especially telling; although states like the United States and Israel virtually never officially admit making concessions to ter-rorism, leaders such as Ronald Reagan and Yitzhak Rabin have at times been quite open about the impact of suicide terrorism on their own policy decisions, as we see below.

Finally, our consideration of how terrorists assess the effectiveness of suicide terrorism should also be influenced by our prior understanding of the fanatical nature of the specific terrorists at issue. If the most fanatical groups also make what appear to be reasonable assessments, then this would increase our confidence in the finding that most terrorists would make similar calculations. Hamas and Islamic Jihad are the most crucial case, because these groups have been considered fanatical extremists even by comparison with other terrorists.[4] Thus, detailed examination of how Hamas and Islamic Jihad leaders assessed the coercive value of suicide at-tacks during the 1990s is especially important.

THE APPARENT SUCCESS OF SUICIDE TERRORISM

Perhaps the most striking aspect of recent suicide terrorist campaigns is that they are associated with gains for the terrorists' political cause about half the time. As Chapter 4 shows, of the thirteen suicide terrorist cam-paigns that were completed during 1980–2003, seven correlate with signifi-cant policy changes by the target state toward the terrorists' major political goals. In one case, the terrorists' territorial goals were fully achieved (Hezbollah versus U.S./F, 1983); in three cases, the terrorists' territorial aims were partly achieved (Hezbollah versus Israel, 1983–85; Hamas ver-sus Israel, 1994, and Hamas versus Israel, 1994–95); in one case, the target government entered into sovereignty negotiations with the terrorists (LTTE versus Sri Lanka, 1993–94 and 2001); and in one case, the terrorist organization's top leader was released from prison (Hamas versus Israel, 1997). Six campaigns did not lead to noticeable concessions (Hezbollah's second effort against Israel in Lebanon, 1985–86; BKI's attacks against Indian leaders in Punjab in 1995; a Hamas campaign in 1996 retaliating for an Israeli assassination; the LTTE versus Sri Lanka, 1995–2002; and both PKK campaigns). Even a 50 percent success rate is remarkable: international military and economic coercion generally works less than a third of the time, and is especially rare for groups with few other options.[5]

So these seven concessions, or at least apparent concessions, help to explain why suicide terrorism is on the rise. In four of the cases, the target government's policy changes are clearly due to coercive pressure from the terrorist group. The American and French withdrawal from Lebanon was perhaps the most clear-cut coercive success for suicide terrorism. In his memoirs, President Ronald Reagan explained the U.S. decision to withdraw: "The price we had to pay in Beirut was so great, the tragedy at the barracks was so enormous. . . . We had to pull out. . . . We couldn't stay there and run the risk of another suicide attack on the Marines."[6]

The Israel Defense Forces (IDF) withdrawal from most of southern Lebanon in 1985 and the Sri Lankan government decisions in 1994 and 2001 to negotiate with the LTTE were also widely understood to be direct results of the coercive punishment imposed by Hezbollah and LTTE respectively. In both cases, the concessions followed periods in which the terrorists had turned more and more to suicide attacks. Since Hezbollah and the LTTE employed a combination of suicide attack and conventional attack, one can question the relative weight of suicide attack in coercing the target states. However, there is little question in either case that punishment pressures inflicted by these terrorist organizations were decisive in the outcomes. For instance, as a candidate for the November 9, 1994, presidential election in Sri Lanka, Mrs. Chandrika Kumaratunga explicitly asked for a mandate to redraw boundaries so as to appease the Tamils in their demand for a separate homeland in the island's northeast provinces. She said, "We definitely hope to begin discussions with the Tamil people, with their representatives — including the Tigers — and offer them political solutions to end the war . . . [involving] extensive devolution." This would, Kumaratunga said, "create an environment in which people could live without fear."[7]

The other three concessions, or arguable concessions, are less clear-cut.

All three involve Hamas campaigns against Israel. Not counting the ongoing second intifada, Hamas waged four separate suicide attack campaigns against Israel, in 1994, 1995, 1996, and 1997. One, in 1996, did not correspond with Israeli concessions. This campaign was announced as retaliation for Israel's assassination of a Hamas leader; no particular coercive goal was announced, and it was suspended by Hamas after four attacks in two weeks. The other three all do correspond with Israeli concessions. In April 1994, Hamas began a series of suicide bombings in retaliation for the Hebron Massacre, committed by Baruch Goldstein in February of that year. After two attacks, Israel decided to accelerate its withdrawal from Gaza, which was required under the Oslo agreement but which had been delayed. Hamas then suspended attacks for five months. From October 1994 to August 1995, Hamas (and Islamic Jihad) carried out a total of seven suicide attacks against Israel. In September 1995, Israel agreed to withdraw from certain West Bank towns that December, which it earlier had claimed could not be done before April 1996 at the soonest. Hamas then suspended attacks for five months until its retaliation campaign during the last week of February and first week of March 1996. Finally, from March to September 1997, Hamas conducted a suicide attack campaign that included an attack about every two months. In response, Israeli prime minister Benjamin Netanyahu authorized the assassination of a Hamas leader in September 1997. The attempt, in Amman, Jordan, failed and the Israeli agents were captured. To get them back, Israel agreed to release Sheikh Ahmed Yassin, the spiritual leader of Hamas. This was not a concession to the terrorists' territorial goals, and there is no evidence that Hamas interpreted the release in any way different from the standard view, namely that it was the product of American and Jordanian pressure. Accordingly, the key Hamas campaigns that might have encouraged the view that suicide terrorism pays were the 1994 and 1995 campaigns, which were associated with Israel's military withdrawals from Gaza and the West Bank. Terrorists' assessments of these events are evaluated in detail.

THE CRUCIAL CASE OF HAMAS

The Hamas and Islamic Jihad suicide campaigns against Israel in 1994 and 1995 are crucial tests of the reasonableness of terrorists' assessments, because these are the groups most frequently cited as aiming at unrealistic goals and therefore as basically irrational. Many observers characterize

Hamas and Islamic Jihad as fanatical, extreme both within Palestinian society and among terrorist groups in general. In both the 1994 and 1995 cases, terrorist leaders claimed that Israeli concessions increased their confidence in the coercive effectiveness of suicide attack. However, there is an important alternative explanation for Israel's concessions in these cases: the Israeli government's obligations under the Oslo Accords. The 1994 and 1995 campaigns are also of special interest because they helped to encourage the most intense ongoing campaign, the second intifada against Israel, and may also have helped to encourage al-Qaeda's campaign against the United States.

Examination of these crucial cases demonstrates that the terrorist groups came to the conclusion that suicide attack accelerated Israel's withdrawal in both cases. Although the Oslo Accords formally committed Israel to withdrawing the IDF from Gaza and the West Bank, Israel routinely missed key deadlines, often by many months, and the terrorists came to believe that Israel would not have withdrawn when it did, and perhaps would not have withdrawn at all, but for the coercive leverage of suicide attack. Moreover, this interpretation of events was hardly unique. Numerous other observers and key Israeli government leaders themselves came to the same conclusion. To be clear, Hamas may well have had motives other than coercion for launching particular attacks, such as retaliation, gaining local support, or disrupting negotiated outcomes it considered insufficient.[8] However, the experience of observing how the target reacted to the suicide campaigns appears to have convinced terrorist leaders of the coercive effectiveness of this strategy.

To evaluate these cases, we need to know: (1) the facts of each case; (2) how others interpreted the events; and (3) how the terrorists interpreted these events. Each campaign is discussed in turn.

ISRAEL'S WITHDRAWAL FROM GAZA, MAY 1994

The Facts

Israel and the Palestine Liberation Organization signed the Oslo Accords on September 13, 1993. These obligated Israel to withdraw its military forces from the Gaza Strip and the West Bank town of Jericho beginning on December 13 and ending on April 13, 1994. In fact, Israel missed both deadlines. The major sticking points during the implementation negotiations in fall and winter of 1993–94 were the size of the Palestinian police force (Israel proposed a limit of 1,800, while the Palestinians demanded 9,000) and jurisdiction over certain criminal matters, especially whether Israel could retain a right of hot pursuit with respect to Palestinian attackers who might flee into Palestinian-ruled zones. As of April 5, 1994, these issues had not been resolved. Hamas then launched two suicide attacks, one on April 6 and another on April 13, killing fifteen Israeli civilians. On April 18, the Israeli Knesset voted to withdraw, effectively accepting the Palestinian positions on both disputed issues. The suicide attacks then stopped and the withdrawal was actually conducted in a few weeks starting on May 4, 1994.[9]

These two suicide attacks may not originally have been intended as coercive, since Hamas leaders had announced them in March 1994 as part of a planned series of five attacks in retaliation for the February 24 Hebron Massacre, in which an Israeli settler killed twenty-nine Palestinians, and had strong reservations about negotiating a compromise settlement with Israel.[10] However, when Israel agreed to withdraw more promptly than expected, Hamas decided to forgo the remaining three planned attacks. There is thus a circumstantial case that the attacks coerced the Israelis into being more forthcoming in the withdrawal negotiations, and both Israeli government leaders and Hamas leaders publicly drew this conclusion.

Israeli and Other Assessments

There are two main reasons to doubt that terrorist pressure accelerated Israel's decision to withdraw. First, one might think that Israel would have withdrawn in any case, as it had promised to do in the Oslo Accords. Second, one might point out that Hamas was opposed to a negotiated settlement with Israel. Taking both points together, therefore, Hamas's attacks could not have contributed to Israel's withdrawal.

The first of these arguments, however, fails to address the fact that Israel had already missed the originally agreed deadline and as of early April 1994 did not appear ready to withdraw at all if that meant making concessions on the size of the Palestinian police force and legal jurisdiction over terrorists. The second argument is simply illogical. Although Hamas objected to surrendering claims to all of historic Palestine, it did value the West Bank and Gaza as an intermediate goal, and certainly had no objection to obtaining this goal sooner rather than later.

Most important, other observers took explanations based on terrorist pressure far more seriously, including the person whose testimony must count most, Israeli prime minister Yitzhak Rabin. On April 13, 1994, Rabin said:

> I can't recall in the past any suicidal terror acts by the PLO. We have seen by now at least six acts of this type by Hamas and Islamic Jihad. . . . The only response to them and to the enemies of peace on the part of Israel is to accelerate the negotiations.[11]

On April 18, 1994, Rabin went further, giving a major speech in the Knesset explaining why the withdrawal was necessary:

> Members of the Knesset: I want to tell the truth. For 27 years we have been dominating another people against its will. For 27 years Palestinians in the territories . . . get up in the morning harboring a fierce hatred for us, as Israelis and Jews. Each morning they get up to a hard life, for which we are also, but not solely responsible. We cannot deny that our continuing control over a foreign people who do not want us exacts a painful price. . . . For two or three years we have been facing a phenomenon of extremist Islamic terrorism, which recalls Hezbollah, which surfaced in Lebanon and perpetrated attacks, including suicide missions. . . . There is no end to the targets Hamas and other terrorist organizations have among us. Each Israeli, in the territories and inside sovereign Israel, including united Jerusalem, each bus, each home, is a target for their murderous plans. Since there is no separation between the two populations, the current situation creates endless possibilities for Hamas and the other organizations.[12]

Independent Israeli observers also credited suicide terrorism with considerable coercive effectiveness. The most detailed assessment is by Efraim Inbar:

> A significant change occurred in Rabin's assessment of the importance of terrorist activities. . . . Reacting to the April 1994 suicide attack in Afula, Rabin recognized that terrorist activities by Hamas and other Islamic radicals were "a form of terrorism different from what we once knew from the PLO terrorist organizations." . . . Rabin admitted that there was no "hermitic" solution available to protect Israeli citizens against such terrorist attacks. . . . He also understood that such incidents intensified the domestic pressure to freeze the Palestinian track of the peace process. Islamic terror-

ism thus initially contributed to the pressure for accelerating the negotiations on his part.[13]

Arab writers also attributed Israeli accommodation to the suicide attacks. Mazin Hammad wrote in an editorial in a Jordanian newspaper:

> It is unprecedented for an Israeli official like Y. Rabin to clearly state that there is no future for the settlements in the occupied territories. . . . He would not have said this [yesterday] if it was not for the collapse of the security of Israel. . . . The martyrdom operation in Hadera shook the faith of the settlers in the possibility of staying in the West Bank and Gaza and increased their motivation to pack their belongings and dismantle their settlements.[14]

Terrorists' Assessments

Even though the favorable result was apparently unexpected by Hamas leaders, given the circumstances and the assessments voiced by Rabin and others, it certainly would have been reasonable for them to conclude that suicide terrorism had helped accelerate Israeli withdrawal, and they did.

Hamas leader Ahmed Bakr said, "What forced the Israelis to withdraw from Gaza was the intifada and not the Oslo agreement," while Imad al-Faluji judged:

> All that has been achieved so far is the consequence of our military actions. Without the so-called peace process, we would have gotten even more. . . . We would have got Gaza and the West Bank without this agreement. . . . Israel can beat all Arab armies. However, it can do nothing against a youth with a knife or an explosive charge on his body. Since it was unable to guarantee security within its borders, Israel entered into negotiations with the PLO. . . . If the Israelis want security, they will have to abandon their settlements . . . in Gaza, the West Bank, and Jerusalem.[15]

Further, these events appear to have persuaded terrorists that future suicide attacks could eventually produce still greater concessions. Fathi al-Shaqaqi, the leader of Islamic Jihad, said in April 1995:

> Our jihad action has exposed the enemy weakness, confusion, and hysteria. It has become clear that the enemy can be defeated, for if a small faithful group was able to instill all this horror and panic in the enemy through confronting it in Palestine and southern Lebanon, what will happen when the

nation confronts it with all its potential[?] . . . Martyrdom actions will escalate in the face of all pressures. . . . [They] are a realistic option in confronting the unequal balance of power. If we are unable to effect a balance of power now, we can achieve a balance of horror.[16]

ISRAEL'S WITHDRAWAL FROM WEST BANK TOWNS, DECEMBER 1995

The second Hamas case, in 1995, tells essentially the same story as the first. Again a series of suicide attacks was associated with Israeli territorial concessions to the Palestinians, and again a significant fraction of outside observers attributed the concessions to the coercive pressure of suicide terrorism, as did the terrorist leaders themselves.

The Facts

The original Oslo Accords scheduled Israel to withdraw from the Palestinian-populated areas of the West Bank by July 13, 1994, but after the delays over Gaza and Jericho all sides recognized that this deadline could not be met. From October 1994 to April 1995, Hamas, along with Islamic Jihad, carried out a series of seven suicide terrorist attacks that were intended to compel Israel to make further withdrawals, and suspended attacks temporarily at the request of the Palestinian Authority after Israel agreed on March 29, 1995, to begin withdrawals by July 1. Later, however, the Israelis announced that withdrawals could not begin before April 1996 because bypass roads needed for the security of Israeli settlements were not ready. Hamas and Islamic Jihad then mounted new suicide attacks on July 24 and August 21, 1995, killing eleven Israeli civilians. In September, Israel agreed to withdraw from the West Bank towns in December (Oslo II) even though the roads were not finished. The suicide attacks then stopped and the withdrawal was actually carried out in a few weeks starting on December 12, 1995.[17]

Israeli and Other Assessments

Although Israeli government spokesmen frequently claimed that suicide terrorism was delaying withdrawal, this claim was contradicted by, among others, Prime Minister Rabin. Rabin explained that the decision for the second withdrawal was, like the first in 1994, motivated in part by the goal of reducing suicide terrorism:

INTERVIEWER: Mr. Rabin, what is the logic of withdrawing from towns and villages when you know that terror might continue to strike at us from there?

RABIN: What is the alternative, to have double the amount of terror? As for the issue of terror, take the suicide bombings. Some 119 Israelis . . . have been killed or murdered since 1st January 1994, 77 of them in suicide bombings perpetrated by Islamic radical fanatics. . . . All the bombers were Palestinians who came from areas under our control.[18]

Similarly, an editorial in the Israeli daily *Yediot Aharonot* explained:

> If the planners of yesterday's attack intended to get Israel to back away from the Oslo accord, they apparently failed. In fact, Prime Minister Y. Rabin is leaning toward expediting the talks with the Palestinians. . . . The immediate conclusion from this line of thinking on Rabin's part—whose results we will witness in the coming days—will be to instruct the negotiators to expedite the talks with the Palestinians with the aim of completing them in the very near future.[19]

Terrorists' Assessments

As in 1994, Hamas and Islamic Jihad came to the conclusion that suicide terrorism was working. Hamas's spokesman in Jordan explained that new attacks were necessary to change Israel's behavior:

> Hamas, leader Muhammad Nazzal said, needed military muscle in order to negotiate with Israel from a position of strength. Arafat started from a position of weakness, he said, which is how the Israelis managed to push on him the solution and get recognition of their state and settlements without getting anything in return.[20]

After the agreement was signed, Hamas leaders also argued that suicide operations contributed to the Israeli withdrawal. Mahmud al-Zahar, a spokesman for Hamas, said:

> [T]he [Palestinian] Authority told us that military action embarrasses the PA because it obstructs the redeployment of the Israeli's forces and implementation of the agreement. . . . We offered many martyrs to attain freedom. . . . Any fair person knows that the military action was useful for the Authority during negotiations.

Moreover, the terrorists also stressed that stopping the attacks only discouraged Israel from withdrawing. An early August Hamas communiqué read:

> They said that the strugglers' operations have been the cause of the delay in widening the autonomous rule in the West Bank, and that they have been the reason for the deterioration of the living and economic conditions of our people. Now the days have come to debunk their false claims . . . and to affirm that July 1 [a promised date for IDF withdrawal] was no more than yet another of the "unholy" Zionist dates. . . . Hamas has shown an utmost degree of self-restraint throughout the past period. . . . but matters have gone far enough and the criminals will reap what their hands have sown.[21]

TERRORIST GROUPS LEARN FROM ONE ANOTHER

The tremendous increase in suicide terrorism over the last two decades is primarily due to terrorist groups learning from each other's coercive successes. The original source of the global spread of suicide terrorism was the success of Hezbollah in driving Israel, France, and—especially—the United States out of Lebanon in the early 1980s. These successes persuaded the Tamil Tigers, Palestinian terrorist groups, and al-Qaeda that suicide terrorism would be an effective tool for reaching their own goals. The world we live in today was created in large part by the decisions of three governments twenty years ago.

The inspiration for the Tamil Tigers' first suicide attack, in 1987, came from Lebanon. In the late 1970s and early 1980s, the LTTE sent fighters to train with the PLO and other terrorist groups in Lebanon's Bekaa Valley. Prabhakaran was especially impressed by Hezbollah's 1983 suicide attack against the U.S. Marine barracks in Lebanon and concluded that the same tactic could be employed to compel the Sri Lankan government to accept Tamil independence. As Prabhakaran says, "Tamil Eelam [the Tamil homeland] can be achieved in 100 years. But if we conduct Black Tiger [suicide] operations, we can shorten the suffering of the people and achieve Tamil Eelam in a shorter period of time."[22]

Palestinian terrorist groups were also encouraged by their assessments of the success of Hezbollah's coercive efforts to believe that suicide terrorism would be an effective way of coercing Israel. The Islamic Jihad leader Ramadan Shallah argued in November 2001:

The shameful defeat that Israel suffered in southern Lebanon and which caused its army to flee it in terror was not made on the negotiations table but on the battlefield and through jihad and martyrdom, which achieved a great victory for the Islamic resistance and Lebanese people. . . . We would not exaggerate if we said that the chances of achieving victory in Palestine are greater than in Lebanon. . . . If the enemy could not bear the losses of the war on the border strip with Lebanon, will it be able to withstand a long war of attrition in the heart of its security dimension and major cities?[23]

Palestinian terrorists are now applying the lessons they have learned. In November 2000, Khalid Mish'al explained Hamas's strategy for the second intifada, which was then in its early stages:

Like the intifada in 1987, the current intifada has taught us that we should move forward normally from popular confrontation to the rifle to suicide operations. This is the normal development. . . . We always have the Lebanese experiment before our eyes. It was a great model of which we are proud.

Even before the second intifada began, other Hamas statements made a similar point:

[T]he Zionist enemy . . . only understands the language of Jihad, resistance and martyrdom, that was the language that led to its blatant defeat in South Lebanon and it will be the language that will defeat it on the land of Palestine.[24]

Al-Qaeda, too, drew encouraging lessons from Hezbollah's accomplishments against American troops in Lebanon. In March 2003, Osama bin Laden said:

[T]he Islamic nation today possesses tremendous forces sufficient to save Palestine and the rest of the Muslim lands. . . . I should like to remind you of the defeats suffered by a number of the great powers at the hands of the Mujahideen. . . . the defeat of the American forces in the year 1402 of the Muslim calendar [1982] when the Israelis invaded Lebanon. The Lebanese resistance sent a truck full of explosives to the American Marines' center in Beirut and killed over 240 of them.[25]

The bottom line is that the ferocious escalation of the pace of suicide terrorism that we have witnessed in the past several years cannot be considered irrational or even surprising. It is simply the result of the lesson that terrorists have quite reasonably learned from their experience of the previous two decades: suicide terrorism pays.

THE LIMITS OF SUICIDE TERRORIST COERCION

Despite the encouraging lessons that suicide terrorist groups have learned, there are sharp limits to the types and scale of concessions that terrorists are likely to gain. Punishment, using anything short of nuclear weapons, is a relatively weak coercive strategy because modern nation-states generally will accept high costs rather than abandon important national goals, while modern administrative techniques and economic adjustments over time often allow states to minimize civilian costs. The most punishing air attacks with conventional munitions in history were the American B-29 raids against Japan's sixty-two largest cities from March to August 1945. Although these raids killed nearly 800,000 Japanese civilians—almost 10 percent died on the first day, in the March 9, 1945, fire-bombing of Tokyo, which killed more than 85,000—the conventional bombing did not compel the Japanese to surrender.[26]

Suicide terrorism makes adjustment to reduce damage more difficult than for states faced with military coercion or economic sanctions. However, it does not affect the target state's interests in the issues at stake. As a result, suicide terrorism can coerce states to abandon limited or modest goals, for example, by withdrawing from territory of low strategic importance, or, as in Israel's case in 1994 and 1995, by a temporary and partial withdrawal from a more important area. However, suicide terrorism is unlikely to cause targets to abandon goals central to their wealth or security, for example, by allowing a loss of territory that would weaken the economic prospects of the target state or strengthen the target state's rivals.[27]

Suicide terrorism makes punishment more effective than in traditional military campaigns. Targets remain willing to countenance high costs for important goals, but administrative, economic, or military adjustments that will prevent suicide attack are harder to make, while suicide attackers themselves are unlikely to be deterred by the threat of retaliation. Accordingly, suicide attack is likely to present a threat of continuing limited civilian punishment that the target government cannot completely eliminate, and the upper bound on what punishment can gain for coercers is recognizably higher in suicidal terrorism than in international military coercion.

The data on suicide terrorism from 1980 to 2003 support this conclusion. While suicide terrorism has achieved modest or very limited goals, it has so far failed to compel target democracies to abandon goals central to national wealth or security. When the United States withdrew from Lebanon in 1984, it had no important security, economic, or even ideological interests at stake. Lebanon was largely a humanitarian mission and not viewed as central to the national welfare of the United States. Israel withdrew from most of Lebanon in June 1985, but remained in a security buffer on the edge of southern Lebanon for more than a decade afterward, even though seventeen of twenty-two suicide attacks occurred in 1985 and 1986. Israel's withdrawals from Gaza and the West Bank in 1994 and 1995 occurred at the same time that settlements increased and did little to hinder the IDF's return, so these concessions were more modest than they may appear. The Sri Lankan government did conduct apparently serious negotiations with the LTTE from November 1994 to April 1995, but did not concede the Tamils' main demand, for independence. The war continued until 2001, when the Sri Lankan government again agreed to negotiations over the future status of Tamil homelands. These negotiations are still going on.

Thus, the logic of punishment and the record of suicide terrorism suggest that, unless suicide terrorists acquire far more destructive technologies, suicide attacks in the service of more ambitious goals are likely to fail and will continue to provoke more aggressive military responses.

PART II

THE
SOCIAL
LOGIC
OF
SUICIDE
TERRORISM

6

Occupation and
Religious Difference

THE TARGETS OF modern suicide terrorist campaigns have been democratic states which have stationed heavy combat troops on the territory that
the terrorists viewed as their national homeland. What accounts for this?
Why do some foreign occupations result in suicide terrorism, while others
do not? Why, for instance, did Hezbollah in the 1980s and the Tamil
Tigers in the 1990s rely on suicide terrorism to achieve self-determination
for their local communities, whereas the ETA, which sought independence for Spain's Basques, did not?

Existing accounts of suicide terrorism focus on personal alienation,
mass unemployment, social humiliation, or religious totalitarianism. Each
of these fits aspects of some cases, but all miss the central feature of modern suicide terrorist campaigns.

My hypothesis is that the taproot of suicide terrorism is nationalism—
the belief among members of a community that they share a distinct set of
ethnic, linguistic, and historical characteristics and are entitled to govern
their national homeland without interference from foreigners.[1] Since the
French Revolution, nationalism has been a powerful force in international politics. It has created nation-states, undermined multinational
empires, and contributed to some of the bloodiest struggles in history. Nationalism is also the main reason why local communities resist foreign occupation. Some occupations inflame nationalist sentiments more than

others; the hottest situations arise when the predominate religion in the occupier's society is different from the predominate religion in the occupied
society. Under the conditions of a foreign occupation, religious *difference*—
more than Islam or any other particular religion—hardens the boundaries
between national communities and so makes it easier for terrorist leaders
to portray the conflict in zero-sum terms, demonize the opponent, and
gain legitimacy for martyrdom from the local community. That is, religious
difference helps to create conditions that encourage resistance movements
to use suicide terrorism. Although it is not the bedrock cause of national
resistance and may not be a necessary or sufficient condition for suicide
terrorism, religious difference significantly increases the risk that a nationalist rebellion against foreign occupation by a democratic state will escalate to the use of suicide terrorism.

The first section of this book explained why suicide terrorism makes
strategic sense for terrorist leaders. This chapter and the next two explain
the social logic of suicide terrorism—that is, the conditions under which it
gains mass support and which, in turn, determine when suicide terrorist
campaigns can occur. Suicide terrorist campaigns are more likely when
(1) a national community is occupied by a foreign power; (2) the foreign
power is of a different religion; (3) the foreign power is a democracy. Of
nine occupations that have generated suicide terrorist campaigns, eight
met all three conditions, and the last, of the Kurds in Turkey, met two of
the three.[2] Further, with respect to the fourteen nationalist rebellions that
have taken place since 1980 and that were directed against a democracy
with a different religion, these three conditions account for the presence
or absence of suicide terrorism in all fourteen, once concessions to ordinary rebellion alone are taken into account. Suicide terrorism occurred in
seven, while the rebels were able to gain concessions without resorting to
suicide terrorism in the other seven. By contrast, only one of twenty-two
nationalist rebellions that did not meet all three criteria produced a suicide terrorist campaign—again, the Kurds in Turkey. The next two chapters add robustness to the theory by tracing the causal effects of the three
key variables through numerous important cases, including al-Qaeda.

WHAT IS TO BE EXPLAINED?

Suicide terrorism is an extreme strategy for national liberation. Although
isolated incidents do occur, the overwhelming majority of suicide terrorist

attacks take place as part of organized, coherent campaigns in which individual after individual, or team after team, voluntarily kill themselves as a means to kill the maximum number of people in the target society in order to compel that state to end a foreign occupation of their homeland.

Protracted campaigns of suicide terrorism require significant community support, for three reasons. The first does not necessarily require wide popular support, but the other two do.

First, community support enables a suicide terrorist group to replenish its membership. Other kinds of terrorists can try to husband their human resources by hiding from society, but suicide terrorist organizations cannot operate without losses. Most suicide attackers are walk-in volunteers, and thus the terrorist organization must have a relatively high profile so that it is easy to find, especially if the flow of volunteers is to be maintained over time or expanded substantially, as has happened in several suicide terrorist campaigns.[3] Hence, suicide terrorist organizations have strong incentives to become deeply embedded in social institutions such as schools, universities, charities, and religious congregations. However, since the number of suicide attackers is never large—the most active suicide terrorist group, the Tamil Tigers, used 143 suicide attackers between 1987 and 2001—sufficient volunteers might be obtainable from a relatively narrow subpopulation of the national community. So replenishment in itself requires deep, but not necessarily wide, popular support.

Second, community support is essential to enable a suicide terrorist group to avoid detection, surveillance, and elimination by the security forces of the target society. Given that recruitment needs oblige them to keep a relatively high profile, suicide terrorist groups cannot prevent many members of the local community from gaining basic information that would be useful to the enemy (for instance, the identity of recruiters, common locations for recruitment, and even locations of frequently used safe houses, means of communication, and other logistics).[4] As a result, without broad sympathy among the local population, suicide terrorist groups would be especially vulnerable to penetration, defection, and informants. They must therefore be popular enough that society as a whole would be willing to silence potential informants. Everyone may know who the terrorists are. No one must tell.

Third, and most important, community support is necessary for martyrdom. If at all possible, terrorist groups need their suicide attackers to be accepted as martyrs by the wider community. This is important because individuals are more likely to volunteer if they can expect to be accorded high status after their deaths than if their sacrifices will go unnoticed. In addition, if the community refuses to accept that the suicide attackers qualify as martyrs, their acts risk condemnation as socially unacceptable. Such condemnation could undermine support for the terrorist campaign.

Martyrdom—death for the sake of one's community—is a social construct. An individual may wish to become a martyr and may voluntarily sacrifice his or her life to achieve this aim. However, it is the community that designates the qualifications for martyrdom and judges whether the self-sacrifice of specific individuals meets the requirements for this special status. Communities commonly reserve a prominent place for the names of their martyrs. Streets and schools are named in their honor. Monuments list their names. But adding new names is up to the community. An individual can die. Only a community can make a martyr.

By using elaborate ceremonies and other means to identify the death of a suicide attacker with the good of the community—such as high-profile funerals, "martyr videos," and murals and graffiti—suicide terrorist organizations can promote the idea that their members should be accorded martyr status. Such propaganda may influence social responses to suicide terrorism. Still, it is the community as a whole, not the terrorists, that decides to whom it will accord the status of martyr.[5]

Evidence from prominent cases suggests that mass support for suicide terrorist campaigns usually goes far beyond a tiny fringe. Hard data are limited, since active rebellions usually make it impossible to conduct accurate polls. However, we do have reliable data directly on the issue in one case, that of the Palestinians. Since the mid-1990s, surveys of Palestinians living in the West Bank and Gaza have shown levels of popular support for suicide terrorist attacks against Israel rising from roughly a third of respondents in 1994 to 1999 to more than two thirds since the start of the second intifada in 2001.[6] We also have indirect evidence of mass support in three other cases. A poll of Saudis taken after September 11, 2001, found that over 95 percent of respondents agreed with Osama bin Laden's objection to American forces in the region, although the respondents were not asked specifically about suicide terrorism.[7] In Sri Lanka, after more than a decade of suicide attacks by the Tamil Tigers, a survey of Tamils in 2002 found that 47 percent supported the use of force to achieve an independent homeland.[8] In Iraq, American estimates of the number of "active supporters" of the Sunni insurgency grew from 5,000 in spring 2004 to 20,000 by fall 2004, while in January 2005 the Iraqi government estimated the number as 100,000.[9] The main exception is the PKK's suicide terrorism in

Turkey, which lacked wide support in the occupied community and was also the least aggressive suicide campaign, killing twenty-two people in fourteen attacks.[10]

The close conjunction between community support and protracted campaigns of suicide terrorism compels us to ask how such violent behavior can become acceptable and supported by a society at large. From the perspective of the terrorist organization, the central problem in suicide terrorism is to persuade the local community to re-define acts of suicide and murder as acts of martyrdom on behalf of the community. There are powerful prohibitions against suicide in virtually every society. (Although Muslims have committed more suicide attacks than non-Muslims, Muslim societies' norms against suicide are among the strongest in the world, as Chapter 9 shows in detail.) Hence, terrorist organizations must typically overcome deep religious and social norms in order to persuade their communities to support suicide campaigns. Absent a foreign military presence that threatens core elements in a community's national identity, such a transformation of communal norms is likely to be rare.

A NATIONALIST THEORY OF SUICIDE TERRORISM

A theory that predicts when suicide terrorism will occur and when it will not must focus on the occupied community's support for individual self-sacrifice; that support, in turn, is affected by the relationship between the identity of the foreign occupier and nationalist sentiments in the occupied community.

De ning "Occupation"

For the purpose of understanding suicide terrorism, it is imperative to view occupation from the perspective of the resistance movement (e.g., terrorists, revolutionaries), because it is the behavior of the local actors, not the foreign power, that determines whether suicide terrorism occurs. Whether the foreign power regards itself as a "stabilizing" ally rather than an "occupying" power is not relevant.

"Occupation" means the exertion of political control over territory by an outside group.[11] The critical requirement is that the occupying power's political control must depend on employing coercive assets—whether troops, police, or other security forces—that are controlled from outside the occupied territory. The number of troops actually stationed in the occupied territory may or may not be large, so long as enough are available, if necessary, to suppress any effort at independence. The best test is the political decisiveness of foreign-controlled coercive power: if the local government requires the power of foreign "stabilizing" troops or police in order to maintain order—or if most of the local community believes that this is the case—then, from the perspective of the resistance, these foreign troops are occupying forces that are preventing a change of government that would otherwise occur. The contention that the foreign troops are occupying forces is made stronger if the local government is engaged in actions that benefit the foreign power at the expense of the local populace.[12]

By this standard, Saudi Arabia, Kuwait, and Qatar all qualify today, because (1) U.S. combat troops have been present on their soil or in nations immediately adjacent to them for over a decade; and (2) owing to the United States' strong economic interest in maintaining the flow of oil from the Persian Gulf, the troops might well be used to prop up these pro-Western regimes if necessary. The other Persian Gulf regimes—Bahrain, the United Arab Emirates, and Oman—also qualify, since U.S. troops are available in neighboring countries. In short, the presence of heavy American military power—tens of thousands of frontline combat troops since 1990—on the Arabian Peninsula constitutes a foreign occupation, certainly in the eyes of opponents of the local regimes. This is so even if the United States disputes the characterization.

The Value of the Homeland

Although foreign occupation of any territory creates a motivation for resistance, the prospect of the homeland being occupied and ruled by foreigners usually constitutes an especially severe provocation to nationalist sentiments. Once a community no longer governs its homeland, it loses the ability to protect the political, economic, and social interests of its members. Worse, the occupiers may threaten the local community's ability to perpetuate the special characteristics that purportedly form the basis of its distinct national identity.[13] Even when the constituent elements of a community's identity are contested—as is often true apart from any external threat—the fact of an occupation means that the future trajectory of the "nation" is no longer determined by the members of the community, who now must compete with the powerful foreigners who are in political control of the territory most associated with the community's identity. In such a situation, people who love their nation can come to feel intense loathing toward the nation occupying their homeland and may develop a heroic sense of duty to inflict terrible punishment on the enemy society in order to compel it to leave. Accordingly, people and communities often go to extreme lengths to regain self-determination, that is, the ability to maintain and reproduce a community's national heritage without interference from others.

Even in today's globalizing world, the territory that national groups perceive as the birthplace of their community usually evokes special commitment. Although boundaries may be ambiguous and history may be contested, the homeland is imbued with memories, meanings, and emotional attachments. The homeland is also a space on which to establish political power. As Guntram H. Herb says, "Over time, as a group occupies and narrates a particular territory, a transformation occurs. Instead of the group defining the territory, the territory comes to define the group."[14]

Even when many or most members of the local community were not especially nationalist before, foreign occupation commonly unifies them by creating a sense of shared threat. The foreign forces' efforts to police the occupied territory or to suppress even mild resistance often kill or injure the innocent as well the guilty, because the occupiers' intelligence about the loyalties and behavior of the local population is often poor, and as a result the occupiers may resort to indiscriminate use of heavy firepower. This, in turn, can lead members of the occupied community to believe that their lives are being treated as more expendable than are the lives of occupation forces. These conditions often intensify nationalist commitment and help to explain the willingness of individuals to sacrifice personal interests to fight and die for the nation.[15] As Frantz Fanon famously said of Algerian resistance to French occupation:

> Individualism is the first to disappear. . . . Henceforward, the interests of one will be the interests of all, for in concrete fact *everyone* will be discovered by the troops, *everyone* will be massacred—or *everyone* will be saved. The motto "look out for yourself," the atheist's method of salvation, is in this context forbidden.[16]

The Importance of the Occupier's Identity

National identities are constructed in relation to other nations. Without a boundary based on purported differences between "us" and "them," nationalism could not exist. If there is no "them," there is no "us." Further, a national identity can only be defined fully in relation to a particular other nation and a particular moment in time. Understandings of the nation's special properties depend in part on the nature of the purported differences that separate one's own nation from the other, and on understandings of both the history and the current state of relations between the two nations. When one country is in political control of another, the national identities of both communities usually include more negative images of the other than do the identities of the same two nations when they are at peace. The boundary between the nations hardens, as well.

The main exception is when the occupied community would face an even greater threat from a different foreign enemy, if it were not occupied. As David Edelstein has shown, the threat from the Soviet Union dampened nationalist resistance to the American occupation of Germany and Japan during the Cold War and created a powerful basis for the establishment of deep institutional bonds that reinforced cooperation among the alliance partners.[17]

Absent a superior external threat, however, the identity of the foreign occupier is normally the most important "other" in relation to the occupied community. A group's identity comprises the distinct set of attributes that a body of individuals believes it has in common. These attributes include not only common objective elements, such as language, history, customs, and institutions, but also people's subjective self-identification. Although nationalism depends on the belief that a community has a unique set of ethnic, linguistic, religious, and other cultural traits that separate it from other communities, all communities do not differ equally across prominent social characteristics. People living in Chicago may view themselves as a Chicagoans, Irish, Catholics, Americans, Westerners, and Christians. They may share many attributes with people living in Dublin (Irish heritage, Catholic, Westerner, Christian), some attributes with people living in Berlin (Westerner, Christian), and few attributes with people living in Sudan.

The wider the difference between the identities of the foreign occupier and of the local community—the fewer prominent attributes they share—the more the local community is likely to view the occupier as "alien," the more it will fear that the occupation will lead to radical and permanent transformation of its national characteristics, and the more it will seek to end the occupation at almost any price. The occupying power already is stronger than any military force in the occupied community—otherwise, the condition of occupation would not exist—and so has the power to damage its political, economic, social, and religious institutions with inevitable effects on other aspects of local culture as well. Even if the occupier does not directly use this power, it necessarily poses an existential threat to the ability of the local community to determine and perpetuate its national identity. Accordingly, we should expect national resistance in general, and suicide terrorism in particular, to be greater in an "alien occupation," when there are few social attributes in common between the foreign rulers and the local community, than in a "kindred" occupation, when both share many social attributes.

"Alien" Occupation and Religious Difference

What, exactly, defines an "alien" occupation? In principle, there are no hard-and-fast rules. Since national identity is partly subjective, it is susceptible to manipulation, at least over long periods of time. In practice, however, some national attributes are likely to be more important than others in distinguishing the social relationship between an occupier and the local community.

For example, ancestral heritage, customs, and language are less crucial than one might at first expect. These attributes almost always differ between a foreign occupier and a local community, so using them to distinguish alien occupation from kindred occupation would largely collapse the meaning of these concepts together. Political ideology, often viewed as a crucial difference between nation-states, is also less important in the context of an occupation, precisely because the occupation itself defines the most salient political difference between the groups: the occupier controls the government, while the local population does not.

Although exceptions can occur, religious difference is probably the most important attribute separating the identity of foreign rulers from the local community.[18] The reason is not that some occupied communities are more intensely religious than others. The reason is also not that some religions guard their independence more fiercely than others. Rather, the fact that the occupier is associated with a different religion *in itself* enables specific dynamics that can increase the fear that the occupation will permanently alter the ability of the occupied community to determine its national characteristics—secular as well as religious.[19]

The main mechanism is exclusivity. The harder the boundary between groups—the more exclusive are membership rules—the more extreme is the "us" versus "them" dichotomy. Religion is normally more exclusive than other national differences (except for race) under the conditions of an occupation and so often becomes the principal defining boundary between an occupier and the local community. People can learn the occupier's language without abandoning their own, and can even participate in many social practices associated with the occupier's society without rejecting their own, but a person cannot be a member of two religions at once, except under the rarest circumstances. (Indeed, most of the world's major religions prohibit simultaneous practice of or membership in another religion.)[20] Even when members of the occupied community have no religious commitment at all, religious difference tells them that they and other members of their society are not part of the occupier's society, while the need for national cohesion for resistance to an occupation intensifies this sense of difference between the two communities. Such nonreligious individuals need not be motivated by a new commitment to the predominant religion of "us" (although some may), but can be motivated simply against the clearly defined "other."

Religious Versus Linguistic Differences

To explain the mechanism of exclusivity, it is helpful to compare the effects of religious difference and linguistic difference on the intensity of nationalist sentiments under the conditions of an occupation. Many scholars of nationalism argue that language differences are more important to the formation of national identities than are religious differences. Language helps demarcate nations, commonly through its impact on economic incentives. In an industrial or post-industrial world, most people are employable only in places where they speak the locally dominant language. A—or perhaps the—most important difference between Germans and Danes is that neither could function well economically in the other's country.[21]

How identities are constructed, however, is different in peace and in war.[22] When external threats to national self-determination are low, language differences may be more important than religious differences in constructing the boundaries between one's own nation and others. When threats to self-determination are high, such as when the nation is at war, or extreme, as when it is under foreign military occupation, the relative importance of religious and linguistic differences reverses. To be clear: *under the circumstances of a foreign occupation, the relative importance of religious and linguistic differences normally reverses and religious difference can inflame nationalist sentiments in ways that encourage mass support for martyrdom and suicide terrorism.*

In an intense conflict, religious differences make for a harder—more exclusive—boundary than do language differences. Under foreign occupation, individuals can learn the enemy's language without changing their membership in their own community, but anyone who converts to the enemy's religion will be understood as having defected from his or her own nation to the enemy nation. The reason that this matters in a foreign occupation is rarely that anyone fears that mass conversion to the occupier's religion will sharply diminish the numbers of the occupied community. Of the eight occupations with a religious difference that are studied in this book, there were few or no such conversions in any of them.[23] Rather, the fact that such conversions are virtually unthinkable helps demonstrate just how exclusive religious differences become under occupation conditions.

When occupation hardens communal boundaries along a religious difference, there are three factors that manifestly intensify nationalist resistance and encourage mass support for extreme self-sacrifice required for suicide terrorism.

1. *Zero-Sum Conflict.* The presence of a religious difference reduces room for compromise between the occupying power and the occupied community, because the conflict is seen as zero-sum. Local resources (land, water, minerals) are divisible and the occupier has the power to redistribute them. The more the occupier is viewed as a distinct entity, the more members of the occupied community—secular and religious—are likely to fear that any redistribution of those resources would come at their expense. Hence, to the population of an occupied land, the most tangible evidence of increased autonomy is a retreat by the occupying power in its control of these resources. As Chapter 8 shows, Hezbollah could recruit many secular Lebanese (and several Christians) as well as Islamists to carry out suicide attacks, largely because of the common belief that Israel would use Lebanese resources at the expense of the community as a whole.

Moreover, religious symbols themselves often become focal points in occupations involving a religious difference, precisely because the central structures and ground associated with a particular religion are genuinely indivisible across a religious divide. Churches, mosques, temples, and monasteries are sacred spaces that cannot be shared with another religion and always have some restrictions on access or behavior that are considered inviolable.[24] Also, religious symbols are normally central in the histories, memories, and emotional attachments that most members of the society—secular and religious—share. Few secular Jews, even among those who would hand over the West Bank and Gaza to Palestinian control, would also willingly surrender Jerusalem. One LTTE suicide attacker was motivated by the thought that the Sinhalese Buddhists would destroy the Hindu temples near her village, even though she had never visited them.

2. *Demonization.* Religious difference can enable extreme demonization—the belief that the enemy is morally inferior as well as militarily dangerous, and so must be dealt with harshly.[25] To most people brought up in any religion, the dogmas and practices of any other religion will seem strange, perhaps inexplicable or pointless, and possibly immoral. This sense of moral difference can heighten fears that the occupying forces may use their superior power to indiscriminately kill members of their own community. Further, most religions claim to possess superior insight into ultimate truths, from which it follows that devotees of any other religion must be misguided, amoral, immoral, or even actively evil. Especially when nationalist sentiments are intensified by war or foreign occupation, the religious inferiority of the enemy can promote a feeling that he is less than fully human. These problems are often made worse by resistance leaders who often exploit religious differences to depict the enemy in as negative a way as possible to mobilize mass support for the resistance. Although any cultural difference between rivals can be manipulated by resistance leaders, religious difference is ready-made for the purpose because it goes to the heart of the moral code attributed to the opponent.

Demonization encourages the two main features of suicide terrorism—the willingness to die and the willingness to kill innocents. The more a foreign occupation threatens a community's national identity, the more patriotic sentiments can inspire members of the occupied community to voluntarily accept great personal sacrifice to maintain the community's original identity. The more the foreign culture is viewed with scorn and revulsion, the more malignant sentiments can justify cruel treatment of even innocent members of the foreign society.

Accordingly, even individuals with no religious commitment at all can support and sacrifice for a national rebellion against a foreign occupier identified with a religion different from the local community's. The Tamil Tigers, a secular group drawn from Hindu families in Sri Lanka, used suicide terrorism to gain national independence largely because they do not accept the decision by the Sinhalese majority that Buddhism should be the dominant religion for the island as a whole.

3. *Legitimacy for Martyrdom.* Religious difference lends greater credibility to extremist groups who seek to use the language of martyrdom to legitimate their violence. The main problem for a community wishing to applaud the self-sacrifice of a martyr is that the act is a direct violation of one of the most common and absolute community norms, the prohibition against suicide. Since the suicide taboo is usually grounded in religious doctrine, if those same doctrines can be re-interpreted to justify self-inflicted death in certain circumstances, then this directly undermines the basis for the suicide taboo, at least in those circumstances.

A religious difference does not solve the extremists' problem, but it reduces the degree of manipulation necessary to re-define acts of suicide and murder as acts of martyrdom for the defense of the community. There are two reasons for this. First, the rhetoric intended to mobilize resistance to occupations with a religious difference is likely to use religious terms, even among secular groups. Although both secular and religious groups honor "martyrs," the idea of martyrdom is religious in origin and remains primarily a religious concept even today.[26] "Martyrdom" means death for the sake of faith, and it or closely related terms are common to all the world's major religions as the sole exception to the prohibition on voluntary death. For instance, the Jewish concept of *Kiddush ha-Shem* — "sanctification of God's Name" — is an exception to the prohibitions against suicide and is reserved for individuals who voluntarily died for their religion.[27]

Second, a religious difference is itself a common standard for martyrdom. Although other qualifications vary, all the world's primary religions hold that the main indicator that one has died for faith is that one has been killed by someone from outside the faith, who is part of a community hostile to the faith. A Jew cannot be martyred by a Jew, a Muslim by a Muslim, or a Christian by a Christian, barring highly exceptional circumstances — for example, that the killer was part of a heretical community acting to undermine the faith.[28] To be sure, the mainstream understanding of martyrdom in all the world's religions still prohibits a person from killing himself or herself. If, however, a religious schism exists and the enemy is viewed as from an alien faith, one of the common qualifications for martyrdom is fulfilled and the suicide terrorist group need only argue that the difference between high-risk missions and self-inflicted-death missions against the foreign enemy should be overlooked. Under the conditions of foreign occupation, manipulation of the normal definition of martyrdom can succeed, because what matters is persuading the community to temporarily suspend the prohibition against voluntary death with respect to those who die for the sake of the community, not to accept voluntary death as legitimate beyond this circumstance.

Together, these effects of religious difference can increase mass support for suicide terrorism in three direct ways: by increasing people's willingness to support rebellion; by increasing support for killing any members of the enemy community, even those who would otherwise be considered innocent; and by convincing some individuals that they have a duty to kill as many of the enemy as possible even at the cost of their own lives.

We cannot measure quantitatively how much these mechanisms increase the likelihood of suicide terrorism. What we can say is that the presence of a religious difference tends to promote suicide terrorism in ways that a language difference would not.

Last Resort Against Democratic Opponents

Although public attention is understandably drawn to the rhetoric of suicide terrorist groups themselves, the central issue in explaining the onset of suicide terrorism is not why one or several extremist leaders call for suicide operations against an occupier, but why the occupied community as a whole would lend significant support to calls for martyrdom.

Expediency is a key factor in determining when a community will promote martyrdom for the sake of national liberation. For a community to re-define what counts as legitimate martyrdom requires the broad acceptance of new interpretations of existing norms, a process that would make little sense if a community already had an effective strategy to achieve self-determination through more conventional means. Hence, we should expect that, even in cases of religious difference, suicide terrorism would be a last resort, typically coming once more conventional means of resistance have been exhausted or were obvious non-starters in the first place.

Occupation is a situation in which there is extreme asymmetry between the strength of the occupier and the strength of the local community. This power asymmetry virtually rules out conventional military confrontation, because the occupied community no longer controls sufficient territory and resources to train, arm, or equip large military formations. In many cases, the power asymmetry is so stark that even minimally organized resistance cannot get off the ground.[29]

When resistance does occur, the most common strategy is guerrilla warfare. This strategy was used frequently to resist imperial control in the twentieth century and is still the main strategy of rebellion in the world today.

Although guerrillas often seek self-determination from government forces, guerrilla resistance commonly escalates into deliberate attacks against innocents associated with the foreign occupier. Partly, the reason is the nature of guerrilla warfare. Guerrillas are too weak to confront the occupier's military forces directly. Instead, they aim to gradually wear down the occupier, fighting in small units dispersed over large areas in order to steadily inflict losses over a protracted period of time, rather than seeking to destroy those forces in major battles.[30] As a result, the line between isolated and easily targeted combatants, and noncombatants, is blurred in guerrilla warfare.

If guerrilla resistance succeeds and the foreign power leaves, then the local community again has no reason to resort to more extreme measures. However, if guerrilla resistance does not succeed (or is not feasible from the outset), then resistance leaders face a sharp choice: accept rule by what may now be an even more hostile occupier, or escalate to more extreme measures. Over the past twenty years, suicide terrorism has increasingly become the choice for groups that choose to escalate rather than quit.

This helps to explain an important fact about suicide terrorist groups. Many people assume that suicide terrorist groups are similar to ordinary terrorist groups—small in number, committed to a strange cause that is unpopular within their own local community—and that such groups are choosing between ordinary forms of terrorism and suicide attack. However, suicide terrorist groups and ordinary terrorist groups have quite different organizational profiles and relationships to their local community.[31] Suicide terrorism rarely evolves from tiny bands of ordinary terrorists, but instead commonly arises from broad-based nationalist liberation movements, those that typically have pursued guerrilla warfare and found that a guerrilla strategy is inadequate to achieve their nationalist aspirations. In other words, suicide terrorist groups are not choosing between ordinary terrorism and suicide terrorism, but are deciding whether to use suicide attack as an extension of a broader guerrilla warfare strategy. This is why suicide terrorism often appears to be a strategy of "last resort."

The evolution from guerrilla warfare also helps to account for the willingness of suicide terrorists to target noncombatants. Although this is the most horrifying element in the strategy, most resistance movements have already come to view the targeting of noncombatants as legitimate before they resort to suicide attack. Indeed, often the main purpose of a suicide attack is to inflict the maximum damage possible on the target society, a goal that suicide terrorists share with many guerrilla resistance movements. The reason that suicide terrorists inflict more horrific damage is not that they have suddenly become willing to target civilians, but that they are now willing to use suicide attack to do so.

If an occupied community pursues the goal of self-determination rationally, it will adopt the strategy most likely to restore its ability to perpetuate and configure national characteristics in the long run. Violent resistance is often not the best choice, either because the power asymmetry between the occupier and local community is so great that even modest rebellion would surely fail or because it would provoke such extreme retaliation against the community that the group could cease to exist. Democracies are commonly thought to be vulnerable to coercive pressure and less willing than authoritarian states to use extremely harsh repression, such as mass extermination. Scholars have recently shown that democracies are not as soft as commonly believed.[32] However, unless this widespread perception changes, the coercive strategy of suicide terrorism is most likely against a foreign power with a democratic political system than other regime types.

The Absence of Concessions. The logic of last resort against democratic regimes leads to an important precondition for suicide terrorism. Since suicide terrorism is mainly a strategy to compel democracies to make concessions that will enable a community to achieve self-determination, if the democracy does make concessions toward the terrorists' political cause, then we would expect the suicide terrorism to decline, pause, or stop altogether, depending on the magnitude of the concession. Similarly, if the democracy makes concessions to rebels using guerrilla warfare or ordinary terrorism, then we would not expect the rebellion to escalate to suicide terrorism.

Alternative Explanations

The nationalist theory of suicide terrorism argues that under foreign occupation by a democratic country, nationalist sentiments are heightened by differences in religion, which leads to community support for martyrdom, which results in suicide terrorism. However, it is theoretically possible that the causal process could run in the opposite direction, in either of two ways. First, since national identities are socially constructed by discourse, practice, or both, it is possible that rebellion itself, or even suicide terrorism, could contribute to the strengthening of a national identity that was previously weak or absent. This could mean that suicide terrorism is produced largely as an output of a self-reinforcing spiral rather than as the outcome of the mainly linear causal process that I claim. Empirically, however, in seven of the nine occupations that have produced suicide terrorism, the national identities of the occupied communities were well formed long before the beginning of the rebellion.[33]

The two arguable cases are the Palestinians and al-Qaeda. Some scholars contend that Palestinian national identity was relatively weak until it was solidified by the first intifada, of 1987–1992.[34] However, this still places both the hardening of communal identity and the beginning of the rebellion prior to the start of suicide terrorism, which was first used by Palestinians in 1994.

Al-Qaeda appeals to national identities on three levels—Arabian, pan-Arab, and pan-Muslim.[35] Of these, Arabian national identity was well formed long before the existence of al-Qaeda. Pan-Arab and pan-Muslim identities also pre-date al-Qaeda, although pan-Arab nationalism remains a relatively weak force and pan-Islam weaker still.[36] It is possible that the activities of al-Qaeda and Western responses to them could have the effect of strengthening one or both of these identities.

Second, even if we can show that nationalism usually precedes both rebellion and suicide terrorism, it could still be possible that the terrorism might inspire mass support for the rebellion, instead of the other way around.[37] Empirically, however, in eight of the nine occupations that led to suicide terrorism, large-scale rebellion either preceded the first suicide terrorist attack or was simultaneous with it. In six cases, rebellion preceded suicide terrorism by several years. In two cases, both began nearly simultaneously. Hezbollah began its guerrilla resistance to the United States, France, and Israel in November 1982 and committed its first suicide attack in the same month. In Iraq, virtually simultaneous guerrilla warfare and suicide attacks began as the United States began to take control of the country in April 2003.

The only exception is al-Qaeda, whose first suicide attack—against American troops in Saudi Arabia in 1995—was not an outgrowth of a local rebellion. Indeed, al-Qaeda hopes to use suicide terrorism to inspire rebellion in Saudi Arabia and other Arab countries, although it has not yet succeeded in this. Al-Qaeda did, however, have a substantial guerrilla organization as early as 1988 in Afghanistan, and its first attack on U.S. forces took place in 1992, when it sent 250 fighters to combat them in Somalia. Although al-Qaeda's suicide terrorism was not an outgrowth of a popular rebellion, formation of a guerrilla army did pre-date its first suicide terrorist attack by seven years.

Thus, in six cases rebellion led to terrorism, in two cases they happened nearly simultaneously, and in one case mass rebellion did not precede the use of suicide terrorism, although the creation of a substantial military organization outside the country did.

In short, in occupations that have generated suicide terrorism, the causal effects run mainly in the direction that I claim: from nationalism to rebellion and terrorism.

ALTERNATIVE CAUSAL PATHWAYS OF SUICIDE TERRORISM

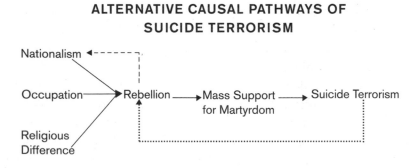

Solid arrows represent the theory proposed in this book.

The dashed arrow represents a causal path that sometimes influences the production of national identity, but that plays little role in determining when suicide terrorism campaigns occur.

The dotted arrow represents a causal path that al-Qaeda and perhaps other terrorist organizations have hoped will occur, but that has not done so.[38]

TESTING THE THEORY

To test my theory, I employ a methodology that combines the features of focused-comparison and statistical-correlative analysis using the universe of foreign occupations, 1980–2003. Correlative analysis of this universe enhances confidence that my theory can predict future events by showing that the patterns predicted by the theory actually occur over a large class of cases. Detailed analysis of historical cases enhances confidence that the correlations found in the larger universe are not spurious—that is, that my theory accurately identifies the causal dynamics that determine outcomes.

Testing the theory requires three steps. First, relevant historical evidence must be identified. Second, the theory must be put into operational terms to provide falsifiable predictions that can easily be observed in historical cases. Third, the predictions of the theory must be compared with the evidence.

This study investigates the universe of foreign occupations in which a democratic state controlled the homeland of a distinct national community (other than the majority in the democratic state) for the period 1980 to 2003, fifty-eight cases in all. The definition of "occupation" is deliberately broad, including not only cases in which a democratic state moved military forces across an internationally recognized boundary to govern the homeland of another community but also the far larger number of cases in which a democratic state controlled the homeland of a distinct national minority within its own borders.

Using this broad definition of "occupation" provides a strong test of the role of religious difference in determining the degree of self-sacrifice by rebel groups. First, it enhances confidence that the findings are not due to the effect of selecting a narrow class of cases, because it tests the theory against all instances in which a local community could plausibly view itself as under foreign occupation. Second, it allows the analysis to control for the effect of prior rebellion on the onset of suicide terrorism. Since rebellion is common in response to a foreign occupation preceded by a military invasion but less common when a distinct minority is ruled by a different majority community within a state, including both situations enhances confidence that the study can determine whether the presence or absence of a nationalist rebellion is a prior condition for suicide terrorism. Finally, the broad definition of "occupation" enhances the robustness of my study by reducing the likelihood that there are a great number of missing cases that would contradict my findings.

Cases were identified according to three criteria. First, cases are restricted to those in which the foreign rulers had military or security forces operating on the ancestral homeland of a local community that constitutes a majority in that area. Minority or diaspora communities, such as Jews and Gypsies in Europe, would not be able to establish control of local communities under any circumstances and so are excluded.

Second, cases are limited to the period 1980 to 2003. The early 1980s appear to be a watershed with respect to suicide terrorism. Although one might expect to find instances in earlier conflicts, such as the Algerian civil war in the 1950s, the Vietnam War in the 1960s, or even the Lebanese civil war or Iranian Revolution in the 1970s, this is not the case. Hence, cases prior to 1980 have no variation on the dependent variable, making it impossible to determine cause and effect.

Third, cases are restricted to occupations by states with a democratic political system, and specifically those with a system of contested national elections, open to a substantial fraction of citizens, for at least five continuous years during the period.[39] As Chapter 4 shows, all suicide terrorist campaigns have been targeted against democracies. My study uses a generous definition of "democracy," excluding only states whose experience with national elections is so limited that terrorist groups could not reasonably hope to affect the policy of the occupying state through attacks that punish its citizens in order to pressure elected officials.

The two independent variables in the study are the existence of a religious difference and the existence of rebellion between the foreign occupier and the local community. Religious differences are coded using standard lists of primary religions and major sectarian differences, which include Buddhism, Christianity, Confucianism, Hinduism, Islam, Judaism, Sikhism, Shinto, and Taoism as well as tribalism and agnosticism. Some lists also include other religions, such as Baha'i, Jainism, Shamanism, and Zoroastrianism, but adding these would not change the results of this study.[40] "Rebellion" counts any organized resistance by a militant group beyond political protests or other forms of non-violent civil disobedience.

The dependent variable is the presence or absence of a suicide terrorist campaign.

To select cases and code the independent variables, I relied mainly on the "Minorities at Risk" database. This database already codes every country in the world for almost the entire period for the concentration of distinct minorities within states, level of rebellion by the minorities, and existence of religious difference between the minority and majority in the states.[41] I supplemented this database with a list of foreign occupations consequent on invasion during the period as well as with additional material to bring the database up to the present.[42]

The key question in assessing the significance of correlations between independent and dependent variables is how they compare with chance. There are two possible outcomes, a suicide terrorist campaign and no suicide terrorist campaign, and four possible combinations of independent variables: religious difference and rebellion; religious difference and no rebellion; no religious difference and rebellion; and no religious difference and no rebellion. Accordingly, we can readily determine whether the suicide terrorist campaigns did or did not occur along with these combinations of independent variables and whether these results differ from what would be obtained by simply flipping a coin.

The nationalist theory of suicide terrorism predicts that suicide terrorism would occur in tandem with only one of the combinations of independent variables—that is, when there is both a religious difference and rebellion. This theory correctly predicts 49 of 58 cases, a result that is statistically significant at the highest common benchmark of .001, meaning that it could be achieved by chance less than once in 1000 times.[43]

TABLE 11. Suicide Terrorism and Democratic Occupations, 1980–2003

	Religious Difference	No Religious Difference
Rebellion	7/14	1/9
No Rebellion	1/15	0/20

Sources: See Appendix for cases and coding of variables.

Further, the predictive value of the nationalist theory of suicide terrorism is even higher once we consider the role of concessions in limiting the rise of suicide terrorism. In seven of the fourteen cases involving a rebellion and a religious difference, the rebels were able to gain concessions without resorting to suicide terrorism. In the other seven cases, prior concessions were either not made or were quickly withdrawn, and the rebels went on to use suicide terrorism in an attempt to gain concessions they otherwise could not get. This means that if we expand the conditions of suicide terrorism from the initial three—foreign occupation, by a democratic state, with a religious difference—to include the presence of concessions to rebellion alone, the nationalist theory of suicide terrorism accounts for 14 of 14 cases (see Table 12) in which all four conditions were met and 56 of 58 cases overall.

TABLE 12. Concessions and Causal Factors of Suicide Terrorism

Case	Democratic Occupation	Nationalist Rebellion	Religious Difference	Prior Concessions	Suicide Terrorism
1. Lebanese Shia vs. U.S./ France/Israel	X	X	X		X
2. Tamils vs. Sri Lanka	X	X	X		X
3. Palestinians vs. Israel	X	X	X		X
4. Sikhs vs. India	X	X	X		X
5. Kashmiris vs. India	X	X	X		X
6. Chechens vs. Russia	X	X	X		X
7. Iraqi rebels vs. U.S.	X	X	X		X
8. Chittagong Hill Tribes vs. Bangladesh	X	X	X	X	
9. Tripuras vs. India	X	X	X	X	
10. Assamee vs. India	X	X	X	X	
11. Nagas vs. India	X	X	X	X	
12. Moros vs. Philippines	X	X	X	X	
13. IRA vs. Great Britain	X	X	X	X	
14. Mayal-Muslims vs. Thailand	X	X	X	X	

Explanation of concessions: The Chittagong Hill Tribes signed a peace agreement with Bangladesh in 1997, granting them autonomy over local public administration and law and order; the Tripuras signed a peace agreement with India in 1988, granting them greater participation in state government and compensation for loss of tribal lands to new settlers; the Assamese signed an agreement with India in 1985, granting them greater political representation in local government and more control over immigration into the region, and several rounds of negotiations for further limits on immigration occurred in 1992 and 2000; the Nagas signed a cease-fire agreement with India in 1997 and autonomy negotiations have been under way since; the Philippines granted the Moros region on Mindanao substantial autonomy with its own executive, legislative, and judicial branches in 1990; Thailand adopted a series of policies in the 1980s that increased linguistic, religious, and economic benefits for Malay-Muslims; the British government brokered a series of peace negotiations with the parties in Northern Ireland beginning in 1989 that led to the 1998 "Good Friday Accords" for a power-sharing government. In these cases, concessions rarely completely ended the violence, but often diminished it, and reduced community support for it.

Sources: Chaim Kaufmann, "Possible and Impossible Solutions to Ethnic Civil Wars," *International Security*, vol. 20, no. 4 (Spring 1996), p. 160; Ted Robert Gurr, "Ethnic Warfare on the Wane," *Foreign Affairs*, vol. 79, no. 3 (May/June 2000), pp. 52–64; idem, "Peoples Against States," *International Studies Quarterly*, vol. 38, no. 3 (September 1994), pp. 369–75; Alexander B. Downes, "Separate States or a State of Autonomies," *Security Studies* (forthcoming); Subir Bhaumik, "Negotiating Access: Northeast India," *Refugee Survey Quarterly*, vol. 19, no. 2 (2000); "India's Turbulent Northeast," *South Asia Monitor*, no. 35 (July 5, 2001); Linda J. True, "Balancing Minorities: A Study of Southern Thailand," SAIS Working Paper, no. WP/02/04 (May 2004); and Roger MacGinty and John Darby, *Guns and Government: Management of the Northern Ireland Peace Process* (New York: Palgrave, 2002).

CONCLUSION

This chapter develops a theory of the causes of suicide terrorism, contending that nationalist rebellion and religious difference between the rebels and a dominant democratic state are the main conditions under which the foreign occupation of a community's homeland is likely to lead to a campaign of suicide terrorism as part of a national liberation strategy. Testing this theory in the relevant universe of cases since suicide terrorism became prominent twenty-five years ago provides strong verification for this proposition. Since 1980, religious difference has accounted for much of the variance in the pattern of when nationalist rebellions against occupation by a democratic state evolve into suicide terrorist campaigns.

Although these findings give us confidence that future cases are likely to follow a similar pattern, we should not overread the evidence. Suicide terrorism is a relatively recent phenomenon and it generates significant coercive pressure against democratic states. Moreover, religious identity is partly a subjective experience and so is vulnerable to manipulation by local elites as they seek ways to mobilize support for nationalist causes. Accordingly, we cannot rule out the possibility that future terrorist organizations would succeed in carrying out suicide campaigns even when the religious difference between the foreign rulers and occupied community is narrower than in past cases. On the basis of existing data, however, we would anticipate that suicide terrorism is more likely to spread when there is a religious difference than when there is not.

We also want to know more about the relationship between religious difference and suicide terrorism. Most important is further evidence that the results of this analysis are not spurious and that the causal dynamics expected by the theory actually appear in individual cases. For these purposes, the detailed case studies in the next chapters are required.

7

Demystifying al-Qaeda

AL-QAEDA'S SUICIDE TERRORIST campaign against the United States and its allies is a critical test of my nationalist theory of suicide terrorism. In this case, the growing American military presence on the Arabian Peninsula created a fear of an "alien" occupation in a number of countries that the terrorists view as their homelands. That fear has encouraged popular support for martyrdom as a strategy of national resistance to the presence of American troops in the region. However, there is an important alternative explanation for al-Qaeda's behavior—the religious commitment of individual members of the organization, a commitment that could encourage Islamic fundamentalists from across the world to pursue martyrdom as an end in itself. Of course, the fact that al-Qaeda does indeed recruit Islamic fundamentalists from a number of countries lends plausibility to the religious explanation.

Thus far, the main problem with understanding the root causes of al-Qaeda's terrorism is that our knowledge of the group's membership and organizational structure has been woefully incomplete. The first wave of knowledge about al-Qaeda appeared during the late 1990s and in the immediate aftermath of the September 11, 2001, attack. Much of this literature provides valuable details on the history of Osama bin Laden's militant activities from his first guerrilla campaign against the Soviet Union in Afghanistan through his rising militancy against the United States as he moved from Saudi Arabia to Sudan to Afghanistan in the 1990s.[1] Although there are brief references to al-Qaeda's recruitment, a major weakness in the first wave is the lack of good understanding of who joins and how many there are. Estimates vary from many thousands to many hundreds.[2]

Our knowledge of al-Qaeda's membership is now improving. Over the past several years, new research has collected detailed information about the demographic characteristics of known al-Qaeda terrorists. The most comprehensive assessment is by Marc Sageman, who collected the name, nationality, and other demographic information of 172 al-Qaeda terrorists.[3] Sageman's work provides important insight into the friendship bonds among al-Qaeda terrorists that appear to pre-date their joining the movement; this suggests that pre-existing social networks may play an important role in who becomes a terrorist and how cells are organized.[4] However, the data are less valuable for assessing patterns in the nationality of al-Qaeda terrorists, since the size of al-Qaeda membership remains unknown. Without reliable information about the underlying distribution of those who join al-Qaeda, we cannot know whether the counted terrorists represent a biased sample and, especially, whether the count overrepresents or underrepresents important countries. This problem is especially difficult because many "terrorists" may never engage in a violent operation and many who do may avoid detection altogether.

The following study examines the universe of al-Qaeda's suicide terrorists, collected as part of the Chicago Project on Suicide Terrorism. Because suicide terrorist attacks are so remarkable and well reported, we can be highly confident that our count of al-Qaeda suicide terrorists is complete, which avoids the problem of counting the group's terrorists in general. Most important, we can explain the crucial set of recruits that make al-Qaeda the highly lethal threat we face today.

Examination of al-Qaeda's pool of suicide terrorists—the seventy-one individuals who actually killed themselves on missions for al-Qaeda from 1995 to 2003—shows that the presence of American military forces for combat operations on the homeland territory of the suicide terrorists is stronger than Islamic fundamentalism in predicting whether individuals from that country will become al-Qaeda suicide terrorists. Islamic fundamentalism may play a modest role in recruiting militants, since al-Qaeda suicide terrorists are twice as likely to come from Muslim countries with Islamic fundamentalist populations compared to Muslim countries with tiny or no Islamic fundamentalist populations. However, al-Qaeda suicide terrorists are ten times more likely to come from Muslim countries where there is an American military presence for combat operations than from other Muslim countries. Further, al-Qaeda suicide terrorists are twenty times more likely to come from Muslim countries with both American military presence for combat operations and Islamic fundamentalist populations compared to other Muslim countries.

Overall, this means that American military policy in the Persian Gulf was most likely the pivotal factor leading to September 11. Although Islamic fundamentalism mattered, the stationing of tens of thousands of American combat troops on the Arabian Peninsula from 1990 to 2001 probably made al-Qaeda suicide attacks against Americans, including the horrible crimes committed on September 11, 2001, from ten to twenty times more likely.

This finding also sheds new light on al-Qaeda's mobilization appeals. Although many in the West are tempted to discount the statements of Osama bin Laden and other al-Qaeda leaders as empty rhetoric or irrational images of reality, it is important to study the group's mobilization appeals if we are to understand what motivates recruits to join the cause.

Examination of al-Qaeda's mobilization rhetoric suggests a picture of the organization that is at variance with the conventional wisdom. Al-Qaeda is less a transnational network of like-minded ideologues brought together from across the globe via the Internet than a cross-national military alliance of national liberation movements working together against what they see as a common imperial threat. For al-Qaeda, religion matters, but mainly in the context of national resistance to foreign occupation. The fact that the United States and its allies are predominately non-Islamic societies makes it easier for al-Qaeda's leaders to exploit their own religion to justify the use of martyrdom operations as the main weapon for national liberation.

Of course, we cannot say with certainty that this detailed argument is the main impetus for the individuals who volunteered to carry out suicide missions. This would require not simply collecting the last statements of these individuals, but subjecting them to cross-examination, obviously impossible for dead terrorists. What we can say is that the pattern of who ultimately decides to die for al-Qaeda's cause is remarkably consistent with the argument that al-Qaeda leaders make. Above all, this suggests that the United States can only bolster al-Qaeda's appeal if it pursues military policies that actually confirm the group's portrayal of American intentions.

AMERICAN MILITARY PRESENCE VERSUS ISLAMIC FUNDAMENTALISM

Al-Qaeda's Islamic Beliefs

"Islamic fundamentalism" is commonly used for any Muslim movement that seeks to establish an Islamic state, meaning a political system in which Islam is the official religion and the laws governing society are based on Islamic texts as understood by Islamic clerics. Further, Islamic fundamentalists are often portrayed in academic as well as popular circles as inherently militant. One scholar of the Middle East writes:

> [T]he modern Islamic movement is authoritarian, anti-democratic, anti-secular, and a protest movement of the economically deprived. Islamic fundamentalism is an aggressive revolutionary movement as militant and violent as the Bolshevik, Fascist, and Nazi movements of the past.[5]

This common conception of Islamic fundamentalism, however, paints with too broad a brush. Islamic fundamentalism comprises a wide variety of movements that offer Islam as a total way of life and adhere to an interpretation of certain Islamic scriptures that they view as infallible.[6] Only a tiny fraction of those who subscribe to these movements have engaged in acts of violence. Even if it were the cause of Islamic militancy, defining Islamic fundamentalism as necessarily violent would collapse the independent and dependent variables in a way that would turn our problem into a tautology—that is, we would end up saying that Osama bin Laden is militant because he is militant.

Further, different Islamic fundamentalist movements do not accept each other as true Islamists and are so ideologically separate from each other that they would have great difficulty working together. The Muslim world is broadly divided between Sunnis and Shias, who disagree about the rightful lineage of religious authority in the generations after the Prophet Mohammed, much the same way that Catholics and Protestants disagree about the religious authority of the Pope.[7] Shia Muslims live mainly in Iran (63 million) and Iraq (15 million), while the overwhelming majority of other Muslims are Sunni. Although many Shias as well as many Sunnis see a need for an Islamic revival in their personal lives and in the governance of their societies, the two groups' visions of just government are not the same; Shia would not accept a Sunni Islamic state as truly Islamic, and vice versa.[8]

Osama bin Laden practices a Sunni form of Islamic fundamentalism called Salafism, and al-Qaeda is a specifically Sunni movement.[9] No follower of Iranian or Iraqi Shi'ism has ever become an al-Qaeda suicide terrorist. Accordingly, broad interpretations of Islamic fundamentalism that elide the Shia-Sunni split would lead to the result that Islamic fundamentalism does not cause al-Qaeda's terrorism, but in a trivial way. Moreover, collapsing all these movements together would confuse policy makers about what they most want to know: whether the brand of Islamic fundamentalism practiced by Osama bin Laden and other leaders of al-Qaeda is the main cause of their militant terrorism against the United States.

Salafism is distinct from other forms of Sunni fundamentalism. *Salaf* is the Arabic word for "ancient ones" and refers to the companions of the Prophet Muhammad. For a Salafi, Islamic authority rests only in the scriptures of the Prophet (the Quran) and in the words and deeds of the Prophet as documented by his companions (the texts called Sunna, a part of the Hadith), while all the more recent interpretations are considered as suspect deviations, corrupted by non-Islamic influences, that dilute the authentic message of God.[10] Other Sunni fundamentalisms, such as Sufism, accommodate recent interpretations, which can reflect tolerance for local non-Muslim practices and customs, and are considered heretical by Salafis.[11]

Salafism is not monolithic, has no worldwide organization, and is not necessarily militant. Rather, it defines a variety of movements that share a desire to create an Islamic revival that would privilege ancient authority over modern interpretations of Islam. For instance, Wahhabism is the official ideology of Saudi Arabia and serves as the basis of the state's mandatory public education system. Saudi Wahhabism focuses on bringing Muslims back to a strict and literal imitation of the Islam of the Prophet and his companions, but discourages violence as a legitimate means for achieving this aim.[12] In Egypt, the Muslim Brotherhood was founded in 1928 as a self-declared Salafi movement. Although one of its most famous theologians, Sayyid Qutb, took the position in the 1950s and 1960s that militancy against apostate Islamic regimes was a sacred duty, the Egyptian Muslim Brotherhood has distanced itself from Qutb since the 1970s and its official mission statement today emphasizes the goal to bring about its Salafi ideals through peaceful political change.[13] In Pakistan, the Deobandist version of Salafism was espoused in the madrassas that educated the Taliban, but Deobandism itself originated in India, where the movement stays out of politics and stresses strict adherence to ancient texts as a personal responsibility.[14]

These movements do not agree on all basic religious tenets. For instance, they vary in their understanding of how the Islamic concept of *shura* (consultation) should be applied, with different movements varying the weight given to the views of *ulama* (Islamic clerics) and other matters. Nonetheless, scholars of Islamic fundamentalism generally consider them as part of the puritanical Salafi tradition in Sunni Islam. For instance, the widely respected scholar Seyyed Hossein Nasr says:

> There is an older puritanical and often rationalistic reform movement, or rather set of movements, that seeks to return to a strict application of the *Sharī'ah* . . . in the name of an early puritanical Islam considered to have been lost by later generations. To this category belongs the Wahhābī movement . . . the Salafiyyah of Syria . . . and the Muhammadiyyah of Indonesia. . . . One can also include the Ikhwān al-muslimīn [Muslim Brotherhood], founded in Egypt, . . . a movement that is still strong in many Islamic countries, especially Egypt and the Sudan, and the Jamā'at-i islamī of Pakistan.[15]

Recognizing the complexity of Salafism is important, because al-Qaeda leaders are not the product of a single Salafi movement. Osama bin Laden was educated in Wahhabi schools while growing up in Saudi Arabia, while Ayman al-Zawahiri joined the Muslim Brotherhood as a youth in Egypt.[16] Of course, both are now militant Salafis, fully embrace the ideas of Qutb, and have sought to focus the energies of Islamic militants against the United States. Important scholars and policy makers have observed these facts and come to the conclusion that the ideology of Salafism is a principal cause of al-Qaeda's terrorism.[17] The central question is whether this is true.

Standards for Measuring Salafism

Salafism could be said to cause al-Qaeda's terrorism if exposure to Salafi beliefs predisposed individuals to carry out acts of terrorism for the group. Al-Qaeda is a self-identified Salafi group, so all of its members are necessarily at least tolerant of Salafism. Although we have little information about the detailed religious beliefs of any of the seventy-one al-Qaeda suicide attackers, we should assume that all were influenced by Salafism, barring new information to the contrary.

The important issue is whether pervasive exposure to Salafism prior to joining al-Qaeda predisposes individuals to become terrorists in the first place. Pervasive exposure to any ideology occurs when there are persistent efforts by committed believers of the creed to persuade others to accept it. For a religious creed like Salafism, the intensity of persuasive efforts experienced by typical individuals in a given community would depend on factors such as whether the state is openly committed to promoting Salafism, prevalence of schools with Salafi curricula and mosques with Salafi clerics, and public support for Salafi political parties. Salafi proponents often use well-known identity markers, calling themselves "Salafi," "People of Hadith," and "those who follow the way of Sunna and Jamma," in addition to espousing specific tenets of the creed.[18]

Although these measures can assess the intensity of influence only roughly and are certainly not a complete list of possible sources of religious influence, they can provide reasonably good estimates of the size of "Salafi-influenced" populations in different Muslim countries. This, in turn, allows us to judge whether al-Qaeda suicide terrorists are more likely to come from the most Salafi-influenced societies than from other Muslim countries.

This approach will probably miss thin scatterings of Salafi institutions in the midst of overwhelmingly non-Salafi countries, but finding tiny numbers of isolated Salafis is not the purpose. What we want to know is whether Salafi-influenced individuals are more likely to join al-Qaeda. If they are, then countries with large Salafi-influenced populations should yield more recruits than countries with fewer Salafi-influenced people or with so few that our measures cannot even detect them.

Standards for Measuring American Military Presence

My theory argues that foreign occupation by a democratic state, national resistance, and religious difference are the main causal factors leading to the rise of suicide terrorist campaigns. In the case of al-Qaeda versus the United States, there is no doubt that there is a religious difference between the rivals and no doubt that the United States is a democracy. The main issue is the boundary for what should count as foreign occupation by the United States.

The standard I use is American military presence, defined as heavy combat operations on the homeland of Sunni Muslim majority countries for a sustained period prior to the onset of al-Qaeda's suicide terrorist campaign against the United States in 1995. If American military presence, so defined, has expanded to include still more countries during the course of al-Qaeda's suicide campaign, then I include those new countries as well, since they could also serve as recruiting grounds for al-Qaeda's ongoing suicide campaign. "American military presence" includes cases where American combat forces are based in the country or where the United States provides an explicit or widely understood security guarantee that could be implemented using its forces in an adjacent country. It does not include cases where American military advisers are present or where the country's military and the U.S. military conduct joint training exercises.

This standard comports with the meaning of "occupation" in Chapter 6, because it defines American military presence from the perspective of the terrorists, who are likely to fear the possibility that foreign control may be imposed by force and to suspect that security "guarantees" actually indicate American intention to defend the regime against revolution. This is Osama bin Laden's view of the role of U.S. troops on the Arabian Peninsula; it is not the perspective of the United States, which, in most of the relevant cases, would see itself as supporting an allied government.

By this standard, Saudi Arabia, Oman, the United Arab Emirates, Bahrain, Kuwait, Qatar, and Turkey all qualify, because the United States has stationed combat troops on the soil of each, or in adjacent countries, continuously since 1990.[19] Afghanistan and Uzbekistan also qualify, since the United States has stationed combat troops on their soil since 2001. I do not count Jordan or Yemen, because it is not clear that the United States would defend Jordan and it certainly does not guarantee the integrity of Yemen. I also do not count Pakistan, Turkmenistan, or Tajikistan, since the United States does not base combat forces in any of these countries nor does it guarantee their security.[20] Since 1990, the United States has not stationed heavy combat forces in any other Sunni Muslim country.

Al-Qaeda's Suicide Terrorism

From 1995 to 2003, seventy-one al-Qaeda suicide terrorists actually completed their missions, killing themselves in order to carry out operations to kill others. We know the nationality of sixty-seven. All but one of these came from a Sunni Muslim country. The other was from Lebanon and his religion is not known for certain.

An examination of the sixty-six al-Qaeda suicide terrorists who were known citizens of Sunni-majority countries shows that American military presence is a stronger factor than Salafi fundamentalism in predicting who dies for al-Qaeda's cause.

Salafi influence probably does not matter much, because there is not a statistically significant difference—odds better than random chance—

between the proportion of Muslims from countries with sizable Salafi-
influenced populations who are al-Qaeda suicide terrorists and the proportion of Muslims from other Sunni countries who are al-Qaeda suicide
terrorists.

Table 13 reports the size of the Salafi-influenced population in every
Sunni-majority country with a population of 1 million or more (there were
no al-Qaeda suicide terrorists from smaller countries) as of about 2000. In
countries with Salafi-influenced populations, there are 233 million Salafi-
influenced people and 48 al-Qaeda suicide terrorists, or 1 suicide terrorist
per 5 million Salafi. In countries without Salafi-influenced populations,
there are 205 Sunni Muslims and 18 al-Qaeda suicide terrorists, or 1 per
12 million. Comparing the relative frequency of al-Qaeda suicide terrorists in these two groups of countries, al-Qaeda suicide terrorists are twice as
likely to come from Salafi-influenced populations as from Sunni Muslims
in other countries.

TABLE 13. Salafi Influence and al-Qaeda

Sunni Countries with Salafi-Influenced Populations (population in millions, 2000)

Country	Muslims	Salafi-Influenced	Al-Qaeda Suicide Terrorists
Somalia	10	5	
Algeria	31	19	
Tunisia	10	5	1
Egypt	62	23	2
Sudan	21	21	
Nigeria	68	37	
Afghanistan	25	10	3
Pakistan	149	43	2
Bangladesh	114	14	
Indonesia	185	26	3
Yemen	18	8	3
Saudi Arabia	21	18	34
Jordan	6	2	
Oman	2	2	
Total	722	233	48 1 per 5 million Salafi
			1 per 15 million Muslims

Sunni Countries without Salafi-Influenced Populations*

Country	Muslims	Salafi-Influenced	Al-Qaeda Suicide Terrorists
Morocco	28		12
Mauritania	3		
Senegal	9		
Mali	10		
Guinea	5		
Sierra Leone	3		
Chad	4		
Burkina Faso	6		
Mauritania	3		
Malaysia	13		
Uzbekistan	21		
Turkmenistan	4		
Tajikistan	5		
Kyrgyzstan	3		
Turkey	67		4
UAE	2		2
Kuwait	2		
Syria	15		
Albania	2		
Niger	7		
Total	212		18 1 per 12 million Muslims

*"Sunni countries" are Sunni Muslim majority countries with populations over 1 million. See appendix for Salafi-influenced populations in each.

However, when we examine the effect of the absolute number of the Salafi-influenced population on the absolute number of terrorists from any country, the effect is not statistically significant even at the most generous confidence level of 0.1. On average, there are 3.5 million Salafi-influenced Sunnis per al-Qaeda suicide terrorist, but this includes numerous extreme outliers. Pakistan produced far fewer terrorists and Saudi Arabia and Morocco far more than would be consistent with a direct relationship between Salafism and suicide terrorism. For the numbers to produce a significant relationship, one would have to discount the majority of al-Qaeda suicide attackers.

We can test for alternative ways in which Salafism could cause suicide terrorism, but these also fail to produce significant results. For instance, there is no significant relationship between the percentage of the Salafi-influenced population and the percentage of terrorists from any country. Further, if we look at the entire population of Sunnis in Salafi-influenced countries, any given Sunni is less likely to be an al-Qaeda suicide terrorist than a Sunni in a non-Salafi-influenced country (1 per 15 million versus 1 per 12 million). Hence, there is also probably no spillover effect, where non-Salafis become terrorists because they live in a Salafi-influenced country.[21]

This means that we can discount both of the two main mechanisms that might lead Salafism to cause terrorism. Whether we think the odds of someone becoming an al-Qaeda suicide terrorist increases directly with the size of the Salafi-influenced population or whether the odds increase as a spillover effect of living in a country with a sizable Salafi-influenced population, the odds that someone from a Salafi-influenced country will become an al-Qaeda suicide terrorist are not significantly better than chance.

By contrast, the presence of American combat operations matters substantially. As Table 14 shows, al-Qaeda suicide terrorists are ten times more likely to come from a Sunni country with American military presence than from another Sunni country. These odds are far better than a coin flip, statistically significant at the standard benchmark of .05. This means that the chances that the presence of American combat troops does not increase the risk of someone from that country becoming an al-Qaeda suicide terrorist are less than 5 in 100. Even if the effect of Salafi-influenced populations on al-Qaeda suicide terrorism were assumed to be significant, American military presence would remain five times as powerful as a predictor of al-Qaeda suicide terrorism.

Further, deploying American combat troops to a Salafi-influenced population matters tremendously. As Table 15 shows, al-Qaeda suicide terrorists are twenty times more likely to come from a Salafi-influenced population with American military presence than from another Sunni country, a result that is statistically significant at the standard benchmark of .05. Moreover, statistical analysis shows that this high level of risk is due simply to the addition of American military presence to Salafi-influenced population, not to a special feature of the interaction of the two. Even if the effect of Salafi-influenced populations on al-Qaeda suicide terrorism were as-

TABLE 14. American Military Presence in Sunni Countries and al-Qaeda

Sunni Countries with American Combat Operations		
Country	*Muslims (millions)*	*Al-Qaeda Suicide Attackers*
Afghanistan	25	3
Saudi Arabia	21	34
Turkey	67	4
Uzbekistan	21	0
UAE	2	2
Oman	2	0
Kuwait	2	0
Total	140	43 1 per 3.2 million
All Other Sunni Countries		
Total	794	23 1 per 35 million

sumed to be significant, American military presence in a Salafi-influenced country would remain ten times as powerful as Salafism alone as a predictor of al-Qaeda suicide terrorism.

TABLE 15. American Military Presence in Salafi Countries Versus Other Sunni Countries and al-Qaeda

Countries with Salafi-Influenced Populations and American Combat Operations		
Country	*Muslims (millions)*	*Al-Qaeda Suicide Attackers*
Afghanistan	25	3
Saudi Arabia	21	34
Oman	2	0
Total	48	37 1 per 1.3 million
All Other Sunni Countries		
Total	886	29 1 per 31 million

Overall, examination of the nationalities of al-Qaeda's suicide terrorists from 1995 to 2003 shows that American military policy in the Persian Gulf was most likely the pivotal factor leading to September 11. This is not to say that al-Qaeda is not committed to Islamic fundamentalism or that it draws no important transnational support. The fact that we can assume that al-Qaeda's suicide attackers have been committed Islamists is sufficient reason to think that Islamic fundamentalism is at least a weak force driving the movement, even if this is not borne out by the statistics. However, it is important to recognize the fundamental role played by American military policy. Although there may well have been excellent reasons for their presence, the stationing of tens of thousands of American combat troops on the Arabian peninsula from 1990 to 2001 most likely made al-Qaeda suicide attacks against Americans, including the atrocities committed on September 11, 2001, from ten to twenty times more likely.[22]

U.S. Foreign Policy and al-Qaeda's Transnational Suicide Terrorists
American military presence accounts for a large fraction of al-Qaeda suicide attackers—forty-three of sixty-seven overall (including the one from Lebanon), or 64 percent. What accounts for the remaining attackers?

Examination of the pool of al-Qaeda's suicide terrorists from Table 16 reveals an important pattern: al-Qaeda's transnational suicide terrorists have come overwhelmingly from America's closest allies in the Muslim world and not at all from the Muslim regimes that the U.S. State Department considers "state sponsors of terrorism." There are twenty-four al-Qaeda suicide terrorists not associated with American combat presence. Of these, nineteen, or 79 percent, come from Muslim regimes strongly allied with the United States and none from the Muslim regimes that the United States considers most hostile.

This pattern gives us important information about the main sources of al-Qaeda's transnational appeal for suicide operations against the United States. However, it cannot be subjected to tests for statistical significance. The number of transnational al-Qaeda suicide attackers is so small that a few outliers could distort the results. Still, examining the extreme ends of the spectrum of American foreign policy toward Muslim regimes is perfectly legitimate—this is done routinely in assessing American voting behavior. While there may be substantial variation in the middle range of a causal variable, we gain important information by looking at how a relationship performs when the factor is extremely high or extremely low,

TABLE 16. U.S. Foreign Policy and al-Qaeda Suicide Attackers, 1995–2003

American Combat Presence		*U.S. Backed Regimes*	
Saudi Arabia	34	Egypt	2
Turkey	4	Pakistan (post-2001)	2
Afghanistan (post-2001)	3	Indonesia (E. Timor)	3
UAE	2	Morocco	12
Total	43		19

*U.S. "Terrorist States"**		*Other*	
Iraq	0	Yemen	3
Iran	0	Tunisia	1
Libya	0	Lebanon	1
Syria	0		
Sudan	0		
Afghanistan (pre-2001)	0		
Total	0		5

Sources: Chicago Project on Suicide Terrorism, University of Chicago, 2005; "State Sponsored Terrorism" (Washington, D.C.: U.S. Department of State, 2005).

*Muslim countries. Cuba and North Korea are also considered state sponsors of terrorism.

which allows us to make judgments about the part of the relationship that is easiest to define.

Although we cannot assess the strength of American support for all Muslim regimes, we can be certain that support for all those listed on the U.S. Department of State's list of state sponsors of terrorism is at the extreme low end and that support for Egypt, Pakistan (post-2001), Indonesia, and Morocco qualifies as at the high end. These four states have all received substantial American military and economic assistance over the past two decades.

Egypt receives about $2 billion of America's $14 billion annual foreign aid budget, in large part as payment for making peace with Israel in 1978. Of that, about $1.3 billion goes to military assistance. Only Israel receives more U.S. aid than Egypt. As for Morocco, the United States has been a staunch supporter of its authoritarian government, providing more than

$1 billion worth of arms as well as $1.3 billion in security and economic assistance programs to the Kingdom in its fight with the Polisario guerrillas in the Western Sahara from 1976 to 1991. The United States has also supported the Kingdom's decision to postpone indefinitely its promised popular referendum on the final status of the area. With respect to Pakistan: the United States provided over $300 million in aid to Islamabad in 2001 in return for its support in the war on terrorism and considers the current government among its closest allies in that effort. In Indonesia, the American military provided important logistical support for the Australian-led military intervention in 1999 that ended the violence and created a Catholic majority state in East Timor.[23]

Further, al-Qaeda's suicide terrorists from these four countries are associated either with efforts to topple the national government or with national liberation movements to establish greater political autonomy for local Muslim populations. In Egypt, Islamic militants—including the Islamic group associated with Ayman al-Zawahiri, al-Qaeda's second in command—have used violence in attempts to overthrow the local government more or less continuously since the late 1970s, including the assassination of President Anwar al-Sadat in 1981 and the attempted assassination of President Hosni Mubarak in 1995. In Pakistan, President Pervez Musharraf has faced numerous assassination attempts since joining America's war on terrorism in 2001. In Morocco, one of the survivors of the fourteen-member al-Qaeda suicide bomb squad that attacked targets associated with American and other Western citizens in Casablanca in May 2003 said during his trial that he "hoped to blow himself up" during the strikes because he was "not happy with the political situation in Morocco." From 1999 to 2001, Indonesian Muslim militias waged an intense campaign of indiscriminate violence to stop East Timor, a predominately Catholic region, from gaining independence.[24]

The striking result from this analysis is that nineteen (79 percent) of al-Qaeda's transnational suicide terrorists—those not associated with American military presence—are from four Muslim countries, all of which have regimes that are close allies of the United States and all of whose suicide terrorists are associated with the cause of national liberation in their own countries. This suggests that al-Qaeda's truly transnational appeal for martyrdom is thin and springs mainly from nationalist causes.

The data on al-Qaeda's transnational suicide terrorists also casts doubt on the argument that the group's core support emanates from Islamic fundamentalism. The five countries with the largest Salafi-influenced populations are Pakistan (43 million), Nigeria (37 million), Indonesia (26 million), Egypt (23 million), and Sudan (21 million). Altogether, these countries account for 64 percent of the world's total Salafi-influenced population (150 million), but only 29 percent of al-Qaeda's transnational suicide terrorists (seven of twenty-four).

Overall, analysis of al-Qaeda's suicide terrorists shows that its most lethal forces are best understood as a coalition of nationalist groups seeking to achieve a local change in their home countries, not as a truly transnational movement seeking to spread Islam or any other ideology to non-Islamic populations. Religion matters, but mainly in the context of national resistance.

AL-QAEDA'S APPEAL: FOREIGN OCCUPATION AND RELIGIOUS DIFFERENCE

Al-Qaeda's recruitment rhetoric emphasizes alliance politics among separate national groups, not the construction of a transnational network to spread Islamic fundamentalism or in opposition to democracy in general. Over the years, Osama bin Laden's main call has been for Islamic groups reacting separately against American military presence or U.S. support for their local governments to create, in essence, a cross-national military coalition against the United States. Indeed, bin Laden's principal organizational innovation has been to reorient various local resistance movements away from their local grievances in the short term so as to bring an accumulation of violence against their common enemy, the United States. Because there is a religious difference between the United States and all these groups, and because none are militarily strong enough to stand up to American power on their own, al-Qaeda leaders can portray the United States as a religiously motivated aggressor, posing a common threat to occupy and transform their societies, and can appeal for collective martyrdom operations as the only means of protecting the self-determination of the threatened communities.

"Veiled Colonialism"

The linchpin in al-Qaeda's appeal for separate nationalist liberation movements to unify their efforts against the United States is the idea of "veiled colonialism." America's ambitions, bin Laden and other al-Qaeda leaders claim, are not limited to the Arabian Peninsula, but include the suppression and control of other Muslim societies, especially those near Israel. These societies face not direct military occupation, but "veiled colonialism" in which the United States supports repressive regimes that serve the interests of the "Crusader-Zionist alliance." One of al-Qaeda's most detailed documents, issued on the Internet to explain its attacks against the Saudi regime in May 2003, says:

> The Muslim countries today are colonized. Colonialism is either direct or veiled. . . . masking colonialism . . . is exactly what happened in Afghanistan when the United States occupied that country and installed an Afghan agent, Hamid Karzai. . . . There is no difference between the Karzai of Yemen, the Karzai of Pakistan, the Karzai of Jordan, the Karzai of Qatar, the Karzai of Kuwait, the Karzai of Egypt, and the long list of Karzai traitors ruling the Muslim countries.

The document also explains that "veiled colonialism" is tantamount to the occupation and political control of the country:

> The ruler of a country is the one that has the authority in it. . . . The real ruler is the Crusader United States. The subserviency of [Muslim] rulers is no different from the subserviency of the amirs or governors of provinces to the king or the president. The rule of the agent is the rule of the one who made him his agent.

Finally, it contends that "veiled colonialism" threatens full military occupation:

> It is important to know that the colonialist enemy might give up veiled colonialism and establish, through its armies, colonialism where there is little fear of resistance or the agent leadership could not achieve the interests of colonialism or had deviated—even in a small way—from its hegemony. For this reason, the United States chose to invade Iraq militarily and might choose to invade any Muslim country near or far from Iraq at any time. . . . [If the United States can run a country's] radar equipment, the AWACs reconnaissance aircraft, and the air, land and sea command and control centers, it can occupy a country whenever it wants, and this is exactly what the United States is doing in Saudi Arabia.[25]

To see how al-Qaeda seeks to persuade the members of its coalition to rely on martyrdom operations to meet this threat, it is helpful to understand more about the image of American motives and strategy as portrayed by Osama bin Laden and his associates.

Religious Difference and al-Qaeda's Case for Martyrdom

The politics of religious difference is central to al-Qaeda's campaign of suicide terrorism against the United States. Throughout virtually all the statements, interviews, sermons, and books by Osama bin Laden and other al-Qaeda leaders over the past decade, the United States is portrayed as a religiously motivated "Crusader" on an aggressive mission to subdue, occupy, and transform Muslim societies. Although we in the West discount such statements as mere rhetoric, it is important to recognize that the image of an offensive war waged by Christians against Muslims has great emotional and political power. Establishing that the United States is on a Christian crusade to remake the Muslim world enables bin Laden to claim that American foreign and military policies in a variety of countries are part of a coherent plan, that American behavior will become aggressive over time, that national groups in those target countries have a common basis to work together, and that those who die can easily be defined as martyrs for Islam.

America, the "Crusader." Osama bin Laden's statements and interviews almost always begin with a simple, overarching message: the United States is pursuing an offensive mission to control the homelands of Islamic countries in the Persian Gulf and elsewhere, and Muslims in these countries should use force to resist the occupation. In May 1998, when *Frontline* asked why he called for strikes against the United States, bin Laden said:

> The call to wage war against America was made because America has spearheaded the crusade against the Islamic nation, sending tens of thousands of its troops to the land of the two Holy Mosques [Saudi Arabia] over and above its meddling in its affairs and its politics, and its support of the oppressive, corrupt and tyrannical regime that is in control. These are the reasons behind the singling out of America as a target.[26]

Although he also believes that the United States is interested in oil, bin Laden most strikingly characterizes the United States as the leader of a Christian-Jewish alliance that is mainly motivated by religious aims. He

says, "Our enemy is the Crusader alliance led by America, Britain, and Israel." His famous 1998 call to kill Americans is entitled "Jihad against Jews
and Crusaders." He frequently says that it is a mistake "to distinguish between America and Israel."

The use of the word "crusader" is no accident. For many Muslims, the
eleventh-century Crusades were an attempt by Christians to achieve the
key condition for the coming of the Messiah—the return of Israel to
the promised land.[27] Bin Laden often recounts the history of the Crusades
and then identifies the American occupation of the Arabian Peninsula as
the latest effort:

> Our enemy is the Crusader alliance led by America, Britain, and Israel. . . .
> Our hostility is in the first place, and to the greatest extent, leveled against
> these world infidels, and by necessity the regimes which have turned them-
> selves into tools for this occupation. . . . Jordan has American bases and
> American planes occupying it. Egypt also has a number of American bases.
> The six Gulf states are all occupied by American bases.[28]

Bin Laden goes further, asserting that the same specific religious goal—
the creation of Greater Israel—is at the heart of today's Christian-Zionist
alliance:

> One reason behind the symbolic participation of the Western forces . . . is to
> support the Jewish and Zionist plans for expansion of what is called Greater
> Israel. . . . We believe that [the U.S.] administration represents Israel inside
> America. Take the sensitive ministries such as the Ministry of Exterior and
> the Ministry of Defense and the CIA, you will find that the Jews have the
> upper hand in them. They make use of America to further their plans for
> the world, especially the Islamic world. American presence in the Gulf pro-
> vides support to the Jews and protects their rear.[29]

Bin Laden's rhetoric has powerful effects, not only on those specifically
under his direction but also on those who might seek to emulate him. In a
letter to Osama bin Laden intercepted by U.S. intelligence, Abu Mussab
al-Zarqawi, the leader of suicide terrorist attacks in Iraq, also portrays the
United States as motivated by Christian goals:

> The Americans, as you know well, entered Iraq on a contractual basis and
> to create the State of Greater Israel from the Nile to the Euphrates and this

Zionized American administration believes that accelerating the creation of the State of Greater Israel will accelerate the emergence of the Messiah.[30]

America's "World Design." The attribution of religious motives to the United States allows bin Laden to draw a key inference—that American military presence on the Arabian Peninsula is not "temporary," but part of a "world design" that is "aimed at re-dividing the Muslim world." Although some might think that bin Laden is merely using current events to his advantage, in fact he presented his vision of America's grand strategy long before America's war to conquer Iraq in 2003. As early as 1998, bin Laden said:

> There is a [U.S.] plan to divide Iraq into three—one in the north for Muslim Kurds, a state in the middle, and a third in the south. The same applies to the land of the two mosques [Saudi Arabia] where there is a plan to divide it into a state for the two mosques, another state for oil in the eastern region, and a state in the middle. This would make the people of the two mosques always busy trying to earn a living, and would leave a few people in the oil region who can be easily controlled.[31]

In February 2003, bin Laden described the U.S. war against Iraq as the execution of the plan he had already identified:

> The preparations . . . for an attack upon Iraq are but one link in a chain of attacks . . . with the start of the [1991] Gulf War the Americans established important and dangerous military bases which have spread throughout the Land of the Two Holy Places. . . . One of the most important objectives of the new Crusader attack [in 2003] is to pave the way and prepare the region, after its fragmentation, for the establishment of what is known as "the Greater State of Israel," whose borders will include extensive areas of Iraq, Egypt, through Syria, Lebanon, Jordan, all of Palestine and large parts of the Land of the Two Holy Places.[32]

Al-Qaeda's Solution: A Strong Muslim State. Bin Laden and other al-Qaeda leaders stress that the only solution to the common threat they face from a religiously motivated United States is a strong Islamic state, one sufficiently powerful to prevent the United States from implementing its plans involving a number of Muslim countries. This solution not only appeals to bin Laden himself, but is also clearly reflected in detailed statements by other al-Qaeda leaders from countries outside of the Persian Gulf. Consider the famous book *Knights Under the Banner of the Prophet* by al-Zawahiri, an Egyptian who was part of Egypt's Islamic Jihad before joining forces with al-Qaeda:

> Victory for the Islamic movements against the Crusader alliance cannot be attained unless these movements possess an Islamic base in the heart of the Arab region. . . . The jihad movement must adopt its plan on the basis of controlling a piece of land in the heart of the Islamic world on which it could establish and protect the state of Islam. . . . If the successful operations against Islam's enemies and the severe damage inflicted upon them do not serve the ultimate goal of establishing the Muslim nation in the heart of the Islamic world, they will be nothing more than disturbing acts. . . . The restoration of the caliphate and the dismissal of the invaders from the land of Islam . . . must remain the basic objective of the Islamic jihad movement, regardless of the sacrifices and the time involved.

Given the relative weakness of individual Muslim countries, this goal requires that regional groups work together against the United States:

> The struggle for the establishment of the Muslim state cannot be launched as a regional struggle. . . . the Jewish-Crusader alliance, led by the United States, will not allow any Muslim force to reach power in any of the Islamic countries. . . . The struggle against the external enemy [the United States] cannot be postponed. . . . The jihad movement must realize that half the road to victory is attained through its unity . . . before the single enemy. . . . The movement must seek this unity as soon as possible if it is serious in its quest for victory.[33]

American Society Is the Vulnerable Point. Although al-Qaeda depicts the U.S. government as a religiously motivated aggressor, it does not ascribe religious motives to American or Western society in general. In fact, Western society is described as corrupted by materialism, a fact that al-Qaeda believes can be used to drive a wedge between Western publics and their governments. Thus, central to al-Qaeda's strategy is the use of coercion that would impose high costs on civilians in order to compel them to pressure their governments to reverse course.

Bin Laden describes America as a paper tiger that can be coerced by inflicting modest costs on its society:

America is a great power possessed of tremendous military might and a wide-ranging economy, but all this is built upon an unstable foundation which can be targeted, with special attention to its obvious weak spots. If America is hit in one hundredth of those spots, God willing, it will stumble, wither away and relinquish world leadership and its oppression. A small group of young Islamic fighters managed . . . to provide people with proof of the fact that it is possible to wage war upon and fight against a so-called "great power" . . . because they used Jihad . . . any means which brings victory is worthwhile.[34]

We believe that America is weaker than [Soviet] Russia and from what we have heard from our brothers who waged jihad in Somalia, they found to their greatest surprise the weakness, frailness and cowardliness of the American soldier. When only eight of them were killed they packed up in the darkness of night and escaped without looking back.[35]

[T]he Islamic nation today possesses tremendous forces sufficient to save Palestine and the rest of the Muslim lands. . . . I should like to remind you of the defeats suffered by a number of the great powers at the hands of the Mujahideen. . . . [For example,] the defeat of the American forces in the year 1402 of the Muslim calendar [1982] when the Israelis invaded Lebanon. The Lebanese resistance sent a truck full of explosives to the American Marines' center in Beirut and killed over 240 of them.[36]

Hence, the military objective is to impose costs that will compel the United States to withdraw from Muslim countries. As al-Zawahiri states:

The masters in Washington and Tel Aviv are using the regimes to protect their interest and to fight the battle against the Muslims on their behalf. If the shrapnel from the battle reaches their homes and their bodies . . . they will face one of two bitter choices: Either [they] personally wage the battle against the Muslims, which means that the battle will turn into clear-cut jihad against infidels, or they reconsider their plans after acknowledging the failure of the brute and violent confrontation against Muslims. Therefore, we must move the battle to the enemy's grounds to burn the hands of those who ignite fire in our countries.[37]

Martyrdom Operations Against Religious Persecution. Al-Qaeda's statements emphasize that "martyrdom operations" are the best tactics against the United States. Al-Zawahiri, al-Qaeda's second in command, says:

> To adjust to this new reality [the "Crusader alliance" led by the United States] we must prepare ourselves for a battle that is not confined to a single region. . . . The mujahid Islamic movement must escalate its methods of strikes and tools of resisting the enemies. . . . In this regard, we concentrate on the following:
> 1. The need to inflict the maximum casualties against the opponent, for this is the language understood by the West, no matter how much time and effort such operations take.
> 2. The need to concentrate on the method of martyrdom operations as the most successful way of inflicting damage against the opponent and the least costly to the Mujahedin in terms of casualties.
> 3. The targets as well as the type and method of weapons used must be chosen to have an impact on the structure of the enemy and deter it enough to stop its brutality, arrogance, and disregard for all taboos and customs. It must restore the struggle to its real size.
> 4. To reemphasize what we have already explained, we reiterate that focusing on the domestic enemy alone will not be feasible at this stage.[38]

Those who carry out suicide operations against the United States are considered martyrs for the simple reason that they are fighting against religious oppression. Bin Laden says in his famous "Declaration of War against the Americans Occupying the Land of the Two Holy Places" (1996):

> Under [today's] circumstances, to push the enemy—the greatest Kufr [infidel]—out of the country is a prime duty. . . . [D]ue to the imbalance of power between our armed forces and the enemy forces, a suitable means of fighting must be adopted. . . . [Our] youths know that their rewards in fighting you, the USA, are double their rewards in fighting someone else not from the people of the book [i.e., the Bible]. They have no intention except to enter paradise by killing you. An infidel . . . cannot be in the same hell with his righteous executioner. . . . These youths are commendable and praiseworthy. They stand up tall to defend the religion. . . . It is a duty on every tribe in the Arab Peninsula to fight, Jihad, in the cause of Allah and to cleanse the land from those occupiers.[39]

CONCLUSION

My theory of the origins of suicide terrorism captures the core features of al-Qaeda. The theory contends that nationalism and religious difference between the rebels and a dominant democratic state are the main conditions under which the "alien" occupation of a community's homeland is likely to lead to a campaign of suicide terrorism. Examination of al-Qaeda's pool of suicide terrorists and of its mobilization appeals shows that American military policy is stronger than Islamic fundamentalism in recruiting individuals willing to carry out suicide terrorist operations against the United States. Truly transnational al-Qaeda suicide terrorists are few, while the overwhelming majority emanate from a narrow range of Muslim countries, those with American combat troops stationed on or immediately adjacent to their soil and those that received substantial backing by the United States. American military policy in the Persian Gulf was the pivotal factor leading to September 11. Although Islamic fundamentalism mattered, the stationing of tens of thousands of American combat troops on the Arabian Peninsula from 1990 to 2001 probably increased the risk of al-Qaeda suicide attacks against Americans, including the events of September 11, 2001, ten to twenty times.

The main implication for the security of the United States is simple: if al-Qaeda's truly transnational support were to dry up tomorrow, the group would remain a robust threat to the United States. However, if al-Qaeda no longer drew recruits from the Sunni Muslim countries where there is a heavy American military presence or where the government receives strong U.S. support, the remaining transnational network would pose a far smaller threat and might well simply collapse.

This finding also has important implications for American policy toward Iraq: the longer American combat forces remain in the country, the greater the risk that the Iraqi suicide terrorists will seek to mount operations to kill Americans in the United States. Although fostering democracy is important, the United States should carefully reconsider the role of military power in its long-term policy toward achieving this goal in Iraq.

We still want to know whether the causal dynamics predicted by my theory exist in a broad range of other foreign occupations in which national resistance has escalated to suicide terrorism, and are absent in foreign occupations that did not. This is the subject of the next chapter.

8

Suicide Terrorist Organizations
Around the Globe

MY THEORY ARGUES that national resistance to foreign occupation, a democratic political system in the occupying power, and a religious difference between the occupied and occupying societies are the main causal factors leading to the rise of suicide terrorist campaigns. Thus far, this book has shown that modern suicide terrorism is best understood as a strategy used by groups seeking to compel democratic states to withdraw military forces from territory that they consider their national homelands. It also explains why a *difference* in the predominate religion of the two societies — not the religion of the occupied nation, Muslim or otherwise — is a main cause for why some foreign occupations by a democratic state escalate to suicide terrorism and others do not. This theory is strongly supported by evidence from across the universe of nationalist rebellions since 1980 and by the examination of al-Qaeda in the previous chapter.

Whether my theory is persuasive, however, depends on whether the dynamics that make religious difference important are also present in other suicide terrorist campaigns. To show that this is the case, I must demonstrate that the history of disputes that have escalated to suicide terrorism involves primarily the clash of two religions. In other words, the evidence must show that a religious difference routinely enabled terrorist leaders to gain significant public support for suicide terrorism by painting the conflict in stark zero-sum terms, demonizing the opponent, and gaining legitimacy for martyrdom. The evidence must also show that these dynamics were not the product of any one religion or class of religions, and that they occur even when the terrorist group is not itself religious.

It is not easy to establish that religious difference is a key factor enabling suicide terrorism. Since religious difference is a static phenomenon—it is either present or absent, but does not widen or narrow during the lifetime of an occupation—we cannot compare a change in this factor with the timing of a suicide terrorist campaign to demonstrate the relationship between cause and effect in any individual case. Further, many differences normally exist between societies, while only a relatively small number of occupations have resulted in suicide terrorism. As a result, comparisons between cases where suicide terrorism did occur and cases where it did not will usually involve societies that differ in so many basic ways that it is probably impossible to disentangle the effects of a religious difference (or the lack thereof) from other possible causal factors.

However, these limits also suggest a research design. If we study a group of cases of suicide terrorism that differ greatly in the number of different religions they involve, then we can gain confidence—precisely because so many other cultural differences would also exist—that the effects of religious difference, if they can be shown, have causal weight. Further, we can look to include certain accidents of history that overcome the problem of cross-case comparison. If the same national community finds its homeland occupied at different times by two different occupying powers, one of which shares the occupied community's religion and one of which does not, then comparison of these two cases provides useful causal information. We do have one such pair, in Sri Lanka, and this study includes it. Finally, we can examine the one case in which suicide terrorism occurred without a religious difference (the Kurdish PKK versus Turkey) to see if the dynamics of this single case should fundamentally alter our understanding of the origins of suicide terrorism in general.

Within each case, we can examine the discourse of terrorist organizations and other leaders of an occupied community to see how much weight they put on religious difference, compared with other factors, in explaining why the community should support suicide terrorism. If such appeals do yield numerous recruits who are willing to commit acts of suicide terrorism, then this method can provide important information about what leaders in an occupied community *believe* can best elicit mass support for the purpose. If such appeals yield recruits from a range of secular and religious backgrounds, then this approach can tell us that a common

perception of the threat posed by the occupying power, rather than ideological uniformity in the occupied community, is the more important factor. When added to the information about the strong association between
religious difference and suicide terrorism from our examination of the universe of recent rebellions against democracies in Chapter 6, this process-
tracing approach can increase the number of observations relevant to the
causal logic and so increase our confidence in the theory as a whole.[1] The
more the discourse of leaders and suicide terrorists centers around the specific mechanisms by which we expect religious difference to matter, the
more confidence we gain.

Which cases merit deep examination? Nine occupations led to suicide
terrorism; of these, eight involved a religious difference and one did not.
Although it would naturally be helpful to study them all, this is not practical given the depth of analysis required and the limits of information available for some cases. Al-Qaeda, of course, has been studied in the previous
chapter.

To make the inquiry manageable, this study selects four cases of suicide
terrorism with a wide range of religious differences, Lebanon, Sri Lanka,
Punjab, and Turkey. Overall, this study includes the interplay of six different religions. Lebanon in the 1980s involved Shia Muslims versus Israeli
(Jewish) and Western (Christian) opponents; Sri Lanka in the 1980s and
1990s involved Tamils (Hindu) versus the Sinhalese (Buddhist) government; and Punjab in the 1990s involved Sihks versus the Indian (Hindu)
government. This design can also easily incorporate the one paired comparison that does offer relatively tight control on the effect of religious difference. During the course of the Sinhalese-Tamil dispute, the Indian
government (Hindu) sent thousands of troops to occupy the Tamil community (Hindu) from 1987 to 1990, an interlude during which the Tamil
resistance temporarily abandoned the use of suicide terrorism. This study
also includes the one occupation without a religious difference that led to
suicide terrorism, the Kurdish PKK (Sunni) versus the Turkish government (Sunni).

All of the case studies are structured similarly to show the pattern of
cause and effect both within and across cases. Since the purpose is to identify the effect of foreign occupation on the popularity of individual self-
sacrifice and suicide terrorism within the local community, I organize
each case around three main issues: (1) the nature and extent of the foreign occupation; (2) the extent of community support for self-sacrifice to

end the occupation; and (3) how terrorist and other community leaders exploited the existence of a religious difference to mobilize popular support for martyrdom.

SUICIDE TERRORISM IN LEBANON

Hezbollah, the loose federation of militant Shia groups that sprang up in Lebanon in the early 1980s, is the first modern suicide terrorist organization. From 1982 to 1986, Hezbollah conducted thirty-six suicide terrorist attacks involving a total of forty-one attackers against American, French, and Israeli political and military targets in Lebanon. Among these was the spectacular attack on the U.S. Marine barracks in Beirut on October 23, 1983. Altogether, these attacks killed 659 people, most of whom were off-duty soldiers in no position to defend themselves, such as the 241 U.S. Marines who were killed as they slept on that fateful day in Beirut. Even today, Hezbollah's campaigns of suicide terrorism continue to influence events. Although al-Qaeda, the Liberation Tigers of Tamil Eelam in Sri Lanka, and Palestinian suicide terrorist groups have killed more people, Hezbollah's prominent success in compelling the United States, France, and Israel to withdraw military forces from territory that the terrorists view as their homeland has played a major role in encouraging today's most deadly suicide terrorists.

What caused the emergence of suicide terrorism in Lebanon? The most common explanation is Islamic fundamentalism. Hezbollah, so the argument goes, was founded on the basis of radical Islamic principles that gained ascendancy following the Islamic revolution in Iran in 1979, and extreme devotion to radical Islam accounts for the willingness of its members to achieve personal salvation through martyrdom operations.[2] The tendency of most news stories at the time to stress the Islamic identity of the attackers encouraged the perception that Islamic fundamentalism is the root cause of suicide terrorism in Lebanon.

However, this is not the case. New information about the identity of the suicide attackers presents a fresh picture that casts the role of Islamic fundamentalism in a new light. I spent a year leading a team of researchers who collected detailed evidence on the ideological and other demographic characteristics of suicide terrorists. The results show that at least thirty of the forty-one attackers do not fit the description of Islamic funda-

mentalism. Twenty-seven were communists or socialists with no commitment to religious extremism; three were Christians. Only eight suicide attackers were affiliated with Islamic fundamentalism; the ideological
affiliation of three cannot be identified. Moreover, although Iran did provide money and other support to the Lebanese resistance fighters, the rise
of Hezbollah and large popular support for the movement were directly
caused by a clear external event, Israel's massive occupation of southern
Lebanon in 1982. Further, although religion was a recruiting tool, examination of the logic of martyrdom articulated by Hezbollah and other
Lebanese political leaders overwhelmingly justified suicide terrorist acts,
commonly called "self-martyr" operations, as an extreme measure necessary to end foreign occupation of the homeland, while explicitly ruling out
such acts as an end in themselves or for other, even religious, goals.

Contrary to the conventional wisdom, I argue that religious *difference*—
not Islam—played the key enabling role in causing suicide terrorism in
Lebanon. Although foreign occupation created the necessary basis for
armed resistance, the religious schism between the occupiers' societies
and the occupied society enabled resistance leaders to inflame nationalist
sentiments to the point that the occupied community supported and glori-
fied suicide terrorism. Fear of a religiously motivated occupier, more than
anything in Islam, encouraged a significant level of community support
for extreme self-sacrifice to end the occupation.

Israel's Occupation of Lebanon

Lebanon is on the Mediterranean coast, north of Israel and west of Syria.
In the 1980s, it had a population of approximately 2.6 million people,
composed of about 40 percent Shia Muslims, 25 percent Sunni Muslims,
15 percent Maronite Christians, 8 percent Greek Orthodox and Catholics,
and 7 percent Druze (a religion unique to Lebanon).[3]

Before the 1980s, there were no suicide terrorist attacks in Lebanon.
This is true even though the Shia community had long been politically
and economically disadvantaged compared with other groups in the country, even though a fierce civil war occurred in 1975–76, and even though
many Lebanese Islamic fundamentalists were heartened by the revolution
in Iran in 1979. Indeed, before the summer of 1982, Hezbollah did not
exist.

In the 1970s, the most important Shia militant organization was
Harakat Amal, a nationalist movement founded in the Shia heartland of
South Lebanon in 1975. Amal leaders advocated the restructuring of the

Lebanese political system to prevent the subordination of Shia interests to other groups' and, after 1975, organized militias to protect the security of villages in south Lebanon during the civil war. The Amal political platform called for equality of all citizens, social justice, and a non-sectarian commitment to national unity; it did not propose the creation of an Islamic state in Lebanon. By early 1982, Amal was the most powerful organization within the Shia community and perhaps the largest organization in the country, numbering in the tens of thousands.[4]

On June 6, 1982, Israel launched a major invasion of Lebanon. Within days, six and a half divisions of the Israel Defense Forces, comprising 78,000 troops, 1,240 tanks, and 1,520 armored personnel carriers, occupied large parts of the south of the country up to Beirut. Israel's military objectives were three: first, to destroy the PLO's 15,000 troops, who had resided in the south of the country since leaving Jordan in the early 1970s; second, to force the PLO leadership near Beirut to abandon Lebanon; and third, to compel Syria's 30,000 troops, 612 tanks, and 150 armored personnel carriers, which had moved into the center and east during the 1975 civil war, to leave the country. By September, Israel had succeeded in ousting the PLO to Tunisia and thereafter reduced IDF troop strength to 20,000, promising to leave Lebanon only if Syrian troops did likewise (which there was no reason to expect). From this point on, Israel began to implement a long-term plan to stabilize Maronite Christian control over the government in Beirut, and appeared to settle in for a prolonged occupation of Lebanon.[5]

Hezbollah came into being in the immediate aftermath of Israel's invasion. In late June 1982, Hussain Mussawi, a secular Shia leader who was second in command of Amal, and his followers broke away from Amal, proclaiming that its collaboration with Israel's program of expansion was unacceptable. This group formed "Islamic Amal," a movement that professed support for an Islamic state on the model of Iran, and was soon joined by a contingent of 800 to 1,000 Pasdaran (Revolutionary Guards) that Iran dispatched to Lebanon in July. As best we can tell, Mussawi and his followers appear to have formed the core of what later became known as Hezbollah. This group established a headquarters in the Bekaa Valley and, over the coming months, sought to inspire active resistance among the Shia to the Israeli invaders.[6]

At first, Hezbollah appears to have had little popular support. In the summer of 1982, the Shia supported Israel's invasion even though Israel's initial military operations probably killed 3,000 to 5,000 civilians and left

70,000 to 80,000 homeless in the Shia's homeland in southern Lebanon.[7] Although the Shia were broadly sympathetic to the Palestinian cause, after a decade of increasing tensions between the Shia and the PLO, many were more than willing to stand aside while Israel ejected the Palestinians from their country.

However, the Shia community's early reaction was not long-lived and fundamentally reversed as Israeli troops remained in Lebanon. As Magnus Ranstrop says, "Although the Lebanese Shia community initially welcomed Israel's decision to eradicate the PLO presence, any Shia euphoria soon developed into resentment and militancy following the realization that Israel would continue to occupy southern Lebanon."[8] This sense of foreign occupation deepened as thousands of American, French, and other Western troops arrived in the country in August 1982, even though their purpose was to stabilize the country and reduce violence.

As more and more Shia came to resent and resist Israel's occupation, Hezbollah—never tight-knit—expanded into an umbrella organization coordinating the resistance operations of a loose collection of groups with a variety of religious and secular aims. Lebanese militants grew from a handful in the summer of 1982 to more than 7,000 members over the next few years. What made the rise of Hezbollah so rapid was not its association with Iran or other sources of international support, but the fact that it evolved from a reorientation of a number of pre-existing social groups in Lebanon. Hezbollah's main factions, such as the Mussawi faction within Amal, the Lebanese Da'wa Party, the Association of Muslim Ulama in Lebanon, and the Association of Muslim Students, all existed in the 1970s.[9] However, Israel's invasion of Lebanon created new circumstances that allowed these groups to form a new overarching purpose. As Hezbollah's general secretary, Sheikh Hassan Nasrallah, explains:

> This new group or new framework had the conditions for its formation before the Israeli invasion. But the invasion accelerated its existence, and Hezbollah was born as a resistance force in the reaction to the occupation. . . . [C]ontrary to the accusations . . . that it was Iranian—it was a Lebanese decision, founded by a group of Lebanese with a Lebanese leadership, Lebanese grassroots, and the freedom fighters are Lebanese. . . . Hezbollah was at its inception centered on resisting the occupation, nothing else. . . . Naturally, we asked for assistance. From any party. . . . From then on the relations began with Syria and Iran.[10]

The main impetus for the growth of Hezbollah was Israel's increasingly deep control and regulation of the local villages of the Shia community in southern Lebanon. Israel began arresting local Shia leaders in the fall of 1982, and formalized this effort in January 1983 by creating the "Organization for a United South," which sought to supplant the existing Amal leaders in the thirty largest villages in southern Lebanon with Israeli-backed village committees. These committees were to mount local militias that would work alongside Israeli forces. Israel's occupation thus dashed the hopes of self-determination among many Shia. As Augustus Norton observes, "Having begun to throw off the shackles of the PLO presence, the Shia community was not about to wrap itself in the chains of Israel's occupation."[11]

The timing of Hezbollah's suicide operations parallels the rise of Israel's control of the Shia community. Starting in November 1982, Hezbollah carried out the first of thirty-six suicide terrorist attacks against American, French, and Israeli political and military targets in Lebanon through 1986. As discussed more fully in Chapter 10, these attacks involved suicide terrorists from a wide range of ideological commitments—communists, socialists, and even some Christians in addition to Islamists—united in the purpose of ending Western and Israeli occupation of the country.

Community Support for Martyrdom

Community support for martyrdom played a key role in encouraging individuals to become suicide terrorists. Although they varied in other ways, the individuals who carried out suicide terrorist attacks in Lebanon attached tremendous importance to how the community would understand and remember their actions. The overwhelming majority of these individuals left detailed statements, either in writing or on video, that they expected to be made public after their death.[12] Most of these testaments did become public soon after the individual's mission and circulated widely among the Shia community, either in newspapers or as items available in local markets. Of course, we should assume that the terrorist organization was instrumental in producing them; indeed, many are quite professional. The key fact, however, is that they were created with the local community in mind. Among ordinary suicides, less than 20 percent leave suicide notes and virtually none of these are directed at the community at large.[13]

The prevalence of "martyr" testimonials indicates that the suicide terrorists and their organization attach great importance to establishing themselves as martyrs in the eyes of their community. In many, the individuals use the word "martyr," either to describe those who went on similar missions in the past or to name what they hoped to become. They also explain why their actions are directly related to foreign occupation, often explicitly describing Israeli military forces as barbaric invaders who must be ousted from the country at any price. Few, if any, suicide terrorists would bother making such statements if they felt that community support for their actions was unimportant.

Compare two such statements. The first is by Sanaa Muhaidly, a seventeen-year-old Sunni girl belonging to a secular political party who was one of the first to issue a videotape explaining her motives. Although she mentions her hope of going to paradise, what is most prominent is her association of self-sacrifice with the need to free her community from foreign occupation:

> I have witnessed the calamity of my people under occupation. With total calmness I shall carry out an attack of my choice hoping to kill the largest number of the Israeli army. I hope my soul will join the souls of the other martyrs. I have not died, but am moving alive among you. . . . [D]o not cry for me, do not be sad for me, but be happy and smile. I am now planted in the earth of the South irrigating and quenching her with my blood and my love for her.[14]

The second statement was made by the "Islamic Jihad"—a name clearly intended to evoke religious commitment—shortly after the bombing of the Marine barracks in Beirut. However, it, too, stresses nationalist resistance to a foreign occupation and seeks to encourage other Lebanese to follow in this path:

> We have carried out this operation against the fortresses of reactionary imperialism to prove to the world that their naval and artillery firepower does not frighten us. We are soldiers of God and we are fond of death. We are neither Iranians nor Syrians nor Palestinians. We are Lebanese Muslims who follow the principles of the Koran.[15]

These "martyr" statements did not fall on deaf ears in the Shia community. The trajectory of the number of suicide terrorists increased markedly over time—from one in 1982, to eight in 1983 and 1984, to thirty-two in 1985 and 1986. Many Lebanese suicide terrorists were walk-ins, who had little connection to terrorism before they carried out their suicide missions. All claimed in their final statements to have been volunteers and none of the forty-one made an effort to surrender to Israeli forces rather than carry out their mission.

There is also important evidence of public support for martyrdom. We cannot provide precise figures, since no opinion surveys of the Shia community were taken during the period. However, there were highly visible signs of pervasive public support for and commemoration of "martyrs" who killed themselves to kill American, French, and Israeli troops. Major city streets were named in honor of these fallen heroes; their pictures were widely used as positive symbols in political discourse; and large public rallies were commonly held in their honor on annual public holidays and at other special events.[16] Such public commemoration continues to this day. Among the best sources of information about Hezbollah leaders' thinking are the speeches given on "Martyrs' Day," held annually on November 11 to venerate Hezbollah's first suicide attacker, who killed himself in an attack on an Israeli military post on that date in 1982.

Even in the absense of opinion polls, these facts suggest that Lebanon's suicide terrorists are probably widely respected as "martyrs" by their local community. By contrast, there are no visible signs of public disaffection with Hezbollah's suicide operations. No community leader or movement condemned Lebanon's suicide attackers, either at the time or since.

The Importance of Religious Difference

Foreign occupation was a necessary condition for the Shia community to support national resistance at all. However, the politics of religious difference likely played a key enabling role, functioning as an important reason why Israel's occupation in particular led to public support for suicide terrorism to end it. Specifically, the Jewish-Muslim divide enabled Lebanese resistance leaders to portray Israel's occupation as an existential threat to the Shia community and thereby persuade large segments to re-define suicide and murder as legitimate, even commendable, acts of martyrdom for the common good. Under the conditions of occupation, a religious difference tends to harden the boundary between "us" and "them," amplifying tendencies to view the conflict in zero-sum terms, to demonize the enemy, and to legitimate those who sacrifice to kill the enemy as martyrs.

Depicting Israel as a Religious Threat. To create the momentum for a protracted campaign, Hezbollah and other Shia leaders encouraged public support for suicide operations. These leaders gave literally hundreds of public speeches and interviews explaining the need for what they call "self-martyr" operations; many of these texts have been translated into English. The main purpose of this public discourse was to persuade the local community at large to accept that acts normally qualifying as suicide and murder should be redefined as martyrdom and legitimate self-defense, and to encourage some members to volunteer for these operations.

Although Islam plays a role, the main theme of the overwhelming number of these speeches is that Israel is motivated by its own religion to seize Lebanon's resources for use by Jews at the expense of the Muslim inhabitants. From Hezbollah's perspective, the state of Israel is a religious monolith, characterized above all by a uniform commitment to Judaism and a doctrine of territorial expansion with biblical justification. Although Israelis see themselves as distinguished by debate and division, Hezbollah defines Israel as the one state in the world that grants citizenship strictly on the basis of religious membership and so as based on inherently exclusionary political principles. Hezbollah refers to Israel as a "Zionist" or "Jewish" entity, never as a secular state tolerant of all religions.[17]

"Greater Israel." In Hezbollah's view, Israel's occupation of southern Lebanon was merely the first step in using Lebanon's resources in the service of "Greater Israel." This characterization of Israel's game plan is at the heart of Hezbollah's famous "Open Letter" of February 1985. The "Open Letter" was the official mission statement describing the purposes of the organization:

> Israel . . . poses a great danger to our future generations and to the destiny of our nation, especially since it embraces a settlement-oriented and expansionist idea . . . to build Greater Israel, from the Euphrates to the Nile. . . . [W]e view the recently voiced Jewish call for settlement in south Lebanon . . . as part of the expansionist scheme.[18]

Hezbollah leaders describe the United States and the West in general as "European Christendom," and so as staunch allies in support of Israel's religious mission. Sayyid Muhammad Husayn Fadlallah, often called Hezbollah's spiritual leader, said:

> We believe there is no difference between the United States and Israel; the latter is a mere extension of the former. The United States is ready to fight

the whole world to defend Israel's existence and security. The two countries are working in complete harmony, and the United States is certainly not inclined to exert pressure on Israel.[19]

Although the group appealed to history, Hezbollah's main evidence for its analysis was simply the course of recent events. In 1982, Israel remained in Lebanon after accomplishing its main objective of ousting the PLO, was subsequently joined by the United States and other European forces, and was already settling Jews on the West Bank and Gaza. From there, it was a short leap for Hezbollah to assert that Israel's main purpose in Lebanon was to seize control of the Litani River and to uproot local Shia from the land so as to resettle Jews there in the future.[20]

Demonization. Hezbollah's repeated reference to Israel as espousing a different religion also served as the basis for portraying the Israeli state and society as evil incarnate, based on a moral code fundamentally different and inferior to that of the Shia community. Israelis are not simply painted as occupiers or settlers, but as barbarians willing to take the lives of Muslims without hesitation. Hezbollah's "Open Letter" says:

> America, its Atlantic Pact allies, and the Zionist entity . . . invaded our country, destroyed our villages, slit the throats of our children, violated our sanctuaries, and . . . committed the worst massacres against our nation. . . . In a single night the Israelis and the Phalangists executed thousands of our sons, women and children in Sabra and Shatila . . . a massacre perpetrated with the tacit accord of America's European allies.[21]

Demonization encouraged community support not only for great self-sacrifice, but also for acts that break normal community norms against killing innocents. From Hezbollah's perspective, atrocities committed by Israeli forces during the occupation are condoned by Israeli society as a whole, since Israeli citizens pay taxes and provide other support to the occupation forces.[22] By breaking down the distinction between Israeli military forces and society, Hezbollah also broke down the distinction between combatants and non-combatants, essentially holding all Israelis accountable for immoral acts committed in Lebanon. In this way, acts that would normally count as murder—terrorism against innocents—were redefined as legitimate self-defense for the common good.

Legitimacy for Martyrdom. The religious schism also facilitated Hezbollah's claims that the community should accord the status of martyr to those who committed suicide attacks against Israeli and Western targets. Islam has a long history of martyrdom, defined as dying at the hands of a non-Muslim, and many disputes with Jews and Christians. For Hezbollah, the main issue in qualifying its suicide attackers as "martyrs" was overcoming the Islamic injunction against voluntary death. What is striking is that the group achieved this goal without issuing a single official religious edict (*fatwa*) sanctioning suicide as a method of attack but relied simply on public discourse to make the case for martyrdom.

Hezbollah leaders argued that "self-martyrdom" operations qualified as part of religious conflict on the basis of their instrumental value in ending the occupation, not by the individual's desire for personal salvation or as an end in themselves. Fadlallah made the fullest public case. First, he justified these operations on the ground of the imbalance of power between the Shia and their enemies: "If an oppressed people does not have the means to confront the United States and Israel with the weapons in which they are superior, then they [can use] unfamiliar weapons." Second, he dismissed the special nature of a voluntary suicide attack: "Muslims believe that you struggle by transforming yourself into a living bomb like you struggle with a gun in your hand. There is no difference between dying with a gun in your hand or exploding yourself." Third, the attacks must provide significant leverage to defeat the enemy: "The self-martyring operation is not permitted unless it can convulse the enemy"; otherwise, suicide attacks would be "mere acts of self-martyrdom," which are forbidden. Only if these conditions are met, an individual's "sacrifice can be part of jihad, a religious war" against an enemy of a different religion.[23]

The suicide attackers themselves bolstered their claims to the status of "martyr." Many, even those with secular backgrounds, stressed in their final testimonials that they were motivated by the religious identity of the enemy. Wajdi Sayegh, a nineteen-year-old member of the Syrian Socialist National Party, said "we have no enemy who fights us to take our rights and homeland but the Jews"; Sana Youssef Mhaydali, a sixteen-year-old member of the Communist Party who was the first female suicide bomber, explained her motive as "to liberate the south from the occupation of the Zionist terrorists . . . who are not like us"; Bilal Fahs, an eighteen-year-old member of the Communist Party, spoke about "liberation from occupation as Jihad and obligation"; and Khaled al-Azrak, a twenty-year-old member of the SSNP, said his "main motive" was "to liberate this land from the Jewish enemies."[24]

SUICIDE TERRORISM IN SRI LANKA

The Liberation Tigers of Tamil Eelam are the world's leading suicide terrorist organization. From 1987 to 2001, the Tamil Tigers carried out 76 suicide terrorist attacks involving a total of 143 male and female Black Tigers—many operating in teams—against a variety of political, economic, and military targets in Sri Lanka. These figures represent more suicide attacks than any other terrorist organization and more total suicide attackers than from all of the Palestinian suicide terrorist groups combined. The Black Tigers achieved an extraordinary degree of tactical success, killing a total of 901 people, including two world leaders—India's former prime minister Rajiv Gandhi in 1991 and Sri Lanka's President Ranasinghe Premadasa in 1993. The Tamil Tigers also achieved significant coercive success, twice compelling the Sri Lankan government to engage in serious sovereignty negotiations.

From the standpoint of explaining suicide terrorism, what matters is not the exact date that the Tamil Tigers shifted from ordinary armed resistance organized around guerrilla warfare tactics to the use of suicide operations. The key question is what enabled the Tigers to conduct protracted campaigns of suicide terrorism involving a stream of many individuals who willingly accepted certain death in order to carry out their missions.

Two main explanations have been offered thus far. The first argues that local competition between the LTTE and other Tamil guerrilla groups encouraged the LTTE to use the extreme tactic of suicide to distinguish itself from its rivals.[25] The second explanation stresses the "cult-like" behavior of the group in which the Tamil Tigers separate their fighters from the general population and brainwash recruits to follow the leader's orders without conscious choice.[26]

The principal implication of both these arguments is that the sources of the Tamil Tigers' use of suicide terrorism lay in the internal dynamics of the group and have little to do with the political grievances of Tamil society or the relationship between the Tamils and their Sinhalese opponents. Yet, neither explanation is consistent with the facts. The argument that rivalry with other Tamil guerrilla groups accounts for the LTTE's use of suicide terrorism fails because the Tigers had already eliminated all of their major rivals and many of their smaller ones by 1987 and so had already become the preeminent political and military power within the Tamil community before the onset of suicide operations.[27] The argument that the LTTE is a cult isolated from Tamil society is also off the mark. Tiger recruits scoff at the idea that coercion determines their willingness to make extreme self-sacrifice. As a woman cadre in the political and intelligence wing of the LTTE said:

> It's very hard to force anyone to make this kind of sacrifice. A lot of us know what we are getting into by joining. We've heard it from friends and relatives who have joined. . . . And besides, if we forced people to join the LTTE and fight the Sri Lankan army, how could we possibly trust our own cadres to carry out a mission in battle?[28]

As we see below, evidence shows that the Tamil community does support martyrdom as a means of national resistance.

I argue that the logic of religious difference provides a more compelling explanation. Fear of religious persecution, not internal dynamics within Tamil society or the LTTE, largely accounts for the pervasive use of suicide terrorism in this case. In Sri Lanka, the Sinhalese majority are predominately Buddhists, while the Tamil minority is overwhelmingly Hindu and Christian. Especially after the new Sinhalese constitution took effect in 1972, the Tamil community has increasingly come to believe that the Sinhalese government is deliberately pursuing policies that seek to stamp out core attributes of Tamil national identity, and that Buddhist religious goals are the driving force behind this program. In response, the Tamil community has supported higher and higher intensities of armed resistance and individual self-sacrifice in order to preserve the ability to perpetuate its national heritage without interference from others. Suicide attack became the signature weapon of the LTTE's national liberation strategy when all other means had failed.

Sinhalese Occupation of the Tamil Homeland
Sri Lanka is an island-state off the coast of India. In 1990, it had a population of about 17.2 million people, composed of 74 percent Sinhalese (predominately Buddhists), 18 percent Tamils (mainly Hindu), and 8 percent other (mostly Muslims). The Tamil minority are concentrated in the northern and eastern regions and call this land "Tamil Eelam," the term for their

ancestral homeland since Hindus first began migrating to the island in the sixth century B.C.[29]

Sri Lanka first experienced suicide terrorism in July 1987, in the form of a suicide truck bombing carried out by the LTTE against a Sinhalese military barracks and modeled after the spectacular suicide bombing of the U.S. Marine barracks in Lebanon in 1983. Before this point, there were no suicide attacks in Sri Lanka, even though the Tamil community had been politically and economically disadvantaged since the island achieved independence from British colonial rule in 1948 and became a functioning democracy governed by the Sinhalese majority. Indeed, before the early 1970s, Tamil militancy hardly existed.[30]

In the 1970s, Sinhalese and Tamil relations changed markedly. In 1972, the Sinhalese government adopted a new constitution that accorded Buddhism "the foremost place" and directed the state "to protect and foster" it. In the late 1970s, the government started a series of large agricultural projects that asserted new, uncontested rights to Tamil lands. By 1989, these projects had resettled 163,000 people (92 percent Sinhalese and 7 percent Muslim) on Tamil lands; in other words, the settlers constituted a group roughly 7 percent the size of the Tamil population living in the north and eastern regions of the country (about 3 million people).[31] A defining moment for Tamil perceptions of the consequences of Sinhalese dominance occurred in July 1983. Following an LTTE assault on a Sri Lankan army camp that killed thirteen soldiers, a major riot broke out against Tamils living in Colombo. Hundreds of Tamils were killed, more than 100,000 fled the city, and—perhaps the most significant event—the Sri Lankan government waited days before calling in security forces to restore order.[32]

The rise of Tamil militancy parallels the increasing Sinhalese encroachment on Tamil culture and resources. Numerous Tamil militant organizations sprang up during the debate over the new constitution. The LTTE started as a handful of mainly college students in 1972 and formally took the name in 1976, but was only one of dozens of new Tamil guerrilla groups.[33] Following the 1983 riots, the LTTE and a small number of other Tamil militant groups dramatically surged in size. The LTTE grew from fewer than fifty armed militants engaged in minor acts of violence to an estimated 3,000 guerrillas who began conducting large-scale military operations against a variety of Sri Lankan military and political targets. At the same time, the LTTE solidified its dominance as the main Tamil insurgent organization, effectively coopting or destroying its Tamil rivals by late

1986. In response, the Sri Lankan army began operations to root out the Tamil militants, culminating in a major offensive against armed insurgents against the LTTE's headquarters in the main Tamil town, Jaffna, in the first half of 1987.[34]

The Tamil Tigers' first suicide attack was carried out by a special unit devoted to this purpose called the "Black Tigers." This suicide attack was part of the effort to stymie the Sri Lankan military offensive against Jaffna. On July 5, 1987, a Black Tiger named Captain Miller drove a truck full of explosives into the Sri Lankan army camp in Vadamarachi and exploded the vehicle and himself near a military barracks, reportedly killing seventy Sri Lankan soldiers. The inspiration for the attack came from Lebanon. In the late 1970s and early 1980s, the Tamil Tigers had sent fighters to train with the PLO and other terrorist groups in Lebanon's Bekaa Valley. Prabhakaran was especially impressed by Hezbollah's 1983 suicide attack against the U.S. Marine barracks in Lebanon and concluded that the same tactic could be employed to compel the Sri Lankan government to accept Tamil independence.[35]

Shortly thereafter, however, an external event changed the conflict. In August 1987, India sent troops to Sri Lanka in an effort to broker a peace agreement called the Indo–Sri Lankan Accord. Although initially supported by the Tamils, including the LTTE, the agreement collapsed when the Tamil militants refused to surrender their weapons prior to the implementation of a popular referendum over the ultimate status of the Tamil regions of the island. From October 1987 to April 1990, the Indian army sought to disarm the LTTE by force, but ultimately abandoned the mission when both the LTTE and Sri Lankan government joined forces against it. Although the LTTE fought the Indian army tenaciously, it did not launch a single suicide attack during the period of Indian occupation.[36] From 1990 onward, the civil war between the Tamils and Sri Lankan government resumed with more force than ever.

Community Support for Martyrdom

The Tamil Tigers' protracted and extensive use of suicide terrorism probably could not have occurred without sustained popular support from the Tamil community. Indeed, the LTTE's reliance on suicide tactics goes far beyond the 143 Black Tigers who can be classified as suicide attackers according to our narrow definition (individuals who killed themselves while trying to kill others). Another 100 or so Black Tigers also carried out suicide missions in which they died at the hands of Sinhalese troops but made no effort to escape and are recorded in the group's commemorative albums as individuals who knew they would surely die during the mission. Moreover, the Tamil Tigers require something no other major militant group has ever required: that every member, male and female, wear a vial of cyanide, refreshed every few months, on a leather thong around the neck. At the moment when capture appears inevitable, a Tamil Tiger is obligated to bite down on the vial. The shards of glass lacerate the gums and send the deadly poison directly into the bloodstream, causing death in about two minutes. Over the past two decades, more than 600 Tamil Tigers have committed suicide in this way. Only a few have ever been captured alive, many having their stomachs pumped before the poison took effect.[37]

Expectation of community support is a key reason so many individuals are willing to commit suicide for the Tamil Tigers. Those who carried out suicide attacks for the LTTE attached great importance to how the community would interpret and remember their actions. Prior to their missions, the Black Tigers keep their identity a closely guarded secret so as to avoid providing the Sinhalese with useful intelligence. After their missions, however, their identities are revealed in highly public displays of commemoration, their stories are published in Tamil newspapers and in special commemorative albums circulated by the organization, and the individuals themselves take steps, even during their actual missions, to ensure their identity will be publicized. Black Tigers routinely carry on their missions a laminated identity card with their picture, name, and designation as a Black Tiger; the information is often written in English and Sinhalese as well as Tamil. The card reads: "I am filled with a huge explosive. If my journey is blocked I will explode it. Let me go."[38] This may help their mission, but it almost guarantees identification and publicity afterward.

The importance LTTE cadres attach to community support for martyrdom is also evident in public interviews. As Nandini, a female LTTE fighter, said in 1995:

As Black Tigers, they are a physical embodiment of self-determination and liberation. They employ their lives as missiles armed with the kind of determination and purpose that is unmatched by any conventional weapon that the Sinhala forces may deploy. There lies the strength and honor of our Black Tigers.

Nandini went on to explain her reasons for accepting as beneficial for the community the practice of choosing death over capture:

> If I am captured and I give up ten names of people in the movement, they'll capture and torture those ten to get a hundred names, and after capturing a hundred people they can capture a thousand people, and so on. In this way, a movement can be destroyed. So if you ask me why I should give up my own life [by taking cyanide]? At the time when we are captured alive by the enemy, when I die, as a single individual who gives up her life, I have the capacity to protect not only the lives of several other people but I am also able to protect the movement and the liberation struggle as a whole.[39]

The leaders of the Tamil Tigers also attach great importance to establishing individuals who commit suicide attacks as martyrs in the eyes of the Tamil community. In numerous speeches, Black Tiger operations are centrally linked to the common welfare. Prabhakaran, the leader of the group, is famous for saying, "Tamil Eelam can be achieved in 100 years. But if we conduct Black Tiger operations, we can shorten the suffering of the people and achieve Tamil Eelam in a shorter period of time."[40] Like other suicide terrorist groups, LTTE seeks to glorify suicide attackers immediately after their death by displaying their pictures on posters and holding public processions with pomp and pageantry (singing is common) in their honor. Since 1990, the LTTE has held annual public ceremonies to venerate its "martyrs." In Jaffna, July 5 is called "Heroes' Day" in memory of the first Black Tiger attack. On this day, Prabhakaran gives a speech commemorating the Black Tigers and others who have made especially heroic sacrifices for the cause of Tamil independence. In 1993, he said: "Our martyrs die in the arena of struggle with the intense passion for the freedom of their people, for the liberation of their homeland and therefore the death of every martyr constitutes a brave act of enunciation of freedom."

However, the LTTE goes further. Black Tigers often have their own monuments, built near public spaces in Tamil towns. The largest is the life-size statue of Captain Miller that sits near a well-traveled intersection in Jaffna. Others are distinctive conical structures with memorabilia on a platform, sometimes surrounded by a small pond or a park or fence to provide space for the community to lay flowers in honor of the person.[41]

These displays are conscious efforts to cultivate broad public support for martyrdom. Peter Schalk, who has closely studied the LTTE, observes:

A total mobilization of people and institutions for the bureaucratization and institutionalization of Tamil nationalism is evident in the organization of hero veneration . . . an attempt to fortify and enforce resistance on an ideological level. . . . [V]eneration of heroes promotes the idea of representational dying for civilians and . . . is mainly directed towards the future of armed resistance against the enemy.[42]

Beyond participation in public ceremonies, there is evidence of broad Tamil public support for martyrdom in the context of national resistance. Numerous journalists and scholars who have visited Jaffna report that the local population supports suicide operations and commemorates LTTE martyrs. As A. J. V. Chandrakanthan reports, "The suicide squads of the LTTE . . . I have seen hundreds of shrines erected in Jaffna by the friends and relatives of those LTTE [suicide] cadres."[43]

Further, although we do not have surveys on suicide terrorism per se, we do have surveys on Tamil support for armed resistance and we know that the LTTE's suicide terrorism was common knowledge among the Tamil population. Indeed, the LTTE itself constituted a significant fraction of the total Tamil population, numbering 10,000–15,000 during the 1990s, or some 1 in 100 fighting-age Tamils. Hence, popular support for armed resistance should be read as sympathy, if not active support, for suicide operations.

Surveys show that Tamil community support for the LTTE remained strong long after the Tigers began to use suicide operations, with a near majority supporting the use of armed force for independence even after more than a decade of protracted suicide operations.

TABLE 17. Tamil Support for National Resistance

	Favor	Oppose
Independence, 1986	72%	10%
Armed force, 2002	47%	52%

Sources: Ambalavanar Sivarajah, *Politics of Tamil Nationalism in Sri Lanka* (New Delhi: South Asian Publishers, 1996), pp. 159–58; Mia Bloom, *Dying to Kill* (New York: Columbia University Press, 2005), Chapter 3.

Overall, these facts suggest that Tiger suicide terrorists are respected as martyrs by their local community. By contrast, there are no visible signs of

public disaffection with the Black Tigers or any other Tigers who voluntarily died for the cause. Tamil leaders have publically disagreed with the
leader of the LTTE, but none have ever condemned Tiger suicide attackers.

The Importance of Religious Difference

Sinhalese occupation of Tamil lands created the core necessary condition
for the Tamil community to support national resistance at all. However,
the politics of religious difference helped to intensify the resistance and to
encourage public support for suicide terrorism. Specifically, the Sinhalese-
Hindu divide enabled Tamil resistance leaders to portray the Sinhalese
military presence in the Tamil homeland as an existential threat to the
Tamil community and thereby persuade large segments to redefine suicide and murder as legitimate—even commendable—acts of martyrdom
for the common good.

Depicting the Sinhalese State as a Religious Threat. Although race, language, and Sinhalese policies are important, the most prominent factor driving Tamil community support for individual self-sacrifice is fear of Buddhist
extremism. Especially since the establishment of the new state constitution
in 1972, prominent Tamil leaders have consistently claimed that the Sinhalese government is motivated by the goal to extend Buddhism into the
Tamil regions of the island, a religious game plan that justifies treating the
Tamil people harshly, which in turn justifies extreme self-sacrifice as necessary to meet the threat.[44] The link between Sinhala Buddhism and the government's policies toward the Tamil community is commonly made in
speeches by Tamil leaders and even by independent scholars.

At an international conference on the Tamil struggle in 1988, a variety
of Tamil leaders spoke about the origins, underlying motivations, and
basic aims of the growing Sinhalese repression of the Tamil community.
Brian Senewiratne spoke on "Sinhala-Buddhist Chauvinism and the Bud-
dist Clergy":

> There is a deep-rooted perception among the Sinhalese that Sri Lanka is a
> Sinhalese-Buddhist country. . . . The strongest advocates of this Sinhala
> chauvinism have been sections of the Buddhist clergy. These hardline ex-
> tremists who can markedly influence the Sinhalese-Buddhist majority have
> collaborated with the opposition of whatever political hue to prevent suc-
> cessive Sri Lankan governments from implementing any realistic devolu-

tion of power to the Tamils. . . . Sinhalese-Buddhist ethno-religious chauvinism and its strongest advocates, the Buddhist clergy, are the most important factors that prevent a solution to the Sri Lankan ethnic conflict.[45]

Sarath Amunugama explained the religious origins of the Sinhalese Buddhist claims to the Tamil homeland:

According to Sinhala-Buddhist tradition . . . Sri Lanka is the island consecrated by the Buddha himself as the land in which his teachings would flourish. . . . [I]t was believed that the Buddha had visited the island thrice. One of these visits was to Nagadipa in the northernmost part of the Jaffna peninsula. The north was thereby firmly established within the sacred geography of Buddhists.[46]

Other speakers said that the view of the Sinhalese settlers as "alien" was due specifically to the religious schism between the communities.[47]

Western scholars also attribute the main source of the Sri Lankan conflict to Sinhala Buddhism. David Little of Harvard writes:

In reaction to colonialism and emerging nationalism, the factors of race, language, and historical origins gained prominence as marks for distinguishing the Sinhala people from Tamils and others. But it was the religious factor—the sacred legends synthesized by Buddhist monks into the *Mahavamsa* and the other chronicles—that gave special authority to the Sinhala as a "chosen people" and thereby entitled them, from their point of view, to preserve and protect the special status, the proper preeminence, of the Sinhala Buddhist tradition in Sri Lankan life.[48]

In Tamil discourse, the main evidence of Sinhalese religious motives comes from recent speeches by prominent Sinhalese political leaders. One Sinhalese cabinet minister proclaimed in 1980:

Sri Lanka is inherently and rightfully a Sinhalese state. . . . This must be accepted as a fact and not a matter of opinion to be debated. By attempting to challenge this premise, Tamils have brought the wrath of the Sinhalese on their own heads; they have themselves to blame.[49]

Another Sinhalese leader said in 1981:

The link between the Sinhala race and Buddhism is so close and inseparable. . . . There is no Buddhism without the Sinhalese and no Sinhalese without Buddhism. . . . [T]he culture of the Sinhalese is Buddhist culture . . . the flag of the Sinhalese is the Sinhalese Buddhist flag.[50]

Sinhalese expressions of a commitment to Buddhism to the exclusion of Tamil culture continued through the 1990s.[51]

Zero-Sum Conflict. Tamil discourse portrays the Sri Lankan government policy as based on a grand plan to increase Sinhalese control over Tamil resources as a means to eradicate the core elements of Tamil society. One LTTE publication states:

Successive Sri Lankan governments aimed at the annihilation of the national entity of the Tamils. . . .This oppression was not simply an expression of racial prejudice, but a well-calculated genocidal plan aimed at the gradual and systematic destruction of the essential foundations of national community. . . . The most vicious form of oppression calculated to destroy the national identity of the Tamils was the state aided aggressive colonization which began soon after "independence" and has now swallowed nearly three thousand square miles of Tamil Eelam. This planned occupation of Tamil lands by hundreds of thousands of Sinhala people aided and abetted by the state was aimed to annihilate the geographical entity of the Tamil nation.[52]

In his "Heroes' Day" speeches, Prabhakaran routinely emphasizes the zero-sum nature of the conflict:

The strategic objective of [Sinhala chauvinism] is to annihilate the national identity of the Tamils by destroying their life and property and their land and resources.[53]

Demonization. Tamil discourse portrays Sinhala Buddhism as a religion with a moral code fundamentally different from the Tamils'. The discourse explicitly claims that this religious difference is the underlying reason why Tamils should expect harsh treatment at the hands of the Sinhalese. Implicit, of course, in this line of argument is a none-too-subtle message that Tamils should feel justified in treating the Sinhalese harshly in return. One recent Tamil history reads:

To a Sinhalese, the word "Jathiya" means the Sinhala Nation [which] claims as its right, the domination of the whole island. This concept also aspires to establish a Sinhala Buddhist country over the whole island and the use of the Sinhalese language and Buddhist religion in all walks of state life. . . . The subscription of [the] average Sinhalese to the idea of exclusivity relieves him from any compulsion and the need to seek out and subscribe to a value system that accommodates the mutual rights of all people in a federally structured or any other type of polity. This situation is no different from the situation that prevailed in Nazi Germany in the early thirties, and the term "Jathiya" shares a common experience with the German word Volk during the time of the Nazis.[54]

Prabhakaran rarely passes up an opportunity to emphasize the moral differences that drive the brutal treatment of Tamils by the Sinhalese:

The Sinhala-Buddhist racist ideology, with its roots buried in Sri Lankan Buddhism, has perversely spread throughout the Sinhala social formation and penetrated deep into the Sinhala political system. . . . [T]he culprit behind the tyrannical oppression of the Tamils is Sinhala Buddhist racism.[55]

Legitimation of Martyrdom. The LTTE is a secular group that disavows Tamil religious motivations as a driving force behind national resistance. This makes it all the more important to recognize how much even this secular group depends on religious notions of martyrdom to mobilize public support for suicide operations.

Scholars have gone to Jaffna to study how the LTTE constructs the culture of martyrdom. While these studies confirm that the Tamil Tigers see themselves as "beyond religion," they also explain that the LTTE's notions of martyrdom are deeply rooted in traditional religion of the Tamil community. A. J. V. Chandrakanthan writes about the shrines to the Black Tigers:

. . . Heroic death founded with the fire of Tamil nationalism has given birth to a new set of terms, almost all derived from the ancient Tamil religion of Saivism; indeed within the North and East, Tamil nationalism has the appeal of a new religious movement. . . . People bedeck these "shrines of Martyrs" with offerings of flowers and oil as they normally do in their temples or holy shrines.[56]

Peter Schalk, a prolific scholar of LTTE martyrdom, writes:

> The self-understanding of the LTTE is that it is beyond religion. . . . [How-
> ever], the LTTE selectively revives religious concepts relating to a martyr
> cult. . . . The LTTE sacralizes its aim, *cutantiram* ("independence"), by de-
> claring it to be a *punita ilatciyam* ("holy aim"). . . . They lean towards reli-
> gion because religion has what they lack, tradition.[57]

Schalk goes on to explain that the LTTE word *tiyakam* ("abandonment") for "martyrdom" is rooted in the Hindu religion and means "the
voluntary abandonment of life in the very act of taking life, in the act of
killing . . . a rather specific Indian form of martyrdom [with] roots in the
last section of the Bhagavadgita."[58]

This is not to say that Hindu martyrdom is mainly militaristic. In fact,
mainstream understandings of Hindu martyrdom portray individuals who
qualify for this status as personally nonviolent. Like most religions, however, Hinduism contains examples of violent martyrs who lie on the margins of its religious history, similar to the Christians who fought in the
Crusades, and whose violence received religious sanction from the Pope.
Under the pressure of external threat, these marginal readings can be
brought into the mainstream of discourse by leaders searching for ways to
motivate local populations to support their activities.

How effective is Tamil martyrdom discourse? We do not have much independently corroborated information about the motivations of individual
LTTE fighters. However, what we do know is consistent with the logic of
religious difference as a central cause of the extraordinary willingness of
the Black Tigers to kill themselves to accomplish their missions. According to a major general of the Sinhalese army:

> A young female suicide cadre apprehended by the Security Forces revealed
> some fascinating details. Her knowledge was that "Eelam" was a country
> with a Tamil majority and a Sinhala minority. Sinhala people were carrying
> out terrorist attacks on Tamils. She had been shown the Nallur Kandasamy
> Temple in Jaffna and told that the Sinhala terrorists are planning to destroy
> the temple and construct a Buddhist temple instead.[59]

In sum, there is good evidence that religious difference is a central
component of the LTTE's concept of self-sacrifice for national resistance
and that it plays a key role in Tamil popular support for suicide terrorism.

That suicide terrorism did not occur during the years of Indian occupation, and that the element of religious difference was markedly absent from resistance discourse during this period, adds further weight to this finding.

The Absence of Suicide Terrorism During India's Occupation

The Indian intervention provides an important opportunity for within-case comparison. Although the Tamil Tigers carried out suicide terrorist attacks against their Sinhalese opponents both before and after the Indian intervention, there were no suicide attacks against the Indian troops by the LTTE or any other group. Why not? As I argue, the main reason is not a difference in the severity of the occupation or in the LTTE's confidence in defeating It, but the absence of a religious difference between the foreign occupier and local occupied community. While the Tamils (Hindu) fear that the Sinhalese (Buddhists) are seeking to implement a religiously motivated program to transform the core characteristics of their national community, the Tamils (Hindu) did not view the Indian army (Hindu) as a religiously motivated occupier seeking to transform their society—and this is the most likely reason why one case led to suicide terrorism but the other did not.

Although beginning as a small peacekeeping mission, the Indian military presence in Sri Lanka soon escalated into a broad operation to occupy most of the territory that the Tamils considered their homeland. The Indian forces inflicted significant civilian casualties in an effort to replace the leaders of the Tamil resistance with more moderate leadership. Following the Indo–Sri Lankan Accord in July 1987, the Indian government originally sent about 7,000 troops to the island for the purpose of collecting weapons from the 3,000 or so Tamil Tigers and other militants, who initially seemed to accept voluntary disarmament as a precursor to a political settlement. The Tamil militants, however, refused to surrender their weapons. In October, the Indian army launched its first major offensive to capture the LTTE stronghold of Jaffna.

By March 1988, the number of the Indian troops deployed to Sri Lanka had increased to more than 100,000, nearly three times the size of the entire Sinhalese army of 35,000. The mission of the Indian forces was to occupy and destroy LTTE strongholds throughout Sri Lanka, which in practice meant saturating the population centers across the Jaffna peninsula and other Tamil regions of the island in order to confine the LTTE to the jungles. As an Indian general leading the operations said, "Our strategy is to continuously occupy the LTTE bases and hide-outs, to keep them in a state of continuous disruption and disorganization."[60]

Especially during the first year, the vast size of the India military presence was a source of extreme pessimism among Tamil militants. In comparing the LTTE's military prospects against the Indian and Sinhalese forces, one Tamil militant wrote in April 1988: "IPKF [the Indian Peacekeeping Force] is more dangerous than the Sri Lankan Army. Our LTTE are capable enough, brave enough, potent enough to defeat the Sri Lankan Army, but not the Indian Army."[61]

At the same time, the Indian army inflicted significant casualties among Tamil civilians. To minimize its own casualties, the Indian army made extensive use of air power and heavy artillery, even in populated areas. Although estimates vary, Indian forces killed somewhere between 3,000 and 4,000 Tamil civilians, depopulated large areas, and raped untold numbers of Tamil women. These numbers represent a level of civilian damage at least as great as during the worst periods of fighting between the Tamils and Sri Lankan forces.[62] One observer concluded that the Indian army "proved to be much more heavy-handed in their treatment of the people than their Sri Lankan counterparts."[63] Civilian casualties also became a source of bitter hatred. One LTTE statement read:

> What horrified the Tamil people was the brutal and ruthless manner the Indian troops conducted the military campaign in callous disregard to human life and property. . . . Innocent civilians, including women and children were massacred in a most barbaric manner. Houses were destroyed, temples desecrated, and shops looted. The worst crime committed by the Indian troops was the rape of the Tamil women. Hundreds of Tamil women were raped brutally and most of them were done to death after sexual violence. This brutality deeply wounded the sentiments of the people and the hate for the Indian army became widespread. The IPKF received the motto as the Innocent People Killing Force.[64]

Indian occupation of the Tamil homeland failed to eradicate armed resistance. Although the Indian army controlled most of the Tamil population centers, the LTTE grew from 3,000 cadres in the summer of 1987 to more than 10,000 by the time the Indian forces abandoned the mission in early 1990. India's prolonged and extensive occupation of large parts of Sri Lanka effectively alienated the Sinhalese as well. A large fraction of the 1,155 Indian troops who died were killed by weapons provided to the

Tamil rebels by the government in Colombo following its decision in April 1989 to compel the Indian army to leave the island.[65]

Yet the Indian occupation did not elicit suicide attacks. The same LTTE that had carried out its first "Black Tiger" suicide operation against the Sinhalese in July 1987, and that would use such operations extensively against the Sinhalese in the 1990s, did not launch a single suicide attack against the Indian army.

The main reason appears to be the absence of religious difference between the Hindu Indian army and the mainly Hindu Tamil population.[66] At the same time that fighting between the Indian forces and Tamil militants was at its peak, even the most militant Tamils continued to stress the inherent ability of the Indians and the Tamils to work together toward a mutual understanding that would not challenge the core goals of either.

In October 1987, just after India's initial offensive against Jaffna, the LTTE stated:

> Neither the Tamil people nor the LTTE anticipated, even in their wildest dreams, a war with India. For the Tamils, India was their protector, guardian and saviour and the presence of the Indian troops was looked upon as an instrument of peace and love. For the LTTE, India was their promoter, a friendly power who provided sanctuary and armed assistance, an ally who respected its role in the liberation war and recognized its political importance. Therefore, the Indian decision to launch a war against the LTTE shook the Tamil nation by surprise and anguish.[67]

In April 1988, the keynote speaker at a major international conference, who strongly condemned Sinhalese aggression against the Tamils, said this about the Indian sympathies with the Tamil cause reflected in the Indo–Sri Lankan Accord:

> There is a refreshingly frank admission that the Tamil community has a distinct cultural and linguistic identity. . . . This is followed by a critical confession that the northern and eastern provinces have been the historic home of the Tamil-speaking peoples. . . . Of course, IPKF excesses, if continued, may make them a hated horde.[68]

In April 1990, following the departure of India's troops from Sri Lanka, the leader of the LTTE, Prabhakaran, spoke passionately of his desire to reestablish good relations between Tamil and Indian peoples and leaders:

We are not a hostile force to the Indian government or to the Indian people. We opposed the misguided policies of the former Indian administration and resisted the military intervention. We do not want the government of India to interfere, politically or militarily, in our problems. The policy makers in Delhi should realize that the legitimate struggle of our oppressed people will not in any way contravene the geo-political concerns of India nor will it undermine the internal stability of the Indian state. We fervently hope that on the basis of this understanding the new Indian administration would make sincere efforts to restore friendly ties with our organization.[69]

Although the absence of religious difference appears to have mitigated the threat the Tamils perceived from the Indian intervention and so reduced the popular support for extreme self- sacrifice that would lead to a protracted campaign of suicide terrorism, one piece of evidence from this case does suggest that religious difference is not an inviolable threshold. On May 19, 1991, an LTTE suicide attacker assassinated Rajiv Gandhi while he was campaigning for re-election as India's prime minister on a platform of returning the Indian army to Sri Lanka. The Indian army did not return and the LTTE did not carry out any other instances of suicide attack against Indian targets.

THE SIKHS AFTER THE GOLDEN TEMPLE MASSACRE

On August 31, 1995, a suicide bomber leapt at Beant Singh, the chief minister of the state of Punjab in India, as he was leaving his car outside of the secretariat building in the capital city of Chandigarh. The attack killed Minister Singh, fifteen of his security guards and aides, and the bomber himself, identified as Dilawar Singh, a young man in his early twenties who had left a note to his accomplices saying that his act was "in memory of the martyrs." This was the first successful suicide attack associated with the Sikh terrorist group called the Babbar Khalsa International, which publicly claimed the attack as a step toward the goal of Sikh independence in Punjab. The episode presaged a number of attempted suicide attacks that continued through January 2000.[70]

This is a borderline case of a campaign of suicide terrorism. Although there was only one successful attack, the fact that the same Sikh terrorist group carried out at least one other possible (ambiguous) suicide attack and organized other follow-on suicide attacks that were foiled only as a result of early detection by local police indicates that the lone successful attack was part of a protracted effort. Moreover, if we look beyond our narrow definition of a suicide attack—the attacker kills himself in order to kill others—there are other instances of suicidal violence by Sikh militants precipitated by the virulent nationalism of the 1980s and 1990s. The key question is whether the relatively low level of suicide terrorism by Sikh militants is due to substantially the same causes as more ambitious suicide terrorist campaigns.

The answer is yes. Examination of this case shows that the rise of suicide terrorism among Sikh militants is part of a national liberation movement that failed to achieve its aims through ordinary means of armed resistance. During the 1980s, the Sikh community experienced increasing control by the Indian government, including the prominent presence of the Indian army in Punjab. Militants portrayed the situation as a military occupation that would lead to the transformation of the Sikh national identity by an alien power, and this produced widespread community support for armed resistance and self-sacrifice to return to the status quo ante. Precisely when ordinary armed resistance seemed to have failed, Sikh militants turned to suicide terrorism as a last resort. They appear to have abandoned that effort when it, too, failed to yield significant results for their cause.

Indian Military Presence in Sikh Homeland

The Sikh homeland is in the Punjab province of India, whose population in 1991 was approximately 20 million, 61 percent Sikh and 37 percent Hindu.[71] Punjab ranks among the top three of India's twenty-five states in per capita income and is the lowest in percentage of population below the poverty line. The Sikh religion was born in Punjab when its founder, Guru Nanak (1469–1539), abandoned Hinduism's polytheism, idol worship, and caste system in favor of a simple and strict monotheism that propounded the oneness of God, rejected the worship of idols, and emphasized the equality of all people. The distinctiveness of Sikhism grew during the hundred years of British colonial rule in Punjab (1849–1947). The Sikhs remained loyal during the mutiny of the Indian army in 1857, after which the British relied heavily on Sikh soldiers to maintain control in India, giving special economic privileges to the Sikhs and creating companies and regiments that consisted entirely of Sikhs.[72]

Although the Sikh nationalist party, the Akali Dal, often accused Hindus of discrimination, the Congress Party included a sufficient number of

Sikhs that the Akali Dal was unable to get more than 30 percent of the vote in the five elections for the Punjab legislative assembly from 1967 to 1980.[73] From 1981 to 1984, there were a number of incidents involving violence against Sikhs, which led to mass protests organized by the Akali Dal, which led to still more violence and agitation. In October 1983, following a wave of terrorist attacks against Hindus, Prime Minister Indira Gandhi dissolved the Punjab legislative assembly and placed the province under the direct control of the central government.

The Golden Temple Massacre and the Aftermath. On June 3, 1984, the Indian army launched "Operation Blue Star," a massive attack on the Golden Temple in Amritsar, the sacred heart of the Sikh religion and the most important symbol of the Sikh homeland. The purpose of the attack was to root out a group of Sikh militants led by Sant Jarnail Singh Bhindranwale. After a day-long battle, the Indian army successfully took control of the temple, killing Bhindranwale and at least 492 other Sikhs and destroying large parts of the main temple complex, including the Akal Takht, the principal shrine. Immediately after Operation Blue Star, the Indian army conducted Operation Woodrose, a broad effort to arrest militants. Woodrose involved forced entry into thousands of Sikh homes, most of whose inhabitants had committed no crime.

Operation Blue Star outraged large numbers of Sikhs. Within days of the attack, whole units of Sikh soldiers began to mutiny, creating the most serious crisis within the Indian army since independence. Numerous armed Sikh groups demanding an independent homeland emerged either newly formed or greatly invigorated, and widespread killings and guerrilla resistance followed. Overall, some 18,000 people died in Punjab as a result of communal violence from 1981 to 1993, the overwhelming majority in the years after the Golden Temple massacre.[74]

Although the Sikh fighters did not immediately use suicide terrorism in the strict sense, there were instances of suicidal violence directly related to the Golden Temple massacre. Bhindranwale was widely celebrated as a martyr who had voluntarily died in defense of the Sikh community. His portrait now hangs in Sikh homes alongside those of other famous Sikh martyrs, and the story of his last moments closely associates him with them. Sihk nationalists know the story of Baba Deep Singh, who is said to have carried his head, severed in battle against Afghans, to the Golden Temple as an act of superhuman devotion. As the Indian army advanced on his position, Bhindranwale is reported to have made no effort to escape, saying, "I am privileged to be able to give my head right here."

On October 31, 1984, Indira Gandhi was assassinated in reprisal for ordering the attack on the temple. The killers were two of her Sikh bodyguards, who were on what appears to have been a suicide mission. After shooting Gandhi, the two assassins did not try to escape but instead dropped their weapons, saying: "Whatever we had to do, we have done; now you can do what you like." They were then shot by other security personnel.[75]

Operation Blue Star and its aftermath led to a broad mobilization of the Sikh community that substantially increased the size and violence of the Sikh insurgency. Prior to this point, the largest pro-Khalistan (Sikh independence) demonstration was probably a rally in March 1981 involving 200 or so people. Although the Indian government made numerous small concessions to Sikh autonomy in the aftermath of the Golden Temple massacre—including withdrawal of the standing orders giving the Indian army special powers to act in Punjab; payment to relatives of innocents killed; rehabilitation of army deserters; and release of political detainees—ordinary armed resistance did not subside until the mid-1990s, and observers remain concerned that new acts of oppression could easily re-ignite nationalist sentiments.[76]

Community Support for Martyrdom

From 1984 through the 1990s, thousands of young men and hundreds of women joined the Sikh independence movement. This wave of recruits substantially increased the size of a number of militant organizations, including the Babbar Khalsa International, the Khalistan Commando Force, the Khalistan Liberation Force, the Bhindranwale Tiger Force of Khalistan, and radical factions of the All-India Sikh Students Federation, all of which had been only tiny groups on the margins of the Sikh community before this point. The reported number of those killed on both sides was 598 in 1986; the toll rose to 3,788 in 1990, 4,768 in 1991, and 3,629 in 1992, before dropping sharply.[77] After this point, the Sikh militants appear to have changed tactics, with the first possible (but unconfirmed) suicide attack in 1993, the first confirmed suicide attack in 1995, and at least two failed attempted suicide attacks in 1999 and 2000.

Although religion was a powerful recruiting tool, the desire for personal salvation is less important in Sikhism than the contribution an individual makes to the perpetuation of the Sikh community on earth. Unlike Islam and some other religions, Sikh martyrs do not look forward to an eternal life in paradise. The emphasis is on this world. G. S. Mansukhani, who wrote a popular primer on Sikhism, instructs that "those who know the art of true living also know that of true dying. True living is dying to the self, the ego, and living up to God. True dying is the privilege of the brave."[78]

Sikh nationalists expressly called for the community to accept the necessity of individual self-sacrifice in order to achieve the goal of political independence from India. Bhindranwale himself proclaimed, "When they say the Sikhs are not separate, we'll demand separate identity—even if it demands sacrifice."[79] Just months after the Golden Temple massacre, the well-known Sikh nationalist S. Dharam wrote:

> The only option that can meet the aspirations of the Sikhs and that would be acceptable to them under the existing state of affairs is to have an independent and sovereign State of their own so that they can live with self-respect and dignity and have freedom of faith to practice their religion without interference and domination by others. . . . The Sikhs may have to pay a heavy price for it; they may have to lay down the lives of thousands of brave young Sikhs. . . . It is any day better to fight and die a brave man's death than to be a slave of the communal and atrocious Hindu regime, which is already committing genocide of Sikhs and is bent upon exterminating them from the face of India.[80]

In 1985, the Khalistan activist Ganga Singh Dhillon gave a prominent speech in which he proclaimed:

> We are not just looking for a piece of land. We are looking for a territory where Sikhs can protect their women and children. Where a Sikh can become a master of his own destiny—where our religious shrines are not allowed to be run over by army tanks. You can call it an independent Punjab, a sovereign state, or Khalistan. What we are asking for is a homeland for the Sikh nation.[81]

Wassan Singh Zaffarwal, leader of the Khalistan Commando Force, said:

> The worst thing was that we couldn't bring to the attention of the world what had happened to us. There was no place for us to go. . . . Prior to June

1984, we used to talk about the Anandpur Sahib resolution because it contained the right to self-determination within India. After 1984 we needed our own independent home. The government that could kill hundreds, send thousands to prison, rape our women and generally humiliate our people, there could never be a compromise with them! We now needed an independent home for the Sikhs.[82]

These appeals for self-sacrifice to achieve self-determination for the Sikh nation met with substantial community support. Even before the actual attack on the Golden Temple, the fear that Indian security forces would defile the shrine by entering it in order to arrest Sikh militants provoked strong responses from the community. From March to May 1983, more than 115,000 Sikhs took an oath "to make any sacrifice in protection of the Golden Temple."[83]

Sikh militants believed they enjoyed broad community support for their actions, and especially for self-sacrifice to achieve independence for their community. Harpal Singh, a Sikh militant discussing the death of his brother, who had been killed by Indian troops, said:

They were proud. Because when a boy or girl dies for Khalistan, dies for our religion, we say it's a martyrdom. We celebrate martyrdom and honor those who martyred for the cause. . . . [H]undreds of people came to remember my brother. My whole village and my whole society honored him. You have to understand that even our enemies praise the way we sacrifice our lives if necessary. Someone who offers his life for the people becomes part of them, strengthens them. A sincere martyrdom is a very good thing, we think. That is why in the end we will succeed. Nobody can beat us for devotion.

A friend of Harpal Singh added: "That's the price of getting your own country. If you can't pay it, you don't deserve a country."[84]

Guerrillas were often supported by ordinary villagers. The leader of the Khalistan Commando Force said, "Wherever we went, people gave us beds to sleep on while they themselves slept on the floor. . . . We felt that those who gave us shelter and food were our families. When our clothes were torn or too dirty, they would give us their own."[85] Wassan Singh Zaffarwal of the Khalistan Commando Force said:

What was positive was that wherever I went people wanted to do something. They did not want to sit back. Wherever we went, villagers would give us

money and beg us to go forward, not backwards. My family didn't stop me
in my activities. I had their full support. When people saw us sticking together they thought we're not finished yet.[86]

A key manifestation of community support for self-sacrifice by the Sikh
militants was the widespread practice of holding public ceremonies in celebration of the "heroic fighters" who died fighting the Indian state. These
ceremonies were typically advertised in local newspapers and drew large
audiences. According to Joyce Pettigrew, who spent months living in Sikh
communities in Punjab in 1989 and 1990, the relevant militant group
would issue an announcement for "Martyrdom Congregations" reading:
"It is a wonderful thing for the brave to die in the cause of truth. . . . During the present-day struggle . . . [name given] from [village given] became
a martyr. . . . The last rites of [name] will be performed at [time and place].
We appeal to all the Sikh congregations to participate in the peace of the
departed soul."[87] As a result of these public ceremonies, Sikh fighters were
not viewed as victims, social misfits, or dysfunctional individuals, but as
honorable martyrs whose death merited social appreciation, both for the
individuals who die and their families.

The Importance of Religious Difference

The underlying religious difference between the Sikh and Hindu communities helps to explain why Sikh resistance became so extreme in the aftermath of the Golden Temple massacre. For Sikh nationalists, India's attack
was not simply the product of an overly aggressive army or an insensitive
political leader, but indicated the general willingness of Hindus to allow
the more radical elements within their society to perpetrate violence
against the Sikh community.

The key difference between the two religions is that Sikhism is
monotheistic, Hinduism polytheistic. Hindus follow a strict caste system,
which determines the standing of each person. The caste one is born into
is the result of the karma from his or her previous life. Sikhs believe in
samsara, karma, and reincarnation as Hindus do, but reject the caste
system. They believe that everyone has equal status in the eyes of God.

The best articulation of the Sikh nationalist view is S. Dharam's explanation of the "root cause" of the conflict between the Sikhs and the Hindus:

The Arya Samajis are the root cause of the present conflict between Hindus
and Sikhs of Punjab and Haryana. Arya Samaj is India's most fanatical cult,

which attacks and slanders almost all the religions, Sikhism [and others]. . . .
Anti-Sikh policies and activities of Arya Samaj are responsible for alienating
the Sikhs from Hindu society and pushing more Sikhs into saying that they
are not Hindus. . . . The Arya Samaj's doctrine of fanaticism and their slan-
dering of the Sikhs' Gurus naturally infected the minds of certain sections
of the Punjabi Hindus who started opposing various rightful demands put
up by the Sikhs for the welfare of Punjab. Thus even though on the surface
there would appear to be various causes leading to the present state of ten-
sion between the Hindus and Sikhs, yet the fact is that the basis of all further
causes leading to the present state of conflict is the hostile attitude of the
Punjabi Hindu against Sikhs as a result of influence of the Arya Samaj on
them.[88]

In the end, the logic of martyrdom is a response to the perceived willingness of the occupier to allow extremists to transform the local community. The main argument of Sikh nationalists is not that they have an
inherent right to their own state. Rather, it is that Hindu extremists, pro-
tected by a Hindu state, will dominate the Sikhs unless the community
achieves independence:

The Sikhs today stand at the cross-roads of their history where they face the
danger of being over-run by the fanatic and barbaric forces of Hinduism. . . .
The state is in the tight grip of the Indian Army . . . and every Sikh living in
it is a suspect in the eyes of security forces. . . . Big Brother has classified
these Sikhs as "dangerous people" who . . . need to be "subjugated." For
achieving this subjugation, Big Brother permits its forces to use any methods howsoever heinous or horrid they may be.[89]

In 1996, the leading Khalistan leader, Simranjit Singh Mann, stressed
that the Sikh rebellion was not merely based in religion, but was a struggle
to "protect the Sikh community" from the influences of Hindu activists.
Other activists in the Khalistan movement frequently declare their desire
to "protect the Sikh faith from Brahminical tyranny."[90]
Wassan Singh Zaffarwal, leader of the Khalistan Commando Force:

Our ideology is clearly intended to bring about our liberation as individuals
and as a people. There is no need to follow any other alien system of
thought. We have our own values. Our history and *bani* [scripture] inspires
us.[91]

Jasvinder Singh, a member of the KCF:

We were, ourselves, aware of our *shahidi* [martyrdom] and sacrifices but we always thought India to be our country. We never questioned it! . . . At the time of Operation Blue Star, I was 16. . . . Suddenly all our villages were surrounded by the army. . . . We started realizing we are not safe—neither ourselves nor our religion. Later, when we went to the [Golden Temple], we saw the marks of the bullets. Bloodstains were still visible. . . . [The Indian government] ruined them [the temple buildings] in order to rid the Sikh mind of the notion that they are a nation. Many buildings were destroyed simply to destroy the culture. I and many other young people began to think, on seeing this, that neither we nor our religion could be safe in a country that did this. . . . Everyone understood that if it means saving Sikhism, one had to sacrifice.[92]

Jarnail Singh Hoshiarpur, a senior leader of the KCF:

Ours is a national struggle. It is simply that people want to be free. We want to get rid of Brahmanic imperialism. They eat our Punjab.[93]

Dr. Gurmit Singh Aulakh, president of the Council of Khalistan:

The Hindu government of India, whether run by the Congress Party or by the BJP [Bhartiya Janta Party], wants minorities either subservient to Hinduism or completely wiped out. The Indian government and its allies have tried to weaken the Sikh religion by saying that Sikhism is part of Hinduism. If that is true, why have they murdered so many Sikhs? . . . Guru Nanak was born Hindu, so they proclaim Sikhism to be part of Hinduism. Yet Guru Nanak said that he was "neither Hindu nor Muslim." Jesus was born Jewish. Does that mean that Christianity is merely part of Judaism?[94]

THE PKK'S SUICIDE TERRORISM IN TURKEY

From 1996 to 1999, the Parti Karkaren Kurdistan, or Kurdish Workers Party, carried out fourteen suicide attacks, each with one attacker, against government buildings and Turkish military targets, killing twenty-two people in addition to the attackers themselves. The PKK's suicide terrorism is remarkable in three respects. First, it qualifies as the least aggressive modern suicide terrorist campaign, killing on average fewer than two persons per attack, compared with the average of twelve in the universe of suicide terrorist attacks since 1980. Second, the individual PKK suicide terrorists sought remarkably little publicity, leaving no final testimonials in writing or on video, and the organization rarely promoted the life stories of the attackers. Third, few if any of the suicide attackers appear to have been walk-ins. Although suicide terrorist organizations almost always replenish their ranks as the suicide campaign unfolds, the PKK's suicide attackers were long-serving members of the organization and their number was not augmented by grassroots volunteers.

From the perspective of explaining suicide terrorism, the important question in the case of the PKK is less why it occurred than why it remained so limited. Although the PKK's suicide terrorism occurred while the Kurdish homeland was under Turkish military occupation, the origins of the PKK's suicide terrorism, more so than any other case, are most likely due to a narrow commitment to the group's leader, Abdullah Ocalan. While in jail, Ocalan called for his followers to conduct suicide attacks as a means to compel the Turkish government to release him. Coercion failed and the attacks stopped when Ocalan asked his followers to abandon the effort. He remains in custody.

The interesting question is why suicide terrorism did not escalate in the Kurdish case. Some have thought that suicide terrorism occurs mainly as a product of internal group dynamics. Once started, so the argument goes, suicide terrorism can feed on itself, fomenting a wider rebellion or an escalation in suicide attacks.[95] If so, then the sources of suicide terrorism are mainly inside the group and are only slightly related to external circumstances such as foreign occupation or religious difference. To be sure, the PKK's suicide terrorism shows that internal group dynamics can cause some suicide terrorist attacks. However, there is a more important observation. Even if internal dynamics account for the PKK's suicide terrorism, these attacks did not precipitate a groundswell of national resistance and in fact mark the tail end of the Kurdish national rebellion, which lasted from 1984 to 1999. Why is this so?

The limits of suicide terrorism among the Kurds are likely due to the absence of a religious difference in this case. In the 1980s and 1990s, the Turkish military occupied large parts of the Kurdish homeland and used harsh measures to suppress the PKK. However, this was far from intensifying Kurdish support for the nationalist rebellion. Indeed, the vast majority of the Kurdish population appear to have sided with the Turkish government, while support for the rebellion actually declined over time. A key reason appears to be the commonality of religion across the two communities. Although Kurds and Turks speak different languages, both are predominately Sunni Muslims. This religious similarity forms the basis of significant cross-community assimilation, which continues even now.

Turkey's Military Occupation

The Kurds are a predominately Sunni Muslim people with a distinct family of languages, numbering some 20 million to 25 million as of 1995. Their homeland, "Kurdistan," spans southeastern Turkey, northeastern Iraq, and parts of Syria and Iran. Approximately 6 million to 9 million Kurds reside in Turkey, where they make up about 15 to 20 percent of the total population and constitute a large majority in the southeast.[96]

The Kurds have a long history of violence in the Middle East. The 1984 civil war in Turkey started when the PKK, based at the time in northern Iraq, launched a series of raids across the border and sought to control various Kurdish rural towns.[97] The Turkish government responded with heavy-handed counterinsurgency tactics including large military operations (some involving up to 35,000 troops) in the Kurdish areas of the country. The Turkish government claims that from 1984 to 1999, some 5,000 Kurdish civilians died during its military operations to suppress the PKK; independent observers estimate that the number is probably closer to 35,000.[98] The government also forcibly "resettled" at least 362,000 Kurds, reducing the rural population of the southeast by 12 percent during the period.[99] Although the Turkish army withdrew from many rural Kurdish towns in the early 1990s, it continued counterinsurgency operations against the PKK in the region through late 1998.[100]

Community Support for Independence

The PKK's main goal was to establish an independent Kurdish state. At its peak, the PKK appears to have numbered from 5,000 to 10,000 armed guerrillas and may have had passive support from tens of thousands more.[101] Although this represents deep support by a small fraction of Kurds, there is good reason to doubt that the PKK, or the Kurdish independence movement as a whole, had much popular support.

An extensive analysis of Kurdish public opinion on independence has been conducted by Matthew Kocher. Since public opinion surveys were not taken during the conflict, he analyzes vote returns for Kurdish parties in Turkey's three parliamentary elections in the 1990s. These elections, which are generally considered to have been free and fair, show only a modest absolute level of support for Kurdish parties associated with independence, and that level declines over time. Although this is not direct information on popular support for the PKK, it is highly unlikely that the general Kurdish population would more strongly support armed insurgency to achieve independence than it would the goal of independence itself.

TABLE 18. Vote for Kurdish Parties in Turkey's Elections, 1991–99

	1991	1995	1999
Turkey	20.8%	4.2%	4.7%
Kurdish Provinces	28.6%	16.2%	19.1%

Source: Matthew Kocher, "The Decline of PKK and the Viability of a One-State Solution in Turkey," *International Journal on Multicultural Societies*, vol. 4, no. 1 (2002), pp. 145–46.

The Absence of Religious Difference

Although foreign occupation had the effect of hardening communal identities in Lebanon, Sri Lanka, and Punjab, this did not happen in the Kurdish case. During the civil war, millions of Kurds continued to live in the cities of eastern Turkey and to attend public schools in which Turkish is the mandatory language, while hundreds of thousands of Kurdish males continued to accept conscription in the Turkish army.[102] Turkey has erected few barriers to the advancement of Kurds in the state bureaucracy, business, and politics; individuals of Kurdish descent have been mayors of major cities (including Istanbul) and parliamentarians (the foreign minister in 1995).[103] In a 2001 survey, 12 percent of Turkish citizens identified Kurdish as their mother tongue, but only 4 percent identified themselves as "primarily Kurds" rather than "primarily Turks."[104] Although ethnic mobilization surely occurred, there is a pattern of successful integration of Kurds into Turkish society, a pattern absent from foreign occupations that led to suicide terrorism.

The reason is not that Turkey's occupation policies were especially benign. In fact, the rate of occupation-related civilian deaths and disruption to the occupied community is higher in Turkey's Kurdish regions than in Punjab and only moderately lower, given the high absolute level of damage, than in Lebanon and Sri Lanka.[105]

Rather, the main reason that the Kurds did not mount an aggressive campaign of suicide terrorism is probably that the linguistic difference that defines the Kurdish nation does not lend itself to the sharp boundary between "us" and "them" that can occur when rivals are divided by religion. Turkey's Kurds are predominately bilingual, speaking their mother tongue at home and on social occasions but using Turkish for business, in school, and to follow the news. Indeed, Kurdish is primarily spoken; few textbooks or other literature is available in the language.[106] Since the adoption of Turkish as a second language does not require Kurds to abandon their mother tongue, the categories of "Kurd" and "Turk" are not mutually exclusive.

Moreover, the fact that the Kurdish nation spans a variety of ethnic groups—Arabs in Syria, Persians in Iran, and tribal clans in Turkey—tends to blur the boundaries of the nation. To be sure, Kurdish historians seek to draw a stark definition between "us," the Kurds, who are the oldest people in the region and who speak a distinct language, and "them," outsiders like the Ottomans (Turks) who came later. They also stress that the Kurds are endowed with certain special characteristics (mainly, language). However, Kurdish historians also emphasize that the Kurdish nation is the product of reciprocal influence with other peoples, especially Arabs and Persians. Weakening the lines that demarcate the nation is especially important, since many Kurds are not Sunni Muslims but Shia, including about 30 percent in Turkey (the Alevi). As one scholar of Kurdish nationalist discourse explains, "The Other and the Self are defined without actually considering the question of where the limits of these categories are."[107]

Overall, this analysis confirms that the absence of a religious difference tends to limit suicide terrorism. Although the PKK was still able to carry out a series of suicide terrorist attacks, support for Kurdish independence and for the PKK's resistance movement remained limited to a small fraction of the Kurdish population and the phenomenon of mass support for martyrdom did not occur.

CONCLUSION

Religion plays a role in suicide terrorism, but mainly in the context of national resistance. Moreover, the effects of religion that matter do not lie mainly in Islam or in any other single religion or culture. Rather, they lie mainly in the dynamics of religious difference. In Lebanon, Sri Lanka, and Punjab the presence of a religious schism—different in each case—

between the occupying power and the occupied community produced a common set of mechanisms that enabled resistance leaders to mobilize significant levels of popular support for "martyrs" who carried out suicide terrorist attacks. By contrast, the absence of a religious clash in Turkey limited Kurdish support for the PKK's suicide terrorism. This does not mean that religious difference is a hard, necessary condition for suicide terrorism. The growing coercive power of suicide terrorist attacks to compel modern democracies to alter their policies may tempt many kinds of national resistance movements to use suicide terrorism in the future. However, the important role of religious difference in the campaigns of suicide terrorism over the past two decades suggests that the risk of suicide terrorism is higher when a foreign occupation by a democratic state also involves a religious difference.

PART III

THE INDIVIDUAL LOGIC OF SUICIDE TERRORISM

9
—

Altruism and Terrorism

WHAT MOTIVATES INDIVIDUAL suicide terrorists? Are suicide attackers driven by economic helplessness, social anomie, religious indoctrination, or something else?

The individual logic of suicide terrorism has been hard to grasp, because many are looking at it through the wrong lens—the lens of ordinary suicide. For the past two decades, journalists, scholars, and other researchers have written a multitude of accounts that seek to explain the individual logic of suicide terrorism by assembling the life narratives of specific suicide bombers. These life narratives follow a familiar pattern. Typically, the writer begins by interviewing the suicide bomber's immediate family, friends, and other close associates, asking detailed questions about the personal history and psychological condition of the individual. From these interviews, the suicide attacker's life story is stitched together, often with painstaking effort to identify the key moments of transition that "caused" the person to wish to die and so to willingly accept a suicide terrorist mission. Finally, there is a summary statement—often to the effect that, much to the writer's surprise, no clear "moment of transition" could be found.[1]

One can quibble about the method or complain about its thoroughness of execution in hard-to-study areas of the world. However, this method, which experts call psychological autopsy—is exactly the one used to explain the many cases of ordinary suicide that we read about every day.[2] Moreover, the life narratives of many suicide terrorists are quite complete, some more complete than accounts of everyday suicides. Although we do want more information, and surely want the best experts to analyze it, this chapter argues that there is a conceptual gap that confounds efforts to explain what motivates individual suicide terrorists.

An important obstacle to resolving the puzzle of the individual logic of suicide terrorism is the tendency to think that all suicides arise from similar causes. In our everyday lives, we have come to expect that "suicide" carries a particular set of meanings. People who "commit suicide" are people "seeking to die," often because they wish to "escape emotional pain." Our personal experience tends to reinforce this common understanding. Every day, ordinary suicides are reported in the newspapers. These reports commonly include some account of why the person committed suicide, and the answer is often linked to an identifiable personal trauma or mental illness, usually reported by a family member or close associate. When the occasional suicide occurs that does not fit this pattern, it is easy to think that we just have not learned enough about the case, and also easy not to think about it at all.

Our experience with ordinary suicide leads to a common misunderstanding about suicide terrorists: that many are seeking to end their lives in any case and are merely taking an opportunity to die in an especially theatrical way. This presumption is a mistake. Many suicide terrorists are acting on the basis of motives fundamentally different from those that underlie ordinary suicide and would probably not commit suicide absent the special circumstances that create these motives.

Using Emile Durkheim's famous study of suicide in nineteenth-century Europe, this chapter broadens our understanding of suicide to include circumstances that we do not encounter every day but that are closely relevant to suicide terrorism (and other forms of suicide). It also applies this broader conceptual framework to elucidate the motives of actual suicide terrorists.

Suicide can take multiple forms. The most common, "egoistic suicide," occurs when an individual is excessively isolated from society, cannot cope with intense psychological trauma, and chooses voluntary death as a means to escape this painful existence. The less common and fundamentally different "altruistic suicide" occurs when high levels of social integration and respect for community values cause otherwise normal individuals to commit suicide out of a sense of duty. The extremely rare "fatalistic suicide" happens when individuals are confined under conditions of such excessive regulation, oppressive discipline, and seclusion from society that they can be made to carry out extreme acts through what lay people call brainwashing.

This new conceptual lens helps us to see the distinctive qualities of suicide terrorism. Many suicide terrorists are acting out of altruistic motives, not the egoistic motives that are typical of almost all other suicides. Numerous suicide terrorists are acting at least partly to serve their community's interest in fighting the national enemy. These individuals are rarely brainwashed into accepting such missions through the heavy indoctrination associated with the recent mass suicides by religious cults, but accept the task much like a soldier who accepts a "suicide mission" in an ordinary war.

THE INDIVIDUAL LOGIC OF SUICIDE

Suicide occurs when an individual deliberately acts to kill himself. Although it is common to assume that the supreme motive of the individual in committing suicide is to seek death as an end in itself, there are other motives for voluntary death. A mother sacrificing her life to save her child, a soldier jumping on a hand grenade to protect his buddies, or a shipwrecked sailor giving his last pint of water to others—these individuals may not wish to die, but they are the cause of their own death as surely as Ernest Hemingway when he put a shotgun to his head. The common quality in these cases is not motive, but a conscious choice to take an action that the individual knows, at the moment of acting, will result in certain death. These instances of voluntary death are clearly distinct from other individual behaviors and other categories of death (involuntary, unexpected, and so on) and so are properly considered under the same discrete category of individual behavior commonly called suicide.

In general, suicide can take one of three forms. These are distinguished by the type of motive as well as by the degree of an individual's integration into society.

Egoistic suicide occurs when individuals simultaneously experience a high degree of personal trauma and a low degree of attachment to society.[3] Life is full of personal traumas and major disappointments—painful personal illness, ugly public disclosures of private matters, distressful divorces, anguishing career failures—and the number of these commonly mounts with age. As Durkheim explains, individuals normally weather personal strains with the help of family members, close personal friends, or involvement in community activities, all of which create important reasons to endure personal pain for the benefit of others and also reduce the sense that one must suffer alone. However, the more detached individuals are from society, the less intense is their sense of duty to others and the more likely they are to see no reason to endure life's sufferings. The root cause of egoistic suicide is not found in the specific suffering the individual faces, but in the fact that the individual confronts this suffering alone. Accordingly, egoistic suicide is usually a private act.[4]

Social detachment can sometimes occur abruptly, causing even individuals with a long history of dense social bonds to commit suicide. The sudden loss of a job, death of a close friend, loss of a fortune, or gush of wealth can leave a person estranged from his accustomed social ties and devoid of a sense of purpose. In the aftermath of sudden social isolation, the present can seem valueless and the future to offer no hope of greater satisfaction. The shock of life without purpose leaves one vulnerable to impulsive decisions for voluntary death, which is why suicide so often rises with personal bankruptcy, divorce, widowhood, and instant wealth.

Durkheim thought abrupt change of circumstances was so important that he created a special category for such suicides, "anomic suicide." However, the mechanisms leading to voluntary death for anomic and egoistic suicide are the same, personal trauma combined with social isolation. They differ only in the duration of detachment—chronic in egoistic suicide, acute in anomic. Hence, I will often use the single term "egoistic" to refer to both phenomena and "anomic suicide" only when assessing whether an abrupt change of circumstance can account for suicide terrorism.

If egoistic suicide originates from extreme personal detachment, the second basic type—altruistic suicide—emanates from nearly the opposite condition: excessive integration of the individual into society. Sometimes, individuals are intensely attached to their community. Parents want their families to survive. Soldiers value the success of their units. Citizens are devoted to their countries. In such situations, society can exert pressure on the individual to make personal sacrifices, including the sacrifice of one's life, for purely collective goals. The mother who insists on living when her death would have saved her child, the soldier who runs out on buddies under fire, the citizen who will not make the supreme sacrifice for his country—these individuals lose public respect and are therefore discouraged from doing so. By contrast, individuals who kill themselves rather than allow harm to members of their community gain social prestige and receive encouragement by this fact. Unlike egoistic suicide, altruistic suicide is likely to be a public act. Accordingly, the more a person values his community, the more likely he is to kill himself for the sake of the community, as Durkheim wrote, *"because it is his duty."*[5]

Although Durkheim found numerous examples of altruistic suicide among the customs of various societies, the paradigmatic case was suicide among military servicemen.[6] In general, during the nineteenth century, suicide rates in European militaries were much higher than for the civilian population of the same age. This fact was difficult to explain by social isolation, since military institutions are highly cohesive and often respected by the surrounding society. Hardship also accounted poorly for military suicides, since the rate tended to accelerate with prolonged service, when individuals should be most accustomed to the rigors of a soldier's life. Rather, the main cause was simply a close attachment of the individual to the group. As Durkheim wrote:

> Influenced by this predisposition, the soldier kills himself at the least disappointment, for the most futile reasons, for a refusal of leave, a reprimand, an unjust punishment, a delay in promotion, a question of honor, a flush of momentary jealousy or even simply because other suicides have occurred before his eyes or to his knowledge.[7]

The third form of suicide is fatalistic suicide.[8] This occurs when the individual is subjected to such oppressive regulation of personal beliefs that suicide (or any behavior) is the result of "ineluctable and inflexible" pressure to carry out the act. Today, we might reasonably call this brainwashing—the use of excessive regulation and oppressive discipline to strip individuals of the capacity for independent thought and so leave them vulnerable to following directions against their self-interest. To sap an individual's capacity for free will, intensive thought reform or "reeducation" programs generally require that the members of a small group be kept in extreme isolation from the surrounding society for prolonged periods of time. In this situation, an individual can lose all concern for the wider society and value conformity with the small group above all else.[9] "Suicide pacts" are a common instance of fatalistic suicide, because they generally occur among individuals who are almost exclusively bonded to each other.

Fatalistic suicide differs fundamentally from altruistic suicide, which does not require either heavy indoctrination to change pre-existing beliefs or exclusive bonds to a small group. Although altruistic suicide involves social pressure, the individual retains a significant capacity for choice in the personal decision to accept or reject a social obligation and is not secluded from the surrounding society. Indeed, the condition of sustained isolation from wider society would contradict the logic of altruistic suicide, which depends on mass approval, not oppressive discipline, as the main factor guiding an individual's actions. In the end, the core difference between altruistic suicide and fatalistic suicide is the attitude of the surrounding society to the act. In altruistic suicide, society venerates the person who commits the act as a martyr or hero that others should emulate. In fatalistic suicide, society treats the individuals as lost souls and condemns the act as something repulsive and bizarre that should never happen again.

"Egoistic," "altruistic," and "fatalistic" suicide are logically separate classes of behavior. They also correspond to distinct manifestations of suicide in the world today. The ordinary suicides that we encounter in our daily lives are mainly egoistic. The recent famous mass suicides among various religious cults are examples of fatalistic suicide. Many suicide terrorists are committing altruistic suicide.

TABLE 19. Forms of Suicide

	Egoistic Suicide	Altruistic Suicide	Fatalistic Suicide
Individual's relationship to society	Isolation	Integration	Separation
Individual's relationship to small groups	Isolation	Participation	Immersion
Society's view of the act	Unacceptable	Approved	Unacceptable
Suicide plan	Private, alone	Public, team or alone	Secluded, en masse
Motive	Escape personal pain	Promote common good	Conformity to group
Real-world example	Ordinary suicide	Suicide terrorism	Cult suicide

Ordinary Suicide. Our understanding of ordinary suicide helps to explain why so many investigators search the life narratives of suicide terrorists for evidence of major depression, personal trauma, and social isolation. Most of the suicides familiar to us are indeed egoistic. The misunderstanding is not to do with the facts of ordinary suicide, but with the presumption that suicide terrorists are basically the same as ordinary suicides.

The overwhelming feature of ordinary suicides is that the victims were chronically or abruptly detached from society. Ordinary suicide is most often a private, lonely act. Publicity is rarely sought and commonly shunned. Overall, suicide typically accounts for just over 1 percent of all deaths in the United States and other countries. The great majority occur in the victim's home, in prisons, and in hospitals, places in which the victim can predict periods of privacy that reduce the risk of public disclosure before the act is complete. Only a minority (15–20 percent) of completed suicides leave notes, and these are usually intended for family rather than for the wider public.[10]

The primary risk factors for ordinary suicide are conditions that would lead individuals to become shut off or to shut themselves off from society. Some 95 percent of ordinary suicides are accompanied by one or more risk factors that are related to depression, physical disease, low levels of social contact, alcohol dependency, past suicide attempts, and gender:

- 80 percent of all suicides are males

- 45–66 percent suffer major depression; often recently hospitalized for mental disorders

- 49 percent have no close friends and belong to no social organizations

- 30 percent have a severe physical illness

- 30 percent have a history of attempted suicide

- 25 percent are alcoholics, often with prolonged dependence[11]

This is not to say that there are no still deeper antecedent conditions that lead individuals to become shut off or to shut themselves off from society.[12] It is to say, however, that unconnected individuals—especially elderly men who have recently lost their wives—kill themselves vastly more often than do people who are anchored to church, family, or community networks.[13]

Cult Suicide. The dynamics of fatalistic suicide provide an excellent account for the well-known recent instances of mass suicides among religious cults and other small messianic movements. On November 18,

1978, more than 900 followers of Jim Jones committed suicide by drinking cyanide-laced Kool-Aid in the jungle of Guyana, an event that may be the largest mass suicide in history. On April 19, 1993, David Koresh and seventy-six followers took their own lives at their compound ten miles outside Waco, Texas, rather than submit to arrest by the FBI. In October 1994, December 1995, and March 1997, a total of seventy-four members of the Order of the Solar Temple killed themselves in separate incidents in Switzerland and Quebec. On March 26, 1997, thirty-nine members of the religious cult Heaven's Gate killed themselves in a mansion in Rancho Santa Fe, outside San Diego. On March 18, 2000, some 230 members of a Ugandan doomsday cult called the Movement for the Restoration for the Ten Commandments of God sang hymns while dousing themselves with gasoline and setting themselves on fire.

The groups all had charismatic leaders. However, charismatic leadership alone is far too common among the numerous political, economic, religious, social, and other groups that exist in every community to provide a sufficient explanation for such extreme willingness of individuals to follow a leader's direction to destroy themselves. Moreover, most people in any society are subject to the influence of multiple charismatic and persuasive leaders; often they are exposed to the influence of a number of such leaders—in schools, churches, and workplaces, and in their families—within the span of a few weeks. Hence, the simple fact of charismatic leadership does not explain why particular people followed a specific leader at a given moment to such an extreme.

The groups mentioned above also were all religious. However, religious belief and intense religious faith are pervasive elements in most societies and so cannot alone account for the willingness of certain individuals to completely surrender their independent judgment to the decisions of a given leader. Moreover, these groups had a great variety of complex, idiosyncratic belief systems, a fact that casts significant doubt on the idea that particular religious beliefs lead to mass suicidal behavior. Further, to the extent that these groups shared any specific religious beliefs in common, it is a distant association to Christianity that can be found in the backgrounds of many of their leaders and members.[14] Given Christianity's strict prohibition against suicide, this should have militated against the mass suicides rather than encouraged them.[15]

Instead, the key factor that these mass suicides have in common is that the members of the groups lived in physical isolation from the surrounding society. Sociologists tell us that the key feature of a cult is not the content of its belief system or the presence of persuasive leaders, but the existence of a hard boundary separating a self-contained group from the society at large. A hard boundary is important because it enables highly intrusive control. In this situation, leaders can observe and regulate the behavior of their followers across the full range of cognitive, emotional, sexual, and other personal experiences in the rigid manner necessary to maintain a system of shared beliefs that is markedly at variance with the surrounding culture. The boundary separating the group from the wider society typically becomes the key defining feature of the group and so is highly valued by its members. This is why there is often an aggressive or self-destructive response when outsiders seek to breach it.[16]

All of the groups whose members committed mass suicide in the past thirty years lived under highly restrictive conditions that established a hard boundary between the group and the surrounding society. The members of Jim Jones's People's Temple, the Branch Davidians, Heaven's Gate, the Solar Temple, and the Uganda doomsday cult all were required to transfer all their personal wealth to the group, to live for years in dormitories or other communal settings that were physically separate—often remote—from wider society, and to engage in bizarre and eccentric practices that marked them as members of the group, reinforced its social isolation, and the group's progressively undermined individual autonomy. These practices included castration, vows of silence, polygamy, public confession, and communal punishment of transgressions. The timing of the mass suicide commonly corresponded to an imminent threat of intrusion by outsiders.[17]

Although produced more than a hundred years ago, Durkheim's models of suicide remain most useful in studying ordinary suicide and cult suicide today. They are also highly illuminating with respect to suicide terrorism.

SUICIDE TERRORISM IN THE WORLD

Many acts of suicide terrorism are a murderous form of what Durkheim called altruistic suicide. Although one might object to using the term "altruistic" to describe a behavior clearly intended to kill others, it is important to remember that our purpose is to explain what causes a suicide attacker to willingly kill himself in order to complete the mission. The murder of innocents is surely evil. Explaining it hardly justifies it. However, the homicidal dimension of the act should not cause us to overlook an important cause leading to it—that many suicide terrorists are killing themselves to advance what they see as the common good.

The circumstances of numerous suicide attackers support this finding. In contrast to persons who commit egoistic suicide, numerous suicide attackers are integrated into society, espouse collective goals for their missions in highly public ceremonies, and raise their social status and their families' by executing the act. Further, suicide terrorist groups exhibit few of the defining features of the religious cults whose members have committed recent mass suicides. Far from creating hard boundaries between the groups and surrounding society, the groups generally make strenuous efforts to integrate into the community, and the surrounding society often approves of the group's behavior. This is not to say that there are no instances of egoistic suicide among suicide terrorists. Some do exist and more may not yet have been detected. However, the data we have show that suicide terrorism is (1) surely not predominantly egoistic; (2) not likely fatalistic; and (3) probably mostly committed by people who are anchored to community or friendship networks.

Standards of Assessment

It is not easy to evaluate the role of egoism and altruism in suicide terrorist attacks. Given the impossibility of interviewing suicide terrorists who actually completed their missions, psychological autopsies based on reconstruction of life narratives are a logical substitute. But these are likely to remain open to charges of intentional or inadvertent bias even if professionals trained in survey methods had far greater access than they do to the families and associates of suicide terrorists. However, we can approach the problem another way. Since we know the circumstances of ordinary suicide, it is possible to compare them to conditions related to suicide terrorism. If the rate of ordinary suicide is not markedly higher in the countries most associated with suicide terrorism, and if the circumstances of suicide terrorist attacks differ significantly from ordinary suicide, this provides strong evidence that suicide terrorism is not overwhelmingly egoistic, because it could not be explained simply by the base rate of ordinary suicide in that particular society. Further, if the circumstances of suicide terrorism closely approximate key measures of altruistic behavior, then this provides positive evidence for the existence of altruistic suicide terrorism.

The analysis below follows this comparative method. It identifies four patterns that, together, demonstrate that altruistic motives likely account for a substantial portion of suicide terrorism. First, the rate of ordinary suicide is not normally high in countries most associated with suicide terrorism; this undermines the notion that a cultural predisposition for egoistic suicide accounts for this phenomenon. Second, although ordinary suicide sometimes increases abruptly during violent nationalist rebellions associated with suicide terrorism, an important counterexample—Palestinian suicide terrorism since 2000, which has not been accompanied by a rise in ordinary suicide—indicates that even the anomic variant of egoistic suicide does not account overwhelmingly for suicide terrorism. Third, there is a particular method of suicide terrorism—the team attack—that is more likely associated with altruistic than with egoistic motives. Fourth, the social construction of the "altruistic motive" in suicide terrorism is not mainly a product of the separation of the group from society, as is common in recent mass suicides by religious cults, but is typically the result of a close integration of suicide terrorist groups with the surrounding society. The following sections present the evidence for each of these assessments.

Suicide Terrorism Is Not Overwhelmingly Egoistic

Ordinary, egoistic suicide could account for suicide terrorism if the societies most associated with this form of violence were culturally predisposed to tolerate voluntary death. This, however, is not the case. Whether understood as social practices or as the tenet of a specific religion, cultural tolerance for ordinary suicide does little to account for suicide terrorism. Over the past two decades, suicide terrorism has occurred among Muslims in a variety of countries, among Tamils in Sri Lanka, and among Sikhs in India. With the exception of Sri Lanka, the incidence of suicide terrorism is highest where ordinary suicide rates are low. In Sri Lanka, the higher rate of ordinary suicide is more likely due to the protracted civil war than to cultural factors.

Muslim suicide terrorism is the most important case. Whether secular or religious, Muslims are associated with a majority of suicide terrorist attacks. However, Muslims are not especially likely to commit suicide. If anything, there are strong data that suggest Islam reduces the likelihood of suicide.

Suicide rates in Muslim societies are among the lowest in the world, significantly below those in Christian and even Jewish societies. Since the 1950s, the World Health Organization has tracked suicide rates for its member states, of which there are now more than 100. While suicide terrorism has grown over the past twenty years, rates of ordinary suicide among Muslims have remained relatively flat. During this period, the global average rate for suicide ranged from 11 to 15 per 100,000, with the highest rates in Eastern Europe, from an average of 24 per 100,000 in Poland to more than 70 per 100,000 in Russia and Lithuania. Muslim countries had consistently far lower annual suicide rates, with Jordan, Egypt, Iran, and Syria typically experiencing less than 1 suicide per 100,000 population and Kuwait, Turkey, Azerbaijan, Albania, and Bahrain fewer than 5.[18]

There is good reason to think these data are reliable.[19] Muslim suicide rates are based on official death certificates from states with a wide range of political systems and are commonly confirmed by independent scholarship.[20] Moreover, Western countries and Israel, whose coroners would have little reason to under-report suicide rates among Muslims, also consistently report lower suicide rates for this community. In 2000, Israel counted deaths due to "intentional self-harm" for Muslims at a rate of 3 per 100,000, compared with 8 for Jews.[21]

Among Sikhs in Punjab, ordinary suicide is also rare. During the 1980s and 1990s, the highest suicide rate in Punjab was 2.77 per 100,000 in 1997, following a spate of suicides by destitute farmers, a figure that is lower than the world average of 11 and also lower than India's average of 8.48.[22]

Tamils in Sri Lanka are the one case in which high rates of ordinary suicide dovetail with suicide terrorism. During the 1980s and 1990s, suicide rates in Sri Lanka were typically among the ten highest in the world, ranging from 35 to 48 per 100,000. Tamils committed ordinary suicide at least as frequently as the national average, according to independent studies of specific villages in the Tamil regions of the island.[23]

Culture, however, is probably not the main explanation for the high rates of Tamil suicide over the past two decades. Sometimes the harsh conditions associated with heavy-handed military occupation and violence can lead to a rise in anomic suicide, and indeed, conflict-induced anomic suicide probably accounts for high Tamil suicide rates. As the chart below shows, Sri Lankan suicide rates were relatively low for decades following World War II and only shot up after 1983, the year of the famous riots against Tamils in Colombo that led to a vast expansion of civil violence across the island. During this violence, hundreds of thousands of Tamils and Sinhalese were displaced, often into wretched camps, and many regions were plunged into extreme poverty. Surveys by the World Health Organization have found high rates of depression, anxiety, and other psychological disorders in these destitute areas, and academic studies have found both Sinhalese and Tamil rural villages to have especially high rates of ordinary suicide.[24]

CHART 4. SUICIDE RATES IN SRI LANKA, 1880–1997

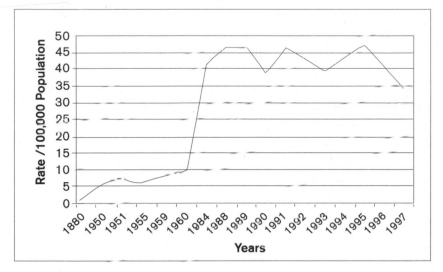

Source: Sri Lanka, Department of Police, Division of Statistics, as reported in Neil Thalagala, "Attempted Suicides" (Ph D. dissertation, University of Colombo, Sri Lanka, 2000), p. 42.

Limits of Anomic Suicide

Foreign occupation and violent nationalist rebellions can create the conditions for anomic suicide. Forced displacement, extreme brutalization, and death of family members or friends can cause individuals to suddenly lose purpose and opt for voluntary death. Thus, it is possible that suicide terrorism could be mainly a side effect of an underlying rise in the rate of anomic suicide in the occupied society.

Conditions of personal anomie may well have influenced some individuals to carry out suicide terrorist attacks. In the next chapter, we will survey the demographic characteristics and backgrounds of the more than 460 suicide terrorist attackers who actually completed their missions. Of these, we can document that at least sixteen were individuals who had a family member or close friend killed by the foreign enemy. There are probably more. The Chechens make such great use of female suicide attackers who have lost husbands or children that there is a colloquial name for them—the Black Widows.

Anomic suicide, however, is probably not the principal basis for individual suicide terrorism, for three reasons. First, some suicide terrorist campaigns target an enemy who is not inflicting heavy violence on the terrorists' homeland territory. For instance, U.S. forces stationed on the Arabian Peninsula during the 1990s did not kill any citizens of Saudi Arabia or other states in the Persian Gulf, but more than half of all al-Qaeda suicide attackers, from the first such mission in 1995 through 2003, came from these countries.

Second, some suicide terrorist campaigns begin and escalate after the damage inflicted by the foreign forces has peaked and then waned to much lower levels. When Israel invaded Lebanon in June 1982, most of the damage that its forces inflicted on the local Shia community (forced displacement, civilian casualties, and so on) took place in the following several months. However, the first Hezbollah suicide terrorist attack against the Israelis did not occur until November 1982, and the vast majority of attacks did not occur for years after that. Revenge could have motivated some Lebanese attackers, but our usual understanding of anomie would seem to predict the opposite trajectory—a high incidence of suicide attack during 1982, followed by a decline as Israeli violence against the Shia waned.

Third and most important, there is at least one case in which the rate of suicide attacks rose so far and so quickly that it cannot be accounted for by an increase in anomic suicide. From late 2000 through 2003, Palestinian terrorist groups carried out more than thirty suicide attacks per year, compared to an average of fewer than four per year during the 1990s. At the same time, the number of ordinary suicides among the Palestinians hardly changed; it actually declined slightly, from thirty-six in 2000 to twenty-nine in 2003.[25] For a rise in anomic suicide to account for Palestinian suicide terrorism in these years, one would have to assume that terrorist groups were able to identify and recruit every new case of an individual willing to commit suicide anyway. Given how difficult it is for family members to anticipate suicides, and given that ordinary suicides generally occur in private, this is highly implausible.

Overall, egoistic and anomic motives are insufficient to account for the individual logic of suicide terrorism. Altruistic motives, either alone or in conjunction with others, likely play an important role.

Signi cantly Altruistic Suicide

A striking fact about suicide terrorism is that it often occurs in teams. In fact, many suicide attacks involve multiple individuals working together for weeks, sometimes even months, to gather intelligence, plan, and re-hearse a joint mission. Team suicide attacks, by their nature, are based on extensive social interaction and require unity of purpose, features that are more likely associated with altruistic than egoistic motives.

Team suicides or "suicide pacts" are extremely rare among ordinary sui-cides. Virtually all of the suicides we encounter every day involve individ-uals acting alone, often withdrawing from social contact altogether to die a private death. The act of suicide is rarely witnessed. Suicide pacts ac-count for less than 1 percent of all suicides in the United States, Western Europe, and elsewhere. The great majority are pairs of individuals with a long-standing romantic relationship, typically either married couples one of whom is in failing health, or young lovers unable to marry.[26]

By contrast, suicide terrorists commonly operate in squads. Over the past twenty-five years, there have been at least 462 suicide terrorist attack-ers who actually completed the mission, killing themselves. Of these, 212, or 46 percent, carried out suicide attacks in which they were part of a joint mission against the same target or targets in close proximity. Some groups use team attacks more than others. Al-Qaeda has deployed 89 percent of its suicide attackers in teams, the Chechens 73 percent, the Tamil Tigers 64 percent, the Palestinians 21 percent, the Lebanese 20 percent, and the

CHART 5. TEAM VERSUS SINGLE SUICIDE ATTACKERS

Percentage by Mode of Attack

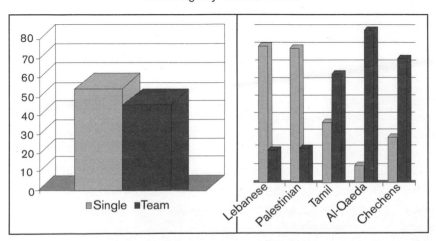

PKK none.[27] Although more work is needed to examine the variation, the groups that must deploy attackers over the greatest distances or against the hardest targets also rely the most on team attacks (al-Qaeda, Chechens, and Tamil Tigers). This suggests that operational considerations may influence how these organizations deploy their attackers.

The prevalence of team suicide attacks strongly indicates the presence of altruistic motives among a significant number of suicide attackers. Even if all suicide attackers had some personal motive to die, suicide attackers who work together as a team must also be motivated, at least partly, to achieve a collective purpose, the completion of a group mission that serves a cause beyond their own personal death.

Egoistic and anomic motives are insufficient to account for team suicide attacks, for two reasons. First, few resemble ordinary suicide pacts. Some team suicides involve individuals with pre-existing social bonds, such as school mates, friends living together, and members of the same civic organization.[28] However, many appear to have had little, if any, social interaction before they began to prepare for the mission. Romantic bonds appear to play little role. Only about 25 percent of all team attacks involved exactly two suicide attackers, and less than 5 percent were male-female pairs. There are no reports of a romantic connection between any team attackers.

Second, team attackers are unlikely to be collections of individuals who were spurred by purely egoistic or anomic motives, people who would have committed suicide anyway without also sharing an altruistic motive for the act. Our understanding of ordinary suicide largely rules out the notion that a large fraction of suicidal individuals would expend considerable energy forming teams, or coordinating their actions, or directing their actions at a particular object. Ordinary suicides are so often lethargic and consumed with their own personal problems that a great number would abandon the team attack at an early stage, if they could come together as a group at all.

The existence of team suicide attacks does not mean that all members of a squad were motivated purely by altruism. Mixed motives surely exist among the hundreds of suicide attackers. However, a significant degree of altruism is probably a necessary condition. If many suicide terrorists attack under conditions rarely possible for ordinary, egoistic suicide, and if individual commitment to a collective goal characterizes those conditions, then altruistic motives are probably necessary for at least one important category of suicide terrorism.

Of course, suicide terrorists who attack in single-person missions may also have altruistic motives. In fact, suicide terrorists often claim, in martyr videos and other last testaments, to be motivated by altruism. Absent extensive psychological autopsies, it is impossible to verify these individual claims of altruistic motives. However, the widespread existence of team suicide attacks suggests that many, possibly most, suicide terrorists are motivated, crucially if not wholly, by a collective purpose.

If not for the presence of an altruistic motive, numerous suicide attacks would probably not occur. This raises the question: what gives rise to the altruistic motive?

The Social Construction of Altruistic Martyrdom

Altruistic motives are heavily influenced by social approval. Although one could believe that an action would benefit others even if those others did not agree with the judgment, an individual is more likely to conclude that an act is beneficial if society actually supports and honors it. In fact, social approval is central to the logic of altruistic suicide as Durkheim conceived it. Whereas an egoistic suicide seeks to escape pain that society would normally expect a person to endure, the altruistic suicide willingly accepts a voluntary death precisely because society supports and honors the act.[29]

The altruistic motive in suicide terrorism also depends on social approval. Suicide terrorist organizations are commonly thought of as "religious cults," as if they consisted of individuals separated from their surrounding communities and with aspirations fundamentally different from those of society at large. This is a mistake. A suicide terrorist organization is generally an integral part of society rather than a separate entity. Indeed, members of the group typically go to great lengths to deepen their social ties, to participate actively in social institutions, and to adopt customs that display communal devotion. For its part, the local society commonly honors individuals who carry out suicide terrorist attacks. As a result, it is impossible to understand the conduct, motivation, and self-perception of individual suicide attackers without considering the importance of the intimate ties that generally exist between suicide terrorist organizations and their communities.[30]

Suicide terrorist organizations are bound to their societies by virtue of pursuing political goals viewed as legitimate by the society at large, by their participation in local charities and other institutions that benefit society, and by the use of elaborate ceremonies and other rituals that identify the death of a suicide attacker with the good of the community. These close social bonds do not create altruistic individuals. However, they do create the conditions under which individuals who wish to sacrifice for their community can be confident that their self-sacrifice will be viewed as altruistic.

Hezbollah in Lebanon Although we do not have precise figures, there is broad agreement among those who have studied Hezbollah closely that "within a matter of months, this small group had become a mass movement" with broad community support.[31] From 1982 to 1986, Hezbollah grew from a handful to more than 7,000 members. During the 1980s and even up through the present day, large segments of the Shia community in Lebanon engage in highly visible rituals and ceremonies that commemorate "martyrs" who have committed acts of suicide terrorism against American, Israeli, and other international targets. Major city streets are named in honor of these fallen heroes, their pictures are widely used as positive symbols in political discourse, and large public rallies are commonly associated with yearly public holidays and other special events that are held in their honor.

Far from being an isolated cult, Hezbollah devotes considerable effort to social services for the community as a whole. Practically from the beginning of its first resistance operations against Israeli and Western troops occupying Lebanon, the leaders of Hezbollah started cultural centers, orphanages, clinics, and welfare centers in Beirut and numerous villages in southern Lebanon. In 1982, Hezbollah started a Financial Assistance Committee, an organization that granted 130,000 scholarships and aided 135,000 needy families with interest-free loans over the next several years. In 1985, secretarial and sewing courses were set up to provide the handicapped with a means of subsistence. In 1986, the Islamic Health Organization, a Hezbollah offshoot, built two major hospitals to care for the local community. As Judith Harik puts it, "by the mid-1980s social services and welfare foundations were *de rigueur*."[32]

Provision of social services substantially enhances the legitimacy of Hezbollah as a movement devoted to the collective welfare of the Lebanese population; this work is probably second in importance only to resistance against the occupation itself. Indeed, Hezbollah's legitimacy seems to have rested more on the establishment of social services than on religious affinity. According to a poll conducted in the late 1980s, only 36 percent of southern Lebanese believed in the inevitability of Islamic unity, but 53 percent took advantage of social services provided by Hezbollah and 67 percent viewed this group as more legitimate than the national government.[33]

To create the momentum for a protracted campaign, Hezbollah and other Shia leaders encouraged altruistic support for suicide operations. These leaders gave literally hundreds of public speeches and interviews explaining the need for what they call self-martyr operations. The main purpose of this public discourse by leaders of Hezbollah and other Shia groups is to persuade the local community at large to accept that acts normally qualifying as suicide and murder should be re-defined as martyrdom and legitimate self-defense, and to encourage some community members to volunteer for these operations.

Although religion plays a role, the main theme of these speeches is that martyrdom operations are a justifiable response to the specific circumstance of a foreign occupation. In speech after speech, by leader after leader, it is the real-world circumstances of foreign occupation that define how religious norms should be interpreted, not an individual's desire for personal salvation independent of this context. The argument is often made at considerable length, and for good reason. Islamic societies have strong norms that strictly prohibit suicide, so Lebanese leaders must work hard to create broad support for suicide terrorism. This is reflected in the volume and length of their discourse on the subject.

The main argument is that martyrdom is justified by its instrumental value in protecting the local community from a foreign occupation and not as an end itself. An individual, the argument goes, has a purpose on earth and so should end that purpose only for another legitimate purpose. Ending a foreign occupation that would oppress the local community is viewed as a possible legitimate purpose, but only if the self-sacrifice would in fact contribute toward that end.

Hezbollah's discourse on martyrdom relies on three themes that jointly work to make this argument: (1) the purpose of martyrdom operations is to end the foreign occupation of the Shia homeland; (2) martyrdom operations are needed for this purpose because of the imbalance of conventional military power between the occupiers and the occupied community; and (3) martyrdom operations are in fact likely to achieve this goal because the target society is susceptible to coercive pressure.

1. Response to Occupation The first theme is that the central purpose of martyrdom operations—and the principal reason for the armed resistance generally—is to end the occupation of the Shia homeland by American, Israeli, and other Western military forces.

In 1985, Hezbollah's famous "Open Letter" declared:

America and its allies and the Zionist entity . . . have attacked our country, destroyed our villages, massacred our children, violated our sanctities, and installed over our heads criminal henchmen. . . . We have risen to liberate our country, to drive the imperialists and the invaders out of it, and to determine our fate by our own hands.[34]

2. <u>Conventional Inferiority Mandates Self-Sacrifice</u> The second major theme in the discourse on martyrdom emphasizes that suicide operations are justified as a last resort made necessary by the Shia community's inferiority in conventional weapons compared to Israel and Western military power. As the secretary general of Hezbollah explained:

Speaking about the experience . . . in Lebanon, in order to carry out an operation with an outcome of 8 or 9 dead soldiers, it would need training, equipping, observations, frontier groups, rockets, explosives. . . . After all these preparations, the outcome would only be 3 or 4 deaths due to the strong fortifications of the enemy. On the other hand, one single [martyr] without any training or experience, driving a bus without any military backups or supporting groups, was able to kill 8 or 9, wound 21, and scare the entire "Israeli" entity.[35]

3. <u>The Enemy Is Vulnerable to Coercive Pressure</u> The third theme in Hezbollah's discourse on martyrdom underscores the expectation that Israel and other Western enemies occupying Lebanon would be susceptible to coercive pressure through suicide attack. Hezbollah's "Open Letter" states:

With the blood of its martyrs and the struggle of its heroes, the Islamic resistance has been able to force the enemy for the first time in the history of the conflict against it to make a decision to retreat and withdraw from Lebanon without any American or other influence.

Fadlallah, Hezbollah's spiritual leader, said:

The self-martyring operation is not permitted unless it can convulse the enemy. The believer cannot blow himself up unless the results will equal or exceed the loss of the believer's soul. Self-martyring operations are not fatal accidents but legal obligations governed by rules.[36]

Finally, Hezbollah has gone to great lengths to ensure that the local community identifies specific suicide terrorist attackers with altruistic motives. In Lebanon, dozens of suicide attackers left testimonials in the form of martyr videos and other last statements. These are widely distributed and strongly reflect altruistic motives. Bilal Fahs wrote before his suicide attack on June 16, 1984, that he sought Lebanon's "liberation from occupation." Wajdi Sayegh wrote before his March 10, 1985, attack that it was "a national and patriotic obligation to fight the occupation." Sana Youssef Mhaydali, probably the first female suicide attacker, explained the motive for her April 9, 1985, attack as "to liberate the south from the occupation of the Zionist terrorists." Before his team suicide attack on July 9, 1985, Khaled al-Azrak said that his "main motive is to liberate this land from the Jewish enemies."[37]

Given Hezbollah's deep commitment to the welfare of Lebanese society and strong association of suicide terrorism with ending a foreign occupation, it is hardly surprising that some individuals willing to sacrifice for their community would voluntarily carry out suicide attacks for this purpose. These circumstances do not create altruistic individuals, but they do create the opportunity for an altruistic individual to contribute to society and to be honored for it.

Hamas Social construction of altruistic martyrdom is also evidenced in popular support for the Palestinian Islamic Resistance Movement, Hamas. Since the mid-1990s, numerous surveys of Palestinians living in the West Bank and Gaza have shown remarkably high levels of popular support for suicide terrorist attacks against Israel—virtually always above a third of respondents and often as high as 70 percent.[38] Moreover, widespread posters, graffiti, and public ceremonies routinely commemorate individual suicide attackers and show that respect for suicide bombing in Palestine goes far beyond a tiny fringe.[39]

Like Hezbollah, Hamas is deeply embedded in the surrounding society, supporting an extensive network of more than forty social welfare organizations. Most were established by Sheik Ahmed Yassin, the founder of Hamas, with a combination of local tithing (*zakat*) and financial support from Muslims abroad. Charitable institutions provide financial subsidies, food, clothing, and shelter. Service organizations provide education, vocational training, libraries, neighborhood sport clubs, and medical relief. In 1997, an estimated 22,615 families received assistance from Hamas-affiliated social welfare organizations, while in 1999 such organizations made up as many as 40 percent of all the social welfare institutions in the West Bank and Gaza. Beneficiaries include orphans, widows, families headed by women whose husbands are imprisoned or permanently disabled, and schoolchildren. Although many are small, some of these organizations are quite large. The Zakat Committee in Gaza has more than fifty employees and provides more than 5,000 people with cash assistance, food, free health care, and interest-free loans for housing and university education.[40]

In an important study, the economist Eli Berman finds that Hamas's network of social service organizations makes an essential contribution to the legitimacy of suicide terrorism among Palestinians. By providing collective goods that are otherwise unavailable, Hamas sends a credible signal that the sacrifices it demands of its members actually benefit the community as a whole. This increases the willingness of individuals who do want to sacrifice for the community to act on this motivation, because they are now confident that their self-sacrifice will in fact be viewed as they intend it.[41]

Hamas's discourse on martyrdom strongly reinforces the altruistic purpose of the group. Like Hezbollah, the main argument is that martyrdom is justified by its instrumental value in protecting the local community from a foreign occupation and not as an end in itself. Statements by the Hamas Political Bureau routinely follow the three-part logic that suicide operations are a response to occupation, mandated by weakness in conventional force, and justified by Israel's vulnerability to coercive pressure.

1. Response to Occupation

The quickened pace of jihad and heroic operations by our mujahidin in al-Qassam Battalions [suicide squads] fits with the Movement's game plan of resistance until occupation is routed and our sacred land liberated.[42]

2. Conventional Inferiority Mandates Self-Sacrifice

INTERVIEWER: "Why not plant a bomb and run?"

HAMAS SPOKESMAN: "There are more fatalities in a suicide attack."[43]

3. The Enemy Is Vulnerable to Coercive Pressure

The Zionist enemy does not understand the language of begging and sub-
mission, which only increase its aggressiveness and arrogance. It only understands the language of Jihad, resistance and martyrdom, that was the
language that led to its blatant defeat in South Lebanon and it will be the
language that will defeat it on the land of Palestine.[44]

Individual suicide bombers routinely leave martyr videos testifying to
the altruistic motive for the suicide attack as a means to end Israeli occupation. Although one might doubt the sincerity of these claims, it is important to recognize that there is a strong material basis for why the Palestinian
community would find them credible: since 1998, Israel has systematically
demolished the homes of suicide bombers' families. Although many reportedly receive cash compensation from Hamas and other groups worth
approximately $10,000, the loss of a home worth many times this value is
a strong signal that the motive for the attack was indeed to promote the
communal good.[45] To this day, Palestinian suicide bombers continue to reveal their identities although it is common knowledge that their families
will suffer harsh consequences.

Liberation Tigers of Tamil Eelam Social construction of altruistic martyrdom is closely associated with the popular support for the Tamil Tigers
among the Tamil population of Sri Lanka. Since the mid-1990s, numerous journalists and scholars who have visited Jaffna, the LTTE's stronghold in the northern region of the country, report that the local population
supports suicide operations and commemorates the LTTE martyrs, called
"Black Tigers." Each year on July 5, thousands attend the "Heroes' Day"
celebration, commemorating the first Black Tiger, whose mission occurred on July 5, 1987, and others since. There are also hundreds of
shrines to individual suicide attackers, kept with flowers and with special
trees planted to represent the martyrs who "planted" their lives for the
land.[46]

The Tamil Tigers also contribute to the social and economic life of the
local society by devoting some of the group's limited resources to social services. In 1987, the LTTE founded the Tamils Rehabilitation Organization
near Jaffna, which has provided thousands of families and individuals with
food, water, resettlement housing, health services, and interest-free loans.

In 1991, the Center for Women's Development was opened, delivering humanitarian relief, vocational training, psychological counseling, and child care to women and children in a series of centers that has expanded over time. In 1992, the Tigers established a police and judicial system in the areas under its control, recruiting female police officers and administrators in a move that expanded the roles of women in Tamil society. In 1993, the Tamil Eelam Bank was established, providing low-interest loans to stimulate small business from salt production to prawn farming.[47]

The LTTE's discourse on martyrdom emphasizes the altruistic motives and instrumental value of self-sacrifice to liberate the local community from Sinhalese occupation.

1. Response to Occupation Prabhakaran, the LTTE leader:

Our martyrs die in the arena of struggle with the intense passion for the freedom of their people, for the liberation of their homeland and therefore the death of every martyr constitutes a brave act of enunciation of freedom.[48]

2. Conventional Inferiority Mandates Self-Sacrifice Nandini, a female LTTE fighter:

As Black Tigers, they are a physical embodiment of self-determination and liberation. They employ their lives as missiles armed with the kind of determination and purpose that is unmatched by any conventional weapon that the Sinhala forces may deploy. There lies the strength and honor of our Black Tigers.[49]

3. The Enemy Is Vulnerable to Coercive Pressure Prabhakaran:

Tamil Eelam can be achieved in 100 years. But if we conduct Black Tiger operations, we can shorten the suffering of the people and achieve Tamil Eelam in a shorter period of time.[50]

To identify the motives of individual Black Tigers with the Tamil community, the LTTE publishes periodicals with profiles of and tributes to the numerous Black Tigers who have carried out suicide attacks over the past twenty years. The broadsheets *Kalathil* and *Erimalai*, printed in the native Tamil language, are widely distributed within the Tamil regions of Sri

Lanka. They are difficult to obtain in the West, but here are several translations.

- Tribute to Captain Miller, the first Black Tiger: "His intention was always
  to rescue the motherland." His mother is quoted: "I am sad that my son
  has died. But he has died for his country. When I think of that, it is pride
  I feel."

- Black Tigress Major Santhana (June 26, 2000): "Major Santhana . . .
  joined the Movement to fight and liberate the Tamils from Sinhalese
  dominance."

- Black Tiger Vasantharaja (December 2000): "This is the most supreme
  sacrifice I can make. The only way we can get our eelam [homeland] is
  through arms . . . even if we die."[51]

In these ways, the LTTE breaks down the boundaries between the
group and the local Tamil community, creating the opportunity for individuals willing to sacrifice for the community to do so through suicide attack. As a study of the LTTE's popular support explains:

Why does the LTTE have so much support among the population? [It] is
the only group that is accepted by the population as "one of our own," "our
boys," even "our sons." . . . The LTTE are the one militant group that has
managed to build up grassroots support and loyalty among the population
for reasons of both ideology and organization and got a grip on the political
and social structure of Jaffna.[52]

Al-Qaeda Social construction of altruistic martyrdom plays an important
role in al-Qaeda's popular support. To be sure, there is a major debate
among Islamists over the morality of suicide attacks, but within Saudi Arabia there is little debate over al-Qaeda's objection to American forces in
the region: over 95 percent of Saudi society reportedly agrees with Osama
bin Laden on this matter. Recent international opinion polls show that bin
Laden enjoys high levels of popular support in other Muslim countries.[53]

Osama bin Laden has been deeply involved with several Islamic social
service organizations and al-Qaeda funds have been used to support their
growth. Among the organizations that bin Laden founded or that his associates have worked for are Human Concern International, the Third

World Relief Agency, Mercy International, and the Islamic International Relief Organization. These organizations are not merely shells or fronts to finance terrorist operations (although they do this). They also carry out significant humanitarian work, providing resources to Muslim refugees, widows, orphans, and the elderly around the world.[54]

Two Islamic charities based in the United States illustrate al-Qaeda's support for Islamic humanitarian efforts. After September 11, 2001, the U.S. government shut down the Global Relief Foundation and the Benevolence International Foundation because of accusations that these organizations provided substantial financing to al-Qaeda. Subsequently, the 9/11 Commission throughly investigated these cases. There is no doubt that the charities provided millions of dollars for humanitarian relief services to aid Muslims in Bosnia, Afghanistan, Lebanon, and Chechnya, including a tuberculosis hospital for children in Tajikistan and a women's hospital in Daghestan. There is also no doubt that al-Qaeda supported the charities. GRF's founders were intimately associated with Osama bin Laden's "Human Services Office," the precursor to al-Qaeda in Afghanistan. The leader of BIF allegedly also had personal ties to bin Laden in the 1980s and 1990s, and the organization received substantial funds from wealthy Saudi donors who are under scrutiny for funding al-Qaeda military operations. However, as the 9/11 Commission concluded: "Despite these troubling links, the investigation of BIF and GRF revealed little compelling evidence that either of these charities actually provided financial support to Al Qaeda."[55]

Al-Qaeda's discourse on martyrdom emphasizes the altruistic motives and instrumental value of self-sacrifice to liberate the local community from U.S. occupation.

1. <u>Response to Occupation</u> In May 1998, Osama bin Laden said:

> The call to wage war against America was made because America has spearheaded the crusade against the Islamic nation, sending tens of thousands of its troops to the land of the two Holy Mosques [Saudi Arabia] over and above its meddling in its affairs and its politics, and its support of the oppressive, corrupt and tyrannical regime that is in control. These are the reasons behind the singling out of America as a target.[56]

2. <u>Conventional Inferiority Mandates Self-Sacrifice</u> In December 2001, al-Zawahiri, al-Qaeda's second in command, underscored:

the need to concentrate on the method of martyrdom operations as the most successful way of inflicting damage against the opponent and the least costly to the Mujahedin in terms of casualties.[57]

3. The Enemy Is Vulnerable to Coercive Pressure In March 2003, bin Laden said:

The Islamic nation today possesses tremendous forces sufficient to save Palestine and the rest of the Muslim lands. . . . I should like to remind you of the defeats suffered by a number of the great powers at the hands of the Mujahideen. . . . [For example,] the defeat of the American forces in the year 1402 of the Muslim calendar [1982] when the Israelis invaded Lebanon. The Lebanese resistance sent a truck full of explosives to the American Marines' center in Beirut and killed over 240 of them.[58]

CONCLUSION

Altruistic motives are significant in the individual logic of suicide terrorism. Many suicide attackers may also wish to escape personal problems, but the egoistic motives that account for ordinary suicides are insufficient, on their own, to explain why many individuals voluntarily carry out suicide terrorist attacks. This is especially true for one category of suicide terrorism—the team suicide attack—that by its nature involves multiple individuals working together for a collective purpose. Moreover, suicide terrorist organizations are not socially isolated groups with socially unacceptable goals, but go to great lengths to embed themselves in their surrounding communities and to pursue socially acceptable political objectives. Although this social construction of altruistic martyrdom does not create altruistic individuals, it does produce the circumstances under which an individual who wishes to sacrifice for the community can be confident that the act is understood in this way. As a result, the altruistic motive is often a necessary if not sufficient condition for suicide terrorism. Absent the altruistic motive, many suicide attacks would probably not occur and many suicide attackers might well seek other opportunities to contribute to their community.

This finding has important implications. First, it suggests that the number of people who would engage in suicide terrorism is potentially much greater than the number of those who are suicidal in the ordinary sense.

Far from the common stereotype of a poor, socially isolated, uneducated religious fanatic, we should expect that suicide attackers are likely to come from a broad cross section of society. As the next chapter shows, a remarkable portion of suicide attackers are indeed secular, employed, reasonably well-educated, and otherwise contributing members of their societies. Although many of us would like to believe that suicide terrorism is limited to a tiny fringe, the fact is that there may be no upper bound on the potential number of suicide terrorists.

Second, the role of altruism in suicide terrorism suggests that there may be a geometric multiplier built into the process of suicide terrorism. Unlike suicides following a stock market crash or mass suicides of a religious cult, the trajectory of suicide terrorism is often an upward slope. From Lebanon in the 1980s to the Palestinians in the second intafada in 2000–2003 to al-Qaeda's attacks in 2002–2003, suicide terrorist campaigns tend to gather pace—and attract more walk-in volunteers—over time. Given the dynamics of altruism, this trajectory is something we should expect in future suicide campaigns.

Finally, the role of altruism means that any attempt to profile suicide terrorists that is based on the known profiles of ordinary suicides is likely to miss a substantial portion. Indeed, since the pool of individuals potentially available in suicide terrorist campaigns is probably not limited to those who would commit suicide anyway, nations under fire may have little choice but to deal with the root causes of suicide terrorism.

10

The Demographic Profile
of Suicide Terrorists

THE MOST COMMON stereotype of a suicide bomber is that of a young man or teenage boy who has no job, no education, no prospects, and no hope. Exactly why such a person becomes a suicide terrorist has been the subject of wide speculation. Some suggest religious fanaticism: a young, impulsive, and inexperienced teenage boy would seem to be easily gulled into believing that if he straps a few sticks of dynamite around his waist and presses a button, he will stroll through the Gates of Paradise, where he will be bedded by virgins. Others suggest social alienation presumed common among criminals: a young man living with the dregs of society might enjoy a variety of deviant pleasures, including the self-satisfaction of a sensational, almost theatrical death during a suicide terrorist attack. Still others suggest mental illness: a demented loner is caught in the throes of a depressive nightmare, possibly besieged by demonic illusions, which makes escape through self-killing a desirable end in itself, especially if it is possible to take out some imaginary tormentors at the same time.[1]

Until now, the main problem in evaluating these competing explanations is that our information about the actual demographic characteristics of suicide attackers has been woefully incomplete. Our information is improving. There is a growing number of new books and articles that detail the life histories of individual suicide terrorists,[2] collect broad data on the backgrounds of terrorists in general and certain groups of suicide terrorists in particular,[3] and present the results of interviewing jailed suicide terror-ists or their families.[4] In general, these studies find that poverty is not as closely associated with terrorism as many have thought and that suicide terrorists are exposed to only thin indoctrination; they are generally walk-in volunteers who receive little training prior to their missions. However, we need to know more.

The key to improving our knowledge about the demographic character-istics of suicide terrorists is to gather information about attackers from across a broad range of suicide terrorist campaigns and regions of the world. Only such a broad examination of suicide terrorists can provide the necessary information to evaluate the still dominant perception that sui-cide terrorists are essentially society's losers—those who have little to live for and so are easily duped into abandoning their lives.

To evaluate this profile, this chapter surveys the available information on the social, religious, educational, and other demographic characteris-tics of all suicide terrorist attackers around the world from 1980 through 2003. Overall, this survey shows that the profile of suicide attackers is nearly the opposite of what many now assume. Suicide terrorists are *not* primarily from religious cults whose members are uneducated, isolated from society, and easily brainwashed into pursuing delusional aspirations. Nor are suicide terrorists mainly from criminal gangs whose members are motivated by youthful impulsiveness, personal satisfaction in harming oth-ers, or the anti-social habits of a life of crime. Nor are suicide terrorists drawn from the ranks of the mentally ill, individuals so depressed that they cannot hold a job, enjoy life, or otherwise lead productive lives and thus seek to die as an end in itself.

In general, suicide attackers are rarely socially isolated, clinically in-sane, or economically destitute individuals, but are most often educated, socially integrated, and highly capable people who could be expected to have a good future. The profile of a suicide terrorist resembles that of a po-litically conscious individual who might join a grassroots movement more than it does the stereotypical murderer, religious cult member, or everyday suicide.

These findings have an important implication for our understanding of what motivates an individual to become a suicide bomber. Although there are important exceptions, these data support the finding in Chapter 9 that suicide terrorism is not usually an act of egoistic suicide by which the indi-vidual seeks relief from a painful existence. Rather, it is commonly a form of altruistic suicide, in which high levels of social integration and respect for community values can lead successful individuals to commit suicide out of a sense of duty.

GATHERING THE FACTS

To advance our understanding of what motivates individuals to become suicide terrorists, we must gather information about the demographic characteristics of past suicide terrorists and we must collect these data systematically. The information we want is relatively straightforward. We want biographical data on the suicide attackers themselves, especially detailed information about their age, gender, ideological and religious affiliation, employment, income, education, and reports of mental illness. The main obstacle is that, although some information can be gathered from English-language sources, much is likely to be available only in native-language newspapers, journal articles, public statements, and other local media. Native-language sources are the venues in which terrorist groups communicate to their most supportive audiences and so they are likely to have the most extensive information about the demographic and general biographical characteristics of suicide attackers. Thus, a survey of native-language sources is likely to shed important light on the extent to which suicide attacks are spontaneous or organized in campaigns, and related to nationalist causes rather than to religious or psychological motives.

To gather these data, I assembled a team of advanced graduate students associated with the University of Chicago who are fluent in the main relevant languages—Arabic, Hebrew, Russian, Tamil—for an intensive survey of regional newspapers, broadcast transcripts, and other materials not currently translated into English. This project also gathered literature documenting individual martyrs from the main suicide terrorist groups themselves—such as Hezbollah, Hamas, and the Tamil Tigers—as well as all publicly available lists of suicide attacks from the main organizations in target countries that collect such data (such as the Israel Defense Forces, Israel's Ministry of Foreign Affairs, and the U.S. Department of State). In addition, this project also amassed all the relevant data that could be found in English, for example in translations by the Foreign Broadcast Information Service and in online collections of English-language newspapers, such as the Lexis database. All information is based on public sources and the raw data are available at the archive for the Chicago Project on Suicide Terrorism housed at the University of Chicago. Although not perfect, these data are more than a "list of lists" and probably represent the most comprehensive and reliable survey now available of the demographic characteristics of suicide terrorists over the past two decades from multiple regions around the world.

This survey defines a suicide terrorist attack in the classic sense of an individual killing himself (or herself) in order to kill others. This counting rule is followed strictly and only those individuals who actually completed the mission and killed themselves are included, because this is the best way to ensure that the individuals surely had the intent to die. The survey therefore does not count high-risk attacks that are sometimes called suicide missions (such as shooting sprees in well-defended areas), suicides to avoid capture (such as taking cyanide to prevent capture by defense forces following an ordinary attack), preemptive kills of suspected suicide terrorists by defense forces, or any mission explicitly authorized by a state (such as North Korean suicide commandos attacking South Korean targets).

Conducting this survey reveals the importance of independent verification and multiple sources of information. Lists assembled by the terrorist groups and by organizations within target countries use loose and sometimes inconsistent counting rules that may make sense for some purposes but that would create confusing results if not corroborated by independent sources. For example, Hamas routinely publishes lists of "martyrs" online. These include many leaders and other members of the organization killed by Israeli security forces in retaliation for their attacks, as well as individuals who committed suicide attacks in the classic sense.

Lists made by target countries are also subject to important inaccuracies. The famous list on the Israeli Ministry of Foreign Affairs website, "Suicide and Other Bombings," is a case in point. As of September 2003, this list counted some 130 events and many of the world's leading journalists and scholars routinely count all of them as suicide attacks. However, the list cites only seventy-three actual suicide attacks—the rest are attempts, captures, preemptive kills, and remote-controlled bombs—and misses nineteen suicide attacks that did occur. (Most likely these were not counted because they did not ultimately succeed in killing Israelis.)

If consistently applied, these loose standards would increase the count of suicide attacks against Israel by 30 percent, would more or less double the count in some important cases such as in Sri Lanka, and would probably make the universe of suicide attacks and attackers uncountable since many, many more cases around the world would have to be included.

CHARACTERISTICS OF MODERN SUICIDE TERRORISTS

Overview

This survey collected the universe of suicide terrorist attackers from 1980 to the end of 2003, a total of 462 suicide attackers in all. Using the methods described above, it was possible to find a wealth of primary demographic data for the overwhelming majority of these attackers, including the names of 333 (72 percent of the total), the ideological affiliation of 384 (83 percent), the sex of 381 (82 percent), and the age of 278 (60 percent). In addition, it was possible to ascertain the principal socioeconomic characteristics of a significant portion of Arab attackers considered as a group. Altogether, there were a total of 232 Arab suicide attackers in the suicide terrorist campaigns in Lebanon, in Palestine, and by al-Qaeda from 1980 to 2003. Of these, the survey identified the education level for 67 and income level for 77.

TABLE 20. Demographic Data on Suicide Terrorists

Total Suicide Attackers, 1980–2003	462

Primary Demographic Data

Names	333
Ideological affiliation	384
Sex	381
Age	278

Socioeconomic Data for Arab Attackers

Arab suicide attackers (Lebanon, Palestine, al-Qaeda)	232
Education level	67
Income level	77

Source: Chicago Project on Suicide Terrorism, 2004

Although one would always like more, these data provide a strong foundation to supply fresh insight into the types of people involved in important past suicide terrorist campaigns, to assess the basic demographic characteristics of the population of suicide attackers as a whole, and to ascertain the socioeconomic features of Arab suicide attackers, both for the group as a whole and in comparison to baselines in the relevant societies.

Fresh Insight: Hezbollah in Lebanon

Hezbollah has long been the paradigmatic case of Islamic fundamentalism driving suicide terrorism, in the view of experts and the public at large.
Although we have also known that Hezbollah was an umbrella organization comprising a variety of disparate sub-groups in a loose working relationship, the complexities of the organization have remained insufficiently
clear to challenge the conventional understanding of the case.[5] Indeed,
the standard stereotype of a suicide bomber as a poor, uneducated religious fanatic largely derived from writings about Hezbollah in the 1980s
and 1990s, which overwhelmingly describe Lebanese suicide attackers in
this way.[6]

The survey of native-language and other sources, however, provides
strong new information that paints a far different image of the individuals
who carried out suicide attacks against American, French, and Israeli
forces in Lebanon from 1982 to 1986. During this period, there were 36
suicide terrorist attacks in Lebanon, involving a total of 41 suicide attackers. For this group, the survey identified the names and sex of 37 (90 percent; 6 were women); the age of 38 (93 percent; 21 years on average); the
marital status of 37 (90 percent overall, of whom 97 percent were single or
not engaged); the ideological affiliation of 38 (93 percent); the education
level of 12 (29 percent overall, of whom 75 percent had secondary or post-
secondary schooling); and the income level of 7 (17 percent).

TABLE 21. Suicide Attackers in Lebanon, 1982–1986

Total attacks	36
Total attackers	41
Names	37 (90%)
Sex	31 men; 6 women
Average age	21.1 years
Marital Status	97% single

Source: Chicago Project on Suicide Terrorism, 2004

The most important new information concerns the ideological affiliation of the suicide terrorists. Hezbollah, its related groups, and the individual attackers themselves were supremely proud of their willingness to
launch suicide attacks to compel Israeli and Western forces to leave their
country. The attackers made numerous martyr videos and left many written statements that were widely distributed and prominently displayed in

their local communities and even collected in commemorative albums. These local sources provide extensive demographic information on the attackers, including pictures. They also contain reliable information about the ideological affiliations of the individuals, since one purpose of these documents was to encourage those with similar ideological affiliations to join the cause.

The survey ascertained the ideological affiliation of 38 of the 41 attackers. Of these, 30 were affiliated with groups opposed to Islamic fundamentalism. Twenty-seven were from communist or socialist groups such as the Lebanese Communist Party, the Lebanese National Resistance Front, the Popular Front for the Liberation of Palestine, Amal, the Syrian Social Nationalist Party, the Arab Socialist Union, the Arab Egyptian League, and the Baath Party—secular groups with no commitment to religious extremism of any kind. Three of the suicide attackers were Christians, including a female Christian high school teacher (Norma Hassan), a Christian factory worker (Elias Harb), and one person from a group called the Vanguard of Arab Christians. Only 8 of the 41 suicide attackers were affiliated with Islamic fundamentalism; all these were from a group called Islamic Jihad. Three were not clearly associated with any ideology. All 38 were native Lebanese.

The following chart summarizes the ideological composition of the Lebanese attackers.

CHART 6. IDEOLOGY OF LEBANESE SUICIDE ATTACKERS

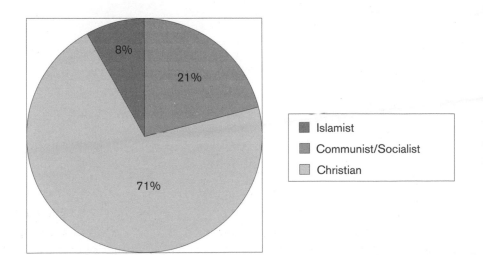

- Islamist
- Communist/Socialist
- Christian

1980s LEBANESE SUICIDE ATTACKERS

Pictures of the suicide attackers are commonplace in the native sources. Many are dressed in Western clothes, with stylish haircuts and even makeup, hardly projecting an image of Islamic fundamentalism. Above are pictures of four of the six female suicide terrorists, including the Christian high school teacher, Norma Hassan, at lower right.

Perhaps the most striking finding is that Lebanese suicide attackers were associated with a wide variety of different ideologies and not the product of a single religious or secular mind-set. Some were longtime members of political groups that existed prior to Israel's occupation of Lebanon in 1982.

Some joined such groups only weeks before their mission. Still others were members of groups with no documented history prior to Israel's invasion.

In the end, what Lebanon's suicide attackers share is not ideology or organizational indoctrination, but simply a common commitment to resist a foreign occupation. Alliances among such disparate groups and individuals are common in nationalist rebellions.

Primary Demographic Characteristics

The survey also provides important information about the age, sex, and ideological orientation of hundreds of individuals who have committed suicide terrorist attacks over the past two decades. Until now, most people have thought that suicide terrorists are overwhelmingly teenage boys who, because of their inexperience and youthful impulsiveness, are easily brought under the spell of a charismatic leader with a religious message. The facts present a different picture.

The survey identified the ages of 278 suicide terrorists, who ranged from 15 (the youngest, a male attacker in Lebanon) to 52 (the oldest, a female attacker in Chechnya), with an average age of 22.7 years. Of these, only 13 percent were between the ages of 15 and 18, while 55 percent were between 19 and 23, and 32 percent—nearly a third—were 24 or older.

CHART 7. AGE OF SUICIDE ATTACKERS, 1980–2003

Percentage by Age Cohort

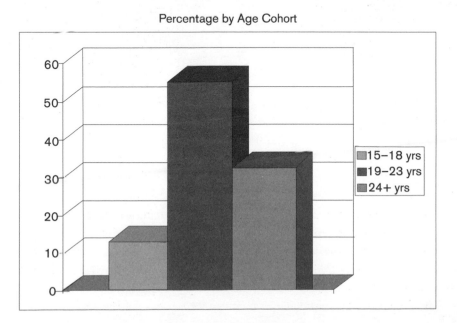

The average age of suicide attackers also varies notably across terrorist groups. Lebanese suicide terrorists were the youngest, averaging 21.1 years old, followed by the Tamil Tigers at 21.9 years, Palestinians at 22.5 years, PKK at 23.6 years, al-Qaeda at 26.7 years, and Chechen rebels at 29.8 years. What accounts for the variation in age across groups is not clear. However, it is unlikely that culture alone does, since the groups with the youngest and oldest average are both from Muslim societies.

CHART 8. AVERAGE AGE OF SUICIDE ATTACKERS ACROSS GROUPS

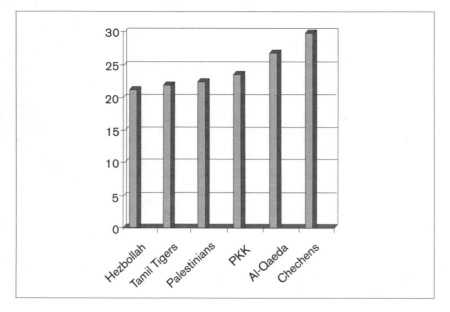

The sex of suicide attackers also varies significantly across suicide terrorist groups. The survey identified the sex of 381 suicide terrorists, of whom 59, or 15 percent, were female. However, some groups use female suicide attackers much more than others. As a proportion of all suicide attackers whose sex could be ascertained during the period 1980 to 2003, al-Qaeda employed no female suicide attackers; the Palestinians used 6 female attackers, or 5 percent; the Lebanese used 6, or 16 percent; the Tamil Tigers used 23, or 20 percent; the Chechens used 14, or 60 percent; and the PKK used 10 female attackers, or 71 percent. Although more work is needed to examine this variation, the groups that used the fewest female suicide attackers (al-Qaeda and the Palestinians) are also the most associated with Islamic fundamentalism (which frowns on female warriors in general). This suggests an interesting hypothesis: Islamic fundamentalism may actually reduce the number of suicide terrorists by discouraging certain categories of individuals from undertaking the act.

CHART 9. PERCENTAGE OF FEMALE SUICIDE ATTACKERS ACROSS GROUPS

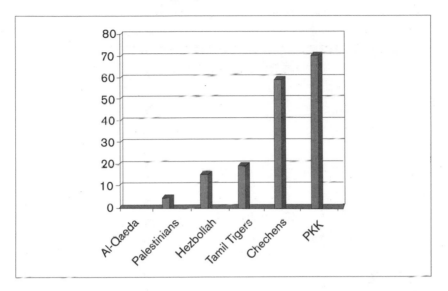

Another important finding about female suicide terrorists concerns their age. Chart 10 compares the ages of groups with both male and female suicide attackers—Hezbollah, the Palestinians, the Tamil Tigers, the Chechens, and the PKK—and shows that women tend to be significantly more mature than their male counterparts. Altogether, the survey identified both the age and the sex of 261 individuals from these five groups. Although the proportion of males and females aged 15 to 18 years was almost identical (13 percent and 14 percent, respectively), female attackers were significantly less likely to be in their late teens and early twenties and more likely to be in their mid-twenties and older. An obvious hypothesis that bears further research is that this age difference reflects the declining marriage prospects for mature women in traditional societies.

Perhaps the most important finding concerns the ideological affiliation of suicide attackers. Altogether, the survey ascertained the religious or ideological affiliation of 384 of the 462 suicide terrorists, accounting for 83 percent of all suicide terrorists worldwide from 1980 to 2003. Comparing

CHART 10. AGE OF SUICIDE ATTACKERS

Percentage by Sex

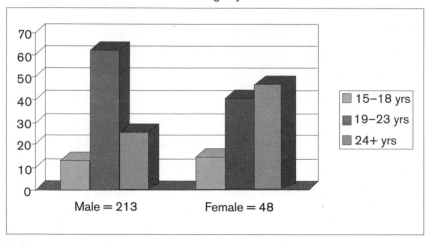

the number of suicide attackers who carried out attacks for secular terrorist groups and for religious terrorist groups, it is clear that the attackers are much more secular than many would expect. Of the 384 attackers for whom we have data, 166, or 43 percent, were religious, while 218, or 57 percent, were secular. Even if we assume that all unaccounted-for attackers (77) were religious, the results would still be a nearly even split— 52 percent religious versus 48 percent secular. Suicide terrorism is not overwhelmingly a religious phenomenon.

In addition, consider the dogs that did not bark. Although the absence of evidence cannot rule out the presence of hard-to-measure factors such as mental illness, major criminal behavior, or other abnormalities, it is highly suggestive to note what was not found among the hundreds of journalistic and other accounts covering the suicide attacks, many of which draw on interviews with family and friends of the suicide attackers. Although there are numerous reports of attackers who were agitated during the execution of the mission, the survey found no documented mental illness, such as depression, psychosis, or past suicide attempts. The survey also found no evidence of major criminal behavior, such as murder, beyond the petty crime normally associated with terrorist groups, such as money laundering (of tiny sums) and theft. The survey found not a single report that a suicide attacker was gay, an adulterer, or otherwise living in a way that would bring shame in a traditional society. In the entire sample, there was a single case of probable mental retardation (a "feeble-minded" Chechen female bomber).

CHART 11. RELIGIOUS VERSUS SECULAR SUICIDE ATTACKERS

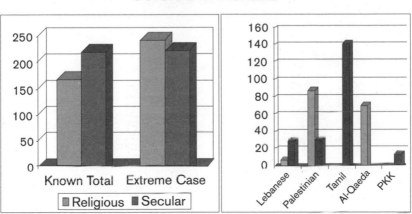

The absence of documented evidence of mental illness does not mean that none of the suicide terrorists experienced personal trauma before undertaking their missions. As shown in Table 22, we know that at least 16 of the 462 did have a family member or close friend killed by enemy military forces and, as I mentioned earlier, the Chechen female suicide attackers are commonly referred to as the Black Widows to make the point that they are seeking revenge for the loss of their family members to Russian military action. In our lexicon of types of suicide, these instances would qualify as possible instances of anomic suicide terrorism. However, even assuming the existence of many others with similar experiences not found in our survey, it would be surprising if as many as a third of suicide terrorists fit this description.

Overall, this survey of the primary demographic characteristics of suicide terrorists casts strong doubt on the prevailing assumptions that individuals who carry out these attacks are primarily religious fanatics, irresponsible adolescents, or sexually frustrated males. Nearly all were well beyond adolescence, most were secular, and many—the overwhelming majority in some groups—were women. None had the pathognomonic characteristic of a suicidal personality: past history of suicide attempts. Rather, the uncomfortable fact is that suicide terrorists are far more normal than many of us would like to believe.

Socioeconomic Status of Arab Attackers
Suicide terrorism is commonly ascribed to poverty; the underlying logic is usually that suicide attackers come from among society's losers, individuals

TABLE 22. Instances of Possible Anomic Suicide Terrorism

Date of Suicide Attack	Name	Group	Sex	Age	Family/Friend Killed in Conflict
1. May 9, 1985	Wafaa Nour E'Din	Lebanese	F	23	Husband
2. July 9, 1985	Ibtissam Harb	Lebanese	F	28	Brother
3. Feb. 5, 1985	Hasan Qasir	Lebanese	M	??	Best friend
4. Apr. 6, 1994	Raid Zakarnah	Palestinian	M	19	Best friend
5. Oct. 19, 1994	Saleh Abdul Rahim	Palestinian	M	25	Brother
6. June 7, 2000	Ajsa Gasujewa	Chechen	F	22	Husband, two brothers/sister
7. July 9, 2001	Nafez Saleh al-Nazar	Palestinian	M	26	Brother
8. Aug. 12, 2001	Mohammed Hamood Bakr Nasr	Palestinian	M	28	Best friend
9. Nov. 29, 2001	Aizan Vakhaevna Gazueva	Chechen	F	18	Husband, two children
10. Dec. 5, 2001	Daoud Abu Sway	Palestinian	M	46	Brother
11. Mar. 29, 2002	Eiat al Achras	Palestinian	F	18	First cousin
12. Mar. 2, 2002	Muhammed Ahmad Darameh	Palestinian	M	19	Two first cousins
13. July 27, 2003	Imam-Said Khachukaeva	Chechen	F	27	Husband
14. Aug. 12, 2003	Khamis Jurwan	Palestinian	M	18	Close friend
15. Aug. 19, 2003	Raid Abu Hamid Ritqa	Palestinian	M	29	Close friend
16. Oct. 4, 2003	Hanadi Jaradat	Palestinian	F	27	Fiancé, brother

Source: Chicago Project on Suicide Terrorism, 2004.

who are so poor now and so unlikely to prosper in the future that they have little to live for and so are more likely to sacrifice a pathetic existence for some illusory blessing. If this explanation were correct, one would expect suicide terrorists to score low on the main indicators of socioeconomic status—education and income level—both in absolute terms and by comparison with their society. However, the socioeconomic facts for an important pool of suicide terrorists—Arab suicide attackers—present a different picture.

Although reliable data on education and income level are difficult to find even in native-language sources, the survey included information about them for a large portion of the 232 total Arab suicide attackers associated with Lebanon, Palestine, and al-Qaeda from 1980 to 2003. This pool of suicide terrorists is especially important, both because it includes the threat immediately facing the United States and some of its key allies and because the conventional stereotype of the suicide bomber as a social loser was largely derived from this context.

Specifically, the survey ascertained the education level of 67 and the income level of 77 Arab suicide terrorists. Education level was divided into three categories: less than secondary school education (that is, no more than an eighth-grade education); secondary education (ninth grade through a secondary degree, in high school or technical school); and post-secondary education (enrollment in any educational institution after secondary school). Income level was also divided into three categories: low-class (unemployed or identified as poor, without a clear source of income); working/middle-class (employed in an identified job that is not normally considered white-collar; such as technician, electrician, security guard, waiter, primary or secondary school teacher, etc.); and professional/high class (employed in an identified job that is normally considered white-collar, such as lawyer or doctor, or identified as a member of a wealthy family). These measures of education and income were selected because they are directly comparable to the common measures used by reputable organizations to assess these factors in the relevant countries.[7]

Overall, Arab suicide attackers are much better educated than the conventional profile would lead one to expect. Chart 12 on the following page compares Arab suicide attackers with their peer groups in Lebanon and Palestine. Ten percent of the attackers in our sample had only a primary school education or less, compared with nearly half in their societies as a whole. Fifty-four percent had some post-secondary education, compared with only a small fraction of their societies.

CHART 12. EDUCATION OF ARAB SUICIDE ATTACKERS
VERSUS PEER GROUPS

Percentage by Income Level

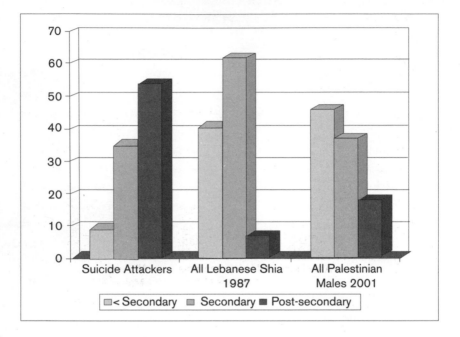

As shown in Chart 13 regarding income, Arab suicide attackers are typically from the working and middle classes and seldom unemployed or poor. Seventeen percent of the attackers in our sample were at the bottom income rung or unemployed, compared to roughly a third in their societies as a whole. Seventy-six percent had working-class or middle-class jobs—technicians, mechanics, waiters, policemen, and teachers, for example—compared to lower levels for these groups in their societies as a whole. It is useful to note that a number of attackers were reported to have left their jobs days or weeks prior to their attacks to carry out the mission, which could explain why they might appear to have been unemployed.

Finally, secular and religious Arab suicide attackers have remarkably similar socioeconomic status, which suggests that religious suicide attackers are not especially uneducated or poor. Chart 14 compares the income and education levels of secular and religious suicide attackers in Lebanon and Palestine. The secular and religious attackers have virtually

CHART 13. INCOME OF ARAB SUICIDE ATTACKERS VERSUS PEER GROUPS

Percentage by Income Level

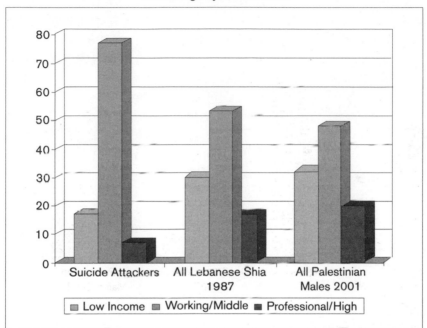

CHART 14. SECULAR VERSUS RELIGIOUS SUICIDE ATTACKERS IN LEBANON AND PALESTINE

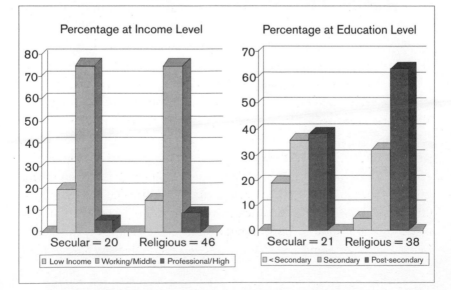

the same income distribution. Religious attackers are highly educated, although the difference is not statistically significant.

The bottom line, then, is that suicide attackers are not mainly poor, uneducated, immature religious zealots or social losers. Instead, suicide attackers are normally well-educated workers from both religious and secular backgrounds. Especially given their education, they resemble the kind of politically conscious individuals who might join a grassroots movement more than they do wayward adolescents or religious fanatics.

11

Portraits of Three
Suicide Terrorists

WE LIKE OUR villains to be wild-eyed monsters. The more the crime violates our sense of humanity, the more we expect the perpetrators to be deviant, repulsive, antipathetic, mentally ill, or deficient in normal human feeling. Of course, associating inhuman acts with inhuman villains does not bring the victims back. It does, however, at least seem to offer an explanation for how horrible atrocities could occur in the first place.

Sometimes this intuition is right. Serial killers such as Charles Manson, Theodore Kaczynski, Jeffrey Dahmer, and Ted Bundy are described by those who know them well as alienated from society, unable to function well in social settings, from dysfunctional backgrounds, and as engaging in highly repulsive acts even apart from murder.[1]

Sometimes, however, those who commit the worst crimes turn out to be quite ordinary in every other respect. The philosopher Hannah Arendt found Adolf Eichmann, the chief administrator of the Nazis' campaign to exterminate the Jews, less a bloodthirsty sadist than a dutiful bureaucrat who was remarkable mainly for his emotional disengagement from the genocide he planned and executed. What stood out was the "banality" of Eichmann's evil, leaving the startling impression that many ordinary Germans could have filled his shoes.[2]

Murderous suicide terrorism is an especially atrocious act, since it violates two of society's primary taboos, the prohibition against killing innocent men, women, and children, and the ban against killing oneself. Suicide terrorism is therefore a double crime against humanity. We also cannot forget the gruesome nature of the injuries and pain that suicide terrorists inflict. These things make it seem all the more sensible that suicide terrorists must be truly deviant human beings.

Academic work on suicide terrorism in the 1980s and 1990s largely supported the view that suicide terrorists are irrational individuals who seek death primarily as an end in itself. Ariel Merari, an Israeli psychologist who has been one of the leading students of suicide terrorism since the early 1980s, characterized the phenomenon as follows: "Terrorist suicide, like any other suicide, is basically an individual act rather than a group phenomenon: it is done by people who wish to die for personal reasons."[3] Jerrold Post, another leading scholar of suicide terrorism and of political psychology, views suicide terrorism as the result of paranoia with psychological roots that can be "traced back to the cradle":

> Some individuals remain fixed in the paranoid position . . . locked in the depressive position—under attack by the internal persecutor, guilt-ridden, and vulnerable to depression. . . . A solution for this "intolerable burden" is to disown the internal persecutor. . . . If he does commit suicide, it is to escape his projected internal prosecutor, his hidden executioner.[4]

Both Merari and Post have characterized suicide terrorists as overwhelmingly uneducated, unemployed, socially isolated single men in their late teens or early twenties. They are the principal authorities whose work underpins the profile of a suicide attacker that is commonly used by law enforcement officials and that is so pervasive in journalistic accounts of this phenomenon.

As we saw in Chapter 10, this demographic profile may fit the relatively few instances of suicide terrorism in the 1980s fairly well. However, examination of the much larger number of suicide attackers during the 1990s and since shows that suicide terrorism does not have a single demographic profile. We now know that suicide terrorists can be college educated or uneducated, married or single, male or female, socially isolated or integrated, as young as fifteen or as old as fifty-two. The individuals who carry out suicide terrorist attacks are typically mentally normal, with good prospects for employment or other advancement in their society, and they enjoy good standing in their communities. They are, in other words, much like ordinary soldiers with a strong sense of duty and a willingness to sacrifice all for the common good of their community.

This chapter examines the individual logic of suicide terrorism and shows that even the worst suicide terrorists are surprisingly ordinary people, motivated not by the desire to seek their own death as an end in itself, but by what they see as their duty to kill significant numbers of the enemy even at the cost of their own lives.

To really understand what makes suicide terrorists do what they do, we would like more than basic demographic information about these individuals; we would like to have detailed biographies and personality studies of each suicide terrorist. However, such comprehensive study is not possible because the detailed information we would need is not available in sufficient detail for most suicide attackers. It is usually available only for the most deadly or famous suicide terrorists—those who killed the most people or who attacked in the most spectacular circumstances—because these are the ones whose acts generate the most investigation, especially press coverage, including news stories in which journalists often interview family members, co-workers, and police officials, asking, "Why was this person willing to die to kill others?"

Accordingly, this chapter focuses on the personal histories of three of the most deadly suicide terrorists over the past two decades:

- Mohammed Atta, who organized and led the September 11, 2001, suicide attacks, the deadliest in history;

- Dhanu, who assassinated Rajiv Gandhi for the Tamil Tigers, the highest-ranking political leader ever killed by a suicide terrorist; and

- Saeed Hotari, a member of Hamas who blew up himself and twenty-one Israelis outside a discotheque in Tel Aviv, one of the worst suicide bombings in Israel.

Focusing on these famous individuals does not bias the analysis in favor of my argument. Just the opposite. To the extent that there is bias in the news accounts of these cases, it is in the other direction, because so many of the investigating journalists, like everyone else, were predisposed to find that such terrible criminals must be irrational, abnormal, or anti-social. Commonly, the news stories are organized to create a psychological portrait that would identify the emotional, delusional, or psychotic factors that drove the person to become a suicide terrorist. However, surprisingly few accounts actually find confirmation of such deviant psychological factors; many of the investigators end by forthrightly admitting that they cannot find the moment of psychological trauma or depression that "changed" the individual into a suicide attacker.[5]

Instead, what stands out is that, to a striking degree, the most deadly suicide terrorists have been almost ordinary people. Atta, Dhanu, and Hotari were not from especially impoverished families. They were not highly impulsive, not subject to delusions, not readily characterized as depressed, not unable to enjoy life, not detached from friends and society. They were also not brought up with a religious fundamentalist education that justified terrorism. Rather, they had friends, observed ordinary norms of social and other behavior in their communities, and generally approached their task with a soldier-like sense of mission. They devoted months to detailed planning for their mission, carried out dress rehearsals, and studied similar missions by others in order to work out the kinks in their own plan. In this, they worked closely with others, either as part of suicide squads or in training regimens that would enhance the effectiveness of their attacks. For them, suicide attack was not an escape — it was a duty. From smiles to statements of satisfaction in their final moments on earth, the world's most deadly suicide terrorists took evident pride in what they saw not as crimes but as sacrifices for their communities.

MOHAMMED ATTA, LEADER OF THE SEPTEMBER 11 HIJACKERS

Mohammed Atta in no way matches the stereotype of the pathetic creature who seeks death and chooses suicide attack as a convenient means of escape. He did not come from a poor family; he was the son of a lawyer. His family lives, to this day, in a Cairo apartment filled with ornate furniture, and has a vacation home on the Mediterranean coast. His two sisters are university professors. Atta himself earned a bachelor's degree in Cairo in 1990 and went to Germany for graduate work in urban studies at Hamburg Technical University, where his professors describe him as a good student.

Nor was he brainwashed into fundamentalist beliefs as a child. By all accounts, Atta was only moderately religious in his youth, as was typical for children of his class growing up in the 1970s and 1980s in Egypt.

As Atta saw it, his motive was his duty to help end the West's "humiliation" of the Islamic world. Atta became an Islamic fundamentalist in Germany in 1995, after he was already well educated and, as far as we can tell, he did not make the turn out of despair. At the time he became committed to the cause, he was steadily making progress toward his professional goals and had the support of his family. He showed no obvious signs of major depression around this time, nor did he suffer any profound trauma that we know of.

The Attack

Together with two friends from Hamburg, Atta organized and led the four hijackings on September 11, 2001, that ended with airliners slamming into the two World Trade Center towers, the Pentagon, and a field in Pennsylvania, killing almost 3,000 people. He flew the first plane personally, as well as coordinating the training and planning for the teams involved in the other attacks (the original concept for the attack was a variant of an older al-Qaeda plan). Although in the immediate aftermath many details were murky, American and German investigators have now assembled a great deal of new information on the origins of the plot from interviews with al-Qaeda operatives captured in Afghanistan, Pakistan, and elsewhere.

Intelligence officials knew that terrorists associated with al-Qaeda had a similar plan for quite some time before the September 11 attacks. In 1995, Philippine police raided the bomb-making laboratory of Ramzi Yousef, who coordinated the 1993 World Trade Center bombing and who is known to have had some activities financed by Osama bin Laden. Although Yousef escaped, the police captured one of his associates, Abdul Hakim Murad, and computer files for an operation called Bojinka ("Loud Bang" in Serbo-Croatian), a plan to blow up eleven U.S. airliners over the Pacific Ocean with remote-controlled bombs and to have a suicide pilot crash one into CIA headquarters at Langley, Virginia. Murad, who had recently earned his pilot's license, confessed that he was preparing for the suicide mission. According to a January 20, 1995, briefing report written by the Manila police, Murad said he came up with the idea during a conversation with Ramzi Yousef. The report states that Murad intended to

board any American commercial aircraft pretending to be an ordinary passenger. . . . Then he will hijack said aircraft, control its cockpit and dive it at the C.I.A. headquarters. . . . There will be no bomb or any explosive that he will use in its execution. It is simply a suicidal mission that he is very much willing to execute.

Murad also said that the plan included secondary targets, including the U.S. Congress, the White House, the Pentagon, and possibly some skyscrapers. The only problem, he said, was that they needed more trained pilots to hit all the targets.[6]

What intelligence officials did not realize was the extent to which al-Qaeda had made progress in training such pilots. In November 1999, Atta and several other Muslims from Hamburg traveled to Afghanistan for several months of training, including an audience with Osama bin Laden, a privilege reserved for those on important missions. It was during this visit, intelligence officials believe, that Atta was presented with a plan inspired by Bojinka. The presenter was probably Khalid Shaik Mohammed, the uncle of Ramzi Yousef, who was an important member of al-Qaeda and who was in Afghanistan at the time. After returning to Germany in February 2000, the Hamburg men took their first concrete steps toward executing the mission, e-mailing thirty-one flight schools in the United States for admission information. Starting in the spring of 2000, Atta and the other pilots involved in the September 11 attacks attended flight schools in California, Arizona, and Florida. They completed their training a year later.

After Atta returned from a short visit to Spain in July 2001, the final phase of the plot began. Over the next several weeks, fifteen Saudis arrived in the United States to provide the "muscle" that would restrain the hijacked jets' crew and passengers while the newly trained pilots flew the airliners into their targets. According to a videotape by bin Laden, these men did not know they were on a suicide mission before they arrived in the United States. On the last night, however, the hijackers appear to have been given handwritten instructions, distributed by Atta, that would have left no doubt as to their purpose. The instructions told the men to shave excess hair from their bodies, to read certain passages of the Quran, and to be happy that "you are on your way to everlasting paradise."[7]

On September 11, the plan went into action. Between 7:58 A.M. and 8:10 A.M., four airliners took off—two from Boston, one from Newark, and one from Dulles Airport in Washington, D.C. An hour later, all four had been hijacked; two were flown into the towers of the World Trade Center, one into the Pentagon, and one into a field in Pennsylvania. Atta and his eighteen accomplices had brought Operation Bojinka into our world.

Atta's Training

Like many other al-Qaeda operatives, Atta spent several months training in Afghanistan, most likely from late 1998 to early 1999. Beyond his meeting with bin Laden and the likelihood that he received instructions on the basic scheme for the September 11 attacks, we do not know the details of his stay. However, the numerous al-Qaeda operatives captured in the recent past have provided extensive information about al-Qaeda's training camps in Afghanistan. Much of the training regimen—the curriculum—was standardized. Accordingly, understanding how al-Qaeda's training camps were run gives us an excellent window into Atta's terrorist training.

Al-Qaeda ran a dozen training camps in Afghanistan, most located in Paktia Province near the border with Pakistan. Camps varied in size. The smallest accommodated some fifteen fighters at a time, and had only one mud brick mosque and fabric tents. The largest trained as many as 300 fighters at once and had numerous permanent buildings plus the wherewithal to support thirty to forty families; these camps even generated their own electrical power.[8]

The most common estimates of the number of fighters who were trained in al-Qaeda's camps between the time bin Laden first went to Afghanistan in 1996 and the time the United States toppled the Taliban regime in November 2001 range from 5,000 to 8,000 individuals. However, even the best estimates are based on interviews with captured al-Qaeda leaders and not on hard records of attendance, so precise counts are unobtainable.

The main purpose of the camps was military training. Although one might suspect that religious indoctrination was a core feature of bin Laden's camps, this was not the case. Recruits were not admitted to the camps unless they were already devout. Most, including Atta, went through a two-month "basic" course with only two weeks devoted to religious education. Like all major religions, Islam prohibits the killing of innocents, a principle that Islamic fundamentalists have "reinterpreted" in order to justify precisely such acts. The purpose of the two weeks of religious lectures was to ensure that the recruits had a common justification rooted in Islam for the acts they were already intent on committing. Mohamed Rashed Daoud al-'Owhali, a defendant tried in the United States for his role in the Kenya and Tanzania bombings in 1998, said that the religious teaching he received in Afghanistan taught him that an individual (not necessarily Muslim) who helped to enact laws against Islam had committed blasphemy and that "it was your right and duty to kill him."[9]

The rest of al-Qaeda's basic training was devoted to the tactical military skills necessary for small numbers of fighters to kill others—effectively, efficiently, and, if possible, spectacularly. Although the length of each phase varied, recruits commonly went through three stages of military training. In the first, lasting about a month, recruits were taught how to use an impressive array of light weapons, such as pistols, sniper rifles, and machine guns. Recruits began the day with morning prayers, devoting the rest of their mornings to rigorous physical exercise and the afternoons to small-arms training and target practice. Next was a two-week course in explosives, teaching fighters how to use plastic explosives, dynamite, and electronic detonators to build bombs, how to use different types of mines, such as anti-personnel and anti-tank mines, and how to conduct reconnaissance and prepare plans for specific attacks. The final several weeks were devoted to the use of heavier weapons, such as mortars, grenade launchers, and anti-aircraft weapons. Some fighters then stayed an additional month for advanced training for specific operations—surveillance techniques for stadiums, bridges, and various buildings, and the use of chemical weapons, with dogs and other animals as subjects.[10]

Atta's State of Mind

Born in 1968 in the town of Kar el Sheikh, Mohammed Atta was the son of a middle-class lawyer and lived much of his youth in the genteel Abdein neighborhood of Cairo. Atta's family would be considered professional by Western standards. His father encouraged all three of his children to pursue advanced secular and professional careers. All three did well in school and showed signs of a strong work ethic and socially commendable ambitions. Mohammed was the youngest. His two older sisters grew up to be a botany professor and a medical doctor, while from a young age Mohammed aimed to become an engineer.

As a boy, Mohammed was encouraged by his family to be moderately religious, observing basic Islamic practices such as daily prayers from the age of twelve or thirteen on. Hundreds of millions of Muslims follow a similar lifestyle. This is normal for Westernized, educated Muslims in Egypt and elsewhere and is hardly the mark of an extremist. In fact, as a teenager, Atta refused to join a basketball league because it was organized by the Muslim Brotherhood, Egypt's main Islamic fundamentalist organization. The Muslim Brotherhood also recruited actively in Atta's engineering department at the University of Cairo, but there is no record that Atta showed any interest. Atta earned respectable, if not outstanding, grades, and graduated in 1990. His father rewarded him with a 1974 Fiat 128 coupe as a graduation present.

In 1992, Atta left Egypt to study for an advanced degree in town planning at Hamburg Technical University in Germany. Like a great many college graduates, he had not been able to find a job in his field in the weak Egyptian economy. His father persuaded him that only a graduate degree from Europe or the United States would allow him to prosper in Egypt.

Within months of his arrival in Hamburg, Atta was able to supplement his studies with a part-time job with Plankontor, a respectable urban planning firm in an upscale section of the city. Although he quietly prayed at the office, often kneeling at midday beside his desk, his co-workers saw him as no different from the millions of other devout and peaceful Muslims in Germany. In these years, Atta seemed to have things going his way. He was accepted at work and school. He spoke to his colleagues about his hopes of eventually returning to Egypt to help build neighborhoods where people could live better lives.

If there was any single point of change, it may have come in 1995, when Atta made his haj to Mecca in Saudi Arabia, a pilgrimage that Muslims are commanded to make at least once in their lives. When he returned to Hamburg in early 1996, Atta wrote a will, dated March 6, 1996, which was found in a suitcase that he left behind when he hijacked American Airlines flight 512 out of Boston years later. The will leaves little doubt that he had become a committed fundamentalist. It dedicates his life and death to Allah and forbids women to visit his grave. Atta's co-workers also report that at about this time he began to grow his beard in the distinctive pattern — around the chin but not over the upper lip — that, at least in North African cultures, is usually the sign of a fundamentalist.

In June 1997, Atta lost his job at Plankontor, partly because of declining business at the firm and partly because the firm had purchased a new computer system that made his drafting work redundant. Atta then left school and Hamburg for fifteen months with little explanation — he said for "family reasons." When he reappeared in October 1998, Atta's mustache-less beard had become thick and long; he founded an Islamic prayer group and moved into an apartment with two other Muslims who would later go on to join him in the September 11 plot. Atta also showed renewed interest in completing his degree, interest he had not shown since beginning his studies in 1992. A year later, in October 1999, Atta formally presented his 152-page thesis on urban planning, earning a top grade. He then traveled to Cairo, degree in hand, for what became his last visit with his family. A month later, he and his roommates headed for Afghanistan to begin dedicated preparations for the September 11 attacks.

Since September 11, perhaps a dozen journalists have conducted several dozens of interviews with Atta's family, his fellow high school students, and his co-workers and professors in Germany. What stands out is not an impulsive, erratic, warped, or pessimistic person with low self-esteem and no social conscience, but almost the opposite. By all accounts, Atta was responsible, industrious, respectful, and willing to uphold rules and regulations. Above all, those who knew Atta best report that he had an emotional steadiness that one might describe as mild or unassuming, and a strong sense of duty as evidenced by his plans at the time he began his studies to use his educational advantages to improve the lot of less well-off urban dwellers back in Egypt. He was principled and meticulous, conscientious and rational.

The only thing that makes Atta unusual is that he eventually decided that his highest duty was to advance the Muslim cause in its struggle with the West by killing Americans even at the expense of his own life. Atta saw himself as a self-sacrificing soldier, and indeed, his psychological history, motivations, and behavior do not appear terribly different from those of the kamikazes or of many soldiers from many cultures who saw their societies as engaged in desperate struggles for survival.[11]

DHANU, TAMIL TIGERS

Dhanu, the single name of a young woman from Jaffna, is the most famous Tamil Tiger suicide bomber. On May 21, 1991, she hid a girdle of grenades beneath her gown, presented a garland to Rajiv Gandhi, India's top political figure, and exploded, instantly killing them both. Dhanu has become a heroine to the women of Sri Lanka's Hindu Tamil minority. The Tigers targeted Gandhi because they feared that, if the Congress under Gandhi were to win the upcoming election, the new government would order the recently withdrawn Indian Peacekeeping Force to return to Sri Lanka to suppress the Tigers' insurgency. For the Tigers, the assassination was a strategic victory. For Dhanu, a remarkably beautiful woman in her late twenties, motivation probably came directly from revenge: reportedly her home in Jaffna was looted by Indian soldiers, she was gang-raped, and her four brothers were killed.

The Attack

Dhanu was the first attacker to use a "suicide belt," and this novelty determined the operational plan of attack. It is not known how the Tigers hit upon the idea. A suicide belt is an undergarment with specially made pockets to hold explosives and triggering devices so that they closely conform to the contours of the human bomb's body. However, there is a close match between Dhanu's suicide belt and one described in a dramatic scene in a Frederick Forsyth best-seller published in 1989, *The Negotiator*. In the novel, kidnappers use a belt bomb to kill the son of the U.S. president. The fictitious belt bomb is virtually identical to the belt worn by Dhanu, which investigators pieced together after the attack. Both belts are three inches wide, made from leather and denim, with a Velcro closure, and with explosives inserted to lie across the backbone. The main difference is the detonation mechanism. The belt in the novel is set off by a remote-control device hidden in the buckle, while the woman assassin had no such device and triggered the bomb herself with a manual switch.[12]

The plan was simple. According to accomplices and messages captured after the attack, the LTTE sent a squad of four assassins to Madras, the largest city in the southern Tamil Nadu region of India, about three weeks before Rajiv Gandhi was scheduled to speak at a major political rally. Dhanu was the designated assassin. It was her job to wear the belt bomb, carry a garland for Gandhi, "accidentally" drop it at his feet, bend over to pick it up, and explode the bomb at the precise moment when Gandhi (and she) would receive its full force. Two members of the squad were to ensure that Dhanu would reach her target. The last served as a cameraman, taking live footage of the attack so that LTTE leaders, cadre, and future recruits could view the mission as it actually happened.[13]

The assassination went off according to plan. However, the cameraman was too close. He died in the blast, and the tape fell into the hands of the Indian police, providing an unusually vivid account that helped elucidate the assassination plot.

On page 228 are two of the ten surviving still frames of the actual attack. The first shows Dhanu at the far left smiling, garland in hand, waiting for the approaching Gandhi. The second shows the last moments of Gandhi's life.

Dhanu's Training

Dhanu belonged to the female suicide bomber unit of the Liberation Tigers of Tamil Eelam that goes by the name Black Tigresses. Since the

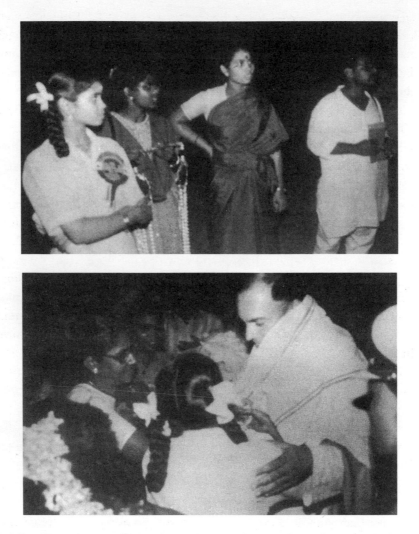

early 1980s, the Tamil population has fought a civil war for independence from the Sinhalese Buddhist majority of Sri Lanka. The Tamil leader Velupillai Prabhakaran formed the LTTE with support and arms from India, and began a terror campaign against the Sinhalese government in which more than 60,000 people have died. Although precise numbers are hard to come by, the LTTE is estimated to number well over 10,000 guerrillas and has had as many as 14,000 during the 1990s. Of these, as many as 4,000 are women.[14]

LTTE guerrillas all manifest a high degree of personal commitment to the cause of independence for their Tamil homeland. The most evident sign is the small cyanide capsule that hangs around the neck of each guerrilla, and that puts him or her only seconds from death. Literally hundreds have died at their own hands, biting through their capsules and consuming the deadly contents rather than accepting capture by the Sinhalese authorities.

The Black Tigresses (and Black Tigers) are different. These units of the LTTE are trained especially for suicide terrorist operations. For them, it is not a matter of committing suicide rather than accepting the humiliation and possible torture that comes with capture. Rather, suicide is an inextricable part of their mission. They are trained to kill others while killing themselves in order to maximize the chances of a successful mission — typically, the assassination of a prominent political leader or the infliction of the most possible casualties on Sinhalese civilians or unsuspecting soldiers.

Members of the LTTE's suicide squads perform only one mission. Their selection and training are dedicated to ensuring that this single mission achieves results — not simply their own death, but the deaths of others.

Dhanu, alias Anbu alias Kalaivani, was from Jaffna, the principal town in the Tamil region of Sri Lanka. She appears to have been a member of the LTTE since the mid-1980s and to have gone through the typical process of becoming a Black Tigress in the late 1980s, possibly after her personal trauma at the hands of Indian troops.

Joining the LTTE's suicide squads involves a number of steps. First, the suicide attackers are carefully selected. Although every LTTE guerrilla is given the option to join these groups, many more are rejected than accepted. At any given point, of the 10,000 or so cadres, there are probably 150 to 200 who are Black Tigresses and Tigers. The main selection criterion is a high level of motivation to complete the mission, a criterion that puts a premium on mental stability over tactical military competence.

Second, the suicide attackers are trained in special camps. They are segregated from the regulars and trained only for suicide missions. The training involves daily physical exercises, arms training, and political classes that all emphasize results. According to reliable reports, the Black Tigresses and Tigers have a simple motto: "You die only once."

Third, LTTE suicide attackers routinely conduct dress rehearsals near the intended location of an attack. They also devote considerable effort to the study of past operations, going so far as to film the actual execution of many suicide missions and to use these films to motivate and train future

suicide attackers. The LTTE's videotape of its first suicide attacker—
a truck bomber who killed eighteen Sinhalese soldiers on July 5, 1987—
reportedly shows the truck rolling through the military camp, exploding,
and strewing the limbs of soldiers for hundreds of yards. These films are
shown to all members of the suicide squads. They leave little doubt that
the LTTE reveres the Black Tigresses and Tigers as heroes and that these
individuals know full well what is expected of them.

How committed are the LTTE suicide commandos? From 1980 to
2001, Black Tigresses and Tigers conducted a total of seventy-six suicide
terrorist attacks. These missions routinely involved backup suicide attackers ready to strike if the primary attacker withdrew at the last minute. However, there is only one known example of a Black Tiger withdrawing from
a mission.[15]

Dhanu's State of Mind

Although detailed information on her mental state is not available,
Dhanu's behavior during the weeks before the assassination does not display signs of depression or personal trauma. Indeed, what we know about
her activities suggests a person enjoying the good things in life. For
Dhanu, her trip to Madras was the first time she had traveled beyond the
Tamil areas of Sri Lanka. Even though much of the three weeks prior to
the attack was devoted to preparations and rehearsals for the mission, she
took advantage of her new surroundings. With money and encouragement
from the LTTE, she went to the market, the beach, and restaurants every
day, enjoying many luxuries rarely found in the jungles of Jaffna. She
bought dresses, jewelry, cosmetics, and even her first pair of glasses. In the
last twenty days of her life, she took in six movies at a local cinema.

Dhanu clearly had nerves of steel. She clearly understood the consequences of her actions and worked hard to ensure that her mission would
surely succeed. Some of the female suicide bombers in Sri Lanka are believed to be victims of rape at the hands of Sinhalese or Indian soldiers, a
stigma that destroys their prospects for marriage and rules out procreation
as a means of contributing to the community. "Acting as a human bomb,"
a Tamil woman told Ana Cutter, the former editor of Columbia University's *Journal of International Affairs*, "is an understood and accepted offer-
ing for a woman who will never be a mother."[16]

SAEED HOTARI, HAMAS

Saeed Hotari is well known in the West Bank. On June 1, 2001, this Hamas terrorist blew himself up outside a disco in Tel Aviv, killing twenty-one Israelis in what remains one of Israel's worst suicide bombings ever. Although many Palestinians support suicide bombings, the interviews given by Hotari's father after his son's mission are especially revealing. Far from lamenting the loss of his son, Hotari's father threw a party to celebrate his son's heroic act to help end Israel's occupation of Palestine. He also had no hesitation in proclaiming that he hoped his other sons would do the same and that he felt "jealous" because he wished he had done the attack

The Attack

On the night of Friday, June 1, 2001, Saeed Hotari took a taxi for the thirty-minute ride from his home in Qaliqilya in the West Bank to the Dolphinarium, a popular discotheque in Tel Aviv. When he got out of the car, Hotari warned the Palestinian driver to leave the area quickly. Although the driver became suspicious, and was in fact an informer for Israeli police intelligence, events unfolded too rapidly for him to act. Hotari immediately walked into the crowd at the entrance to the disco, stopped next to a group of teenage girls, and triggered the deadly mix of explosives and steel ball bearings that he had strapped to his chest. Within seconds, Hotari and twenty-one Israelis were dead.[17]

Hotari's Training

Hotari was recruited by Hamas for his suicide mission in the usual way. At any one time, Hamas has from five to twenty individuals, between eighteen and twenty-three years old, ready to carry out suicide attacks, according to Israeli officials. Although one might think that Hamas's recruitment methods would be a closely guarded secret, Hamas recruiters are quite open about the broad outlines of how the organization identifies, selects, and prepares suicide terrorist attackers.

Mosques are a common recruitment ground. Hamas's leaders say that they routinely mingle with those who attend regular services and look for three qualities in a potential bomber: an intense interest in Islam; a clean criminal record, so as not to raise the suspicions of Israel's secret police; and a strong nerve, to carry out the mission successfully. When the need arises, Hamas leaders initiate a discussion of dying for Allah with small groups of young people and invite those who seem particularly interested to join a special Hamas-led class on Islamic study. After just several weeks, many in such classes willingly volunteer to be suicide bombers, at which point Hamas inquires into the past criminal behavior of the volunteers.[18]

In these classes, the recruits usually spend between two and four hours a day reading and discussing various parts of the Quran. The passages emphasize the birth of the nation of Islam, the importance of faith, the duty of jihad, and Allah's favors for those deemed most faithful.[19]

In most cases, a suicide terrorist in waiting is assigned to his mission only days before it is to occur. As the mission nears, the volunteers are tested for their strength of nerve and their commitment to completing their assigned task. The recruit, sometimes alone and sometimes with several others, is taken to a cemetery. He is told to prepare for death by lying between grave sites for several hours and to wear a white, hooded shroud normally used to cover bodies for burial.[20] Those who remain calm pass the test and are selected for the final preparations.

As part of the preparation, the would-be suicide bomber returns to the cemetery, spending a dozen or more hours in a grave while reciting passages of the Koran. Meanwhile, separate Hamas groups select the target, construct the bomb or the suicide vest, and make preparations to take the bomber to the target. Once at the target site, the recruit is told to remain calm, blend in as much as possible, and, when surrounded by Israelis, press a switch to explode the bomb.[21]

From what we know, Hotari's recruitment followed this path. He fit all of Hamas's criteria. According to his father, Hotari was "a devout Muslim who used to pray, observed fasting and performed all his religious obligations to the letter and spirit." He had no criminal history. In Qaliqilya, Hotari and two other Palestinians attended a mosque where a Hamas leader persuaded them to attend a special class on Islamic study. Hotari and the other two Palestinians carried out their attacks within weeks of each other. Reportedly, Hotari himself watched as his friend Mahmoud Marmash blew himself up on May 18, 2001, in a shopping mall in Netanya.[22]

Hotari's State of Mind

Saeed Hotari, twenty-two, was one of nine children from a poor Palestinian family living in Zarqa, Jordan. He was an observant Muslim who moved to the West Bank two years before the attack in search of a better job.[23]

Although few details of Hotari's life in the West Bank are available, we can gain important insight into the circumstances of his decision from the detailed interviews his father gave to the media after his son's suicide attack.

A month after the attack, the bomber's father, Hassan Hotari, threw a party to celebrate his son's mission. Neighbors hung pictures on their trees of Saeed Hotari holding seven sticks of dynamite. Others put up a sign: "Martyr Saeed Hotari." Still others expressed satisfaction with what the mission accomplished, spray-painting "21 and counting" on a stone wall.

Mr. Hotari was elated by his son's act, eagerly proclaiming: "I am very happy and proud of what my son did and, frankly, am a bit jealous. I wish I had done [the bombing]. My son has fulfilled the Prophet's wishes. He has become a hero! Tell me, what more could a father ask? . . . I hope I have many sons to carry out the same act."[24]

Two years later, the bomber's father lamented the loss of his son. However, he offered no apologies, saying, "There are no apologies from Israelis when our people die."[25] He said that the popular Israeli view that the suicide bombers kill themselves because they are promised seventy-two virgins in the afterlife is a means to avoid considering their real motivations:

> Before they ask me how my son could do something like that, they should ask what the conditions were that led him to do it. Why do people kill themselves? Are they fond of death? Is it a fashion? Since 1948, the Jews have taken more and more of our land. My son wasn't a radical person, he was radicalized by the anger, by the humiliation. Look before your eyes. We are living in a jail. I would be a liar to say I feel sorry for the people who are oppressing us day by day.[26]

In his final statement, Hotari explained why concern about Israeli retaliation does not deter community support for suicide terrorism against Israelis, "If we don't fight, we will suffer. If we do fight, we will suffer, but so will they."[27]

To hear a father so strongly support his own son's suicide in public may be startling and is not the norm among the families of suicide terrorists, but Hassan Hotari is not a lone exception. Palestinian suicide terrorists often make videos describing their motives, but the one by Mahmoud al-Obeid, a college student, age twenty-three, from Gaza, was different. Unusually, the young man's mother, Naima, appeared in the video and was clearly fully aware of what he planned to do. She says to her son: "God willing, you will succeed. May every bullet hit its target, and may God give you martyrdom. This is the best day of my life." Mahmoud replies, "Thank you for raising me." The video was released in early June 2002. Days later, the man died carrying out a suicide attack on a Jewish settlement. After her son's death, Naima told a journalist: "Nobody wants their son to be killed. I always wanted him to have a good life. But our land is occupied by the Israelis. We're sacrificing our sons to get our freedom." She also said that she has nine more children, each of whom has a duty to fight.[28]

CONCLUSION

1 2

A New Strategy
for Victory

UNDERSTANDING THAT SUICIDE terrorism is mainly a response to foreign occupation rather than the product of Islamic fundamentalism has
important implications for how the United States and its allies should conduct the war on terrorism. Since the root cause of suicide terrorism does
not lie in an ideology, even among Muslims, spreading democracy across
the Persian Gulf is not likely to be a panacea so long as foreign combat
troops remain on the Arabian Peninsula. If not for the world's interest in
Persian Gulf oil, the obvious solution—just as it was for Ronald Reagan
when the United States faced suicide terrorism in Lebanon—might well
be simply to abandon the region altogether. This, however, is not possible,
certainly not for the foreseeable future. Thus, the question is: can we find
a lasting solution to suicide terrorism that does not compromise our core
interest in maintaining access to one of the world's key oil-producing regions?

The answer is a qualified yes. Although isolated suicide attacks may still
occur, America and its allies can pursue a strategy for victory that promises
to substantially reduce the likelihood of sustained campaigns of suicide
terrorism without compromising our core international security interests.
To do this, we must recognize the limits both of offensive military action
and of concessions, as well as the value (and limits) of enhanced homeland security efforts. Most of all, we need to recall the virtues of our tradi-

tional policy of "offshore balancing" in the Persian Gulf and return to that strategy. Offshore balancing is the best way to secure our interests in the world's key oil-producing region without provoking more terrorism.

DEFINING VICTORY

Winning the war on terrorism requires a clear conception of victory. The enemy is not "terrorism" per se. This is a tactic that has existed throughout history and that will continue to exist long after the threat to the United States and its allies comes to an end. The enemy that matters is also not the existence of one or a handful of anti-American terrorists, because isolated individual terrorist attacks remain a relatively minor threat to American security. Rather, the threat that can and must be defeated is campaigns of anti-American terrorism—especially suicide terrorism—a sustained sequence of attacks designed to kill large numbers of innocent people by numerous individuals willing to die to achieve this evil purpose.

Two main features distinguish today's anti-American suicide terrorist campaigns. The individual terrorists are most often shadowy, hard-to-find creatures whose existence is rarely known until they strike. They are also most often walk-in volunteers, with little connection to terrorism or any other form of violence until just before they sign up for their missions. Mohammed Atta, the lead hijacker on September 11, was not a member of al-Qaeda prior to going to Afghanistan in order to volunteer for a mission on behalf of the group. Similarly, many al-Qaeda suicide terrorists who carried out their attacks after September 11 were not associated with al-Qaeda until just months prior to their mission, had never been to Afghanistan, and never met Osama bin Laden. These facts have an important implication: even if we could miraculously root out every terrorist now planning to give up his or her life to kill Americans, this would provide little lasting security—so long as more took their place.

Accordingly, the United States must achieve two goals to win the war on terrorism: (1) we must defeat the current pool of terrorists now actively planning to kill Americans; and (2) we must prevent a new, potentially larger generation from rising up. Both are necessary and each must be considered independently, for success in one does not necessarily mean success in the other. Although some have thought that a demonstration of American power would not only root out today's terrorists but make others think twice before joining them, the rise in anti-American suicide terrorism by al-Qaeda since 2002 and in Iraq since 2003 shows that heavy military force does not automatically solve our problems and can make them worse. The trade-off between our two objectives exists because the use of heavy offensive force to defeat the existing generation of terrorists is the most likely stimulus to the rise of the next. For a lasting solution to anti-American terrorism, therefore, America's strategy must defeat the existing pool of terrorists while not encouraging more to take their place.

DEFEATING THE CURRENT GENERATION

While defeating the active generation of suicide terrorists seems daunting, there are important policy lessons to learn from our experience.

The first key point is that offensive military action rarely works. Although military action can disrupt a terrorist group's operations temporarily, it rarely ends the threat. Of the thirteen major suicide terrorist campaigns that had ended as of 2004, only one—the PKK versus Turkey—did so as a result of leadership decapitation, when the leader, in Turkish custody, asked his followers to stop. Depriving al-Qaeda of its Afghan bases was well worth doing, as are our efforts to keep Osama bin Laden on the run and to capture him if we can. Gains from offensive military action, however, must be weighed against costs. Although few, even in the Muslim world, objected to our actions in Afghanistan, our invasion of Iraq has generated new support for anti-American terrorism and given al-Qaeda a new lease on life, especially in Iraq itself and in Saudi Arabia.

The second is that, like offensive action, attempts to resolve threats through concessions must also be handled very carefully, and also may not work. Concessions to the nationalist grievances of the terrorists' community can make it more difficult for the terrorists to recruit new suicide attackers and strengthen the standing of more moderate elites. Partial or gradual, incremental concessions that are dragged out over time, however, are likely to fail. Incremental compromises are often proposed as a way of "building confidence," but they also provide time for spoilers—the terrorists—to commit more violence, undermining support for compromise on both sides. This is what happened to the Israeli-Palestinian Oslo Accords, leading to the second intifada. Hence, concessions make sense only if they actually satisfy most of the national community that the terrorists come from, and are then made all at once in a single step. The issue is not whom to bargain with or how, or even whether any formal agreement is necessary, but careful consideration by the state targeted by terrorism of what stakes it is willing to relinquish, combined with good judgment about the real grievances of the opposing community. Advocates of concessions should also recognize that even genuine resolution of the main dispute will not end terrorism immediately, since any concessions will almost always strengthen the terrorist leaders' belief in their own coercive effectiveness. Denied further popular support, however, the terrorist threat will gradually fade.

Third, even though attaining perfect security against suicide attackers is usually impossible, homeland security must be a part of any solution. Ethnic civil wars can often be stopped by demographic separation because this reduces both means and incentives for the sides to attack each other.[1] This logic applies with even more force to suicide terrorism, since gaining physical access to the target area is the only genuinely demanding part of a suicide operation. Recent evidence from Israel supports the value of separation. In August 2003, Israel completed the first major section of a dense "security fence"—three barriers with other defensive measures—along its border with the West Bank. Palestinian terrorist groups had carried out an average of more than twenty successful suicide attacks over the previous three years, but only six in the following year. The fence probably accounts for much of this decline, since it appears that no suicide attackers got through the barrier, only through still unfinished sections. Hence, Israel now has an optimum strategy combining concessions with defense: abandoning much of the territory it occupies in the West Bank and Gaza, along with erecting physical barriers that prevent access to areas Israel is determined to retain.

The United States must step up border and immigration controls. We have substantially increased background checks of immigrants and visa seekers, and these policies should be maintained. The United States should also take stronger measures to control illegal immigration, especially across its most porous border, with Mexico. In 1996 the United States began building a National Border Fence, comparable to the Israeli barriers, covering a fourteen-mile stretch near San Diego. Extending the fence to cover the entire 1,951-mile border with Mexico would cost about $6 billion, or about the same as one month of U.S. operations in Iraq.[2] Such measures would make it more difficult for al-Qaeda to continue attacks inside the United States.

THE WRONG STRATEGY AGAINST THE NEXT
GENERATION

Since September 11, 2001, the United States has responded to the growing threat of suicide terrorism by embarking on a policy to conquer Muslim countries—not simply rooting out existing havens for terrorists in
Afghanistan but going further, to remake Muslim societies in the Persian
Gulf. Proponents claim that Islamic fundamentalism is the principal
cause of suicide terrorism and that this radical ideology is spreading
through Muslim societies, dramatically increasing the prospects for a new,
larger generation of anti-American terrorists in the future. Hence, the
United States should install new governments in Muslim countries in
order to transform and diminish the role of radical Islam in their societies.
This logic led to widespread support for the conquest of Iraq and is promoted as the principal reason for regime change in Iran, Saudi Arabia, and
other Persian Gulf states in the future.

The goal of this strategy is correct, but its premise is faulty. American
security depends critically on diminishing the next generation of anti-
American Muslim terrorists. However, Islamic fundamentalism is not the
main cause of suicide terrorism, and conquering Muslim countries to
transform their societies is likely to increase the number coming at us.

Spokesmen for the "Muslim transformation" strategy present a sweep-
ing case. Although these arguments are sometimes vague and incomplete,
they all center on the presumption that Islamic fundamentalism is the
driving force behind the growing threat of suicide terrorism. According to
David Frum and Richard Perle, "The terrorists kill and will accept death
for a cause with which no accommodation is possible. That cause is militant Islam." Moreover, these beliefs are not really confined to a radical
fringe, but infect even ordinary Muslims: "And though it is comforting to
deny it, all the available evidence indicates that militant Islam commands
wide support, and even wider sympathy, among Muslims worldwide, including Muslim minorities in the West." For Frum and Perle, "the roots of
Muslim rage are to be found in Islam itself. . . . The Islamic world has
lagged further and further behind the Christian West." While there are
multiple terrorist groups, the common element of Islam makes the threat
monolithic: "The distinction between Islamic terrorism against Israel, on
the one hand, and Islamic terrorism against the United States and Europe,
on the other, cannot be sustained. . . . Worse, the ideology that justifies the
terrible crimes of Hamas and Hezbollah is the same ideology that justifies

the crimes of al-Qaeda." The result is an unlimited threat to dominate the world: "This strain seeks to overthrow our civilization and remake the nations of the West into Islamic societies, imposing on the whole world its religion and its law." The solution, Perle and Frum contend, is regime change: "We must move boldly against [Iran] and against all the other sponsors of terrorism as well: Syria, Libya, and Saudi Arabia."[3]

This argument is fatally flawed. First, al-Qaeda's suicide terrorists have not come from the most populous Islamic fundamentalist populations in the world, but mainly from the Muslim countries with heavy American combat presence. From 1995 through 2003, there have been a total of seventy-one al-Qaeda suicide terrorists. Only 6 percent (4 of 71) have come from the five countries with the world's largest Islamic fundamentalist populations—Pakistan (149 million), Bangladesh (114 million), Iran (63 million), Egypt (62 million), and Nigeria (37 million). By contrast, 55 percent of al-Qaeda's suicide terrorists (39 of 71) have come from Saudi Arabia and other Persian Gulf countries, a region whose population totals less than 30 million, but where the United States has stationed heavy combat troops more or less continuously since 1990.

This comparison of the relative weight of American military presence and Islamic fundamentalism is important. If Islamic fundamentalism is driving al-Qaeda's suicide terrorism, then we would expect a close relationship between the world's largest Islamic fundamentalist populations and the nationality of al-Qaeda's suicide terrorists. However, this is not the case. The world's five largest Islamic fundamentalist populations without American military presence have produced al-Qaeda suicide terrorists on the order of 1 per 71 million people, while the Persian Gulf countries with American military presence have produced al-Qaeda suicide terrorists at a rate of 1 per million, or 70 times more often. Further, even if we narrow our definition of Islamic fundamentalism to Salafism, the specific form associated with Osama bin Laden but not with Iran or even many Sunnis, American military presence remains the pivotal factor driving al-Qaeda's suicide terrorists. As Chapter 7 shows, the stationing of tens of thousands of American combat troops on the Arabian Peninsula from 1990 to 2001 probably made al-Qaeda suicide attacks against Americans, including the horrible crimes committed on September 11, 2001, from five to twenty times more likely. Hence, the longer American troops remain in Iraq and in the Persian Gulf in general, the greater the risk of the next September 11.

Second, Islamic fundamentalism has not created a monolithic terrorism threat against the United States or other Western countries. Islamic fundamentalism does not lead suicide terrorist organizations to cooperate with each other in the ways that matter most—the sharing of suicide terrorists across groups, or one group conducting a suicide terrorist campaign on behalf of another. Hezbollah and Hamas have each waged numerous suicide terrorist campaigns against Israel, but never for each other and never at the same time. Al-Qaeda has never attacked Israel at all, while Hamas has never attacked the United States, and Hezbollah has attacked only Americans in Lebanon. When one studies the various suicide terrorist campaigns by Hezbollah, Hamas, and al-Qaeda what stands out is not that these groups share military resources or act in concert, like a monolithic movement. Instead, what stands out is that each is driven by essentially nationalist goals to compel target democracies to withdraw military forces from their *particular* homeland.

Third, the idea that all Muslims around the world are quietly anti-American because Islam encourages hatred for American values for democracy and free markets does not square with the facts. Indeed, robust evidence shows that American military policies, not revulsion against Western political and economic values, are driving anti-Americanism among Muslims.

Our best information on Muslim attitudes comes from the Pew Global Attitudes surveys. Since 2000, approval of the United States has been declining sharply among Muslims from across a broad cross section of countries—among both Muslims who were initially highly favorable to the United States and those who were not. Even with the slight rise in 2004, America's image even among our closest Muslim allies is now a pale reflection of where it was four years ago.

TABLE 23. Muslims with a Favorable View of the United States

	Percentage of Population			
	2000	*2002*	*2003*	*2004*
Turkey	52	30	15	30
Morocco	77	na	27	27
Pakistan	23	10	13	21
Jordan	na	25	1	5

Source: Pew Global Attitudes Project, "Global Opinion: The Spread of Anti-Americanism," (Washington, D.C.: Pew Research Center, January 2005).

The underlying reason is not discontent with Western political or economic values, which are supported by majorities or near majorities in these countries.

TABLE 24. Muslim Attitudes on Western Economic and Political Values

---

Percentage Favorable

	World Trade	Free Markets	Democracy
Turkey	82	60	57
Morocco	na	na	na
Pakistan	78	50	42
Jordan	52	47	47

Source: Pew Global Attitudes Project, "Views of a Changing World" (Washington, D.C.: Pew Research Center, June 2003).

Rather, the taproot is American military policy. Overwhelming majorities across a range of Muslim countries believe that the United States conquered Iraq to control its oil or to help Israel rather than to end terrorism or promote democracy, and fear that their country might be next.[4]

TABLE 25. Muslim Views of U.S. Motives for Iraq and Future Threat

---

Percentage of Population

	Control Oil	Support Israel	Stop Terrorism	Promote Democracy	U.S. Military Threat to Your Country
Pakistan	54	44	6	5	73
Turkey	64	45	20	9	71
Morocco	63	54	17	15	na
Jordan	71	70	11	7	56

Source: Pew Global Attitudes Project, "Views of a Changing World" (Washington, D.C.: Pew Research Center, June 2003 and March 2004).

Fourth, the idea that Islamic fundamentalism is on the verge of world domination and poses a realistic threat to impose Islamic laws in the

United States and Europe is pure fantasy. Some radicals may harbor such delusions. Some fearmongers may use such delusions to whip up hysteria. But these are delusions nonetheless. The United States and Europe are overwhelmingly Christian countries and, short of physical conquest, will remain so.[5]

Fifth, and most important, an attempt to transform Muslim societies through regime change is likely to dramatically increase the threat we face. The root cause of suicide terrorism is foreign occupation and the threat that foreign military presence poses to the local community's way of life. Hence, any policy that seeks to conquer Muslim societies in order, deliberately, to transform their culture is folly. Even if our intentions are good, anti-American terrorism would likely grow, and grow rapidly.

Consider Iraq. Proponents of Muslim transformation were staunch advocates of the invasion of Iraq in March 2003, fully expecting that American forces would be greeted as liberators rather than as conquerors. The projected resistance was thought to be so light that the number of American troops would be reduced to 30,000 just six months later. Muslims around the world would come to support this policy, because the war would demonstrate America's commitment to democracy and freedom. Two years later, things have not turned out this way.

The resistance to American occupation has grown steadily from April 2003 to the present. Even though the United States kills an average of 2,000 insurgents every month, the size of the insurgency has grown from

TABLE 26. Resistance of U.S. Occupation of Iraq, 2003–2005

	July 2003	January 2004	July 2004	January 2005
Percent of Iraqis favoring near-term U.S. withdrawal	30	30	65	82
Estimated insurgents/ foreign fighters	5,000/300	5,000/300	20,000/400	18,000/600
Foreign Coalition troops (U.S./other)	149,000/21,000	122,000/26,000	140,000/22,000	150,000/25,000

Source: Adriana Lins de Albuquerque and Michael O'Hanlon, "The State of Iraq," *New York Times* (February 21, 2005). Numbers of insurgents and foreign fighters are based on official U.S. estimates.

approximately 5,000 fighters in April 2003 to 18,000 in January 2005. The overwhelming number of these fighters are local Iraqis and their numbers have risen along with popular support for American withdrawal. Foreign fighters make up less than 5 percent, as estimated by U.S. intelligence.

Moreover, suicide terrorism has been a prime weapon. Prior to April 2003, Iraq had never experienced even a single suicide terrorist attack in its history. Since then, the trajectory has been rising, with twenty suicide terrorist attacks in 2003 and more than fifty in 2004. The number is on pace in the first months of 2005 to set a new record for the year. The main targets have been American troops, Iraqi troops, and political leaders thought to be working with the Americans.

The identities of the Iraqi suicide attackers are now murky. This is not unusual in the early years of a suicide terrorist campaign. Hezbollah did not publish many of the biographies and last testaments of its suicide attackers until after the suicide operations had ended, a pattern adopted by the Tamil Tigers in Sri Lanka as well. At the moment, our best information is that the attackers are from two main sources, Sunni Iraqis and foreign fighters, principally from Saudi Arabia. If so, this would mean that the two main sources of suicide terrorists in Iraq—Iraqis and Saudis—are from the countries whose societies are most vulnerable to transformation by the presence of American combat troops. This picture is fully consistent with the theory of suicide terrorism presented in this book.

Democracy is a source of peace. However, spreading democracy at the barrel of a gun in the Persian Gulf is not likely to lead to a lasting solution against suicide terrorism. Just as al-Qaeda's suicide terrorism campaign began against American troops on the Arabian Peninsula and then escalated to the United States, we should recognize that the longer that American forces remain in Iraq, the greater the threat of the next September 11 from groups who have not targeted us before. Even if our intentions are good, the United States cannot depend on democratic governments in the region to dampen the risk of suicide terrorism so long as American forces are stationed there.

DEFEATING SUICIDE TERRORISM

To win the war on terrorism, the United States and other democracies under fire must seek to prevent the rise of a new, larger generation of anti-American terrorists. Given the close association of foreign occupation and suicide terrorism, this goal can be achieved only if the United States substantially alters its military policy toward the Persian Gulf.

The present realities in the region create an important opportunity to develop a new strategy for victory in the war on terrorism. Saddam Hussein's control of Iraq was the core reason that the United States has stationed tens of thousands of combat forces in multiple countries on the Arabian Peninsula since 1990. Republican and Democratic administrations both supported this policy, believing that Saddam's regime posed a threat to Persian Gulf oil and to our allies in the region. Today, this is no longer true. With Saddam Hussein out of power, Iraq is poised to become an American ally. Whether one supported the war in Iraq or not, we should acknowledge that the emergence of Iraq as an American ally creates an opening for the United States to fundamentally recast its military policy toward the region as a whole.

Historically, American strategy for the Persian Gulf rested on the concept of "off-shore" balancing.[6] For decades prior to 1990, the United States recognized that access to Persian Gulf oil was crucial to the world's economy and that threats could emerge from multiple directions, including domestic instability in the region. To meet these challenges, U.S. administrations from Harry Truman's to Ronald Reagan's used foreign assistance to build strong alliances with key local states, while developing the capability to rapidly deploy American combat forces into the region should a crisis emerge. During the 1980s, the United States formed an alliance with Iraq and Saudi Arabia, which not only helped contain the threat from Iran but also built the critical infrastructure that allowed for the rapid deployment of American power to defeat Iraq's aggression against Kuwait in 1990.

Off-shore balancing is again America's best strategy for the Persian Gulf. Now that the United States has removed Saddam Hussein from power and shepherded Iraq through the foundational phases of a democratic transition, American combat presence in the Persian Gulf provides diminishing returns to U.S. security. Whether the transition to democracy in Iraq goes well or not, the mere presence of tens of thousands of U.S. troops in the region is likely to fuel continued fear of foreign occupation that will encourage anti-American terrorism in the future. Hence, our objective should be to withdraw all American combat forces from the region expeditiously, while working with Iraq, Saudi Arabia, and other Persian Gulf states to ensure that they maintain the critical infrastructure for a rapid return of U.S. forces should that prove necessary.

The purpose of off-shore balancing is to preserve access to Persian Gulf oil, not to manage the internal politics of states in the region. To achieve this goal, it is important to have the friendliest possible relations with all three of the major states—Saudi Arabia, Iraq, and Iran—or with at least two of them, if their behavior toward one another makes cooperative relations with all three impossible. This means refraining from the use of military coercion unless one of these countries actually attacks another or otherwise immediately threatens the balance of power in the Persian Gulf. This also means stationing no American combat troops on the ground, but maintaining permanent readiness to intervene massively and rapidly if necessary, including maintaining the current infrastructure of military bases in the region.

The United States may or may not have to fight another Gulf War someday. If we do, the cardinal purpose should be the same as for the first Gulf War in 1991—protecting oil—not the same as the purpose of the second in 2003—regime change. Democratization is the long-run future of states in the Persian Gulf.[7] The United States can play an important role in facilitating democratic transitions at arm's length, just as it did in Eastern Europe in the 1990s and just as it is doing in Egypt and on the West Bank today. However, seeking to impose democracy on Iran or Saudi Arabia by force can trigger nationalist sentiments that encourage anti-American terrorism and large-scale internal turmoil—which, ultimately, threaten America's core interests. Together, Iran and Saudi Arabia have 100 million Muslims—four times the population of Iraq. While we can topple their regimes, postwar reconstruction would be even more complex and debilitating than it has been in Iraq, and preventing chaos from breaking out across the region may become impossible for America's already overstretched army.

Conquest is also not the best policy for dealing with the possibility that Iran may acquire nuclear weapons. Since Tehran could conceal major nuclear facilities, air strikes, the seizure of chunks of territory, or other limited military options cannot guarantee to set back the country's nuclear development. Only a massive invasion to occupy the entire country—three times the size of Iraq—would suffice. Further, the United States should expect Iranian retaliation, either in the region or at home, because the fires that drove the popular revolution against America's ally, the Shah of Iran, in 1979 could be re-ignited with even greater force against an actual invasion. Most important, Iran's political leaders from the Ayatollah Khomeini to today's clerics have never demonstrated a reckless disregard for America's capacity to retaliate for unprovoked aggression against it, and so we have no actual basis to doubt that we could live with a nuclear Iran. In this case, the risks of action outweigh the risks of deterrence. To limit the danger, the United States should join Europe's current effort to encourage Iran to abide by the limits of the Non-Proliferation Treaty by using access to trade as a means of strengthening the moderates in the regime.

Off-shore balancing is America's best strategy, but it is not perfect and has risks. The balance of power among Iraq, Iran, and Saudi Arabia as well as internal instability in these states is likely to pose important challenges for decades to come. However, the United States has powerful economic and diplomatic tools to manage the local balance of power, while removal of American combat forces from the region is likely to diminish the main source of instability to the Saudi regime. Further, American naval power would remain a formidable military instrument for influence in the region, should immediate uses of power prove necessary. Above all, a return to off-shore balancing will send an unmistakable signal that the United States is not in the business of empire, and will thus suck the oxygen out of the atmosphere that breeds anti-American suicide terrorism.

Sometimes the right policy is to sacrifice nonessentials to get the best deal on core interests—in this case, oil—while maintaining the power to enforce that deal. This is what off-shore balancing does. By assuring the local populations in the Persian Gulf that the United States has no imperial designs, it reduces al-Qaeda's power to mobilize popular support, while safeguarding America's core interests in the region. Al-Qaeda leaders could try to tout this as "appeasement," but fewer and fewer will bother to listen.

Ultimately, energy independence would be an even better alternative to off-shore balancing, since it would reduce our stake in the Persian Gulf altogether. To do this, the United States must reduce our dependence on imported oil. Since nearly all American oil fields have passed their peak and are now in decline, energy independence must mean greater reliance on alternative energy sources and conservation—something that is completely up to us.

Victory will take time. The threat of suicide terrorism against Americans has been building for over a decade, and we cannot reverse the underlying causes quickly. For this reason, it is crucial to immediately tighten border and immigration controls, while continuing to use offensive military action against al-Qaeda terrorists whom we locate. At the same time, the United States should lay the groundwork for withdrawing all American troops from the Persian Gulf and should adopt the strategy of off-shore balancing to secure our interests in the region. In the long term, the United States should work toward energy independence, thus reducing the need for heavy involvement in the region as a whole. These measures will not provide a perfect solution, but they can make it substantially more difficult for al-Qaeda to carry out future attacks in the United States, and, ultimately, make it harder to explain to Muslims why they should attack America at all.

For nearly ten years, al-Qaeda suicide terrorists have been dying to win. With the right strategy, however, it is the United States that is poised for victory.

APPENDIX I

SUICIDE TERRORIST CAMPAIGNS, 1980–2003

Completed Campaigns			
Date	*Weapon*	*Target*	*Killed**

Campaign #1: Hezbollah vs. U.S., France

1. Apr. 18, 1983	car bomb	U.S. embassy, Beirut	63
2. Oct. 23, 1983	car bomb	U.S. Marine barracks, Beirut	241
3. Oct. 23, 1983	car bomb	French barracks, Beirut	58
4. Dec. 12, 1983	truck bomb	U.S. embassy, Kuwait City	7
5. Sept. 20, 1984	truck bomb	U.S. embassy, Beirut	24

Campaign #2: Hezbollah vs. Israel

1. Nov. 11, 1982	car bomb	IDF headquarters, Tyre	74
2. Nov. 4, 1983	car bomb	IDF post, Tyre	60
3. Apr. 13, 1984	car bomb	IDF convoy, Tyre	12
4. June 16, 1984	car bomb	IDF post, south Lebanon	0
5. Feb. 5, 1985	car bomb	IDF convoy, Sidon	0
6. Mar. 10, 1985	truck bomb	IDF post, Metulla border crossing	12
7. Mar. 12, 1985	car bomb	IDF convoy, Jezzine, south Lebanon	0
8. Apr. 9, 1985	car bomb	IDF post, Batr al-Shouf	2

Date	Weapon	Target	Killed
9. Apr. 20, 1985	truck bomb	IDF convoy, Qasimiyeh bridge, s. Leb.	12
10. May 9, 1985	suitcase bomb	South Lebanese army checkpoint	2
11. June 15, 1985	car bomb	Lebanese army post, Beirut	23

Campaign #3: Hezbollah vs. Israel and South Lebanon Army

Date	Weapon	Target	Killed
1. July 9, 1985	car bombs	SLA outpost, Hasbaya, south Leb.	15
2. July 9, 1985	car bomb	SLA outpost, Ras al-Biyada	0
3. July 15, 1985	car bomb	SLA outpost, Kifr Tibnit	9
4. July 31, 1985	car bomb	IDF patrol, Arnun, south Lebanon	2
5. Aug. 6, 1985	mule bomb	SLA outpost, Hasbaya	0
6. Aug. 15, 1985	car bomb	Beit Yahon gate	1
7. Aug. 28, 1985	car bomb	SLA outpost, Jezzine, south Lebanon	15
8. Sept. 3, 1985	car bomb	SLA outpost, Honeh	0
9. Sept. 11, 1985	car bomb	SLA outpost, Hasbya	21
10. Sept. 17, 1985	car bomb	SLA outpost, Taibe	30
11. Sept. 18, 1985	car bomb	SLA outpost, Tyre	0
12. Oct. 11, 1985	car bomb	SLA outpost, Jezzine	12
13. Oct. 17, 1985	grenades	SLA radio station	6
14. Nov. 3, 1985	mule bomb	SLA outpost, Khellat El-Khazem	0
15. Nov. 4, 1985	car bomb	SLA outpost, Arnnon, south Leb.	1
16. Nov. 12, 1985	car bomb	Christian militia leaders, Beirut	5**
17. Nov. 26, 1985	car bomb	SLA outpost, Jezzine, south Leb.	7
18. Apr. 8, 1986	car bomb	SLA outpost, Hasbya	15
19. July 17, 1986	car bomb	Jezzine, south Lebanon	10
20. Nov. 20, 1986	car bomb	SLA outpost, Tyre	7

Campaign #4: Liberation Tigers of Tamil Eelam vs. Sri Lanka

Date	Weapon	Target	Killed
1. July 10, 1990	boat bomb	naval vessel, Trincomalee	6
2. Nov. 23, 1990	mines	army camp, Manakulam	1
3. Mar. 2, 1991	car bomb	defense minister, Colombo	20**
4. Mar. 19, 1991	truck bomb	army camp, Silavathurai	5
5. May 4, 1991	boat bomb	naval vessel, Point Pedro	5
6. May 21, 1991	belt bomb	Rajiv Gandhi, Madras, India	1**
7. June 21, 1991	car bomb	defense ministry, Colombo	51
8. Nov. 16, 1992	motorcycle bomb	navy commander, Colombo	3**
9. May 1, 1993	belt bomb	president of Sri Lanka, Colombo	23**

Date	Weapon	Target	Killed
10. Aug. 29, 1993	mines	naval vessel, Kilaly	12
11. Nov. 11, 1993	boat bomb	naval base, Jaffna Lagoon	0
12. Aug. 2, 1994	grenades	air force helicopter, Palali	1
13. Aug. 10, 1994	mine	naval vessel, Kangesanthurai	0
14. Sept. 19, 1994	mines	naval vessel, Sagarawardene	25
15. Oct. 24, 1994	belt bomb	presidential candidate, Colombo	53**

Campaign #5: LTTE vs. Sri Lanka

Date	Weapon	Target	Killed
1. Apr. 19, 1995	scuba divers	naval vessel, Trincomalee	16
2. July 16, 1995	scuba divers	naval vessel, Jaffna peninsula	0
3. Aug. 7, 1995	belt bomb	government bldg., Colombo	22
4. Oct. 17, 1995	scuba divers	naval vessel, Trincomalee	9
5. Oct. 20, 1995	mines	2 oil depots, Colombo	23
6. Nov. 11, 1995	belt bombs	army HQ, crowd, Colombo	21
7. Dec. 5, 1995	truck bomb	police camp, Batticaloa	29
8. Jan. 8, 1996	belt bomb	market, Batticaloa	0
9. Jan. 31, 1996	truck bomb	bank, Colombo	91
10. Feb. 13, 1996	scuba divers	naval vessel, Trincomalee	0
11. Mar. 30, 1996	boat bomb	naval vessel, Vettilaikerni	10
12. June 11, 1996	mines	naval vessel, Jaffna	0
13. July 4, 1996	belt bomb	government motorcade, Jaffna	37
14. July 19, 1996	mines	naval gunboat, Mullaittivu	35
15. Oct. 25, 1996	boat bomb	gunboat, Trincomalee	12
16. Nov. 25, 1996	belt bomb	police chief vehicle, Trincomalee	1***
17. Dec. 8, 1996	mines	naval vessel, Trincomalee	0
18. Dec. 17, 1996	motorcycle bomb	police chief, Ampara	1**
19. Mar. 6, 1997	grenades	air base, China Bay	0
20. Oct. 15, 1997	truck bomb	World Trade Centre, Colombo	18
21. Oct. 19, 1997	boat bomb	naval gunboat, northeastern coast	9
22. Dec. 28, 1997	truck bomb	navy chief, south Sri Lanka	0***
23. Jan. 25, 1998	truck bomb	Buddhist shrine, Kandy	11
24. Feb. 5, 1998	belt bomb	air force headquarters, Colombo	8
25. Feb. 22, 1998	boat bombs	2 landing ships off Point Pedro	47
26. Mar. 5, 1998	bus bomb	train station, Colombo	38
27. Mar. 11, 1998	boat bomb	naval vessel, Trincomalee	2
28. May 14, 1998	belt bomb	army brigadier, Jaffna peninsula	1**

Date	Weapon	Target	Killed
29. Sept. 11, 1998	belt bomb	mayor of Jaffna	20**
30. Oct. 30, 1998	boat bomb	naval vessel, Mullaitivu	18
31. Mar. 15, 1999	belt bomb	police station, Colombo	5
32. May 29, 1999	belt bomb	Tamil rival leader, Batticaloa	3**
33. July 29, 1999	belt bomb	Tamil politician, Colombo	1**
34. Aug. 4, 1999	bicycle bomb	police vehicle, Vavuniya	13
35. Aug. 9, 1999	belt bomb	military commander, Vakarai	1
36. Aug. 15, 1999	boat bomb	naval vessel, Trincomalee	10
37. Sept. 2, 1999	belt bomb	Tamil rival, Vavuniya	3
38. Dec. 8, 1999	boat bomb	naval vessel, Point Pedro	4
39. Dec. 18, 1999	belt bomb	president of Sri Lanka, Colombo	24***
40. Dec. 30, 1999	boat bomb	naval vessels, Jaffna lagoon	2
41. Jan. 5, 2000	belt bomb	PM of Sri Lanka, Colombo	12***
42. Mar. 2, 2000	belt bomb	military commander, Trincomalee	1***
43. Mar. 10, 2000	belt bomb	government motorcade, Colombo	23
44. May 22, 2000	belt bomb	political leader, Kantalai	0***
45. June 5, 2000	scuba diver	ammunition ship, northeast coast	5
46. June 7, 2000	belt bomb	industries minister, Colombo	22**
47. June 14, 2000	bicycle bomb	air force bus, Wattala Town	2
48. June 26, 2000	boat bomb	merchant vessel, north coast	7
49. Aug. 16, 2000	belt bomb	military vehicle, Vavuniya	1
50. Sept. 15, 2000	belt bomb	hospital, Colombo	7
51. Oct. 2, 2000	belt bomb	political leader, Trincomalee	23**
52. Oct. 5, 2000	belt bomb	political rally, Medawachchiya	12
53. Oct. 19, 2000	belt bomb	cabinet ceremony, Colombo	0
54. Oct. 23, 2000	boat bombs	gunboat/troop carrier, Trincomalee	2

Campaign #6: Hamas vs. Israel

1. Apr. 6, 1994	car bomb	Afula	9
2. Apr. 13, 1994	belt bomb	Hadera	6

Date	Group	Weapon	Target	Killed

Campaign #7: Hamas/Islamic Jihad vs. Israel

1. Oct. 19, 1994	Hamas	belt bomb	Tel Aviv	22
2. Nov. 11, 1994	Islamic Jihad	bike bomb	Netzarim, Gaza	3

Date	Group	Weapon	Target	Killed
3. Dec. 25, 1994	Hamas	belt bomb	Jerusalem	0
4. Jan. 22, 1995	Islamic Jihad	belt bomb	Beit Lid Junction	21
5. Apr. 9, 1995	Hamas	car bombs	Netzarim, Gaza	8
6. Apr. 9, 1995	Islamic Jihad	car bomb	Kfar Daroum, Gaza	8
7. June 25, 1995	Islamic Jihad	mule bomb	IDF base, Gaza	0
8. July 24, 1995	Hamas	belt bomb	Tel Aviv	6
9. Aug. 21, 1995	Hamas	belt bomb	Jerusalem	5

Date	Weapon	Target	Killed
Campaign #8: BKI vs. India			
1. Aug. 31, 1995	belt bomb	chief minister, Chandigarh, Punjab	16**
Campaign #9: Hamas vs. Israel			
1. Feb. 25, 1996	belt bomb	Jerusalem	25
2. Feb. 25, 1996	belt bomb	Ashkelon	1
3. Mar. 3, 1996	belt bomb	Jerusalem	19
4. Mar. 4, 1996	belt bomb	Tel Aviv	13
Campaign #10: Hamas vs. Israel			
1. Mar. 21, 1997	belt bomb	café, Tel Aviv	3
2. July 30, 1997	belt bomb	Jerusalem	14
3. Sept. 4, 1997	belt bomb	Jerusalem	7
Campaign #11: Kurdistan Workers Party (PKK) vs. Turkey			
1. June 30, 1996	belt bomb	Tunceli	6
2. Oct. 25, 1996	belt bomb	Adana	6
3. Oct. 29, 1996	belt bomb	Sivas	4

Note: There exist several reports of PKK suicides in May and June 1997 during fighting between the PKK and Kurdish militias in Iraq, but coverage does not distinguish suicide attack from suicide to avoid capture.

Date	Weapon	Target	Killed

Campaign #12: PKK vs. Turkey

Date	Weapon	Target	Killed
1. Nov. 11, 1998	belt bomb	Hakkari	0
2. Dec. 1, 1998	belt bomb	Diyarbakir	0
3. Dec. 24, 1998	belt bomb	Van	1
4. Mar. 4, 1999	belt bomb	town square, Batman	0
5. Mar. 11, 1999	belt bomb	government building, Dahuk	2
6. Mar. 27, 1999	grenade	Taksim Square, Istanbul	0
7. Apr. 5, 1999	belt bomb	governor, Bingol	1
8. Apr. 8, 1999	belt bomb	governor, Hakkari	2
9. July 5, 1999	belt bomb	police station, Adana	0
10. July 7, 1999	grenades	Iluh	0
11. Aug. 28, 1999	belt bomb	government building, Tunceli	0

Campaign #13: LTTE vs. Sri Lanka

Date	Weapon	Target	Killed
1. July 24, 2001	belt bomb	international airport, Colombo	8
2. Sept. 15, 2001	boat bomb	naval vessel, north	15
3. Oct. 29, 2001	belt bomb	PM of Sri Lanka, Colombo	3***
4. Oct. 30, 2001	boat bomb	oil tanker, northern coast	4
5. Nov. 9, 2001	belt bomb	police chief, Batticaloa	0***
6. Nov. 15, 2001	belt bomb	crowd, Batticaloa	3

Ongoing Campaigns

Campaign #14: al-Qaeda vs. United States

Date	Weapon	Target	Killed
1. Nov. 13, 1995	car bomb	U.S. military base, Riyadh, S.A.	5
2. June 25, 1996	truck bomb	U.S. military base, Dhahran, S.A.	19
3. Aug. 7, 1998	truck bombs	U.S. embassies, Kenya/Tanzania	225
4. Oct. 12, 2000	boat bomb	U.S.S. *Cole*, Yemen	17
5. Sept. 9, 2001	camera bomb	Ahmed Shah Massoud, Afghanistan	1**
6. Sept. 11, 2001	hijacked airplanes	WTC/Pentagon	2,955
7. Apr. 11, 2002	car bomb	synagogue, Djerba, Tunisia	21
8. May 8, 2002	car bomb	Sheraton Hotel, Karachi	14
9. June 16, 2002	car bomb	U.S. consulate, Karachi	12
10. Oct. 6, 2002	boat bomb	French oil tanker, Yemen	1

Date	Weapon	Target	Killed
11. Oct. 12, 2002	car bomb	nightclub, Bali, Indonesia	202
12. Nov. 28, 2002	car bomb	Hotel Mombasa, Kenya	13
13. May 12, 2003	3 car bombs	Riyadh, Saudi Arabia	34
14. May 16, 2003	car bombs	Casablanca, Morocco	31
15. June 7, 2003	car bomb	German military bus, Kabul	4
16. Aug. 5, 2003	car bomb	Jakarta, Indonesia	15
17. Nov. 8, 2003	car bomb	Riyadh, Saudi Arabia	17
18. Nov. 15, 2003	2 car bombs	2 synagogues, Istanbul, Turkey	25
19. Nov. 20, 2003	2 truck bombs	British embassy, Istanbul, Turkey	31
20. Dec. 25, 2003	2 truck bombs	President Musharraf, Rawalpindi, Pak.	14[***]
21. Dec. 28, 2003	car bomb	airport, Kabul	5

Campaign #15: Chechen Separatists vs. Russia

Date	Weapon	Target	Killed
1. June 7, 2000	truck bomb	Russian police station, Chechnya	2
2. June 11, 2000	truck bomb	military post, Grozny	4
3. July 3, 2000	4 truck bombs	Argun, Naibyora, Gudermes, Urus Martan	57
4. Dec. 8, 2000	truck bomb	Gudermes	1
5. Nov. 29, 2001	belt bomb	military commander, Chechnya	3
6. May 31, 2002	bag bomb	Grozny	4
7. Dec. 27, 2002	2 truck bombs	Grozny	71
8. May 12, 2003	truck bomb	Znamenskoc, Chechnya	59
9. May 14, 2003	2 belt bombs	Suvoro-Yurt, near Gudermes	18
10. June 5, 2003	belt bomb	Mozdok, N. Ossetia	19
11. June 20, 2003	truck bomb	government building, Grozny	0
12. July 5, 2003	2 belt bombs	rock concert, Moscow	16
13. July 7, 2003	bag bomb	Café Imbir, Moscow	1
14. July 22, 2003	belt bomb	checkpoint, Pliyevsky, Ingushetia	0
15. July 27, 2003	belt bomb	assassination attempt, Tstasan-Turt	1[***]
16. Aug. 1, 2003	truck bomb	mil. hospital, Mozdok, N. Ossetia	50
17. Sept. 15, 2003	truck bomb	Russ. HQ, Magas, Ingushetia	5
18. Dec. 5, 2003	bag bomb	train, Kislovodsk, southern Russia	45
19. Dec. 9, 2003	belt bomb	hotel, Moscow	6

Campaign #16: Kashmir Separatists vs. India

Date	Weapon	Target	Killed
1. Dec. 25, 2000	car bomb	Srinagar, Kashmir	8
2. Oct. 1, 2001	car bomb	legislative assembly, Kashmir	30
3. Dec. 13, 2001	gunmen	Parliament, New Delhi	7

Date	Weapon	Target	Killed
4. Apr. 26, 2003	car bomb	Radio Kashmir, Srinagar	2
5. Dec. 25, 2003	2 car bombs	Musharraf, Islamabad, Pak.	14

Date	Group	Weapon	Target	Killed

Campaign #17: Hamas/Islamic Jihad vs. Israel

Date	Group	Weapon	Target	Killed
1. Oct. 26, 2000	Islamic Jihad	bike bomb	Gaza	0
2. Dec. 22, 2000	al-Aqsa	belt bomb	Jordan Valley	3
3. Jan. 1, 2001	Hamas	belt bomb	Netanya, Israel	10
4. Mar. 4, 2001	Hamas	belt bomb	Netanya, Israel	3
5. Mar. 27, 2001	Hamas	belt bomb	Jerusalem	1
6. Mar. 28, 2001	Hamas	belt bomb	Kfar Saba, Israel	2
7. Apr. 22, 2001	Hamas	belt bomb	Kfar Saba, Israel	3
8. Apr. 29, 2001	Hamas	belt bomb	West Bank	0
9. May 18, 2001	Hamas	belt bomb	Netanya, Israel	5
10. May 25, 2001	Hamas	truck bomb	Netzarim, Gaza	0
11. May 25, 2001	Islamic Jihad	car bomb	bus, Hadrea	0
12. May 29, 2001	Hamas	belt bomb	Khamyunis	0
13. June 1, 2001	Hamas	belt bomb	nightclub, Tel Aviv	22
14. June 22, 2001	Hamas	belt bomb	Gaza	2
15. July 9, 2001	Hamas	car bomb	Gaza	1
16. July 16, 2001	Islamic Jihad	belt bomb	Jerusalem	2
17. Aug. 9, 2001	al-Aqsa	car bomb	Jerusalem	0
18. Aug. 9, 2001	Islamic Jihad	belt bomb	Haifa, Israel	15
19. Aug. 12, 2001	Islamic Jihad	belt bomb	Haifa, Israel	0
20. Sept. 4, 2001	Hamas	belt bomb	Jerusalem	0
21. Sept. 9, 2001	Hamas	belt bomb	Nahariya, Israel	3
22. Oct. 7, 2001	Islamic Jihad	car bomb	North Israel	2
23. Oct. 18, 2001	PFLP	car bomb	Nahaloz, Gaza	0
24. Nov. 26, 2001	Hamas	car bomb	Gaza	0
25. Nov. 29, 2001	Islamic Jihad	belt bomb	Gaza	3
26. Dec. 1, 2001	Hamas	belt bomb	Haifa, Israel	11
27. Dec. 2, 2001	Hamas	belt bomb	Jerusalem	15
28. Dec. 5, 2001	Islamic Jihad	belt bomb	Jerusalem	0
29. Dec. 9, 2001	Islamic Jihad	belt bomb	Haifa, Israel	0
30. Dec. 12, 2001	al-Aqsa	belt bomb	Gaza	0

Date	Group	Weapon	Target	Killed
31. Jan. 25, 2002	Islamic Jihad	belt bomb	crowd, Tel Aviv	1
32. Jan. 27, 2002	al-Aqsa	bag bomb	street, Jerusalem	1
33. Jan. 30, 2002	Islamic Jihad	belt bomb	Tulkara, West Bank	0
34. Feb. 16, 2002	PFLP	belt bomb	mall, settlement near Nablus	2
35. Feb. 18, 2002	al-Aqsa	car bomb	Jerusalem	1
36. Feb. 27, 2002	al-Aqsa	belt bomb	IDF checkpoint	2
37. Mar. 2, 2002	al-Aqsa	belt bomb	street, Jerusalem	9
38. Mar. 5, 2002	Islamic Jihad	belt bomb	bus, Afula	1
39. Mar. 7, 2002	PFLP	belt bomb	Ariel, West Bank	0
40. Mar. 9, 2002	Hamas, al-Aqsa	belt bomb	café, Jerusalem	11
41. Mar. 20, 2002	Islamic Jihad	belt bomb	bus, Umm Al Fahm, Israel	7
42. Mar. 21, 2002	al-Aqsa	belt bomb	street, Jerusalem	3
43. Mar. 27, 2002	Hamas	belt bomb	hotel, Netanya	28
44. Mar. 29, 2002	al-Aqsa	belt bomb	supermarket, Jerusalem	2
45. Mar. 30, 2002	al-Aqsa	belt bomb	café, Tel Aviv	1
46. Mar. 31, 2002	Hamas	belt bomb	restaurant, Haifa	16
47. Mar. 31, 2002	al-Aqsa	belt bomb	Efrat, West Bank	0
48. Apr. 1, 2002	al-Aqsa	car bomb	Jerusalem	1
49. Apr. 10, 2002	Hamas	belt bomb	bus, Haifa	7
50. Apr. 12, 2002	al-Aqsa	belt bomb	market, Jerusalem	6
51. Apr. 19, 2002	Islamic Jihad	car bomb	Kissufin, Gaza	0
52. May 7, 2002	Hamas	suitcase bomb	snooker hall, Tel Aviv	16
53. May 19, 2002	PFLP	belt bomb	market, Netanya, Israel	3
54. May 20, 2002	Islamic Jihad	belt bomb	Afula	0
55. May 22, 2002	al-Aqsa	belt bomb	chess café, Tel Aviv	2
56. May 27, 2002	al-Aqsa	belt bomb	market, Tel Aviv	2
57. June 5, 2002	Islamic Jihad	car bomb	bus, Megiddo, Israel	17
58. June 11, 2001	al-Aqsa	belt bomb	restaurant, Herzilya	1
59. June 18, 2002	Hamas	belt bomb	bus, Jerusalem	19
60. June 19, 2002	al-Aqsa	belt bomb	bus stop, Jerusalem	7
61. July 17, 2002	al-Aqsa	2 bag bombs	theater, Tel Aviv	5
62. July 30, 2002	al-Aqsa	belt bomb	café, Jerusalem	0

Date	Group	Weapon	Target	Killed
63. Aug. 4, 2002	Hamas	belt bomb	bus, Safed, Israel	9
64. Sept. 18, 2002	al-Aqsa	belt bomb	bus stop, Umm al-Fahm, Israel	1
65. Sept. 19, 2002	Hamas	belt bomb	bus, Tel Aviv	6
66. Oct. 10, 2002	Hamas	belt bomb	bus stop, Tel Aviv	1
67. Oct. 21, 2002	Islamic Jihad	car bomb	Pardes Hanna, Israel	14
68. Oct. 27, 2002	Hamas	belt bomb	gas station, Ariel	3
69. Nov. 4, 2002	Islamic Jihad/ al-Aqsa	belt bomb	mall, Tel Aviv	2
70. Nov. 21, 2002	Hamas	bag bomb	bus, Jerusalem	11
71. Jan. 5, 2003	al-Aqsa	belt bomb	market, Tel Aviv	23
72. Mar. 5, 2003	Hamas	belt bomb	bus, Haifa	17
73. Mar. 30, 2003	Islamic Jihad	belt bomb	mall, Netanya	0
74. Apr. 24, 2003	al-Aqsa/PFLP	belt bomb	train station, Kfar Saba	1
75. Apr. 30, 2003	Hamas/al-Aqsa	belt bomb	café, Tel Aviv	3
76. May 17, 2003	Hamas	belt bomb	Hebron	2
77. May 18, 2003	Hamas	belt bomb	bus, Jerusalem	7
78. May 18, 2003	Hamas	belt bomb	Wall, Jerusalem	0
79. May 19, 2003	Hamas	bike bomb	IDF, Gaza	0
80. May 19, 2003	Islamic Jihad	bag bomb	mall, Afula	3
81. June 11, 2003	Hamas	belt bomb	bus, Jerusalem	17
82. June 19, 2003	Islamic Jihad	belt bomb	store, Sdeh Trumot	1
83. July 8, 2003	Islamic Jihad	belt bomb	Moshav Kfar Yavetz	1
84. Aug. 12, 2003	Hamas	belt bomb	bus stop, Tel Aviv	1
85. Aug. 12, 2003	al-Aqsa	belt bomb	store, Rosh Haayin	1
86. Aug. 19, 2003	Hamas	belt bomb	bus, Jerusalem	20
87. Sept. 9, 2003	Hamas	belt bomb	café, Jerusalem	7
88. Sept. 9, 2003	Hamas	belt bomb	bus stop, Tel Aviv	9
89. Oct. 4, 2003	Islamic Jihad	belt bomb	restaurant, Haifa	21
90. Oct. 9, 2003	al-Aqsa	belt bomb	IDF office, Tulkarm	0
91. Nov. 3, 2003	al-Aqsa	belt bomb	IDF soldiers, Azun, West Bank	0
92. Dec. 25, 2003	PFLP	belt bomb	bus stop, Gehha Junction	4

Date	Weapon	Target	Killed

Campaign #18: Iraqi Rebels vs. U.S. and Allies

Date	Weapon	Target	Killed
1. Mar. 22, 2003	belt bomb	northern Iraq	4
2. Mar. 29, 2003	car bomb	Najaf	5
3. Apr. 3, 2003	car bomb	checkpoint, west Iraq	3
4. Apr. 10, 2003	belt bomb	Saddam City	1
5. Aug. 7, 2003	truck bomb	Jordanian embassy, Baghdad	17
6. Aug. 19, 2003	truck bomb	U.N. headquarters, Baghdad	22
7. Aug. 29, 2003	car bomb	mosque, Najaf	95
8. Sept. 2, 2003	car bomb	police station, Baghdad	1
9. Sept. 9, 2003	car bomb	U.S. compound, Erbil	3
10. Sept. 22, 2003	car bomb	U.N. headquarters, Baghdad	1
11. Oct. 9, 2003	car bomb	police station, Baghdad	8
12. Oct. 12, 2003	car bomb	Baghdad Hotel, Baghdad	7
13. Oct. 14, 2003	car bomb	Turkish Embassy, Baghdad	1
14. Oct. 24, 2003	car bomb	Baghdad	4
15. Oct. 27, 2003	6 car bombs	5 police stations, Red Cross, Baghdad	35
16. Oct. 28, 2003	truck bomb	police station, Fallujah	4
17. Nov. 12, 2003	car bomb	Italian compound, Nasiriya	26
18. Dec. 10, 2003	car bomb	U.S. military base, Baghdad	0
19. Dec. 14, 2003	car bomb	police station, Khaldiyah	17
20. Dec. 16, 2003	car bomb	police station, Baghdad	8

Isolated Attacks

Date	Group	Weapon	Target	Killed
1. Dec. 15, 1981	???	car bomb	Iraqi embassy, Beirut	30
2. May 25, 1985	Hezbollah	car bomb	emir, Kuwait	0***
3. July 5, 1987	LTTE	truck bomb	army camp, Jaffna Peninsula	18
4. Oct. 19, 1988	Hezbollah	car bomb	IDF vehicle, south Lebanon	8
5. Aug. 9, 1989	Hezbollah	truck bomb	IDF vehicle, south Lebanon	0
6. Nov. 25, 1990	SSNP	suitcase bomb	IDF patrol	0
7. Aug. 15, 1993	???	motorcycle bomb	interior minister, Egypt	3***
8. Jan. 30, 1995	Armed Islamic Group	truck bomb	crowd, Algiers	42
9. Apr. 15, 1995	Hezbollah	belt bomb	IDF convoy, south Lebanon	0
10. Nov. 19, 1995	Islamic Group	truck bomb	Egyptian embassy, Pakistan	16
11. Mar. 20, 1996	Hezbollah	belt bomb	IDF convoy, south Lebanon	1
12. Oct. 29, 1998	Hamas	belt bomb	Gaza	1
13. Nov. 17, 1998	???	belt bomb	Yuksekova, Turkey	0
14. Dec. 29, 1999	Hezbollah	car bomb	south Lebanon	1

??? = unclaimed attacks

*Not including attacker(s).

**Assassination target killed.

***Assassination target survived.

Date	Weapon	Target	Killed

Campaign #18: Iraqi Rebels vs. U.S. and Allies

continued

21. Jan 9, 2004	bicycle bomb	mosque, Baquba	5
22. Jan 14, 2004	car bomb	police station, Baquba	2
23. Jan 18, 2004	car bomb	CPA HQ, Baghdad	25
24. Jan 28, 2004	car bomb	hotel, Baghdad	3
25. Jan 31, 2004	car bomb	police HQ, Mosul	9
26. Feb 1, 2004	2 belt bombs	Kurd pol HQ, Irbil	56
27. Feb 11, 2004	car bomb	recruiting station, Baghdad	47
28. Feb 18, 2004	truck bomb	Polish military base, Hilla	11
29. Feb 23, 2004	car bomb	police station, Kirkuk	13
30. Mar 2, 2004	multiple belt bombs	mosque Karbala	130
31. Mar 18, 2004	car bomb	hotel, Basra	3
32. Apr 21, 2004	car bomb	police station, Basra	50
33. Apr 24, 2004	boat bomb	oil terminal, Basra	0
34. May 6, 2004	car bomb	checkpoint, Baghdad	6
35. May 17. 2004	car bomb	government convoy, Baghdad	8
36. May 22, 2004	car bomb	Interior Minister's house, Baghdad	4***
37. Jun 6, 2004	car bomb	US base, Taji	9
38. Jun 13, 2004	car bomb	US troops, Baghdad	12
39. Jun 14, 2004	car bomb	contractors, Baghdad	8
40. Jun 17, 2004	car bomb	recruiting station, Baghdad	33
41. Jun 24, 2004	car bombs	police stations, Mosul	62
42. July 6, 2004	car bomb	local officials, Khalis	13**
43. July 14, 2004	car bomb	near green zone, Baghdad	7
44. July 17, 2004	car bomb	Justice minister, Baghdad	6***
45. July 19, 2004	truck bomb	police station, Baghdad	10
46. July 26, 2004	bus bomb	recruiting station, Baquba	68
47. Aug 1, 2004	car bomb	police station, Mosul	4
48. Aug 24, 2004	car bomb	Environment Minister, Baghdad	4***
49. Sept 4, 2004	car bomb	police academy, Kirkuk	17
50. Sept 8, 2004	car bomb	US convoy, Fallujah	10
51. Sept 13, 2004	car bomb	police station, Baghdad	47
52. Sept 18, 2004	car bomb	recruiting station, Kirkuk	19

53. Sept 22, 2004	car bomb	recruiting station, Baghdad	6
54. Oct 6, 2004	car bomb	recruiting station, Anah	16
55. Oct 10, 2004	bus bomb	police academy, Baghdad	9
56. Oct 13, 2004	car bomb	US convoy, Mosul	2
57. Oct 23, 2004	car bomb	Iraqi police, US base, West Iraq	16
58. Nov 7, 2004	car bomb	British post, Baghdad	4
59. Nov 17, 2004	car bomb	US Convoy, Beiji	10
60. Nov 18, 2004	car bomb	market, Baghdad	2
61. Nov 29, 2004	car bomb	police station, Ramadi	12
62. Dec 3, 2004	car bomb	US base, West Iraq	2
63. Dec 3, 2004	car bomb	mosque, Baghdad	14
64. Dec 4, 2004	car bomb	police station, Mosul	18
65. Dec 4, 2004	car bomb	police station, Baghdad	8
66. Dec 13, 2004	car bomb	checkpoint, Baghdad	13
67. Dec 19, 2004	bus bomb	bus station, Karbala	62
68. Dec 22, 2004	belt bomb	US mess tent, Mosul	22
69. Dec 28, 2004	car bomb	Shia leaders HQ, Baghdad	15**
70. Jan 3, 2005	car bombs	checkpoints, Baghdad	6
71. Jan 4, 2005	truck bomb	checkpoint, Baghdad	2
72. Jan 5, 2005	car bomb	police academy, Hilla	15
73. Jan 5, 2005	car bomb	checkpoint, Baquba	2
74. Jan 10, 2005	car bomb	police station, Baghdad	4
75. Jan 11, 2005	car bomb	police station, Tikrit	7
76. Jan 18, 2005	car bomb	SCIRI office, Baghdad	1***
77. Jan 19, 2005	car bomb	police station, Baghdad	18
78. Jan 19, 2005	car bomb	mosque, Baghdad	26
79. Jan 21, 2005	car bomb	wedding, Yussufiya	15
80. Jan 21, 2005	car bomb	Australian embassy, Baghdad	2
81. Jan 30, 2005	belt bombs	2 poll stations, Baghdad	10
82. Feb 7, 2005	belt bomb	recruiting station, Baghdad	21
83. Feb 11, 2005	truck bomb	mosque, Baghdad	13
84. Feb 18, 2005	belt bomb	mosque, Baghdad	14
85. Feb 19, 2005	2 belt bombs	checkpoint, funeral, Baghdad	39
86. Feb 19, 2005	belt bomb	Aden square, Baghdad	17
87. Feb 24, 2005	belt bomb	police station, Baghdad	12
88. Mar 2, 2005	2 car bombs	airport, Baghdad	13
89. Mar 9, 2005	car bomb	hotel, Baghdad	1
90. Mar 10, 2005	car bomb	mosque, Baghdad	53
91. Mar 25, 2005	car bomb	checkpoint, Ramadi	11

92. Mar 28, 2005	car bomb	crowd, Hilla	6
93. Mar 31, 2005	car bomb	US convoy, Samarra	3
94. Apr 4, 2005	car bomb	Abu Ghraib prison, Baghdad	0
95. Apr 11, 2005	car bomb	US convoy, Samarra	2
96. Apr 12, 2005	car bomb	Iraqi army troops, Tel Afar	4
97. Apr 13, 2005	car bomb	US/Iraqi army convoy, Mosul	4
98. Apr 15, 2005	2 car bombs	police convoy, Baghdad	15
99. Apr 16, 2005	car bomb	Western convoy, Baghdad	3
100. Apr 16, 2005	car bomb	Restaurant, Baquba	13
101. Apr 19, 2005	2 car bombs	airport, recruiting station Baghdad	5
102. Apr 21, 2005	car bomb	Iraqi Prime Min, Baghdad	1***
103. Apr 24, 2005	car bomb	mosque, Baghdad	15
104. Apr 24, 2005	car bomb	police academy, Tikrit	7
105. Apr 30, 2005	4 car bombs	police patrols, Baghdad	20
106. Apr 30, 2005	3 car bombs	police patrols, Mosul	5
107. May 1, 2005	3 car bombs	police patrols, Baghdad	23
108. May 2, 2005	car bomb	police funeral, Tal Afar	25
109. May 2, 2005	belt bomb	US convoy, Mosul	1
110. May 3, 2005	3 car bombs	police convoy, Baghdad	12
111. May 4, 2005	belt bomb	recruiting station, Erbil	59
112. May 5, 2005	belt bomb	recruiting station, Baghdad	31
113. May 6, 2005	car bomb	market, Baghdad	22
114. May 6, 2005	car bomb	police bus, Tikrit	9
115. May 7, 2005	car bomb	foreign security convoy, Baghdad	18
116. May 9, 2005	car bomb	checkpoint, Baghdad	2
117. May 10, 2005	car bomb	US convoy, Baghdad	6
118. May 11, 2005	belt bomb	recruitment station, Hawija	32
119. May 13, 2005	car bomb	Iraqi army convoy, Baquba	1
120. May 14, 2005	motorbike bomb	US/Iraqi army patrol, Mosul	2
121. May 15, 2005	belt bomb	governor's convoy, Baquba	5
122. May 23, 2005	truck bomb	mayor's office, Tuz Murkhatu	5***
123. May 23, 2005	car bomb	mosque, Mahmoudiya	9
124. May 23, 2005	2 car bombs	Shia leader's home, Tal Afar	33***
125. May 27, 2005	2 car bombs	police patrol, Tikrit	7
126. May 29, 2005	car bomb	Oil ministry, Baghdad	2
127. May 30, 2005	car bomb	policemen, Hilla	27
128. Jun 1, 2005	car bomb	airport checkpoint, Baghdad	15
129. Jun 2, 2005	car bomb	provincial leader, Baquba	4

130. Jun 2, 2005	car bomb	PM's bodyguards, restaurant, Baghdad	11
131. Jun 2, 2005	car bomb	US convoy, Kirkuk	2
132. Jun 2, 2005	belt bomb	crowd, Balad	9
133. Jun 3, 2005	car bomb	police station, Mosul	2
134. Jun 7, 2005	car bomb	Iraqi army station, Hawija	10
135. Jun 13, 2005	car bomb	police patrol, Tikrit	2
136. Jun 13, 2005	belt bomb	crowd, central bank, Kirkuk	20
137. Jun 15, 2005	car bomb	police patrol, Baghdad	8
138. Jun 19, 2005	belt bomb	restaurant, Baghdad	23
139. Jun 19, 2005	car bomb	checkpoint, Tikrit	2
140. Jun 20, 2005	car bomb	security chief's convoy, Halabja	4***
141. Jun 23, 2005	car bomb	US convoy, Fallujah	6
142. Jun 25, 2005	car bomb	police chief convoy, Mosul	4***
143. Jun 26, 2005	belt bomb	Iraqi army base, Mosul	9
144. Jun 26, 2005	belt bomb	police post in hospital, Mosul	5
145. July 2, 2005	belt bomb	policemen, restaurant, Hilla	8
146. July 2, 2005	belt bomb	recruiting station, Baghdad	11
147. July 4, 2005	car bomb	Iraqi army convoy, Fallujah	3
148. July 10, 2005	car bomb	police chief convoy, Mosul	5***
149. July 10, 2005	belt bomb	recruiting station, Baghdad	20
150. July 12, 2005	belt bomb	mosque, Jalowla	2
151. July 13, 2005	car bomb	US troops in crowd, Baghdad	26
152. July 15, 2005	car bomb	residential area, Baghdad	9
153. July 16, 2005	belt bomb	mosque, Mussayib	98
154. July 16, 2005	belt bomb	police station, Mosul	4
155. July 17, 2005	car bomb	US convoy, Mahmoudiya	6
156. July 17, 2005	car bomb	election office, Baghdad	5
157. July 20, 2005	belt bomb	army recruits, Baghdad	6
158. July 24, 2005	truck bomb	police station, Mashtal	40
159. July 25, 2005	bus bomb	checkpoint, Baghdad	12
160. July 29, 2005	belt bomb	army recruits, Rabia	48
161. July 29, 2005	car bomb	police patrol, Baghdad	7
162. Aug 1, 2005	car bomb	US convoy, Hit	1
163. Aug 6, 2005	car bomb	US convoy, Fallujah	1
164. Aug 10, 2005	car bomb	police convoy, Baghdad	6
165. Aug 24, 2005	belt bomb	Coalition station, Baquba	13
166. Sept 7, 2005	taxi bomb	restaurant, Basra	16
167. Sept 14, 2005	bus bomb	Crowd, Baghdad	80
168. Sept 15, 2005	2 car bombs	police convoy, Baghdad	16

169. Sept 16, 2005	car bomb	mosque, Tuz Khormatu	12
170. Sept 19, 2005	car bomb	US convoy, Mosul	4
171. Sept 23, 2005	bus bomb	checkpoint, Hilla	6
172. Sept 25, 2005	bus bomb	Iraqi army convoy, Baghdad	13
173. Sept 27, 2005	belt bomb	recruiting station, Baquba	9
174. Sept 28, 2005	belt bomb	recruiting station, Tal Afar	9
175. Sept 29, 2005	3 car bombs	market near police station, Balad	60
176. Oct 5, 2005	car bomb	mosque, Hilla	24
177. Oct 6, 2005	car bomb	contractors, Baghdad	10
178. Oct 10, 2005	car bomb	checkpoint, Baghdad	6
179. Oct 11, 2005	car bomb	police recruits, Tal Afar	30
180. Oct 23, 2005	car bomb	US convoy, Kirkuk	2
181. Oct 24, 2005	3 car bombs	hotels, Baghdad	20
182. Oct 29, 2005	truck bomb	market, Huwaider	20
183. Nov 2, 2005	car bomb	market, Mussayib	19
184. Nov 9, 2005	car bomb	US troops, Baghdad	4
185. Nov 10, 2005	2 belt bombs	policemen, restaurant, Baghdad	33
186. Nov 18, 2005	2 truck bombs	2 mosques, Khanaqin	67
187. Nov 19, 2005	truck bomb	funeral, Baquba	13
188. Nov 22, 2005	car bomb	police convoy, Kirkuk	17
189. Nov 24, 2005	car bomb	US troops near hospital, Hilla	11
190. Nov 26, 2005	car bomb	police patrol, Samarra	5
191. Dec 7, 2005	2 belt bomb	police academy, Baghdad	36
192. Dec 8, 2005	belt bomb	bus, Baghdad	30
193. Dec 14, 2005	car bomb	UK checkpoint, Baghdad	4
194. Dec 26, 2005	belt bomb	checkpoint, Baghdad	

Chart 15. Suicide Attacks in Iraq

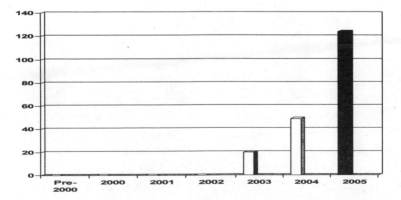

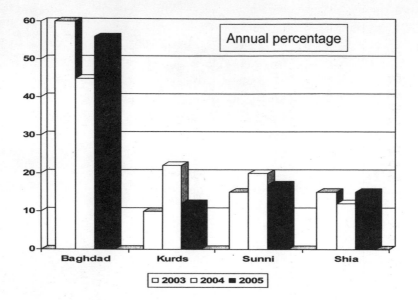

Chart 16. Geography of Suicide Attacks in Iraq

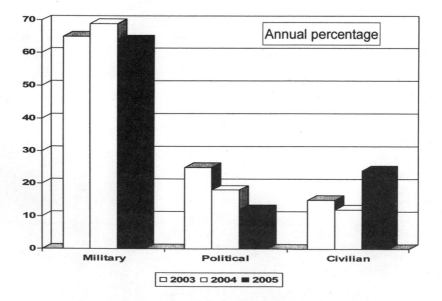

Chart 17. Targets of Suicide Attacks in Iraq

Occupations by Democratic States, 1980–2003

	Case	Years of Violence	Rebellion	Suicide	Religion	Language
1.	Shia vs. U.S./France/Israel	1982–86	guerrilla war	Yes	Muslim vs. Christian	Arabic vs. English/French/Hebrew
2.	Tamils vs. Sri Lanka	1976–2001	guerrilla war	Yes	Hindu vs. Buddhist	Tamil vs. Sinhalese
3.	Palestinians vs. Israel	1968–present	guerrilla war	Yes	Muslim vs. Jewish	Arabic vs. Hebrew
4.	Sikhs vs. India	1980–2000	guerrilla war	Yes	Sikh vs. Hindu	Punjabi vs. Hindi
5.	Kashmiris vs. India	1980–present	guerrilla war	Yes	Muslim vs. Hindu	Kashmiri vs. Hindi
6.	Iraq vs. U.S.	2003–present	guerrilla war	Yes	Muslim vs. Christian	Arabic vs. English
7.	Chechens vs. Russia	1994–present	guerrilla war	Yes	Muslim vs. Orthodox	Chechen vs. Russian
8.	Chittagong Hill Tribes vs. Bangladesh	1972–97	guerrilla war	No	Buddhist/Animists vs. Bengali Muslims	Chakma vs. Bengali
9.	Tripuras vs. India	1978–88, 1990–present	guerrilla war	No	Christian and Buddhist vs. Hindu	Kokborok vs. Hindi
10.	Assamee vs. India	1989–99	guerrilla war	No	Hindu (some Muslim) vs. Hindu	Assamese vs. Hindi
11.	Nagas vs. India	1947–99	guerrilla war	No	Christian vs. Hindu	tribal languages vs. Hindi
12.	Moros vs. Philippines	1972–present	guerrilla war	No	Muslim vs. Christian Malay	multiple languages vs. Filipino
13.	IRA vs. Britain	1968–present	guerrilla war	No	Catholic vs. Protestant	English
14.	Malay-Muslims vs. Thailand	1968–99	guerrilla war	No	Muslim vs. Buddhist	Malay vs. Thai
15.	Kurds vs. Turkey	1984–99	guerrilla war	Yes	both Muslim	dialects of Kurdish vs. Turkish
16.	Amazonian Indians vs. Brazil	1988–95	guerrilla war	No	both Catholic	native languages vs. Portuguese
17.	Bodos vs. India	1979–99	guerrilla war	No	both Hindu	native language vs. Assamese and Hindi
18.	Ind. Miskitos vs. Nicaragua	1981–89	guerrilla war	No	both Catholic	Miskitu (+other ind. langs.) vs. Spanish
19.	Bougainvilleans vs. Papua New Guinea	1987–98	guerrilla war	No	both Christian	19 languages vs. Melanesian Pidgin
20.	Igorots vs. Philippines	1972–86	guerrilla war	No	both Christian	multiple languages vs. Filipino
21.	Basques vs. Spain	1960s–present	terrorism	No	both Roman Catholic	Euskera vs. Russia

	Case	Years of Violence	Rebellion	Suicide	Religion	Language
22.	South Tyroleans vs. Italy	1987	terrorism	No	both Catholic	German vs. Italian
23.	Corsicans vs. France	1975–present	terrorism	No	both Catholic	Corsican vs. French
24.	Basques vs. France			No	both Catholic	French (few speak Euskera)
25.	Al-Qaeda vs. U.S.			Yes	Muslim vs. Christian	Arabic vs. English
26.	Indigenous vs. Argentina			No	both Catholic	some Quechua/Spanish vs. Spanish
27.	Indigenous lowland vs. Bolivia			No	both Catholic	Spanish
28.	Afro-Americans (Haitians) vs. Dominican Republic			No	both Catholic	Creole vs. Spanish
29.	Indigenous highland vs. Ecuador			No	both Catholic	Native language (Chibean) vs. Spanish
30.	Indigenous lowland vs. Ecuador			No	both Catholic	Native language (Quichua) vs. Spanish
31.	Mayans vs. Guatemala			No	both Catholic	26 indigenous languages vs. Spanish
32.	Black Karibs vs. Honduras			No	both Catholic	Garifuna vs. Spanish
33.	Indigenous vs. Honduras			No	both Catholic (some indigenous Protestant)	Miskito and English vs. Spanish
34.	Sardinians vs. Italy			No	both Catholic	Sard vs. Italian
35.	Baluchis vs. Pakistan			No	both Muslim	Baluch and Brahui vs. Arabic
36.	Pashtuns vs. Pakistan			No	both Muslim	Pashto vs. Arabic
37.	Sindhis vs. Pakistan			No	both Muslim	Sindhi vs. Arabic
38.	Indigenous highland vs. Peru			No	both Catholic	80 ind. langs vs. Spanish
39.	Indigenous lowland vs. Peru			No	both Catholic	80 ind. langs vs. Spanish
40.	Ingushes vs. Russia			No	both Orthodox	Ingush vs. Russia
41.	Yakut vs. Russia			No	both Orthodox (some Animist)	remote Turkic language vs. Russian
42.	Honamese (Cholla Provence) vs. S. Korea			No	both Christian and Buddhist	both Korean
43.	Hungarians vs. Slovakia			No	both Christian	Hungarian vs. Slovakian
44.	Catalans vs. Spain			No	both Roman Catholic	Catalan vs. Spanish
45.	Quebecois vs. Canada			No	Catholic vs. Protestant	French vs. English
46.	Ashanti vs. Ghana			No	traditional vs. Christian	Asante vs. English

Case	Years of Violence	Rebellion	Suicide	Religion	Language
47. Ewe vs. Ghana			No	traditional vs. Christian	Ewe vs. English
48. Mossi-Dagomba vs. Ghana			No	Muslim vs. Christian	Gur vs. English
49. Mizos vs. India			No	Christian vs. Hindu	Mizo vs. Hindi
50. Hindus vs. Pakistan			No	Hindu vs. Muslim	Hindi vs. Arabic
51. Tatars vs. Russia			No	Muslim vs. Orthodox	Tatar vs. Russian
52. Avars vs. Russia			No	Muslim vs. Orthodox	Avar dialects vs. Russian
53. Lezghins vs. Russia			No	Muslim vs. Orthodox	3 Lezghin dialects vs. Russian
54. Buryat vs. Russia			No	Buddhist vs. Orthodox	Buryat vs. Russian
55. Kumyks vs. Russia			No	Muslim vs. Orthodox	3 dialects of Kumyk vs. Russian
56. Tuvinians vs. Russia			No	Buddhist vs. Orthodox	Tuvin vs. Russia
57. Northern Hill Tribe vs. Thailand			No	traditional vs. Buddhist	multiple languages vs. Thai
58. Native Americans vs. United States			No	traditional vs. Christian	native languages and English

Source: Ted Robert Gurr, et al., *Minorities at Risk: A Global View of Ethnopolitical Conflict* (Washington, D.C.: United States Institute of Peace Press, 1993), as updated at www.cidcm.umd.edu/inscr/mar/ and augmented by foreign occupations consequent on invasion as well as additional material to bring the data up to date. Occupation is defined from the perspective of a potential resistance movement. The critical requirement is that a democracy controlled the homeland of a distinct national community (other than the majority in the democratic state), a definition that includes cases of national minorities within a democracy's own borders as well as cases in which a democratic state moved military forces across an internationally recognized boundary.

APPENDIX III

Salafism in Major Sunni Muslim Majority Countries

THIS APPENDIX EXPLAINS my estimates of the size of the Salafi-influenced populations in the thirty-four Sunni-majority Muslim countries with populations of 1 million or more. With the exception of one attacker from Lebanon, all al-Qaeda suicide terrorists from 1995 to 2003 were nationals from among these thirty-four countries.

All Islamic fundamentalists believe that society should be organized according to Islamic law (Sharia), which is derived from the acts, statements, and ways of life of Muhammad. All accept the authority of the Quran, the holy book of Islam containing the words of God revealed to Muhammad during his lifetime. They differ on the authority of other sources. The Sunna are the body of sayings and deeds of Muhammad as collected by his companions and written down about sixty years after his death. The Sunna is part of the Hadith, the collection of all laws and stories about Muhammad's way of life as well as later interpretations of apparent contradictions in the early texts, including commentary on appropriate behavior in subsequent events, such as when Muslims lived under other laws.

Salafism is the belief that society should be organized according to the Quran and Sunna only. It is separate from other forms of Islamic fundamentalism, such as Sufism, which are open to more recent sources of Islamic jurisprudence. It is also separate from militant Salafism, which advocates the use of force to achieve Salafi aims.

The category of Salafi-influenced people includes not only committed Salafis but also the population that would be exposed to Salafi beliefs by living in a community with a Salafi ideology. The intensity of exposure to Salafism as experienced by typical individuals in a given community would depend on such factors as whether the government is openly committed to promoting Salafism; the prevalence of schools with Salafi curricula and mosques with Salafi clerics; and public support for Salafi political parties. Hence, these indicators serve as rough measures to estimate the existence of sizable Salafi-influenced populations. The estimates below are for 2000, unless otherwise stated.

Sunni Countries with Salafi-Influenced Populations

Afghanistan: Afghanistan has 25 million Muslims and was governed by the Taliban, with a Salafi ideology, from 1996 to 2001. I count the 10 million Pushtuns, who supported the Taliban, as Salafi-influenced. Source: Kristin Mendoza, "Islam and Islamism in Afghanistan" (Harvard Law School, Afghan Legal History Project, 2004).

Algeria: Algeria has 31 million Sunni Muslims. I count 19 million, or 60 percent of the population, as Salafi-influenced, on the basis of the Islamic Salvation Front (FIS) gain of 60 percent of the vote in provincial elections in 1991, after which military suppression prevented a national FIS victory and triggered the Algerian civil war. Scholars of Algerian Islamism say that the FIS is mainly Salafi. According to an ICG Middle East Report, "The FIS was largely constituted by elements drawn from the dissident wing of the Salafiyya and the local variants of the Muslim Brotherhood." Similarly, Hugh Roberts says, "Most of the Islamist groups that developed in Algeria in the 1980s belonged in one sense or another to the Salafi trend. . . . By 1990, Salafism . . . was openly oriented and linked to Wahhabism. . . . The founders of the FIS came overwhelmingly from the Salafi trend." Sources: "Islamism, Violence, and Reform in Algeria" (Brussels: ICG Middle East Report, #29), p. 3; Hugh Roberts, "North African Islamism" (London: Development Research Centre, London School of Economics, October 2003), p. 25; and Quintan Wiktorowicz, "Centrifugal Tendencies in the Algerian Civil War," Arab Studies Quarterly, vol. 23, no. 3 (Summer 2001), pp. 65–82.

Bangladesh: Bangladesh has 114 million Sunni Muslims and an elected parliament. I count 14 million as Salafi-influenced, which is the percentage of the vote for two self-proclaimed Salafi parties in 2001, Jamaat-i-Islami with 7.5 percent and Islami Oikyo Jote with 4.5 percent. Sources: Bertil Lintner, "Religious Extremism and Nationalism in Bangladesh," The Bangladesh Observer (September 3, 2002); M. Rashdiuzzaman, "The Election and a New Political Reality in Bangladesh in 2001," *Asian Survey* (January/February 2002), vol. 42, no. 1, pp. 183–91; and Sudha Ramachandran, "Behind the Harkat-ul Jihad al-Islami in Bangladesh," *Asia Times* (December 1, 2004).

Egypt: Egypt has 62 million Sunni Muslims and an authoritarian government with a parliament where 10 percent of the seats are openly contested. I count 23 million as Salafi-influenced, since the Salafi Muslim Brotherhood regularly wins half of the open seats in parliamentary elections and experts generally predict that the Muslim Brotherhood would win over a third in an open election. Hasan al-Banna, the founder of the Muslim Brotherhood in Egypt in 1928, portrayed his purpose as a "Salafi mission" and said his society "follows the way of the noble Quran, takes the path of the Great Prophet, does not deviate from what has come down to us in God's Book, his Messenger's Sunna [companions], and the conduct of the venerable forefathers." In the 1950s and 1960s, Sayyid Qutb developed an explicitly militant version of the Brotherhood's philosophy that Muslim Brotherhood leaders publicly rejected in the 1970s. However, Egypt's Muslim Brotherhood did not reject the call that all Muslims should behave according to the Quran and Sunna over national laws. The 2005 mission statement of Egypt's Muslim Brotherhood declares that it is "a salafi mission" and calls for "the return to Islam, to its pure meanings, to the book of God and the Sunna of his Prophet," seeking "to apply the purified Sunna in all actions." It also says, "The principles that are stated in the book of God and the Sunna of his Prophet . . . [are those] that the Muslim person, Muslim household, Muslim society, Muslim state and Muslim nation must adhere to." Sources: Abdel Azim Ramadan, "Fundamentalist Influence in Egypt," in Marty and Appleby, *Fundamentalism and the State* (Chicago: University of Chicago Press, 1993), pp. 152–83; Ruth M. Beitler and Cindy R. Jebb, "Egypt as a Failing State," (Colorado Springs: USAF Academy, Institute for National Security Studies, July 2003); ICG Middle East Briefing, *Islamism in North Africa II* (April 20, 2004); and www.ikhwanonline.net.

Indonesia: Indonesia has 185 million Sunni Muslims. I count 26 million as Salafi-influenced, which is the vote percentage for self-proclaimed Salafi parties (14 percent) in 2004. The oldest Salafi movement, called Muhammadiyah, was based "exclusively on study of the Quran and the Hadith" and is "committed to purifying Islam and Islamic practices from innovation and idolatrous practices." It was represented by the National Mandate Party, led by the head of Muhammadiyah, which received 6.44 percent of the 2004 vote. A newer Salafi party, the Prosperous Justice Party, which rejects "tolerating deviants" who are "undermining the principles of aqidah [faith]" also gained 7.34 percent of the 2004 vote. Sources: "Indonesia Backgrounder: Why Salafism and Terrorism Mostly Don't Mix," *Asia Report*, no. 43 (September 13, 2004); and James J. Fox, "Currents in Contemporary Islam in Indonesia" (Research School of Pacific and Asian Studies, Australian National University, April 2004), p. 18.

Jordan:

Jordan is virtually all Sunni, with 6 million Muslims and an elected parliament. I count a third, or 2 million, as Salafi-influenced, because Salafis are the dominant clerics, are widespread in every major city, and actively recruit from the Muslim Brotherhood, a moderate movement in Jordan that received 25 to 40 percent of the vote in recent elections. The leading scholar of Salafism in Jordan says, "The Salafi movement is at least as large as the Muslim Brotherhood." Source: Quintan Wiktorowicz, *The Management of Islamic Activism: Salafis, the Muslim Brotherhood, and State Power in Jordan* (Albany, N.Y.: State University of New York Press, 2001), p. 145.

Nigeria:

Nigeria has 68 million Sunni Muslims. I count 37 million as Salafi-influenced. This is the population of the twelve northern provinces, all Muslim, which adopted Salafi courts in 1999. Paul Lubeck says, "Among Muslims in the northern states, the Izala, or Society for the Eradication of Innovation and the Establishment of the Sunna, constitute the most influential revival movement. . . . The inspiration for Izala was Abubakar Gummi . . . principal beneficiary of Saudi and Gulf state patronage in Nigeria. . . . In step with Wahhabi and Islamist reforms in the Muslim world, Gummi declared the practices of Sufi brotherhoods to be innovations that lacked roots in the Quran or the practices (Sunna) of the Prophet and his immediate companions (Salafi)." Sources: Paul Lubeck, et al., "The Globality of Islam: Sharia in Nigeria" (Santa Cruz, Calif.: Center for Global, International and Regional Studies, University of California–Santa Cruz, May 2003), p. 17; "Nigeria: Country Report" (Vienna: ACCORD/UNHCR, 2002); and Ousamane Kane, *Muslim Modernity in Postcolonial Nigeria: A Study of the Society for the Reinstatement of Tradition* (Boston: Brill, 2003).

Oman:

Oman has 2 million Sunni Muslims. I count all as Salafi-influenced, since Islam is the official religion, Sharia is the basis for legislation, and judgments are made according to the tenets of the first century of Islam. "Oman's religious culture has remained loyal to the precepts of the first century of Islam and is ingrained in Omanis today: conservatism, purity. . . ." Sources: "Oman: Political Development" (Washington, D.C.: International Republican Institute, July 1995), p. 10; and Sayed Hassan Amin, *Middle East Legal Systems* (Glasgow, U.K.: Royston, 1985).

Pakistan: Pakistan has 149 million Sunni Muslims and an elected parliament. I count 43 million as Salafi-influenced. This is the total of the populations of the North-West Frontier Province and Baluchistan, governed by the self-proclaimed Salafi Jamaat-i-Islami, which won control of these provincial governments in 2002, and the fraction of the populations that correspond to the voting percentages for the JI in Punjab (3 percent) and Sind (6 percent). Source: European Union Election Observation Mission, "Pakistan National and Provincial Assembly Elections 10 October 2002, Final Report."

Saudi Arabia: Saudi Arabia has 18 million Sunni Muslims and Salafism is the official ideology of the Saudi state. Commonly called Wahhabism, it is reflected in the textbooks used in the mandatory state-run education system. Sources: Christopher M. Blanchard, "The Islamic Traditions of Wahhabism and Salafiyya" (Washington, D.C.: Congressional Research Service, RS21695, August 9, 2004); and *Saudi Arabia Handbook* (Washington, D.C.: Library of Congress, Federal Research Division, 2000).

Somalia: Somalia has a virtually all-Sunni population of 10 million and lacked a central government in the 1990s. I count half of the population as Salafi-influenced, on the basis of the Salafi courts that emerged in Mogadishu and across the country in the mid-1990s, the leaders of which formed a "transitional" national government in 2000. The Islamist movement that serves as the guide for these courts is al-Islah, which borrows its vision from the Egyptian Muslim Brotherhood, receives Saudi funds, and calls for an Islamic state based on a return to the original sources of Islam at the time of the Prophet. Sources: "Somalia: Countering Terrorism in a Failed State" (Brussels: International Crisis Group African Report No. 45, May 23, 2002), p. 18; Ted Dagne, "Africa and the War on Terrorism" (Washington, D.C.: CRS, January 2002); and Abdurahaman Abdullah, "Recovering Somali State: The Islamic Factor" (Montreal: McGill University, Islamic Institute, 2002).

Sudan: Sudan has 21 million Sunnis. I count all as Salafi-influenced, since the ruling National Islamic Front (NIS) is a Muslim Brotherhood–inspired political party committed to Salafi beliefs. The NIS came to power in 1989 to return Sudan to rule by "the Sharia, as embodied in the Quran and Sunna." Official NIS statements say, "The teachings of the Quran as embodied in the political practice of the Prophet Mohammad constitute an eternal model that Muslims are bound to adopt as a perfect standard for all time." According to Abdullah Ali Ibrahim, the leader of NIS, Hasan al-Turbi "has no place for Sufism and Mahism in his enterprise of Islamic revival" and believes that "religion is the eternal and legitimate heritage of Islam comprising the Quran and traditions of the Prophet, the Sunna." Sources: Aharon Layish and Gabriel R. Warburg, *The Reinstatement of Islamic Law in Sudan* (Boston: Brill, 2002), p. 82; and Adullah Ali Ibrahim, "A Theology of Modernity: Hasan al-Turbi and Islamic Renewal in Sudan," *Africa Today*, pp. 195–222.

Tunisia: Tunisia is an all-Sunni state of 10 million with an authoritarian government. I count half of the population as Salafi-influenced, on the basis of the popularity of Ennahada, widely viewed by scholars as the most popular political movement in Tunisia today, even though the government cracked down on it in 1990. Ennahada adheres to Salafi principles, calling for "the rejection of doctrinal or jurisprudential *taqlid* (imitation) and for a return to the original sources, that is the Quran, the Sunna, and the experience of the first three generations of Muslims." Rachid Ghannouchi, the leader, was educated in Salafi schools and said in 1989: "The Quran and the Sunna are the ultimate law that governs the behavior of rulers as well as all Muslims. They are also above any invented law." Sources: Azzam Tamimi, *Rachid Ghannouchi* (New York: Oxford University Press, 2001), p. 42; and Mohamed El-hachmi Hamdi, *The Politicisation of Islam: A Case Study of Tunisia* (Boulder, Colo.: Westview Press, 1998), p. 109.

Yemen: Yemen has a population of 18 million Muslims, of whom 11 million are Sunni and 7 million Shia. I count the 8 million Sunnis in the north as Salafi-influenced, since there are many Salafi institutions and charitable organizations as well as prominent Salafi clerics there. The Shia would not be expected to support Sunni beliefs, while the Sunnis in the south could be expected to resist beliefs of the north following the war that led to unity with the north in 1990. Bernard Haykel says that the "Yemeni government has since the early 1970s adopted and promoted a Salafi understanding of Islam and this has been supported financially by the Saudi government through the so-called Scientific Institutes that have been established throughout the north. . . . [V]irtually every student who was born post-1970 would have been exposed to Salafi teachings of Islam." The government did close some Salafi institutions in the wake of September 11. Sources: Hiroshi Matsumoto, "Yemen Between Democratization and Prolonged Power" (Tokyo: Japan Institute of International Affairs, 2003); Bernard Haykel, *Revival and Reform in Islam* (New York: Cambridge University Press, 2003); and Bernard A. Haykel, personal communication, January 24, 2005.

Non-Salafi Sunni Countries

Albania: The population is 70 percent Sunni. Albania is a secular democratic state with no Salafi political or social movements. Source: *Albania: A Country Study* (Washington, D.C.: Library of Congress, Federal Research Division, 1992).

Burkina Faso: Burkina Faso has a population that is 50 percent Sunni, a working secular democratic government as of 2000, and no significant Salafi political or social movements. Sources: *Country Review: Burkina Faso* (Houston: Commercial Data International, 1999); and "Burkina Faso: International Religious Freedom Report" (Washington, D.C.: U.S. Department of State, 2002).

Chad: Chad's population is 51 percent Sunni Muslim, 35 percent Christian, and 14 percent other religions. Some 10 percent of Muslims in Chad are considered Islamic fundamentalists, who overwhelmingly follow the Tijaniyyah Sufi order. Source: Abdelkerim Ousman, "The Potential of Islamic Terrorism in Sub-Saharan Africa," *International Journal of Politics, Culture, and Society*, vol. 18, nos. 1–2 (December 2004), pp. 87–88.

Guinea: Guinea has a population that is 85 percent Sunni, a secular authoritarian government, and no significant Salafi political or social movements. Sources: J. D. Fage with William Tordoff, *A History of Africa* (New York: Routledge, 2002); and "Guinea: International Religious Freedom Report" (Washington, D.C.: U.S. Department of State, 2003).

Kuwait: The population is 60 percent Sunni, 25 percent Shia, and 15 percent other religions. Kuwait has a secular authoritarian government that experimented with parliamentary elections in the 1990s The self-identified Salafi party, Islamic Popular Alliance, won less than 10 percent of the vote, representing far fewer than 1 million people. Source: Nadia Akil Zaman, "Kuwait's Islamist Movement and Its Role in Contemporary Politics," *CSIS Briefing Notes on Islam, Society, and Politics*, vol. 2, no. 1 (May 1999).

Kyrgyzstan: Kyrgyzstan is a secular authoritarian state. The population is 75 percent Sunni. About half pray only rarely or not at all and those who do identify with Sufi orders. Sources: ICG, "Is Radical Islam Inevitable in Central Asia?"; and Angel M. Rabasa, et al., *The Muslim World After 9/11* (Washington, D.C.: RAND Corporation, 2004).

Libya: Libya has an almost completely Sunni population and an authoritarian government. Muammar al-Qadhafi came to power in 1969 on the basis of his own ideology blending socialism and Islam, which has put his regime at odds with Salafi movements ever since. His government has actively suppressed such movements. Sources: Dirk Vandewalle, *Libya Since Independence* (Ithaca, N.Y.: Cornell University Press, 1998); and Obeidi Amal, *Political Culture in Libya* (Richmond, Surrey, U.K.: Curzon, 2001).

Malaysia: The population is 60 percent Muslim and 40 percent Chinese and Indian. Although Islam is the official religion, there are strong constitutional guarantees for freedom of religion. Parti Islam Se-Malaysia, a Salafi political party calling for the establishment of an

Islamic state with the Quran and Sunna as the constitutional guide for Islamic law, has existed since 1951, but won only 3 percent of the national vote in 2004, representing fewer than 1 million Muslims. Sources: *CIA World Fact Book* (Washington, D.C.: Central Intelligence Agency, 2005); and Rabasa, *The Muslim World After 9/11*.

Mali: The population is 90 percent Sunni. The state is a secular democracy and has no significant Salafi political or social movements. Source: *Country Profile: Mali* (Washington, D.C.: Library of Congress, Federal Research Division, January 2005).

Mauritania: The population is almost entirely Sunni. Islam is the state religion and Sharia the law of the land. Although various Islamic doctrines are prominent (such as Qadiriya and the Tijaniya), these are all based on Sufism or other non-Salafi forms of Islamic fundamentalism. Sources: *A Country Study: Mauritania* (Washington, D.C.: Library of Congress, 1988); and Carlos Echeverria Jesus, "Radical Islam in the Maghreb," *Orbis* (Spring 2004), 1–13.

Morocco: Morocco has an almost entirely Sunni population, an authoritarian government, and a legal system based on a combination of French and Islamic law. King Hassan II suppressed a small Salafi movement in the early 1960s. Since then, Sufism has been the dominant form of Sunni fundamentalism and only a handful of small Salafi schools operate today. Source: Henry Munson, *Religion and Power in Morocco* (New Haven: Yale University Press, 1993).

Niger: Niger has a population that is 80 percent Sunni, a working secular democracy as of 2001, and no significant Salafi political or social movements. Sources: *Country Review: Niger* (Houston: Commercial Data International, 1999); and "Niger: International Religious Freedom Report" (Washington, D.C.: U.S. Department of State, 2002).

Senegal: Senegal has an almost completely Sunni population. Islam is predominately represented by various Sufi orders, mainly the Tijaniya and the Muridiya, and the legal system is a mixture of secular and Islamic law, in which Sharia is applied in matters of marriage, divorce, property, and inheritance. Source: Leonardo A. Villalon, *Islamic Society and State Power in Senegal* (Cambridge, U.K.: Cambridge University Press, 1995).

Sierra Leone: Sierra Leone has a population that is 60 percent Sunni, a working secular democratic government as of 2002, and no significant Salafi political or social movements. Sources: Bankole Thompson, *The Constitutional History and Law of Sierra Leone, 1961–1995* (Lanham, Md.: University Press of America, 1997); and "Sierra Leone: International Religious Freedom Report" (Washington, D.C.: U.S. Department of State, 2002).

Syria: The population is 75 percent Sunni. Syria is a secular authoritarian state. The government suppressed a small Salafi movement in the early 1980s, massacring 20,000 following an uprising in the city of Hama in 1982. Since then, Islamic fundamentalist groups have been largely dormant. Source: Rabasa, *The Muslim World After 9/11.*

Tajikistan: Tajikistan is a secular authoritarian state. The population is 85 percent Sunni. Fewer than half pray regularly and those who do identify with Sufi orders. Sources: ICG, "Is Radical Islam Inevitable in Central Asia?"; and Rabasa, *The Muslim World After 9/11.*

Turkey: Turkey is a secular democracy with no Salafi political parties. Its population is almost completely Sunni. Since the 1970s, Turkey has experienced many popular Islamic movements. Yavuz Hakan states that "Turkish Islam is rooted in Sufism, particularly Naksibendi Sufi orders"; Necmettin Erbakan, the first Islamic prime minister, in 1996–97, emerged from this tradition. Sources: Yavuz M. Hakan, *Islamic Political Identity in Turkey* (London: Oxford University Press, 2003), p. 274; and Yildiz Atasoy, "Islamic Revivalism and the Nation-State Project," *Social Compass*, vol. 44, no. 1 (1997).

Turkmenistan: Turkmenistan's population is 90 percent Sunni. The country has a secular authoritarian government, a long tradition of Sufism, and several important Sufi religious sites. Sources: ICG, "Is Radical Islam Inevitable in Central Asia?"; and Rabasa, *The Muslim World After 9/11.*

United Arab Emirates: UAE has 2 million Sunni Muslims and an authoritarian government. Although Islam is the official religion and Sharia is the basis for legislation, judgments are made according to traditional opinions and analogical reasoning, instead of strict adherence to Sunna or Hadith. Source: *Country Study: United Arab Emirates* (Washington, D.C.: Library of Congress, Federal Research Division, 1993).

Uzbekistan: Uzbekistan is an authoritarian state that outlaws Islamic political parties. The population is 90 percent Sunni, the majority of whom do not pray or attend religious services. Virtually all of the most religious, perhaps 30 percent of the population, identify with Sufi orders. The Islamic Movement of Uzbekistan, a Salafi militant group with possibly several thousand members, arose in the 1990s and was soon repressed by the government. Sources: "Is Radical Islam Inevitable in Central Asia?"; and Rabasa, *The Muslim World After 9/11.*

Notes

INTRODUCTION
CHAPTER 1: THE GROWING THREAT

1. Specifically, the data on suicide terrorism in this book are from the period beginning January 1, 1980, and ending December 31, 2003. Data collection continues and the raw data are available at the archive for the Chicago Project on Suicide Terrorism, housed at the University of Chicago.

2. "Final Instructions to the Hijackers of September 11," reprinted in Bruce Lincoln, *Holy Terrors: Thinking About Religion After September 11* (Chicago: University of Chicago Press, 2003), pp. 93–98.

3. If September 11 is counted, suicide attack accounts for 73 percent of total deaths.

CHAPTER 2: EXPLAINING SUICIDE TERRORISM

1. The word "terrorism" dates from the Jacobin government's "Reign of Terror" (1793–94) to eliminate opposition to the French Revolution, but did not come into common usage until the late nineteenth century, when a group of Russian revolutionaries adopted the term to describe their violent struggle against the tsar's rule. Since then, governments have sometimes been accused of terrorism, either against their own people, to suppress dissent (Soviet show trials in the 1930s), or against enemy states, to compel their surrender in war (British fire-bombing of German cities in World War II). However, "terrorism" still signifies, principally, vi-

olent acts against innocents that are committed by nongovernmental actors—such as revolutionaries, nationalists, or ethnic groups—and are intended to challenge the existing political order.

2. On the definition and goals of terrorism, see Alex P. Schmid and Albert J. Jongman, *Political Terrorism* (New Brunswick, N.J.: Transaction Books, 1988); and U.S. Department of State, *Patterns of Global Terrorism* (Washington, D.C.: U.S. Government Printing Office, 2001). Although one could broaden the definition of "terrorism" to include the actions of a national government intended to cause terror among an opposing population, use of such a broad definition would distract attention from what policy makers would most like to know: how to combat the threat posed by non-state actors to the national security of the United States and our allies. Further, it could also create analytic confusion. Terrorist organizations and state governments have different levels of resources, face different kinds of incentives, and are susceptible to different types of pressures. Accordingly, the determinants of their behavior are not likely to be the same, and thus the two require separate theoretical investigations.

3. Carol Edler Baumann, *Diplomatic Kidnapings: A Revolutionary Tactic of Urban Terrorism* (The Hague: Nijhoff, 1973); Richard Clutterbuck, *Living with Terrorism* (London: Faber & Faber, 1975); Peter St. John, *Air Piracy, Airport Security, and International Terrorism* (New York: Quorum Books, 1991).

4. Brian N. Jenkins, "Will Terrorists Go Nuclear?" Rand Report P-5541 (Santa Monica, Calif.: Rand Corporation, 1975), p. 4.

5. For discussions of destructive terrorism, see David C. Rapoport, *Assassination and Terrorism* (Toronto: CBC Merchandising, 1971); Paul Elliott, *Brotherhoods of Fear* (London: Blandford, 1998); and Barbara W. Tuchman, *The Proud Tower* (New York: Macmillan, 1966). Some popular lists count the Anarchists as suicide terrorists, but the characterization is inaccurate. From 1870 through World War I, Anarchist terrorists assassinated a number of heads of state and attacked institutions associated with bourgeois government and society, using a variety of destructive tactics such as throwing bombs into crowded markets and music halls. Although a number of terrorists were subsequently captured, executed, and touted as martyrs, none carried out attacks in which they killed themselves and few of the attacks would even appear to qualify as suicide missions, since the vast majority of attackers tried to escape. Good accounts include James Joll, *The Anarchists* (Cambridge, Mass.: Harvard University Press, 1979); David Miller, *Anarchism* (London: J. M. Dent, 1984); and George Woodcock, *Anarchism* (Cleveland, Ohio: Meridian Books, 1962).

6. Hunger strikes and self-immolation are not ordinarily considered acts of terrorism, because their main purpose is to evoke understanding and sympathy from the target audience, not to cause terror. For a valuable discussion of moral coercion, see Reinhold Niebuhr, *Moral Man and Immoral Society* (New York: Scribners, 1960).

7. A probable additional instance is the Forty-seven Ronin in late sixteenth-century Japan. For the events, see John Allyn, *The Forty-seven Ronin Story* (Rutland, VT: Charles Tuttle, 1970).

8. The two groups were not identical—the Zealots generally attacked Roman elites, while the Sicarii killed prominent Jews collaborating with Rome—and neither was monolithic, being more a loose movement than a tightly knit network.

9. Prominent examples of the extensive literature on the Zealots and Sicarii include Martin Hengel, *The Zealots* (Edinburgh: T. & T. Clark, 1989); David C. Rapoport, "Fear and Trembling: Terrorism in Three Religious Traditions," *American Political Science Review*, vol. 78, no. 3 (Sept. 1984), pp. 658–77; K. Kohler, "The Zealots," *The Jewish Encyclopedia* (New York: Funk & Wagnalls, 1905); S. Zeitlin, "The Sicarii and the Zealots," *Jewish Quarterly Review*, vol. 57 (1967), pp. 251–70; and Richard A. Horsley, "The Sicarii: Ancient Jewish 'Terrorists,' " *Journal of Religion*, vol. 59, no. 4 (1979), pp. 435–58.

10. Josephus, *Antiquities*, vol. 15, p. 288. Quoted in Hengel, *The Zealots*, p. 257, who also provides a general discussion of martyrdom in the group, pp. 256–69.

11. Bernard Lewis, *The Assassins: A Radical Sect in Islam* (New York: Oxford University Press, 1967), quote from p. 47. See also Marshall G. S. Hodgson, *The Order of Assassins: The Struggle of the Early Nizari Ismailis Against the Islamic World* (The Hague: Mouton & Co., 1955); and W. B. Bartlett, *The Assassins: The Story of Medieval Islam's Secret Sect* (Stroud, Eng.: Sutton, 2001).

12. For excellent coverage of the kamikazes, see Richard O'Neill, *Suicide Squads* (New York: Ballantine Books, 1981); Albert Axell and Hideaki Kase, *Kamikaze: Japan's Suicide Gods* (London: Longmans, 2002); and Rikihei Inoguchi and Tadashi Nakajima, *The Divine Wind* (New York: Bantam Books, 1960). On estimates for the total number of the various kamikaze strikes, see Emiko Ohnuki-Tierney, *Kamikaze, Cherry Blossoms, and Nationalisms* (Chicago: University of Chicago Press, 2002), p. 167. On American casualties, see Hatsuho Naito, *Thunder Gods* (New York: Kodansha International/USA, 1989), p. 25.

13. Tim Pat Coogan, *On the Blanket: The Inside Story of the IRA Prisoners' 'Dirty' Protest* (New York: Palgrave Macmillan, 1997); Jonathan Steele, "Ultimate Sacrifice," *The Guardian* (London), January 20, 1999; Scott Anderson, "The Hunger Warriors," *New York Times* (October 21, 2001).

14. For example, Brian N. Jenkins, *International Terrorism* (Washington, D.C.: Rand Corporation, 1985); Walter Laqueur, *The Age of Terrorism* (Boston: Little, Brown, 1987); and Bruce Hoffman, *Inside Terrorism* (New York: Columbia University Press, 1998).

15. Jerrold M. Post, "Terrorist Psycho-Logic: Terrorist Behavior as a Product of Psychological Forces," Martin Kramer, "The Moral Logic of Hizballah," and Ariel Merari, "The Readiness to Kill and Die: Suicidal Terrorism in the Middle East,"

all in Walter Reich, ed., *Origins of Terrorism* (New York: Cambridge University Press, 1990).

16. Institute for Counter-Terrorism (ICT), *Countering Suicide Terrorism* (Herzliya, Israel: International Policy Institute for Counter-Terrorism, 2001).

17. For earlier studies that question the relationship between Islamic fundamentalism and suicide terrorism, see Merari, "Readiness to Kill and Die," and Ehud Sprinzak, "Rational Fanatics," *Foreign Policy*, no. 120 (Sept.–Oct. 2000), pp. 66–73.

18. Post, "Terrorist Psycho-Logic," and Merari, "Readiness to Kill and Die."

19. Sprinzak, "Rational Fanatics." For a comprehensive review of the deficiencies of efforts to profile terrorists, see Rex A. Hudson, *The Sociology and Psychology of Terrorism: Who Becomes a Terrorist and Why?* (Washington, D.C.: Federal Research Division, Library of Congress, September 1999).

20. Alan B. Krueger and Jitka Maleckova, "Education, Poverty, Political Violence, and Terrorism," BNER Working Paper 9074 (Cambridge, Mass.: National Bureau of Economic Research, July 2002).

21. Mia M. Bloom, "Palestinian Suicide Bombing: Public Support, Market Share, and Ethnic Outbidding," *Political Science Quarterly*, vol. 119, no. 1 (Spring 2004), pp. 61–89.

22. The fraction of Palestinians who supported suicide terrorism against Israeli targets was 24 percent in 1994 and remained in a narrow range near 30 percent until it suddenly rose sharply to 73 percent just as the second intifada began in fall 2000. Jerusalem Media and Communication Centre poll, April 2002. See www.jmcc.org/publicpoll/opinion.html.

23. Most theories in political science focus on causes at one level of analysis and assert that other levels are relatively unimportant. However, suicide terrorism cannot usefully be examined this way, since the phenomenon mainly occurs as part of protracted campaigns that involve interactions among the terrorist organizations, local communities associated with the terrorist organizations, and the individual suicide terrorists themselves. As a result, variation in outcomes cannot be explained without understanding processes at three distinct levels of analysis that must operate in a coherent manner for suicide terrorist campaigns to occur.

PART I: THE STRATEGIC LOGIC OF SUICIDE TERRORISM
CHAPTER 3: A STRATEGY FOR WEAK ACTORS

1. The best source for statistics on terrorism is the U.S. Department of State, "Patterns of Global Terrorism" (Washington, D.C.: 1983–2003), although these reports do not distinguish suicide from nonsuicide attacks.

2. Peter Schalk, "Resistance and Martyrdom in the Process of State Formation of

Tamililam," in Joyce Pettigrew, ed., *Martyrdom and Political Resistance* (Amsterdam: VU University Press, 1997), pp. 61–83.

3. Robert A. Pape, *Bombing to Win: Air Power and Coercion in War* (Ithaca, N.Y.: Cornell University Press, 1996); "Debating Robert A. Pape's *Bombing to Win*," *Security Studies*, vol. 7, no. 1 (Winter 1997–98), pp. 93–214.

4. Martha Crenshaw, "The Causes of Terrorism," *Comparative Politics*, vol. 13 (July 1981), pp. 379–99.

5. Hezbollah's "Open Letter" to the "disinherited of Lebanon and the world" first appeared as a pamphlet in Beirut on February 16, 1985. An English translation appears in Augustus Richard Norton, *Amal and the Shi'a: Struggle for the Soul of Lebanon* (Austin: University of Texas Press, 1987), pp. 176–87.

6. Interview with Fadlallah, *Monday Morning* (December 16, 1985), quoted in Martin Kramer, "The Moral Logic of Hizballah," in Walter Reich, ed., *Origins of Terrorism* (New York: Cambridge University Press, 1990), p. 148.

7. Quoted in Khaled Hroub, *Hamas: Political Thought and Practice* (Washington, D C.: Institute for Palestine Studies, 2000), pp. 265–66, 274.

8. Quoted in Joel Greenberg, "Suicide Planner Expresses Joy over His Missions," *New York Times* (May 9, 2002).

9. Velupillai Prabhakaran, "Heroes' Day" speech, 1997, available at www.eelamweb.com.

10. "Commander Says Chechnya War to Spread to Rest of Russia," *BBC Monitoring International Reports* (November 19, 2003).

11. Statement by World Islamic Front, 1998. Available at www.bas.org.

12. Deborah Sontag, "The Palestinian Conversation," *New York Times Magazine* (February 3, 2002), p. 41.

13. Fathi al-Shaqaqi, secretary general of Islamic Jihad, *Al-Quds* (April 11, 1995), in FBIS-NES-95-70 (April 12, 1995). The Foreign Broadcast Information Service is a public resource provided by the U.S. government that monitors and translates information from foreign news media, and is available in most libraries.

14. Amy Waldman, "Masters of Suicide Bombing: Tamil Guerrillas of Sri Lanka," *New York Times* (January 14, 2003).

15. "LTTE Leader on Sri Lanka's Military Campaign," speech released by International Secretariat of LTTE, London, United Kingdom, May 13, 1998. Available at eelamweb.com.

16. Laurinda Keys, "Tamil Tiger Rebels Well-Equipped for Sri Lankan Civil War," Associated Press (June 7, 2000).

17. David C. Rapoport, "Fear and Trembling in Terrorism in Three Religious

Traditions," *American Political Science Review*, vol. 78, no. 3 (September 1984), p. 672.

18. On the role of the Zealots and Sicarii in precipitating the Jewish revolts against Rome, see Moshe Aberback and David Aberback, *The Roman-Jewish Wars and Hebrew Cultural Nationalism* (New York: St. Martin's Press, 2000), pp. 28–48.

19. Josephus, *Jewish War*, vol. 7, pp. 334, 344, 351. Quoted in Hengel, *The Zealots*, p. 264.

20. Bernard Lewis, *The Assassins: A Radical Sect in Islam* (New York: Oxford University Press, 1967), p. 45.

21. Ibid., p. 58.

22. Albert Axell and Hideaki Kase, *Kamikaze: Japan's Suicide Gods* (London: Longmans, 2002), p. 115

23. Bernard Millot, *Divine Thunder: The Life and Death of the Kamikazes* (New York: McCall Publishing Co., 1971), p. 32.

24. Richard O'Neill, *Suicide Squads* (New York: Ballantine Books, 1981), p. 139.

25. Emiko Ohnuki-Tierney, *Kamikaze, Cherry Blossoms, and Nationalisms* (Chicago: University of Chicago Press, 2002), p. 204.

26. Ibid., p. 228.

27. Quoted in Richard O'Neill, *Suicide Squads* (New York: Ballantine Books, 1981), p.144.

28. Quoted in ibid., p. 144.

CHAPTER 4: TARGETING DEMOCRACIES

1. Richard Perle and David Frum, *An End to Evil: How to Win the War on Terror* (New York: Random House, 2003).

2. The data for the survey are available from the Chicago Project on Suicide Terrorism, University of Chicago. The survey is reliable. A majority of the incidents were openly claimed by the sponsoring terrorist organizations. For almost every incident, we have multiple reports in regional news media or other sources, even though many were not reported in U.S. media. To probe for additional cases, I interviewed experts and officials involved in what some might consider conflicts especially prone to suicide attacks, such as Afghanistan in the 1980s, but this did not yield more incidents. According to the CIA station chief for Pakistan from 1986 to 1988 (Milton Bearden, personal communication, May 23, 2002), "I cannot recall a single incident where an Afghan launched himself against a Soviet target with the intention of dying in the process. I don't think these things ever happened, though some of their attacks were a little harebrained and could have been con-

sidered suicidal. I think it's important that Afghans never even took their war outside their borders—for example, they never tried to blow up the Soviet embassy in Pakistan."

3. In August 1993, a BKI terrorist was killed by his own bomb while struggling with security guard in a theater; it is uncertain whether he intended this as a suicide attack. In 1999, the four members of a BKI suicide squad were all killed while attacking the Punjab headquarters of the RSS, a Hindu nationalist group. In January 2000, Indian police captured BKI terrorists who were preparing suicide bomb attacks.

4. Shaul Mishal and Avraham Sela, *The Palestinian Hamas* (New York: Columbia University Press, 2000), p. 71.

5. Elaine Sciolino, "Saudi Warns Bush," *New York Times* (January 27, 2002). Although support for Osama bin Laden himself is lower than for al-Qaeda's goals to reduce America's role on the Arabian Peninsula, almost half of all Saudis said in a poll conducted after the May 2003 suicide attacks in Riyadh that they had a favorable view of bin Laden's sermons and public statements. The poll surveyed more than 15,000 Saudis from August to November 2003, and was overseen by Nawaf Obaid, a Saudi national security consultant. Reported on CNN.com, June 9, 2004.

6. Khaled Hroub, *Hamas: Political Thought and Practice* (Washington, D.C.: Institute for Palestine Studies, 2000); Andrea Nusse, *Muslim Palestine: The Ideology of Hamas* (Amsterdam: Harwood Academic, 1998).

7. Michael Horowitz and Dan Reiter, "When Does Aerial Bombing Work? Quantitative Empirical Tests, 1917–1999," *Journal of Conflict Resolution*, vol. 45 (April 2001), pp. 147–73.

8. Alexander B. Downes, "Targeting Civilians in War" (Ph.D. diss., University of Chicago, 2004).

9. Adam Przeworski, Michael E. Alvarez, Jose Antonio Cheibub, and Fernando Limongi, *Democracy and Development: Political Institutions and Well-Being in the World, 1950–1990* (Cambridge, UK: Cambridge University Press, 2000); Charles Boix and Sebastian Rosato, "A Complete Dataset of Regimes, 1850–1999" (manuscript, the University of Chicago, 2001); Samuel P. Huntington, *The Third Wave: Democratization in the Late Twentieth Century* (Norman, Okla.: University of Oklahoma Press, 1991).

10. Eric Carlton, *Occupation: The Policies and Practices of Military Conquerors* (New York: Routledge, 1992); Gerhard von Glahn, *The Occupation of Enemy Territory* (Minneapolis: University of Minnesota Press, 1957); Eyal Benvenisti, *The International Law of Occupation* (Princeton, N.J.: University of Princeton Press, 1993); and David M. Edelstein, "Occupational Hazards: Why Military Occupations Succeed or Fail," *International Security*, vol. 29, no. 1 (Summer 2004), pp. 49–91.

11. Benny Morris, *Righteous Victims: A History of the Zionist-Arab Conflict, 1881–2001* (New York: Vintage Books, 2001), pp. 329–43; Baruch Kimmerling and Joel Migdal, *Palestinians: The Making of a People* (Cambridge, Mass.: Harvard University Press, 1994); and Rashid Khalidi, *Palestinian Identity: The Construction of Modern National Consciousness* (New York: Columbia University Press, 1997).

12. These numbers do not count the additional several hundred thousand Israelis who moved into East Jerusalem during the period.

13. Hamas, founded in December 1987, is an Islamic fundamentalist religious, social-services, guerrilla, and terrorist organization that was started by Palestinian followers of the Egyptian-based Muslim Brotherhood. The goals of the Muslim Brotherhood and Hamas include stopping Western imperialism in the Middle East and establishing Islamic states in the region. Palestinian Islamic Jihad is a second, smaller Islamist terrorist organization that stems from the Shi'ite Muslim religious tradition—a minority among Palestinians, who are mainly Sunni.

14. Jerusalem Media and Communication Centre Poll, April 2002, available at www.jmcc.org.

15. Prominent works among the fast-growing literature on al-Qaeda include Anonymous, *Through Our Enemies' Eyes: Osama Bin Laden, Radical Islam, and the Future of America* (Washington, D.C.: Brassey's, 2002); Peter L. Bergen, *Holy War, Inc.: Inside the Secret World of Osama bin Laden* (New York: Simon & Schuster, 2002); Rohan Gunaratna, *Inside al-Qaeda* (New York: Columbia University Press, 2002); and Daniel L. Byman, "Al-Qa'ida as an Adversary," *World Politics* (2004).

16. George W. Bush, "Address to the Nation on the War on Terrorism," November 8, 2001.

17. Osama bin Laden, "Declaration of War Against the Americans Occupying the Two Holy Places," August 23,1996.

18. World Islamic Front Statement, "Jihad Against Jews and Crusaders," February 23, 1998.

19. "Jihadi Iraq, Hopes and Dangers," a document dedicated to Yusuf al-Ayiri, a key al-Qaeda ideologist and media coordinator killed in the May 2003 attack in Riyadh, posted originally on a web page called "Global Islamic Media," and later posted on the web page of the Forsvarets Forskningsinstitutt, the Norwegian Defense Research Establishment. Translated from the Arabic by the Chicago Project on Suicide Terrorism.

20. Excerpts from bin Laden tape, *USA Today* (April 15, 2004).

21. Two other operations attacked a disused synagogue (in Tunisia in April 2002) and Jewish-owned restaurants (in Morocco in May 2003), but no Jews were killed in either instance.

CHAPTER 5: LEARNING TERRORISM PAYS

1. Jerrold M. Post, "Terrorist Psycho-Logic: Terrorist Behavior as a Product of Psychological Forces," and Ariel Merari, "The Readiness to Kill and Die: Suicidal Terrorism in the Middle East," both in Walter Reich, ed., *Origins of Terrorism* (New York: Cambridge University Press, 1990).

2. Alexander George, et al., *Limits of Coercive Diplomacy* (Boston: Little, Brown, 1972); Robert A. Pape, *Bombing to Win: Air Power and Coercion in War* (Ithaca, N.Y.: Cornell University Press, 1996).

3. Robert Jervis, *Perception and Misperception in International Politics* (Princeton, N.J.: Princeton University Press, 1976); Richard Ned Lebow, *Between Peace and War: The Nature of International Crisis* (Baltimore: Johns Hopkins University Press, 1981).

4. Martin Kramer, "Fundamentalist Islam at Large: Drive for Power," *Middle East Quarterly*, vol. 3 (June 1996), pp. 37–49.

5. Robert J. Art and Patrick M. Cronin, *The United States and Coercive Diplomacy* (Washington, D.C.: United States Institute of Peace, 2003).

6. Ronald Reagan, *An American Life* (New York: Simon & Schuster, 1990), p. 465.

7. Philippe Sauvagnargues, "Opposition Candidate," Agence France-Presse (August 14, 1994); "Sri Lanka Opposition Leader Promises Talks with Rebels," *Japan Economic Newswire* (August 11, 1994).

8. Rui De Figueredo and Barry R. Weingast, "Vicious Cycles: Endogenous Political Extremism and Political Violence," paper presented at the annual meeting of the American Political Science Association (September 1998); Andrew Kydd and Barbara F. Walter, "Sabotaging the Peace: The Politics of Extremist Violence," *International Organization*, vol. 56, no. 2 (2002), pp. 263–96; and Mia Bloom, "Palestinian Suicide Bombing: Public Support, Market Share, and Ethnic Outbidding," *Political Science Quarterly*, vol. 119, no. 1 (Spring 2004), pp. 61–89.

9. There were no suicide attacks from April to October 1994.

10. Kydd and Walter, "Sabotaging the Peace."

11. David Makovsky and Alon Pinkas, "Rabin: Killing Civilians Won't Kill the Negotiations," *Jerusalem Post* (April 13, 2004).

12. Yitzhak Rabin, speech to Knesset, *BBC Summary of World Broadcasts* (April 20, 1994).

13. Efraim Inbar, *Rabin and Israel's National Security* (Baltimore: Johns Hopkins University Press, 1999), pp. 141–42.

14. "Hamas Operations Against Israel Said to Continue," *Al-Dustur* (Amman, Jordan), April 14, 1994. FBIS-NES-94-072, April 14, 1994.

15. Ahmed Bakr, "Interview," *The Independent* (London) (March 14, 1995); "Hamas Leader Discusses Goals," *Frankfurter Rundschau* (May 3, 1995). FBIS-NES-95-086, May 4, 1995.

16. Fathi al-Shaqaqi, quoted in "Interview," *Al-Quds* (April 11, 1995), in FBIS-NES-95-70, April 12, 1995.

17. There were no suicide attacks from August 1995 to February 1996. There were four suicide attacks, in response to an Israeli assassination, from February 25 to March 4, 1996, and then none until March 1997.

18. Yitzhak Rabin interview, *BBC Summary of World Broadcasts* (September 8, 1995).

19. "Bus Attack Said to Spur Rabin to Speed Talks," *Yediot Aharonot* (July 25, 1995), FBIS-NES-95-142, July 25, 1995.

20. Michael Theodoulou, "New Attacks Feared," *The Times* (London) (August 21, 1995), FBIS-NES-95-165, August 25, 1995.

21. Hamas Communiqué no. 125, *Filastin al-Muslimah* (London) (August 1995), FBIS-NES-95-152, August 8, 1995.

22. When Israeli forces invaded Lebanon in 1982, they found three Tamil Tigers training in Palestinian camps. On Tamil-Lebanese connections, see G. P. V. Somaratne, "Sri Lanka's Relations with Israel," in Shelton U. Kodikara, ed., *External Compulsions of South Asian Politics* (New Delhi: Sage Publications, 1993), p. 205; M. R. Narayan Swamy, *Tigers of Lanka: From Boys to Guerrillas* (3rd ed.; Delhi: Konark Publishers, 2002), pp. 97–101, 241; Bruce Hoffman and Gordon H. McCormick, "Terrorism, Signaling, and Suicide Attack," *Studies in Conflict and Terrorism,* vol. 27 (2004), p. 259. Prabhakaran quoted in Rohan Gunaratna, "The LTTE and Suicide Terrorism," *Frontline* (India), vol. 17, no. 3 (February 5–8, 2000).

23. Ramadan Shallah interview, *BBC Summary of World Broadcasts* (November 3, 2001).

24. "Hamas Statement," *BBC Summary of World Broadcasts* (July 23, 2000).

25. "Bin Laden's Sermon for the Feast of the Sacrifice," *Middle East Media Research Institute*, Special Dispatch Series, no. 476 (March 5, 2003).

26. Robert A. Pape, *Bombing to Win: Air Power and Coercion in War* (Ithaca, N.Y.: Cornell University Press, 1996).

27. Of course, the concept of "homeland" territory can be socially constructed. In most of the societies that have been targeted by suicide terrorists, the consensus on the boundaries of the national homeland is so broad and deep as to be essentially fixed. The major exception is Israel, whose citizens are engaged in debate over whether the West Bank and East Jerusalem should be considered inalienable parts of the national homeland.

PART II: THE SOCIAL LOGIC OF SUICIDE TERRORISM
CHAPTER 6: OCCUPATION AND RELIGIOUS DIFFERENCE

1. Although there are several competing theories of the formation of national identity, scholars broadly agree that national identity includes the idea that the nation should govern itself because it has a unique set of characteristics that only the community itself can perpetuate. For example, see Ernest Gellner, *Nations and Nationalism* (Ithaca, N.Y.: Cornell University Press, 1983); Benedict Anderson, *Imagined Communities* (New York: Verso, 1991); and Rogers Brubaker, *Nationalism Reframed* (New York: Cambridge University Press, 1996).

2. Kurds and Turks are both mainly Sunni Muslims.

3. See Chapter 9.

4. Even if the terrorists' main base of support is a certain subpopulation, social boundaries within a national community are rarely so sharp that they could prevent information from leaking both ways. In any case, drawing only on a completely separate subpopulation would be undesirable because it would simplify the enemy security forces' problem in suppressing the threat.

5. If important segments of the community were unwilling to accept the equation of suicide attack with martyrdom, the terrorists might find that funerals drew few people, martyr videos went unsold, or murals were painted over.

6. Jerusalem Media and Communication Centre polls, 1995 to 2003.

7. Elaine Sciolino, "Saudi Warns Bush," *New York Times* (January 27, 2002).

8. Mia Bloom, *Dying to Kill* (New York: Columbia University Press, 2005), Chapter 3.

9. "Iraq Battling More Than 100,000 Insurgents," Agence France-Presse (January 3, 2005); the RAND Corporation's terrorism expert Bruce Hoffman called the Iraqi government's estimate of active full-time and part-time supporters a "valid" one. As is normal in insurgencies, passive sympathy is almost surely higher.

10. Kurdish parties in the Turkish parliament received 29 percent of the Kurdish vote in 1991, dropping to 16 percent in 1995 and 1999. Matthew Kocher, "The Decline of PKK and the Viability of a One-State Solution in Turkey," *International Journal on Multicultural Societies*, vol. 4, no. 1 (2002), pp. 131–50.

11. Eric Carlton, *Occupation: The Policies and Practices of Military Conquerors* (New York: Routledge, 1992); Gerhard von Glahn, *The Occupation of Enemy Territory* (Minneapolis: University of Minnesota Press, 1957); Eyal Benvenisti, *The International Law of Occupation* (Princeton, N.J.: University of Princeton Press, 1993); and David M. Edelstein, "Occupational Hazards: Why Military Occupations Succeed or Fail," *International Security*, vol. 29, no. 1 (Summer 2004), pp. 49–91.

12. By this standard, the United States' liberation and occupation of Italy, Ger-

many, and Japan in and after World War II qualifies as occupation, but American military deployments to Great Britain and France during the conflict count as military alliances.

13. Anthony Smith, "Culture, Community and Territory," *International Affairs*, vol. 72, no. 3, pp. 445–58; Yi-Fu Tuan, *Space and Place: The Perspective of Experience* (Minneapolis: University of Minnesota Press, 1977); Walker Conner, "Homelands in a World of States," in M. Guibernau and J. Hutchinson, eds., *Understanding Nationalism* (Oxford: Polity Press/Blackwell, 2001), pp. 53–73.

14. Guntram H. Herb, "National Identity and Territory," in Guntram H. Herb and David H. Kaplan, eds., *Nested Identities: Nationalism, Territory, and Scale* (New York: Rowman & Littlefield, 1999), p. 17. See also James Anderson, "Nationalism and Geography," in James Anderson, ed., *The Rise of the Modern State* (Atlantic Highlands, N.J.: Humanities Press International, 1986), pp. 115–42; Jean Gottmann, *The Significance of Territory* (Charlottesville, Va.: University Press of Virginia, 1973); A. Burghardt, "The Bases of Territorial Claims," *The Geographical Review*, vol. 63 (1973), pp. 225–45; Peter Marden, "Geographies of Dissent: Globalization, Identity, and the Nation," *Political Geography* 16 (1997), pp. 37–64; and David B. Knight, "Identity and Territory," *Annals of the Association of American Geographers*, vol. 72 (1982), pp. 514–31.

15. For an excellent discussion of the ideal of dying for one's country in the age of nationalism, see Ernest H. Kantorowiz, *The King's Two Bodies: A Study in Mediaeval Political Theology* (Princeton, N.J.: Princeton University Press, 1997), pp. 232–72.

16. Frantz Fanon, *The Wretched of the Earth* (New York: Grove Press, 1963), p. 38. Some scholars argue that nationalism plays little role in supposedly "nationalist" rebellions, and that these actually comprise mainly local score-settling that takes advantage of the general disorder of the country. Stathis Kalyvas, " 'New' and 'Old' Civil Wars: A Valid Distinction?" *World Politics*, vol. 54, no. 1 (2001), 99–118, and "The Ontology of 'Political Violence': Action and Identity in Civil Wars," *Perspectives on Politics*, vol. 1, no. 3 (2003), 475–94. However, if local score-settling generally dominated communal loyalties, we should see significant cross-ethnic recruiting for armies, militias, and criminal gangs and as many people killed by co-ethnics as by members of enemy communities. In fact, both conditions are rare. Colonial powers are often so wealthy compared with the local society that they can recruit indigenous troops, but these often prove unreliable when ordered to fight their own community. Chaim Kaufmann, "Rational Choice and Progress in the Study of Ethnic Conflict," *Security Studies*, vol. 14, no. 2 (Jan.–Mar. 2005), forthcoming. Of the nine occupied communities that have produced suicide terrorism, three—the Palestinians, the Tamils, and Kurds—did engage in some internecine fighting during the occupation, but in every case the scale was small compared with the violence between the occupiers and the occupied.

17. Edelstein, "Occupational Hazards."

18. Samuel P. Huntington suggests that people may share a "civilization identity" that encourages conflict regardless of other circumstances. Huntington, *The Clash of Civilizations and the Remaking of World Order* (New York: Simon & Schuster, 1996). However, such broad identities are not driving suicide terrorism and most on his list of civilizations are not using this strategy.

19. In other words, under the conditions of a foreign occupation, the initial causes of the effects of religious difference operate not from the inside of the dominated group, but from the outside—either as what the dominating group uses to put the dominated group in a category of a less than human Other, or what the dominated group finds as what can help bind them in resistance, along with a sense of ethnic or regional identity.

20. Buddhism and modern Shintoism are exceptions to this rule; most interpretations of both do not prohibit a person from engaging in Buddhist or Shinto practice at the same time as practice of another religion. Indeed, substantial numbers of Japanese practice both to some degree. There are also limited exceptions involving simultaneous Hindu and Buddhist practice in Nepal and among Sinhalese in Sri Lanka. None of the relevant societies, however, have produced suicide terrorist campaigns. Although Japan used suicide attacks to try to ward off occupation by a predominantly Christian country, the version of Shintoism that was dominant at the time—State Shinto—was more exclusive than most interpretations either earlier or later. See Klaus Antoni, et al., eds., *Religion and National Identity in the Japanese Context* (Munster: Lit, 2002); Helen Hardacre, *Shinto and the State, 1868–1988* (Princeton, N.J.: Princeton University Press, 1989); and David N. Gellner, *The Anthropology of Buddhism and Hinduism* (New York: Oxford University Press, 2001).

21. Gellner, *Nations and Nationalism,* and David D. Laitin, *Identity in Formation: The Russian-Speaking Populations in the Near Abroad* (Ithaca, N.Y.: Cornell University Press, 1998). There is some tendency for state boundaries to conform to linguistic boundaries, although this is by no means universal. There is also some tendency to conform to religious boundaries even when there is no linguistic difference.

22. War generally hardens national identities. See Chaim Kaufmann, "Possible and Impossible Solutions to Ethnic Civil Wars," *International Security*, vol. 20, no. 4 (Spring 1996).

23. The incentives for conversion to an occupier's religion are not similar to those for learning its language. The value of language competency is mainly economic, as for Palestinian workers who picked up some Hebrew while commuting to jobs in Israel. Conversion would be a more fundamentally political act, one viewed as changing sides in the dispute—if the occupier will allow it, which often it does not.

24. Ron E. Hassner, "To Have and to Hold: Conflicts over Sacred Space and the Problem of Indivisibility," *Security Studies*, vol. 12, no. 4 (Summer 2003), pp. 1–33.

25. Demonization is sometimes called "hypernationalism" in inter-state conflict. See John J. Mearsheimer, "Back to the Future: Instability in Europe After the Cold War," *International Security*, vol. 15, no. 4 (Summer 1990), p. 21.

26. The English meaning of the Greek word "martyr" is "witness." The word "martyr" first became prominent to describe Christians who voluntarily died as they "witnessed" their faith in front of Roman persecutors in the third and fourth centuries. The origins of the concept, however, are older still. See Arthur J. Droge and James D. Tabor, *A Noble Death: Suicide and Martyrdom Among Christians and Jews in Antiquity* (San Francisco: HarperCollins, 1992).

27. Margaret Cormack, ed., *Sacrificing the Self: Perspectives on Martyrdom and Religion* (New York: Oxford University Press, 2002); Arthur J. Droge and James D. Tabor, *A Noble Death: Suicide and Martyrdom Among Christians and Jews in Antiquity* (San Francisco: HarperCollins, 1992); and Fred Rosner, "Suicide in Jewish Law," in Kalman J. Kaplan and Matthew B. Schwartz, *Jewish Approaches to Suicide, Martyrdom, and Euthanasia* (Northvale, N.J.: Jason Aronson, 1998), pp. 61–62.

28. On qualifications for martyrdom, see Anna L. Peterson, *Martyrdom and the Politics of Religion* (Albany, N.Y.: State University of New York Press, 1997); Louis E. Fenech, *Martyrdom in the Sikh Tradition* (New York: Oxford University Press, 2000); Karl Rahner, *On the Theology of Death* (New York: Herder and Herder, 1965); Eugene Weiner and Anita Weiner, *The Martyr's Conviction: A Sociological Analysis* (Atlanta, Ga.: Scholars Press, 1990); and Teresa Okure, et al., *Rethinking Martyrdom* (London: SCM Press, 2003).

29. In May 1945, more than 3 million American and British troops occupied zones in Germany totaling approximately 40 million people and quickly imposed tight controls on the population that rendered even low levels of resistance virtually impossible. James Dobbins, Seth Jones, et al., "America's Role in Nation-Building: From Germany to Iraq" (Santa Monica, Calif.: Rand, 2003); and U.S. Department of State, *Occupation of Germany: Policy and Progress, 1945–46* (Washington, D.C.: U.S. Government Printing Office, 1947).

30. Andrew T. Krepinevich, *The Army and Vietnam* (Baltimore: Johns Hopkins University Press, 1986), pp. 3–10; David Galula, *Counterinsurgency Warfare* (New York: Praeger, 1964); and Douglas S. Blaufarb, *The Counterinsurgency Era* (New York: Free Press, 1977).

31. The organizational profile of suicide terrorist groups is developed at length in Chapter 8.

32. Although authoritarian states have carried out the most extreme cases of civil-

ian victimization, analysis of the universe of such cases shows that democracies are not less likely than authoritarian states to harm civilians. See Alexander B. Downes, "Targeting Civilians in War" (Ph.D. diss., University of Chicago, 2004).

33. In a few cases, such as the Kurds of Turkey and the Palestinians, national identities may have been hardened in part by earlier rebellions long before 1980.

34. Rashid Khalidi, *Palestinian Identity: The Construction of Modern National Consciousness* (New York: Columbia University Press, 1997).

35. It is possible that the identity that is most important to different al-Qaeda members varies. Although these are matters of degree, if one can judge by their statements, Osama bin Laden seems to be most tightly attached to Arabian identity, while Ayman al-Zawahiri seems most concerned about pan-Muslim interests.

36. Although pan-Muslim identity is demarcated by religion, al-Qaeda's conception of it—which centers on a demand for self-determination for the community in all the territories inhabited by its members—matches our ordinary understanding of nationalism. Some scholars argue that language is the single most important marker separating different national identities. See Laitin, *Identity in Formation*. However, instances where nations share a language and are demarcated principally by religion are also common, for example Catholics and Protestants in Northern Ireland; Serbs, Croats, and Bosnians in the former Yugoslavia.

37. By providing encouragement that the occupier can be hurt, by provoking the occupier to retaliate in a manner that enrages many in the terrorists' community, or through other mechanisms.

38. It is important to distinguish situations in which suicide terrorism plays a key part in causing a rebellion—which has not happened—from the role of suicide attacks in demonstrating that important harm can be inflicted on the enemy. The latter can increase the popularity not only of suicide terrorism itself but also of an ongoing rebellion, and it has happened in several cases.

39. For specific criteria to determine regime type, I relied on Adam Przeworski, Michael E. Alvarez, Jose Antonio Cheibub, and Frenando Limongi, *Democracy and Development: Political Institutions and Well-Being in the World, 1950–1990* (Cambridge, U.K.: Cambridge University Press, 2000), and Carles Boix and Sebastian Rosato, "A Complete Dataset of Regimes, 1850–1999," typescript (University of Chicago, 2001). The five-year rule eliminated two cases, Nigeria and Uganda.

40. Recent surveys show that over 80 percent of the world's population self-identifies with one of the dozen classic primary religions. Of the world's 6 billion people in 2000, some 2 billion identified as Christian, 1.3 billion as Muslim, 786 million as Hindu, 362 million as Buddhist, and 18 million as Jews, while some 900 million identified as agnostics or cited various forms of tribal religions. David Barrett et al., eds., *World Christian Encyclopedia: A Comparative Survey of*

Churches and Religions, A.D. *30 to 2000* (New York: Oxford University Press, 2001). This survey counts nineteen major world religions, which are subdivided into a total of 270 large religious groups and many smaller ones.

41. MAR does not include minorities that are not considered "at risk" of conflict with the state. Omitting such minorities makes no difference to the study of suicide terrorism, since no theory would expect them to become involved in rebellions, let alone terrorism. See Ted Robert Gurr, et al., *Minorities at Risk: A Global View of Ethnopolitical Conflict* (Washington, D.C.: United States Institute of Peace Press, 1993), as updated at www.cidcm.umd.edu/inscr/mar/.

42. I also cross-checked the data with other well-known databases, such as James D. Fearon and David D. Laitin, "Ethnicity, Insurgency, and Civil War," *American Political Science Review*, vol. 97, no. 1 (February 2003), pp. 75–90, but these revealed no discrepancies with the information in this study.

43. The statistical analysis of suicide terrorism is based on a logit regression, which included religious difference, prior rebellion, and an interaction term between the two as independent variables. Religious difference and prior rebellion were both significant at the .05 level, and the interaction term was significant at the .001 level, demonstrating that the interaction of religious difference and prior rebellion has an effect beyond the independent effect of each.

By comparison, the same data show that the combination of a linguistic difference and rebellion accounts for 43 of 58 cases. However, this interaction term is not significant. Linguistic difference occurs in 53 of the 58 cases, and is too constant to have much explanatory power. In a logit regression of this relationship, linguistic differences drop out of the equation due to the lack of variation.

CHAPTER 7: DEMYSTIFYING AL-QAEDA

1. Among the best are Peter L. Bergen, *Holy War, Inc.: Inside the Secret World of Osama Bin Laden* (New York: Simon & Schuster, 2001); Rohan Gunaratna, *Inside Al-Qaeda* (New York: Columbia University Press, 2002); Daniel Benjamin and Steven Simon, *The Age of Sacred Terror* (New York: Random House, 2002); and Anonymous, *Through Our Enemies' Eyes: Osama bin Laden, Radical Islam, and the Future of America* (Washington, D.C.: Brassey's, 2002).

2. For instance, Daniel Byman, who has tracked Islamic terrorism for the U.S. government, says that Rohan Gunaratna's estimate of al-Qaeda as having 3,000 members "may be something of an overstatement. . . . The al-Qa'ida core devoted to terrorism or skilled operations beyond simple participation in guerrilla war may be far smaller than is generally realized. . . . probably numbers in the hundreds" (Daniel Byman, "Al-Qa'ida as an Adversary: Do We Understand Our Enemy," *World Politics*, vol. 56, no. 1 [October 2003], pp. 148–49).

3. Marc Sageman, *Understanding Terror Networks* (Philadelphia: University of Pennsylvania Press, 2004), 61.

4. This finding supports a similar analysis of socialist terrorist groups in the 1970s and 1980s. See Leonard Weinberg and William Lee Eubank, "Italian Women Terrorists," *Terrorism*, vol. 9, no. 3 (1987), pp. 241–62.

5. Amos Perlmutter, "Wishful Thinking About Islamic Fundamentalism," *Washington Post* (January 19, 1992).

6. On the meaning of Islamic fundamentalism, see Roxanne L. Euben, *Enemy in the Mirror: Islamic Fundamentalism and the Limits of Modern Rationalism* (Princeton, N.J.: Princeton University Press, 1999), pp. 3–19; and Mansoor Moaddel and Kamran Talattof, *Modern and Fundamentalist Debates in Islam* (New York: Palgrave, 2002), pp. 1–22.

7. For sectarian differences in the Muslim world, see Febe Armanios, "Islam: Sunnis and Shiites" (Washington, D.C.: Congressional Research Service, RS21745, February 23, 2004).

8. Said Amir Arjomand, "Shi'ite Jurisprudence and Constitution Making in the Islamic Republic of Iran," in Martin E. Marty and R. Scott Appleby, eds., *Fundamentalism and the State* (Chicago: University of Chicago Press, 1993), pp. 88–109.

9. Sageman, *Understanding Terror Networks*, pp. 1–60, and Jason Burke, *Al Qaeda: The True Story of Radical Islam* (London: I. B. Tauris, 2003).

10. As Daniel Brown writes: "The guiding principle of Salafi reformism was the conviction that Muslims must emulate the first generation of Muslims, the Salaf al-Salih, and recapture the pure Islam of the Prophet. This could be done only by returning to the basic sources of authority, the Qur'an and the Sunna, for only in these sources can the true essence of Islam be found. . . . It is in rejecting the way the Qur'an and Sunna have traditionally been interpreted and in cutting through the interpretive accretions that classical scholarship had built up around these basic texts that the Salifiyya set themselves apart." Brown, *Rethinking Tradition in Modern Islamic Thought* (New York: Cambridge University Press, 1996), p. 31.

11. Muhammad al-Jibali, *Allah's Rights upon His Servants: Tawhid vs. Shirk* (Cincinnati, Oh.: Al-Quran Was-Sunnahh Society of North America, 1995).

12. On Wahhabism as a form of Salafism, see John L. Esposito, *Unholy War: Terror in the Name of Islam* (New York: Oxford University Press, 2002), pp. 105–7; Christopher M. Blanchard, "The Islamic Traditions of Wahhibism and Salafiyya" (Washington, D.C.: Congressional Research Service, RS21695, August 9, 2004).

13. The 2005 mission statement of Egypt's Muslim Brotherhood declares that it is "a salafi mission" and calls for "the return to Islam, to its pure meanings, to the book of God and the sunna of his Prophet" seeking "to apply the purified Sunna in all actions." It also says, "The principles that are stated in the book of God and the sunna of his Prophet . . . [are those] that the Muslim person, Muslim household, Muslim society, Muslim state and Muslim nation must adhere to"

(www.ikhwanonline.net). Translated from Arabic by the Chicago Project on Suicide Terrorism. For the Salafi roots of the movement, see Abdel Azim Ramadan, "Fundamentalist Influence in Egypt," in Marty and Appleby, *Fundamentalism and the State*, pp. 152–83.

14. Ahmed Rashid, *Taliban: Militant Islam, Oil, and Fundamentalism in Central Asia* (New Haven: Yale University Press, 2000), p. 88; Muhammad Qasim Zaman, *The Ulema in Contemporary Islam* (Princeton, N.J.: Princeton University Press, 2002), p. 11.

15. Seyyed Hossein Nasr, *Islam: Religion, History, and Civilization* (New York: HarperCollins, 2003), p. 180. Similarly, Daniel Brown writes: "The argument that the Sunna should be re-evaluated in light of the Quran is by no means unprecedented in Egypt. . . . The argument survived among . . . the Ikhwan al-muslimin [Muslim Brotherhood]: . . . It is clear that many of the Ikhwan tended to favor the Quran over the Hadith. In other words, they tended to extend the salafi skepticism about the classical madhabs to the Hadith literature itself." Daniel W. Brown, *Rethinking Tradition in Modern Islamic Thought* (New York: Cambridge University Press, 1996), pp. 120–21.

16. Esposito, *Unholy War*, pp. 5, 18.

17. Quintan Wiktorowicz, "The New Global Threat: Transnational Salafis and Jihad," *Middle East Policy*, vol. 8, no. 4 (December 2001), pp. 18–38; Reuven Paz, "The Brotherhood of Global Jihad" (Herzliya, Israel: Project for the Research of Islamic Movements, October 2001).

18. Wiktorowicz, "The New Global Threat," p. 21.

19. For instance, in 2001–2002, America approved $2.7 billion in foreign military sales to Saudi Arabia, a sum equaling approximately 10 percent of Saudi Arabia's defense budget, and the main American command center for the conquest of Iraq in 2003 was Prince Sultan Air Base near Riyadh.

20. Pakistan has allowed U.S. military over-flights and occasional operations of small contingents of American ground forces in combination with Pakistani forces.

21. These results are extremely robust. Even if we assume that there are no Salafi-influenced populations in Egypt, Algeria, and Nigeria, and assume that half of the populations of Morocco and Turkey are Salafi-influenced—assumptions that are individually highly unlikely, as the appendix on Salafism demonstrates, to say nothing of the odds against them collectively—Salafi-influenced population still has no significant effects on the odds of someone from that country becoming an al-Qaeda suicide terrorist.

For these results to be overturned, Pakistan would have to have virtually no Salafi-influenced population. The number I estimate, 43 million, includes the populations of the North-West Frontier Province and Baluchistan, which elected provincial governments in October 2002 ruled by the self-proclaimed Salafi party called Jamaat-i-Islami and in which Osama bin Laden is presumed to have been hiding since he left Afghanistan in 2001.

22. To be clear: At most, al-Qaeda suicide terrorists are twice as likely among Sunni Muslim populations that have been influenced by Salafism than from other Sunni populations. However, they are ten times more likely among Sunni Muslim populations from countries with an American combat presence and twenty times more likely among Salafi-influenced Sunni Muslim populations from countries with an American combat presence than among Sunni Muslim populations in other countries. This means that American combat presence on the Arabian Peninsula increased the expected number of individuals willing to carry out an al-Qaeda suicide attack against Americans, such as the September 11 attack, from ten to twenty times. Assuming that the number of suicide attacks is directly proportional to the number of individuals willing to execute them—a reasonable assumption, since the number of suicide terrorists per al-Qaeda attack has varied only within a narrow range and has been as small as one—then increasing the number of suicide terrorists by a given factor (ten to twenty times) will increase the number of expected suicide attacks by that same factor (ten to twenty times).

23. For statistics on U.S. assistance to Muslim countries, see U.S. Agency for International Development, "U.S. Overseas Loans and Grants," 2005.

24. Nachman Tal, "Islamic Terrorism in Egypt," *Strategic Assessment* (Tel Aviv), vol. 1, no. 1 (March 1998); "Four to Die for Casablanca Bombings," www.aljazeerah.info (August 20, 2003); "Pakistan: Country Report" (London: Immigration and Nationality Directorate, Home Office, United Kingdom, October 2004); Amy Chew, "The Roots of Jemaah Islamiyah" (CNN, February 26, 2004).

25. Quoted from Center for Islamic Studies and Research, "The East Riyadh Operation and Our War with the United States and Its Agents," August 1, 2003, available at www.cybcity.com/newss and translated by the Foreign Broadcast Information Service. The Center for Islamic Studies and Research is an organization known to be part of al-Qaeda and its documents are sanctioned by Osama bin Laden.

26. "Interview with Osama bin Laden," *Frontline* (May 1998).

27. Amin Maalouf, *The Crusades Through Arab Eyes* (London: Zed Books, 1984).

28. "Interview with Osama bin Laden," ABC News (December 24, 1998).

29. "Interview with Osama bin Laden," *Frontline* (May 1998).

30. "Intercepted Letter from Abu Mussab al-Zarqawi to Osama bin Laden" (February 2004) at www.jimmarshall.house.gov/Zarqawi.htm.

31. ABC News, December 1998.

32. "Bin Laden's Sermon for the Feast of the Sacrifice," *Middle East Media Research Institute*, Special Dispatch Series, no. 476 (March 5, 2003).

33. Ayman al-Zawahiri, "Knights Under the Prophet's Banner" (December 2, 2001), part 11. Available at www.fas.org.

34. "Bin Laden's Sermon," Middle East Media Research Institute (MEMRI) (March 5, 2003), available at www.memri.org.

35. "Interview Usama bin Laden," Al-Jazeera (February 23, 1998).

36. "Bin Laden's Sermon," MEMRI (March 5, 2003).

37. Al-Zawahiri, "Knights Under the Prophet's Banner," part 11.

38. Ibid.

39. "Declaration of War Against the Americans Occupying the Land of the Two Holy Places," *Al-Quds Al-Arabi* (London) (August 1996), trans. at www.pbs.org/newshour.

CHAPTER 8:
SUICIDE TERRORIST ORGANIZATIONS AROUND THE GLOBE

1. On qualitative methods in social science, see Gary King, Robert O. Keohane, and Sidney Verba, *Designing Social Inquiry: Scientific Inference in Qualitative Research* (Princeton, N.J.: Princeton University Press, 1994), and Stephen Van Evera, *Guide to Methods for Students of Political Science* (Ithaca, N.Y.: Cornell University Press, 1997).

2. The principal statement of this position remains Robin Wright, *Sacred Rage: The Crusade of Modern Islam* (New York: Simon & Schuster, 1986).

3. The Central Intelligence Agency estimated in 1986 that the religious distribution of the population was 41 percent Shia Muslims, 27 percent Sunni Muslims, 16 percent Maronite Christians, 7 percent Druze, and 8 percent Greek Orthodox and Catholics. On population estimates for Lebanon, see *Lebanon: A Country Study* (Washington, D.C.: Library of Congress, 1987), pp. 48–57.

4. On the rise of Amal, see Augustus Richard Norton, *Amal and the Shi'a: Struggle for the Soul of Lebanon* (Austin: University of Texas Press, 1987); Helena Cobban, *The Shia Community and the Future of Lebanon* (Washington, D.C.: American Institute of Islamic Affairs, American University, 1984); and Juan R. I. Cole and Nikki R. Keddie, eds., *Shi'ism and Social Protest* (New Haven: Yale University Press, 1986).

5. Richard A. Gabriel, *Operation Peace for Galilee: The Israeli-PLO War in Lebanon* (New York: Hill & Wang, 1984), pp. 68–81.

6. Interviews with Hussain Mussawi and the former vice president of Amal, Hasan Hashim, August 1985, in As'ad AbuKhalil, "Ideology and Practice of Hizballah in Lebanon," *Middle Eastern Studies*, vol. 27, no. 3 (July 1991), pp. 391–92, 403.

7. Gabriel, *Operation Peace for Galilee*, pp. 121–25.

8. Magnus Ranstrop, *Hizb'allah in Lebanon* (New York: St. Martin's Press, 1997), p. 30.

9. Shimon Shapira, "The Origins of Hizballah," *The Jerusalem Quarterly*, vol. 46 (Spring 1988), pp. 115–130, at p. 124.

10. Interview with General Secretary Sheikh Hassan Nasrallah, *Middle East Insight* (May–August 1996), pp. 38–39. The Iranian revolution in 1979 evoked broad sympathy among the Lebanese Shia community. However, this did not translate into active political support for either Islamic fundamentalism or Iranian goals. Indeed, some radical Islamic groups lost ground after the Iranian revolution. In 1980, the Lebanese Islamic Da'wa Party, the leading group calling for an Islamic state, ceased to exist as a separate organization and its members joined the more popular Amal movement. Shapira, "Origins of Hezbollah," p. 118.

11. Norton, *Amal and the Shi'a*, p. 114. Norton describes the Organization for a United South on p. 111. For the details of Israel's occupation policies, see Chris Mowles, "The Israeli Occupation of South Lebanon," *Third World Quarterly*, vol. 8, no. 4 (October 1986), pp. 1351–66.

12. At least thirty-one of the forty-one Lebanese suicide terrorists left public testimonials. See Lebanese Resistance Movement, "Martyrdom Operations" (Beirut, no date).

13. See Chapter 9.

14. Quoted in Hala Jaber, *Hezbollah: Born with a Vengeance* (New York: Columbia University Press, 1997), pp. 91–92.

15. Quoted in Robert Fisk, *Pity the Nation: Lebanon at War* (New York: Oxford University Press, 2001), p. 490.

16. For contemporary reports, see "Resistance Swells in Southern Lebanon," *Financial Times* (July 19, 1984); "Shiite Radicals Throng to Sidon for a Big Rally," *New York Times* (February 19, 1985); "Young Lebanese Seek New Martyrdom: Suicide Bombers Emerge as Martyrs," *Washington Post* (May 12, 1985); "Lebanon's Poster King Says 'I Fight with My Paintings,'" Associated Press (September 4, 1985); and "Shiites Posthumously Honor Teen-ager as Suicide Bomber," Associated Press (December 19, 1985).

17. Amal Saad-Ghorayeb, *Hizbu'llah: Politics and Religion* (London: Pluto Press, 2002), pp. 138–40.

18. Norton, *Amal and the Shia*, p. 179.

19. Interview in July 1985, quoted in Martin Kramer, "The Oracle of Hizbullah: Sayyid Muhammad Husayn Fadlallah, Part II," in *Spokesmen for the Despised: Fundamentalist Leaders of the Middle East*, ed. R. Scott Appleby (Chicago: University of Chicago Press, 1997), p. 8

20. Saad-Ghorayeb, *Hizbu'llah*, pp. 140–41.

21. Norton, *Amal and the Shia*, pp. 170–71.

22. Saad-Ghorayeb, *Hizbu'llah*, pp. 144–45.

23. Interviews in 1985 are quoted in Martin Kramer, "The Moral Logic of Hizballah," in Walter Reich, ed., *Origins of Terrorism* (Washington, D.C.: Woodrow Wilson Center Press, 1990), pp. 144–45.

24. These statements are collected in Lebanese Resistance Movement, "Martyrdom Operations" (Beirut, no date); translation by Chicago Project on Suicide Terrorism.

25. Mia Bloom, *Dying to Kill* (New York: Columbia University Press, 2005), Chapter 3.

26. Christoph Reuter, *My Life Is a Weapon* (Princeton, NJ: Princeton University Press, 2002), pp. 157–60.

27. "One by one their rivals and opponents among the Tamil separatist groups succumbed to the relentless violence of the LTTE . . . [which] systematically eliminated all rival groups, culminating in the brutal massacre of the Tamil Eelam Liberation Organization and the killing of its leader, Sri Sabaratnam, between 1 and 3 May, 1986." K. M. De Silva, ed., *Conflict and Violence in South Asia* (Kandy, Sri Lanka: International Center for Ethnic Studies, 2000), pp. 407–8. See also Dagmar Hellmann-Rajanayagam, *The Tamil Tigers: Armed Struggle for Identity* (Stuttgart: Franz Steiner Verlag, 1994), pp. 142–45.

28. Quoted in Yamuna Sangarasivam, "Liberation Tigers of Tamil Eelam and the Cultural Production of Nationalism and Violence" (Ph.D. diss., Graduate School of Syracuse University, May 2000), p. 283. The woman, Nandini, was interviewed in 1994–95 in Jaffna.

29. "Sri Lanka" (Geneva: World Health Organization Global Status Report, 1997). According to the Sri Lankan census of 1981, the country's total population of 14,850,000 comprised 10,985,000 Sinhalese, 2,687,000 Tamil, 1,057,000 Muslim, and 59,000 others. Starting in 1990, the Tamils have encouraged Muslims to leave the areas they consider their homeland, with the result that a majority of Tamils are from Hindu families, while a minority are Christians (mainly Catholics, from the days when Ceylon was a Portugese colony). S. J. Tambiah, *Sri Lanka: Ethnic Fratricide and the Dismantling of Democracy* (Chicago: University of Chicago Press, 1986), p. 4.

30. On the history of discrimination against Tamils, see Sinnappah Arasaratnam, *Sri Lanka After Independence* (Madras: University of Madras, 1986); V. Navaratnam, *The Rise and Fall of Tamil Nation* (Madras: 1991); and A. Jeyaratnam Wilson, *The Break-up of Sri Lanka* (Honolulu: University of Hawaii Press, 1988).

31. Arasaratnam, *Sri Lanka After Independence*, p. 74.

32. T.D.S.A. Dissanayaka, *The Agony of Sri Lanka* (Colombo: Swastika Pvt. Ltd.,

1984), esp. pp. 80–90. The Sri Lankan government reported that 350 Tamils died in the July 1983 riots, which many observers consider a low estimate. Tambiah, *Sri Lanka*, p. 22.

33. The Liberation Tigers of Tamil Eelam was officially formed in 1976 when its leader, V. Prabhakaran, split off from an earlier militant group, the Tamil New Tigers.

34. On the rise of the LTTE, see D. Hellmann-Rajanayagam, *The Tamil Tigers—Armed Struggle for Identity* (Stuttgart: Franz Steiner Verlag, 1994).

35. When Israeli forces invaded Lebanon in 1982, they found three Tamil Tigers training in Palestinian camps. On Tamil-Lebanese connections, see G. P. V. Somaratne, "Sri Lanka's Relations with Israel," in Shelton U. Kodikara, ed., *External Compulsions of South Asian Politics* (New Delhi: Sage Publications, 1993), p. 205; M. R. Narayan Swamy, *Tigers of Lanka: From Boys to Guerrillas* (3rd ed.; Delhi: Konark Publishers, 2002), pp. 97–101, 241; Bruce Hoffman and Gordon H. McCormick, "Terrorism, Signaling, and Suicide Attack," *Studies in Conflict and Terrorism*, vol. 27 (2004), p. 259.

36. Rohan Gunaratna, *Indian Intervention in Sri Lanka* (Colombo: South Asian Network on Conflict Research, 1993), pp. 161–316.

37. Sumantra Bose, *States, Nations, Sovereignty: Sri Lanka, India and the Tamil Eelam Movement* (New Delhi: Sage, 1994), p. 118. Writing five years earlier, O'Ballance similarly estimates that more than 300 Tamil Tigers (or 10 percent of the Tamil Tiger forces) have probably committed suicide in this manner. Edgar O'Ballance, *The Cyanide War: Tamil Insurrection in Sri Lanka, 1973–1988* (London: Brassey's, 1989), p. 126.

38. Hoffman and McCormick, "Terrorism, Signaling, and Suicide Attack," p. 260.

39. Quoted in Yamuna Sangarasivam, "Liberation Tigers of Tamil Eelam and the Cultural Production of Nationalism and Violence" (Ph.D. diss., Syracuse University, May 2000), pp. 310, 330.

40. Quoted in Rohan Gunaratna, "The LTTE and Suicide Terrorism," *Frontline* (India), vol. 17, no. 3 (February 5–8, 2000).

41. "Northeast Prepares to Celebrate Black Tigers Day," www.tamil.net (June 24, 2004); Peter Schalk, "Revival of Martyr Cults Among Ilavar," *Temenos*, vol. 33 (1997), pp. 151–52. The Tigers' "Heroes' Day" speeches are commonly published during "Heroes' Week" in November.

42. Peter Schalk, "Resistance and Martyrdom in the Process of State Formation of Tamil Eelam," in Joyce Pettigrew, ed., *Martyrdom and Political Resistance* (Amsterdam: VU University Press, 1997), p. 82.

43. A. J. V. Chandrakanthan, "Eelam Tamil Nationalism: An Inside View," in A. Jeyaratnam Wilson, *Sri Lankan Tamil Nationalism* (Vancouver: UBC Press, 2000), p. 132.

44. For detailed examination of Tamil fears of cultural transformation, see Bryan Pfaffenberger, "The Cultural Dimension of Tamil Separatism in Sri Lanka," *Asian Survey*, vol. 21, no. 11 (November 1981), pp. 1145–57, and id., "The Kataragama Pilgrimage: Hindu-Buddhist Interaction and Its Significance in Sri Lanka's Polyethnic Social System," *Journal of Asian Studies*, vol. 38 (Feb. 1979), pp. 253–70.

45. Brian Senewiratne, "An Evaluation of Solutions to the Sri Lankan Ethnic Conflict and Sinhala-Buddhist Chauvinism and the Buddhist Clergy." Paper presented at the International Conference on the Tamil National Struggle (London, April 30, 1988). In N. Seevaratnam, *The Tamil National Question and the Indo–Sri Lanka Accord* (Delhi: World Federation of Tamils, 1989), pp. 28, 35.

46. Sarath Amunugama, "Buddhaputra and Bhumiputra? Dilemmas of Modern Sinhala Buddhist Monks in Relation to Ethnic and Political Conflict," *Religion*, vol. 21 (1991), pp. 115–39.

47. "The Sinhalese settlers [in Tamil lands] have come to view the Tamils as alien. Generation upon generation of Sinhalese people have been systematically indoctrinated of the so-called enemy within. The active participation of the Buddhist clergy in the process of identification of the Dravidian enemy has had significant impact. . . . The Tamils have consequently earned the dubious reputation of Buddhism's natural enemy." Sebastian Pillai, "Sinhala Nationalism, the Native Physician, Buddhist Chauvinism and the So-called Enemy," paper presented at the International Conference on the Tamil National Struggle (London, April 30, 1988). In Seevaratnam, *Tamil National Question*, p. 45.

48. David Little, *Sri Lanka: The Invention of Enmity* (Washington, D.C.: United States Institute of Peace Press, 1994), p. 105. For other analyses of the role of Sinhala Buddhism in the Sri Lankan civil war, see Stanley Jeyaraja Tambiah, *Buddhism Betrayed: Religion, Politics, and Violence in Sri Lanka* (Chicago: University of Chicago Press, 1992), and K. N. O. Dharmadasa, *Language, Religion, and Ethnic Assertiveness: The Growth of Sinhalese Nationalism in Sri Lanka* (Ann Arbor: University of Michigan Press, 1992).

49. Nissan, *Sri Lanka: In Change and Crisis* (New York: John Wiley, 1984), p. 176.

50. Bertram Bastiam Pillai, *Survey of Conflicts Among Communities in Sri Lanka in Modern Times* (Madras: Center for South and Southeast Asian Studies, University of Madras, 1995), p. 9.

51. "They refuse to accept the fact that the Sinhalese are the majority of the country. . . . They do not accept that at least the written history of the country and its identity is Sinhala Buddhist. . . . Tamil racism considers the Tamils to be a separate nation in their so-called homeland." Nalin de Silva, *An Introduction to Tamil Racism in Sri Lanka* (Maharagama, Sri Lanka: Chintana Prashadaya, 1997), p. 2.

52. LTTE, "Tamils Fight for National Freedom," memorandum to the seventh summit meeting of nonaligned nations, New Delhi, March 1–15, 1983. In

Towards Liberation: Selected Political Documents of the Liberation Tigers of Tamil Eelam (Sri Lanka: LTTE Publications, 1984).

53. Prabhakaran, "Heroes' Day" speech (Jaffna, July 5, 1995). Available at www.eelamweb.com.

54. A. R. Arudpragasam, *The Traditional Homeland of the Tamils* (Kotte, Sri Lanka: Kanal Publications, 1996), p. 3.

55. Prabhakaran, "Heroes' Day" speech (Jaffna, July 5, 2000). Available at www.eelamweb.com.

56. A. J. V. Chandrakanthan, "Eelam Tamil Nationalism: An Inside View," in A. Jeyaratnam Wilson, *Sri Lankan Tamil Nationalism* (Vancouver: UBC Press, 2000), p. 132.

57. Peter Schalk, "The Revival of Martyr Cults Among Ilavar," *Temenos*, vol. 33 (1997), p. 151.

58. Ibid., pp. 154–55.

59. Major General Sarath Munasinghe, *A Soldier's Version: An Account of the On-going Conflict and the Origin of Terrorism in Sri Lanka* (Colombo: Market Information Systems, 2000), p. 178.

60. For the history of India's deployment, see Gunaratna, *Indian Intervention in Sri Lanka*, pp. 161–316; quote at p. 258.

61. Aladi Aruna, "Disarming the LTTE Is Harmful to Our Interests," in Seevaratnam, *Tamil National Question*, p. 117.

62. From 1981 to 1995, the total death toll for the Sri Lankan conflict, including Sinhalese, Tamil, and Indian losses, is estimated at 26,000. Of these, 6,000 occurred from 1981 to 1987, 8,000 from 1987 to 1990, and 12,000 from 1990 to 1995. Gunaratna, *Indian Intervention in Sri Lanka*, p. 481.

63. De Silva, *Conflict and Violence in South Asia*, p. 247.

64. *You Too India* (Madras, India: Political Wing of the LTTE, 1988).

65. Gunaratna, *Indian Intervention in Sri Lanka*, pp. 237–316.

66. The absence of suicide attacks cannot be explained as due to the character of the Indian political system, since India is also a democracy and has been subjected to suicide terrorism by militants in Kashir, where there is also a religious difference.

67. Gunaratna, *Indian Intervention in Sri Lanka*, p. 240.

68. Justice V. R. Krishna Iyer, "The Sri Lankan Accord," in Seevaratnam, *Tamil National Question*, p. 102.

69. Gunaratna, *Indian Intervention in Sri Lanka*, p. 392.

70. In August 1993, a BKI terrorist was killed by his own bomb while struggling with a security guard in a theater; it is uncertain whether he intended a suicide attack. In 1999, the four members of a BKI suicide squad were all killed while attacking the Punjab headquarters of the RSS, a Hindu nationalist group. In January 2000, Indian police captured BKI terrorists who were preparing suicide bomb attacks. The Babbar Khalsa International also committed numerous acts of non-suicidal terrorism, such as the bombing of the Kanishka aircraft of Air India off the Irish coast in June 1985, killing nearly 200 passengers, and an unsuccessful attempt the same day to blow up another Air India plane originating from Tokyo. B. Raman, "Counter-Terrorism: The Indian Experience," South India Analysis Group, no. 649. See www.saq.org.

71. Arjun Adlakha, "Population Trends: India" (Washington, D.C.: U.S. Department of Commerce, Bureau of the Census, 1997); and Sharda Jain, *Politics of Terrorism in India: The Case of Punjab* (New Delhi: Deep & Deep Publications, 1995), p. 118.

72. Peter van der Veer thus concludes, "The Sikh case is an excellent example of the influence of British colonial policies on the development of communal identity." Van der Veer, *Religious Nationalism: Hindus and Muslims in India* (Berkeley: University of California Press, 1994), p. 55. On the history of Sikh identity, see Khushwant Singh, *A History of the Sikhs: 1839–1964* (Princeton, N.J.: Princeton University Press, 1966), esp. vol. 2; Ram Swarup, "Concept of a Sikh Nation," in Abida Samiuddin, *The Punjab Crisis: Challenge and Response* (New Delhi: Mittal Publications, 1985), esp. pp. 435–36; and Rajiv Kapur, *Sikh Separatism: The Politics of Faith* (Delhi: Vikas Publishing House, 1987).

73. Kapur, *Sikh Separatism,* p. 217

74. P. Wallace, "Political Violence and Terrorism in India," in Martha Crenshaw, ed., *Terrorism in Context* (University Park, Penn.: Pennsylvania State University Press, 1995), p. 394; Joyce Pettigrew, "Martyrdom and Guerrilla Organization in Punjab," *Journal of Commonwealth and Comparative Politics,* vol. 30, no 3 (November 1992), p. 394; and Cynthia Keppley Mahmood, *Fighting for Faith and Nation: Dialogues with Sikh Militants* (Philadelphia: University of Pennsylvania Press, 1997), p. 137.

75. S. Anandaram, *Assassination of a Prime Minister* (New Delhi: Vision Books, 1994), p. 16.

76. Devinder Singh, *Akali Politics in Punjab, 1964–1985* (New Delhi: National Book Organization, 1993), p. 202; Gurharpal Singh, "The Punjab Crisis Since 1984," *Ethnic and Racial Studies,* vol. 18, no. 3 (July 1995), pp. 476–93; Judget S. Chima, "Back to the Future in 2002: A Model of Sikh Separatism in Punjab," *Studies in Conflict and Terrorism,* vol. 25 (2002), pp. 19–39.

77. Harish K. Puri, Paramjit Singh Judge, and Jagrup Singh Sekhon, *Terrorism in Punjab: Understanding Grassroots Reality* (New Delhi: Har-Anand Publications, 1999), pp. 9–12.

78. G. S. Mansukhani, *Introduction to Sikhism* (New Delhi: Hemkunt Press, 1977), p. 51.

79. Quoted in Joyce Pettigrew, "In Search of a New Kingdom of Lahore," *Pacific Affairs*, vol. 60, no. 1 (1987), pp. 1–25.

80. S. S. Dharam, *The Only Option for Sikhs* (Jaipur, India: published by the author, 1984), p. 183.

81. Quoted in Therese Suhashini Gunawardena, "Contesting Khalistan: The Sikh Diaspora and the Politics of Separatism" (Ph.D. diss., University of Texas at Austin, May 2001), p. 65.

82. Interviewed December 1989. In Pettigrew, *Sikhs of the Punjab*, p. 149

83. Melissa Ann Fuller, "Explaining Ethnic Conflict: The Sikh Insurgency in Punjab, 1978–1995" (Ph. D. diss., University of California–Los Angeles, 1999), p. 153.

84. Interviewed in Punjab in 1993; quoted in Mahmood, *Fighting for Faith and Nation*, p. 132.

85. Interviewed in December 1989. In Pettigrew, *Sikhs of the Punjab*, p. 141.

86. Interviewed December 1989. In Pettigrew, *Sikhs of the Punjab,* pp. 148–49.

87. Pettigrew, "Martyrdom and Guerrilla Organization in Punjab," pp. 390–91.

88. Dharam, *The Only Option for Sikhs*, pp. 4–8.

89. Ibid., p. 188.

90. Quoted in Therese Suhashini Gunawardena, "Contesting Khalistan: The Sikh Diaspora and the Politics of Separatism" (Ph.D. diss., University of Texas at Austin, May 2001), p. 66.

91. Interviewed December 1989. In Pettigrew, *Sikhs of the Punjab*, p. 154.

92. Interviewed December 1989. In Pettigrew, *Sikhs of the Punjab*, pp. 168–69.

93. Interviewed December 1989. In Pettigrew, *Sikhs of the Punjab*, p. 182.

94. Dr. Gurmit Singh Aulakh, president, Council of Khalistan, "Vaisakhi Day Message to the Sikh Nation," April 6, 2004. Available at www.Khalistan.com.

95. Robert S. Robins and Jerrold M. Post, *Political Paranoia: The Psychopolitics of Hatred* (New Haven: Yale University Press, 1997).

96. There are no precise figures for Kurds in Turkey, since the government does not count this group separately from others. Estimates range from 6 million to 12 million, with most analysts using lower to middle figures. *Turkey: A Country Study* (Washington, D.C.: Federal Research Division, Library of Congress, 1995); Servet Mutlu, "Ethnic Kurds in Turkey: A Demographic Study," *International Journal of Middle East Studies*, vol. 28 (1996), pp. 517–41.

97. On the origins of the civil war, see Kemal Kirisci and Gareth Winrow, *The Kurdish Question and Turkey: An Example of Trans-State Conflict* (London: Frank Cass, 1997); and Henri J. Barkey and Graham E. Fuller, *Turkey's Kurdish Question* (Lanham, Md.: Rowman & Littlefield, 1998).

98. David McDowall, *A Modern History of the Kurds* (New York: I. B. Tauris, 2000), p. 442.

99. Matthew Kocher, "The Decline of PKK and the Viability of a One-State Solution in Turkey," *International Journal on Multicultural Societies*, vol. 4, no. 1 (2002), pp. 133, 136.

100. Ely Karmon, "The Showdown Between the PKK and Turkey," (Herzliya, Israel: International Policy Institute for Counter-Terrorism, November 1998).

101. Barkey and Fuller, *Turkey's Kurdish Question*, p. 47.

102. Svante E. Cornell, "The Kurdish Question in Turkish Politics," *Orbis*, vol. 45, no. 1 (Winter 2001), pp. 31–47.

103. Barkey and Fuller, *Turkey's Kurdish Question*, pp. 81–85.

104. Murat Somer, "Ethnic Kurds, Endogenous Identities, and Turkey's Democratization and Integration with Europe," *Global Review of Ethnopolitics*, vol. 1, no 4 (June 2002), pp. 86–88.

105. Kurdish deaths averaged 4 per 1,000 compared to 1, 15, and 19 per 1,000 for the Sikhs in Punjab, Tamils in Sri Lanka, and Shia in Lebanon, respectively. See Chapter 4.

106. Barkey and Fuller, *Turkey's Kurdish Question*, pp. 61–65.

107. Konrad Hirschler, "Defining the Nation: Kurdish Historiography in Turkey in the 1990s," *Middle Eastern Studies*, vol. 37, no. 3 (July 2001), p. 156.

PART III: THE INDIVIDUAL LOGIC OF SUICIDE TERRORISM
CHAPTER 9: ALTRUISM AND TERRORISM

1. As the *New York Times*'s Steven Erlanger wrote shortly after September 11, 2001, "the forces that transformed Mohammed Atta are not clear." Steven Erlanger, "An Unobtrusive Man's Odyssey: Polite Student to Suicide Hijacker," *New York Times* (September 15, 2001). Even the best efforts to present the biographies of suicide attackers share a similar tendency to look for deviant psychological factors only to find they are weakly present if at all. See Joyce M. Davis, *Martyrs: Innocence, Vengeance, and Despair in the Middle East* (New York: Palgrave Macmillan, 2003); and Barbara Victor, *Army of Roses: Inside the World of Palestinian Women Suicide Bombers* (Rodale, 2003).

2. D. C. Clark and S. L. Horton-Deutsch, "The Value of the Psychological Autopsy Method for Studying Antecedents of Suicide," in R. W. Maris, et al., *The As-

sessment and Prediction of Suicide (New York: Guilford Press, 1992), pp. 144–82; and K. Hawton, et al., "The Psychological Autopsy Approach to Studying Suicide: A Review of Methodological Issues," *Journal of Affective Disorders*, vol. 50 (1998), pp. 269–76.

3. Emile Durkheim, *Suicide: A Study in Sociology*, trans. John A. Spaulding and George Simson (New York: Free Press, 1951), pp. 210, 215.

4. As evidence for the existence of egoistic suicide, Durkheim showed that suicide rates vary significantly with the degree of social integration. With respect to religious society, he found that the suicide rate is highest among Protestants, whose religion promotes a high degree of individualism, lower among Catholics, whose individual beliefs are more bound by collective authority, and lowest among Jews, whose minority status encourages highly cohesive communities. With respect to political society, he found that suicide rates fall markedly during times of great military conflicts and national emergencies as individuals actively close ranks to confront a common danger. Although drawn from nineteenth-century Europe, these basic patterns in the inverse relationship between suicide rates and social integration are routinely confirmed by contemporary studies of suicide in the United States, Western Europe, and other parts of the world. See Ronald W. Maris, *Pathways to Suicide: A Survey of Self-Destructive Behaviors* (Baltimore: Johns Hopkins University Press, 1981); W. S. F. Pickering and Geoffrey Walford, eds., *Durkheim's Suicide: A Century of Research and Debate* (New York: Routledge, 2000).

5. Durkheim, *Suicide*, p. 219. Emphasis in original.

6. The old Indian custom known as suttee obligated widows to throw themselves onto their husbands' funeral pyres, while North American Indian and other traditional societies commonly required the aged to kill themselves rather than await a natural death.

7. Durkheim, *Suicide*, p. 239. Since Durkheim's day, aggressive suicide prevention programs have reduced the incidence of suicide among the American, British, and other major military forces. Although the level of military suicide is now commonly near the civilian average for the civilian population of the same age, occasional spikes occur, which are often curtailed by aggressive preventive measures. U.S. Centers for Disease Control, "Suicide Prevention Among Active Duty Air Force Personnel—United States, 1990–1999," *Morbidity and Mortality Weekly Report*, vol. 48, no. 46 (November 26, 1999). The fact that military suicide appears to be highly responsive to institutional intervention supports the basic logic of altruistic suicide. If the community encouraging personal sacrifice for the group actually opposes it, then we would expect altruistic suicide to decline.

8. Durkheim, *Suicide*, p. 276.

9. On the conditions for brainwashing and other forms of heavy indoctrination, see Robert Jay Lifton, *Thought Reform and the Psychology of Totalism* (New York: W. W. Norton, 1961); Margaret O. Hyde, *Brainwashing and Other Forms of Mind*

Control (New York: McGraw-Hill, 1977); and Denise Winn, *The Manipulated Mind: Brainwashing, Conditioning, and Indoctrination* (Cambridge, Mass.: Malor Books, 2000).

10. Ronald W. Maris, Alan L. Berman, and Morton M. Silverman, *Comprehensive Textbook of Suicidology* (New York: Guilford Press, 2000), pp. 284–310; Antoon A. Leenaars, *Suicide Notes: Predictive Clues and Patterns* (New York: Human Sciences Press, 1988).

11. Social scientists have identified these risk factors on the basis of voluminous studies of suicide in the United States and other countries. For prominent reviews, see Maris et al., *Comprehensive Textbook*; Ronald Maris, *Assessment and Prediction of Suicide* (New York: Guilford Press, 1992); and Keith Hawton and Kees van Heeringen, *The International Handbook of Suicide and Attempted Suicide* (New York: Wiley, 2000).

12. Prominent among the large literature that seeks to identify deeper psychological and other causes for social detachment leading to suicide are Karl Menninger, *Man Against Himself* (New York: Harcourt, Brace, 1938); Norman Farberow and Edwin S. Shneidman, eds., *Cry for Help* (New York: McGraw-Hill, 1961); and Maris, *Pathways to Suicide*.

13. S. Stack, "New Micro Level Data on the Impact of Divorce on Suicide," *Journal of Marriage and the Family*, vol. 52 (1990), pp. 119–27; and J. Slater and R. A. Depue, "The Contribution of Environmental Events and Social Support to Serious Suicide Attempts in Primary Depressive Disorder," *Journal of Abnormal Psychiatry*, vol. 40 (1981), pp. 275–85. The preponderance of suicide among males may also be due to greater access to firearms, the method of choice in about 60 percent of ordinary suicides.

14. Jim Jones, originally a Methodist minister, combined elements of Pentecostalism with aspects of socialism and communism. David Koresh's Branch Davidians drew from Seventh Day Adventism. Heaven's Gate and the Order of the Solar Temple mixed elements of Protestantism and Catholicism, respectively, with beliefs taken from modern science fiction. The Ugandan doomsday cult was founded by excommunicated Roman Catholics who believed they could predict the end of the world.

15. The Christian prohibition against suicide does not rest on a biblical injunction, but derives from Augustine's interpretation of scripture in the fourth century A.D. Augustine's views have since been taken as authoritative by Catholics and Protestants alike. Arthur J. Droge and James D. Tabor, *A Noble Death: Suicide and Martyrdom Among Christains and Jews in Antiquity* (San Francisco: HarperCollins, 1992).

16. On the importance of boundary control, see Marc Galanter, *Cults: Faith, Healing, and Coercion* (New York: Oxford University Press, 1999); and Janja Lalich, *Bounded Choice: True Believers and Charismatic Cults* (Berkeley: University of California Press, 2004).

17. For detailed histories of the groups, see Lalich, *Bounded Choice*; Thomas W. Keiser and Jacqueline L. Keiser, *The Anatomy of Illusion: Religious Cults and Destructive Persuasion* (Springfield, Ill.: Charles C. Thomas, 1987); Robert Jay Lifton, *Destroying the World to Save It* (New York: Metropolitan Books, 1999), ch. 13; and Micha Popper, *Hypnotic Leadership: Leaders, Followers, and the Loss of Self* (Westport, Conn.: Praeger, 2001).

18. World Health Organization, *World Health Statistics Annual* (Geneva, Switzerland: World Health Organization, 1999).

19. In general, there is reason to question the reliability of data collected on the socially sensitive topic of suicide. Although scholars have found that official statistics tend to under-report suicide, they have not found that this bias is related to religion; all religions prohibit the practice. Unlike counts of some under-reported events, such as rape, suicide counts do not depend on self-reports, but on identification by coroners, who are required to review suspicious and violent deaths. Family meetings with coroners appear to reduce the incidence of reported suicide, a fact that may be related to insurance claims or other factors unrelated to religion. For an exhaustive review of the reliability of suicide rates, finding "no evidence" that "misclassification invalidates the use of societal suicide rates in sociological research," see David Lester, *Why People Kill Themselves: A 1990s Summary of Research Findings on Suicidal Behavior* (Springfield, Ill.: Charles C. Thomas, 1992), p. 88.

20. For example, David Lester, "Islam and Suicide," *Psychological Reports*, vol. 87, no. 2 (October 2000), pp. 692–98; and T. K. Daradkeh and N. Al-Zayer, "Parasuicide in an Arab Industrial Community," *Acta Psychiatrica Scandinavia*, vol. 77 (1988), pp. 707–71.

21. In Canada during the 1990s, immigrant Muslims committed suicide at a rate of 6.3 per 100,000, compared with about 13 per 100,000 for the nation as a whole, according to official Canadian government statistics. "Immigrants Less Prone to Suicide," *The Gazette* (Montreal) (March 30, 2004); "Deaths and Mortality Rates by Cause and Population Groups," *Statistical Abstract of Israel* (Tel Aviv: Central Bureau of Statistics, 2004).

22. K. Gopal Iyer and Mehar Singh, *Indebtedness, Impoverishment and Suicides in Rural Punjab* (Delhi: Indian Publishers Distributors, 2000); Institute for Development and Communication, *Suicides in Rural Punjab* (Chandigarh, Punjab: Himalia Press, 1998).

23. Kaz de Jong, et al., "Assessing Trauma in Sri Lanka" (Amsterdam: Médecins sans Frontières, 2001); and P. De Silva, *Suicides in Sri Lanka* (Kandy, Sri Lanka: Institute of Fundamental Studies, 1996).

24. L. Rathanayeke, "Suicides in Sri Lanka," in Robert Koskey, et al., eds., *Suicide Prevention: The Global Context* (New York: Plenum Press, 1998); and Neil Thalagala, "Attempted Suicides" (Ph.D. diss., University of Colombo, Sri Lanka, 2000).

25. According to the Palestinian Ministry of Health, ordinary Palestinian suicides totaled 36 in 2000, 39 in 2001, 31 in 2002, and 29 in 2003. Palestinian National Authority, *Health Status in Palestine* (Ramallah: Ministry of Health, 2000–2003), mortality appendices.

26. Matthew Nock and Peter Marzuk, "Suicide and Violence," in Keith Hawton and Kees van Heeringen, eds., *The International Handbook of Suicide and Attempted Suicide* (New York: John Wiley, 2000), pp. 449–50.

27. Although some suicide attacks in Iraq appear to be coordinated team attacks, I have left these out of the team attack analysis until more data become available.

28. For extensive documentation of pre-existing social bonds among many al-Qaeda terrorists, see Marc Sageman, *Understanding Terror Networks* (Philadelphia: University of Pennsylvania Press, 2004).

29. For a study of altruistic suicide among the Yuit Eskimos, see A. H. Leighton and C. C. Hughes, "Notes on Eskimo Patterns of Suicide," *Southwestern Journal of Anthropology*, vol. 11 (1955), pp. 327–38.

30. Is there a cultural predisposition toward altruistic behavior among Muslims, Tamils, and Sikhs? Although Western notions of individualism would seem to discourage altruistic behavior, in fact the history of martyrdom is replete with examples of Christian and Jewish martyrs from ancient times through the Protestant Reformation and, some would argue, up to the present day (e.g., evangelical Christians who have died for their religion in Latin America). Hence, a cultural predisposition toward altruism seems no more likely than a cultural predisposition toward suicide to account for suicide terrorism.

31. Shimon Shapira, "Origins of Hizbollah," *The Jerusalem Quarterly*, vol. 46 (Spring 1988), p. 124.

32. Judith Harik, *The Public and Social Services of the Lebanese Militias* (Oxford: Centre for Lebanese Studies, 1994), p. 34. See also Magnus Ranstrop, *Hizb'allah in Lebanon* (New York: St. Martin's Press, 1997), pp. 82–84.

33. Hilal Khashan, "The Developmental Programs of Islamic Fundamentalist Groups in Lebanon as a Source of Popular Legitimation," *Indian Journal of Politics*, vol. 27, no. 3 (1993), pp. 1–13.

34. August R. Norton, *Amal and the Shia* (Austin: University of Texas Press, 1987), p. 170.

35. Sayyed Hassan Nasrallah, secretary general of Hezbollah, speech "In Memory of His Eminence Martyr Sayyed Abbas al-Musawi" (February 16, 2001). Available at www.nasrollah.org.

36. Interview in fall 1985, quoted in Martin Krammer, "The Oracle of Hizbullah: Sayyid Muhammad Husayn Fadlallah, Part II," in R. Scott Appleby, ed., *Spokesmen for the Despised: Fundamentalist Leaders of the Middle East* (Chicago: University of Chicago Press, 1997), p. 12.

37. These statements are collected in Lebanese Resistance Movement, "Martyrdom Operations" (Beirut, no date); translation by Chicago Project on Suicide Terrorism.

38. Jerusalem Media and Communication Centre polls 1995 to 2003. Available at www.jmcc.org.

39. For a recent account of these symbols, see Annemarie Oliver and Paul F. Steinberg, *The Road to Martyr's Square* (Princeton: Princeton University Press, 2004).

40. Sara Roy, "The Transformation of Islamic IGOs in Palestine," *Middle East Report*, 214 (Spring 2000); Riccardo Bocco, et al., "International and Local Aid During the Second Intifada" (Geneva, Switzerland, 2001); and "Islamic Social Welfare Activism in the Occupied Palestinian Territories," *Middle East Report*, no. 13 (April 2003).

41. Eli Berman, "Hamas, Taliban, and the Jewish Underground," NBER Working Paper 10004 (Cambridge, Mass.: National Bureau of Economic Research, 2004).

42. Hamas Political Bureau Statement, *Al-Sabil* (Amman, Jordan), April 19, 1994, in FBIS-NES-94-075 (April 19, 1994).

43. "Standing in Line to Commit Suicide" (interview with Hamas official), *Ma'ariv* (December 30, 1994), FBIS-NES-95-007 (Jan. 11, 1995).

44. Statement issued by the Islamic Resistance Movement (Hamas—Palestine), Sunday, July 23, 2000.

45. From 2000 through 2004, Israel demolished the homes of 675 suicide and other terrorists' families. See Greg Myre, "Israel Halts Decades-Old Practice of Demolishing Militants' Homes," *New York Times* (February 18, 2005).

46. A. J. V. Chandrakanthan, "Eelam Tamil Nationalism: An Inside View," in A. Jeyaratnam Wilson, *Sri Lankan Tamil Nationalism* (Vancouver: UBC Press, 2000); Mia Bloom, *Dying to Kill* (New York: Columbia University Press, forthcoming), Chapter 3.

47. On the LTTE's social services, see Sarath Munasinghe, *A Soldier's Version: An Account of the On-going Conflict and Origin of Terrorism in Sri Lanka* (Colombo, Sri Lanka: Market Information, 2000), pp. 184–87; Adele Balasingham, *The Will to Freedom: An Inside View of Tamil Resistance* (Mitcham, U.K.: Fairmax Publishing, 2001), pp. 269–89; Jaffna District Report (Jaffna: Consortium of Humanitarian Agencies, 2004).

48. Prabhakaran, "Heroes' Day" speech (Jaffna, July 5, 1993). Available at www.eelamweb.com.

49. Quoted in Yamuna Sangarasivam, "Liberation Tigers of Tamil Eelam and the Cultural Production of Nationalism and Violence" (Ph.D. diss., Graduate School of Syracuse University, May 2000), p. 310.

50. See Chapter 8, note 41.

51. Collected and translated by the Chicago Project on Suicide Terrorism.

52. Dagmar Hellmann-Rajanayagam, *The Tamil Tigers: Armed Struggle for Identity* (Stuttgart: Franz Steiner Verlag, 1994), pp. 136, 144.

53. Elaine Sciolino, "Saudi Warns Bush," *New York Times* (January 27, 2002).

54. Anonymous, *Through Our Enemies' Eyes* (Washington, D.C.: Brassey's, 2002), pp. 39–41.

55. National Commission on Terrorist Attacks upon the United States, "Monograph on Terrorist Financing," (Washington, D.C.: House-Senate Joint Inquiry Report on 9/11, 2004), p. 111.

56. Osama bin Laden, *Frontline* interview, May 1998.

57. Al-Zawahiri, "Knights Under the Banner of the Prophet" (December 2001), part 11. Available at www.fas.org.

58. Osama bin Laden, sermon, March 5, 2003. Available at www.memri.org.

CHAPTER 10:
THE DEMOGRAPHIC PROFILE OF SUICIDE TERRORISTS

1. For an excellent review of the literature on these existing explanations, see Rex A. Hudson, *The Sociology and Psychology of Terrorism: Who Becomes a Terrorist and Why?* (Washington, D.C.: Federal Research Division, Library of Congress, September 1999).

2. Valuable recent case histories of suicide terrorists include Joyce M. Davis, *Martyrs: Innocence, Vengeance, and Despair in the Middle East* (New York: Palgrave Macmillan, 2003); and Barbara Victor, *Army of Roses: Inside the World of Palestinian Women Suicide Bombers* (Emmaus, Penna.: Rodale, 2003).

3. Important new surveys of demographic data on terrorists include Marc Sageman, *Understanding Terror Networks* (Philadelphia: University of Pennsylvania Press, 2004); Claude Berrebi, "Evidence About the Link Between Education, Poverty, and Terrorism among Palestinians," Princeton University Industrial Relations Section Working Paper 477 (September 2003); and Alan B. Krueger and Jitka Maleckova, "Education, Poverty, Political Violence, and Terrorism," BNER Working Paper 9074 (Cambridge, Mass.: National Bureau of Economic Research, July 2002).

4. Nicole Argo, "Understanding and Defusing Human Bombs: The Palestinian Case," paper presented at the International Studies Association Annual Convention, Montreal (March 2004); Nasra Hassan, "An Arsenal of Believers: Talking to Human Bombs," *The New Yorker* (November 19, 2001), pp. 36–41; and Ariel Merari, "Social, Organizational, and Psychological Factors in Suicide Terrorism," in

T. Bjorgo, ed., *Root Causes of Terrorism* (London: Routledge, forthcoming).

5. Merari identified many different groups in one of the first detailed surveys. Ariel Merari, "The Readiness to Kill and Die: Suicidal Terrorism in the Middle East," in *Origins of Terrorism*, Walter Reich, ed. (Baltimore: Johns Hopkins University Press, 1990), pp. 192–210.

6. Martin Kramer, "Sacrifice and Fratricide in Shiite Lebanon," in *Violence and the Sacred in the Modern World*, Mark Juergensmeyer, ed. (London: Frank Cass, 1991), pp. 71–89.

7. For example, the most reliable statistics on Palestinian income, from the Israel Social Science Data Center and the Hanf survey "Attitudes and Opinions of Economically Active Lebanese 1981–1987," both divide the data into four categories (poor/low, average, above average, high). I reduce this to a three-point scale by collapsing the two middle categories to diminish the most likely measurement error across the surveys. (Israeli Social Sciences Data Center [ISCD], "Israeli Central Bureau of Statistics: Labor Force Survey in Judea, Samaria and Gaza, 1981–1995," issued by the ISCD and the Hebrew University of Jerusalem, 1995; Theodor Hanf, "Attitudes and Opinions of Economically Active Lebanese 1981–1987," in Hanf, *Coexistence in Wartime Lebanon* [London: I. B. Tauris, 1993].)

CHAPTER 11: PORTRAITS OF THREE SUICIDE TERRORISTS

1. Robert D. McFadden, "Prisoner of Rage: From a Child of Promise to the Unabomber Suspect," *New York Times* (May 26, 1996); "Anatomy of a Serial Killer," *The Observer Magazine* (London) (December 12, 1993); Steven A. Egger, *The Killers Among Us: An Examination of Serial Murder and Its Investigation* (Upper Saddle River, N.J.: Prentice-Hall, 2002); and Richard Tithecott, *Of Men and Monsters: Jeffrey Dahmer and the Construction of a Serial Killer* (Madison: University of Wisconsin Press, 1997).

2. Hannah Arendt, *Eichmann in Jerusalem: A Report on the Banality of Evil* (New York: Viking Press, 1963).

3. Ariel Merari, "The Readiness to Kill and Die: Suicide Terrorism in the Middle East," in Walter Reich, ed., *Origins of Terrorism* (New York: Cambridge University Press, 1990), p. 206.

4. Robert S. Robins and Jerrold M. Post, *Political Paranoia: The Psychopolitics of Hatred* (New Haven: Yale University Press, 1997), pp. 78–79.

5. See Chapter 9, note 1.

6. Matthew Brzezinski, "Six Years Before the September 11 Attacks," *Washington Post* (December 30, 2001); Judith Miller and Don Van Natta, Jr., "In Years of Plots and Clues, Scope of al-Qaeda Eluded US, " *New York Times* (June 9, 2002).

7. For the most recent information on the origins of the September 11 attacks, see Douglas Frantz, et al., "On Plotters' Path to US, a Stop at bin Laden Camp," *New York Times* (September 10, 2002). "Final Instructions to the Hijackers of September 11," reprinted in Bruce Lincoln, *Holy Terrors: Thinking About Religion After September 11* (Chicago: University of Chicago Press, 2003), pp. 93–98.

8. Scott Baldauf, "Portrait of an Al Qaeda Camp," *Christian Science Monitor* (January 17, 2003).

9. *"USA vs. Osama Bin Laden, et al.," Findlaw* (January 8, 2001), at http://news.findlaw.com/hdocs/docs/binladen/binladen030701tt.pdf.

10. On the military training in al-Qaeda's camps, see "US Embassy Bombing Transcript Day 8," *International Policy Institute for Counter-Terrorism* (February 21, 2001); Aukai Collins, *My Jihad* (Guilford, Conn.: Lyons Press, 2002), pp. 25–34; and *"United States vs. Mokhtar Haouari* (LAX Millenium Bombing Case)," *Findlaw* (July 5, 2001), in http://news.findlaw.com/hdocs/docs/haouari/ushaouari070501rassamtt.pdf.

11. For good accounts of Atta's life, see Erlanger, "Unobtrusive Man's Odyssey"; Peter Finn, "A Fanatic's Quiet Path to Terror," *Washington Post* (September 22, 2001); John Hooper, "The Shy, Caring, Deadly Fanatic," *Observer* (September 23, 2001); John Cloud, "Atta's Odyssey," *Time* (October 8, 2001); and Jim Yardley et al., "Portrait of the Terrorist," *New York Times* (October 10, 2001). For a psychological assessment, see Aubrey Immelman, "The Personality Profile of September 11 Hijack Ringleader Mohamed Atta" (unpublished manuscript, Saint John's University, October 11, 2001).

12. Rajeev Sharma, *Beyond the Tigers: Tracking Rajiv Gandhi's Assassination* (New Delhi: Kaveri Books, 1998), pp. 44–46.

13. In addition to Sharma, *Beyond the Tigers*, see Subramanian Swamy, *The Assassination of Rajiv Gandhi* (New Delhi, 2000), pp. 111–41, and Shashi Ahluwalia and Meenakshi Ahluwalia, *Assassination of Rajiv Gandhi* (New Delhi: Mittal Publications, 1991), pp. 1–26.

14. On the LTTE and the Sri Lankan civil war, see V. Navaratnam, *The Rise and Fall of the Tamil Nation* (Madras, 1991); A. Jeyaratnam Wilson, *The Break-up of Sri Lanka: The Sinhalese-Tamil Conflict* (Honolulu: University of Hawaii Press, 1988); Rohan Gunaratna, *Sri Lanka's Ethnic Crisis and National Security* (Columbo, Sri Lanka: South Asia Network on Conflict Research, 1998); and Shyamon Jayasinghe, "The Undertones of the Sri Lankan Conflict," *Contemporary Review*, vol. 277, no. 1617 (October 2000), pp. 216–20.

15. On LTTE training for suicide operations, see Sharma, *Beyond the Tigers*, pp. 119–24; Amy Waldman, "Masters of Suicide Bombing: Tamil Guerrillas of Sri Lanka," *New York Times* (January 14, 2003); Rohan Gunaratna, "The LTTE and Suicide Terrorism" (*Frontline*, February 5–8, 2000); and Manoj Joshi, "On the

Razor's Edge: The Liberation Tigers of Tamil Eelam," *Studies in Conflict and Terrorism*, vol. 19 (January–March 1996), pp. 19–42.

16. Ana Cutter, "Tamil Tigresses," *Slant* (Spring 1998), www.columbia.edu/cu/sipa/pubs/slant.

17. "Informer Drove Bomber to Disco," *Ha'aretz* (June 25, 2001).

18. Harvey Kushner, "Suicide Bombers: Business as Usual," *Studies in Conflict and Terrorism*, vol. 19, no. 4 (October–December 1996), pp. 329–38; Hala Jaber, "Inside the World of the Palestinian Suicide Bomber," *Sunday Times* (London) (March 24, 2002); and Assaf Moghadam, "Suicide Bombings in the Israeli-Palestinian Conflict," *Studies in Conflict and Terrorism*, vol. 26, no. 2 (March–April 2003), pp. 65–92.

19. Nasra Hassan, "An Arsenal of Believers: Talking to 'Human Bombs,' " *New Yorker* (November 19, 2001), p. 41.

20. Jack Kelly, "Devotion, Desire Drives Youths to 'Martyrdom,' " *USA Today* (August 9, 2001); Jeffrey Bartholet, "A Guaranteed Trip to Heaven," *Newsweek* (April 24, 1995).

21. Kelly, "Devotion, Desire."

22. Ibid.

23. Jamal Halaby, "Bomber Went to West Bank for a Better Life," *The Guardian* (London) (June 4, 2001).

24. Jack Kelly, "Devotion, Desire"; Nat Hentoff, "Differing Reactions to Death in Israel," *Village Voice* (August 6, 2001).

25. Mitch Potter, "Three Years of Blood," *Toronto Star* (September 28, 2003).

26. Chris McGreal, "The Bomber's Father," *The Guardian* (London) (September 29, 2003).

27. Potter, "Three Years of Blood."

28. Andrew Silke, "Ultimate Outrage," *The Times* (London) (May 5, 2003).

CONCLUSION
CHAPTER 12: A NEW STRATEGY FOR VICTORY

1. Chaim D. Kaufmann, "Possible and Impossible Solutions to Ethnic Civil Wars," *International Security*, vol. 20, no. 4 (Spring 1996), pp. 136–75; and idem, "When All Else Fails: Ethnic Population Transfers and Partitions in the Twentieth Century," *International Security*, vol. 23, no. 2 (Fall 1998), pp. 120–56.

2. This calculation is based on $3 million per mile, the cost of the National Border Fence—with triple barriers and cameras—that now extends over fourteen

miles on the California-Mexico border near San Diego, which is also the same cost as the Israeli security fence. Blas Nuñez-Neto and Stephen R. Vina, "Border Security: Fences Along the U.S. International Border" (Washington, D.C.: Congressional Research Service, January 13, 2005).

3. David Frum and Richard Perle, *An End to Evil: How to Win the War on Terror* (New York: Random House, 2003), pp. 34, 35, 40, 83, and 106. Frum and Perle also call for regime change in North Korea, although how this is related to their definition of the threat as Islamic fundamentalism is unclear.

4. For extensive evaluation of the growing resentment of American policies in numerous areas around the world, see Stephen M. Walt, *Taming American Power: The Global Response to U.S. Primacy* (New York: W. W. Norton, 2005). For analysis of the consequences of U.S. policy toward Israel, see Stephen Van Evera, "Why the U.S. Needs Mideast Peace," *The American Conservative* (March 14, 2005), pp. 7–10.

5. On the similarity with myths guiding past empires, see Jack Snyder, "Imperial Temptations," *National Interest*, no. 71 (Spring 2003), pp. 29–41; and idem, *Myths of Empire: Domestic Politics and International Ambition* (Ithaca, N.Y.: Cornell University Press, 1991).

6. On off-shore balancing in American foreign policy, see John J. Mearsheimer, *The Tragedy of Great Power Politics* (New York: W. W. Norton, 2001); Robert J. Art, *A Grand Strategy for America* (Ithaca, N.Y.: Cornell University Press, 2003); Barry R. Posen and Andrew L. Ross, "Competing Visions for U.S. Grand Strategy," *International Security*, vol. 21, no. 3 (Winter 1996–97), pp. 5–53; and Christopher Layne, "From Preponderance to Off-Shore Balancing," *International Security*, vol. 22, no. 1 (Summer 1997), pp. 86–124.

7. Samuel Huntington writes, "The overwhelming bulk of the countries where economic conditions supportive of democratization were emerging in the 1990s were in the Middle East and North Africa," and lists Iran and Saudi Arabia among them. Samuel P. Huntington, *The Third Wave: Democratization in the Late Twentieth Century* (Norman, Okla.: University of Oklahoma Press, 1991), p. 314.

Index